Season 2
finding your roots

Season 2

finding your roots

HENRY LOUIS GATES JR.

THE OFFICIAL COMPANION TO THE PBS SERIES

The University of North Carolina Press • Chapel Hill

Designed and set in Miller and Myriad types by Rebecca Evans
Manufactured in the United States of America

The University of North Carolina Press has been a member of the
Green Press Initiative since 2003.

JACKET ILLUSTRATIONS: Henry Louis Gates Jr., photo courtesy of
Peter Simon; Anderson Cooper, photo courtesy of CNN; Ken Burns,
photo courtesy of Cable Risdon; Gloria Reuben, photo courtesy of
Francis Hills; Tina Fey, photo courtesy of WNET; Angela Bassett,
photo courtesy of D'Andre Michael; Deepak Chopra, photo courtesy
of Jeremiah Sullivan; background artwork courtesy of PBS.

Library of Congress Cataloging-in-Publication Data
NAMES: Gates, Henry Louis, Jr., author.
TITLE: Finding your roots, season 2 : the official companion to the
    PBS series / Henry Louis Gates Jr.
DESCRIPTION: Chapel Hill : The University of North Carolina Press,
    [2016] |
Includes index.
IDENTIFIERS: LCCN 2015043771 | ISBN 9781469626185 (cloth :
    alk. paper) | ISBN 9781469626192 (ebook)
SUBJECTS: LCSH: Celebrities—United States—Genealogy. | United
    States—Genealogy. | Finding your roots (Television program)
CLASSIFICATION: LCC CS16 .G364 2016 | DDC 929.1072/073—dc23
    LC record available at http://lccn.loc.gov/2015043771

For Eleanor Margaret Gates-Hatley

L'dor vador

("From generation to generation")

CONTENTS

Season 2

finding your roots

Introduction

One Saturday morning in the early nineties, I found myself awake at about 5:00 in the morning in a hotel room in Salt Lake City. I had lectured the evening before at the Utah Academy of Sciences, Arts and Letters, and because I had flown there from my home here in Cambridge, I was suffering from jet lag, hence the much-too-early wakefulness. My flight home wasn't scheduled to leave until early afternoon. What to do on a Saturday morning in Salt Lake City, Utah? As I lay there in bed, a return to sleep a distant dream, it suddenly occurred to me that I could at long last visit the proverbial Vatican for genealogists all around the world, the Family History Library. Operated by Family Search, which is the genealogical wing of the Church of Jesus Christ of Latter-day Saints, the library is fabled for its astonishingly extensive collection of every sort of record that individuals need to begin to trace their family trees. (For once, "humongous" may be the right word to describe this magnificent place.) I worried that it might be closed on Saturday, for some religious reason, perhaps? (I confess that I was totally ignorant of the customs, beliefs, and practices of the religious group most widely known as the Mormons.) So I called Information, dialed the number of the library, and was very pleased to learn that the Family History Library was open on Saturdays from 9:00 to 5:00.

I arrived at 9:10. Little did I know that what I was about to experience in that amazing library would begin a long process that, by fits and starts, would change the direction of my professional life.

The place was packed, each microfilm and microfiche reader occupied, most often by older women; some older men had planted themselves in front of the machines and were working away, too. I happen to love working in the archive, and I once even owned my own microfilm reader and printer. I didn't notice many young people at that time, but some students (working on their PhDs, I'd learn) started to show up as the day wore on. Every sort of ethnicity and nationality seemed to be represented; in fact, the place looked a bit like a United Nations Elderhostel, pulsating with people who I guessed were Asian, Indian, Euro-American, Christian, Jewish, and Lord knows what else, people of just about every color across the spectrum of hues in the human community's rainbow of skin colors. Glancing around in search of my phenotypic kindred, as by habit I always do upon entering a room, I quickly noted that a fair share of these people were black. That took me completely by surprise—a most pleasant surprise. I was startled to see, even at a glance, how very ecumenical genealogy was.

The feeling that pervaded the room also took me by surprise. A certain electricity of expectation was somehow charging the atmosphere, a bit like the way your hair can tingle when lightning is about to strike nearby. I didn't have the words for this yet, and I wouldn't until this happened: a woman sitting near me in front of a microfilm reader suddenly leapt from her chair, waving her arms. She shouted, "I found her!" Tears streamed down her face. She had found a long-lost ancestor! Several researchers working close by immediately stood up as well, hurried over to her and embraced her, offering their warmest and most heartfelt congratulations. It was as if she had been possessed by the Holy Ghost, the way worshippers were at the Pentecostal Church back home on "Back Street" in Piedmont, West Virginia.

I was dumbfounded. I found the whole scene deeply moving, and I was irrevocably changed.

Soon I was searching, too, searching for the oldest Gates we knew of at that time: Jane Gates, a former slave from Cumberland, Maryland; Jane Gates, my great-great-grandmother. I had "met" Jane Gates, born in 1819 and died in 1888, the day of my grandfather's funeral. Edward St. Lawrence Gates was born in 1879 and buried on July 2, 1960, when I was nine years old. Just after we had buried him at the Rose Hill (Episcopal) Cemetery in Cumberland, we returned to the Gates family home on Greene Street, two doors down from the home that Jane had purchased, for cash, in a predominantly white neighborhood, for herself and her exceptionally fair-skinned, mixed-race children, just five years after slavery ended. You don't have to be Sherlock Holmes to solve the mystery of how a black woman with five mixed-race children—Laura, Alice, Clara, Henry, and Edward, all fathered by the same man, she always told them—was able to make that purchase. Never once did she reveal his name, but more on that a bit later.

My father took my brother, Paul, and me upstairs to his parents' bedroom to show us his father's scrapbooks, full of news clippings about all kinds of crazy things, but especially full of obituaries. Among those obituaries, in the sixth or seventh scrapbook my father riffled through, was the one he had summoned us upstairs to see. It was Jane's. She had died on January 6, 1888, and the short account of her life concluded that she had been "an estimable colored woman." I looked up the word "estimable" much later that evening, just before I went to bed. Two days later, following the colored Fourth of July picnic, I asked my father to buy a composition book for me. And that night, in front of our tiny black-and-white TV, I asked my mother and father question after question about their ancestors and dutifully wrote down all that they told me.

I was hooked.

It was years later that I would learn that what I was hooked on was called genealogy, or ancestry tracing. And I have remained hooked on tracing ancestry—at first just my own, but for the last decade, the ancestry of complete strangers—ever since I was that nine-year-old boy rummaging through a stack of old scrapbooks. That interest, that passion, really, was notched up exponentially when Dr. Rick Kittles of the company African Ancestry introduced me, in the year 2000, to the wonders of ancestry tracing through DNA, by attempting to trace my mitochondrial DNA (abbreviated as mt-DNA). My results indicated that I was descended from a female of Nubian descent. Subsequent tests, however, revealed that my mt-DNA was T2, which meant that I, incredibly (and improbably, to my mind), was descended from a white female whose ancestry traced to northern Europe. She was most likely impregnated sometime during slavery by a black male. Shortly after receiving these stunning results, I suddenly and abruptly (in the middle of the night, in fact) got the crazy idea that I could do a documentary series for PBS and trace the ancestry of African Americans following the paper trail, and then when the paper trail ran cold, analyze the person's DNA to see what it might reveal about the African regional origins of their mother's mother's line and their father's father's line (in the case of males), sort of like redoing Alex Haley's *Roots*, but in a test tube. I had no idea that for so many of my black male guests, their Y-DNA would lead back not to Africa but to Europe. More on that below.

I also assumed that the emotional apex of the reveal would be a guest's African ethnic origins, as determined by Dr. Kittles. That, however, was not to be the case. Don't get me wrong: the black guests in the series were fascinated by what their DNA revealed about their African ancestry. But more often than not, on camera at least, their reaction to this information was surprisingly intellectual. The real emotional high point for our black guests tended to occur when they registered the information that we gleaned about their ancestors not in Africa, but rather their American ancestors, whom we found through detailed, painstaking genealogical research.

Learning the names of the ancestors on their family trees, especially anything at all we could tell them about their enslaved ancestors and the people who owned them, proved to be remarkably charged for many of our guests and often elicited tearful responses. Among the various DNA results we presented to each person, most guests, if not all, seemed to be especially fascinated by the results of a test that wouldn't come into wide commercial use until after 2009: the test of a person's "admixture," their percentages of certain regional genetic mutations over the last five hundred or so years (a figure which comes from the DNA-testing company 23andMe). In the case of the black people featured in both parts of my first genealogy series, *African American Lives*, that meant their percentages of European, sub-Saharan African, and Native American ancestry since the time of Columbus (the percentages depending on the company doing the testing and often varying only slightly). The biggest surprise here was how much more European ancestry African Americans have and, concomitantly, how much less Native American ancestry they have, on average, than they thought they did!

My first three genealogy films aired on PBS in as many years: *African American Lives* in 2006, *Finding Oprah's Roots* in 2007, and *African American Lives 2* in 2008. The format we used soon morphed into *Faces of America*, after a kind person, who identified herself as being of Russian Jewish descent, sent me a letter that encouraged me to think more broadly and to include white people as guests. I embraced that idea enthusiastically. *Faces*, which included guests descended from Asian, Caribbean, European, and Native American ancestors, aired in 2010, and participants in this program also responded much more emotionally to learning about their ancestors through a paper trail than they did to their maternal and paternal DNA haplogroup results. (As we saw with my mitochondrial DNA, T2, the names of haplogroups are rendered as a combination of letters and numbers, such as L3, J2, and so on; subclades, or subgroups of these haplogroups, can go on for a number of digits.) Like the guests in *African American Lives*, guests in *Faces of America* usually found their admixture results quite exciting, especially if these results indicated some regional diversity in their genomes. And thanks to two geneticists at the Broad Institute, David Altshuler and Mark J. Daly, and the wonders of autosomal DNA, we were now able to introduce our guests to their genetic "cousins," to the other people in the series with whom they shared long stretches of identical DNA, meaning that they shared a common recent ancestor on their family trees. This innovative feature proved to be riveting to our guests, and evaluation of autosomal DNA is now a common feature offered to consumers of the three DNA companies that we use to test all of our guests: 23andMe, AncestryDNA, and Family Tree DNA. (African Ancestry tests all of our African American guests.)

The enthusiastic response to *Faces of America* led to the weekly ten-part series called *Finding Your Roots*, season 1 of which aired in 2012 and season 2 in 2014. Season 3 is scheduled to air in January 2016. This book is the companion book to season 2 of that series. Each chapter contains a comprehensive recapitulation of all the information about their ancestors we revealed to that guest in a taped on-camera interview that I conducted, interviews that lasted an average of three and a half hours. And here let me say a word about the nature of our reveals.

With each generation you move up your family tree, the number of your ancestors doubles. Each of us has two parents, and each parent has two parents, so each of us has four grandparents, eight great-grandparents, sixteen great-great-grandparents, thirty-two third great-grandparents, and sixty-four fourth great-grandparents. If we are fortunate enough to take a guest's family tree back to one of his or her, say, eighth great-grandparents, that long-ago ancestor is actually one of a total of 1,024 eighth great-grandparents (ten generations), each of whom we could also identify if the paper trail were perfectly preserved. If the guest whose ancestry we were tracing was born in 1950, my birth year, these ancestors would have been born in about 1650, if we use thirty years as a measure of one generation.

But the paper trail is not perfectly preserved and never will be perfectly restored. Still, each year, with the progressively more extensive and systematic digitizing of records such as national and local censuses, birth and death records, tax records and wills, and so forth, the number of ancestors that a careful, patient researcher can find on her family tree increases, and sometimes increases dramatically.

Even if you find the name of your ancestor, that basic information does not necessarily translate into a story, especially if you are trying to use that story in a film. *Finding Your Roots* is, after all, a television series, not a dry ledger merely listing names, birth dates, and death dates. We have to bring that ancestor's life, well, to life by finding evidence of something interesting that happened to them, something that they did. The number of readily findable ancestors we have to work with varies depending on ethnicity. Let's begin with a look at the family trees for guests with colonial American ancestry. Our genealogists, guided by the brilliant leader of our research team, Johni Cerny, can identify on average between one hundred and one hundred and fifty colonial ancestors, depending on whether they are from New England or Virginia. New England ancestors are easier to document because the New England colonies kept better records, following the same system established by the Church of England. Virginia, however, was founded by corporations that did not regulate record keeping. Genealogists are all too familiar with the obstacles presented in researching the ancestry of this next group: for those of African American, Native American, Jewish, and Middle Eastern descent, as well as for guests with ethnicity from many countries of the former Soviet Union, they can identify on average between twenty and thirty ancestors. (For guests with Jewish ancestry, a rabbinical line could involve many more than this number.) Guests whose four grandparents were born in Ireland tend to list around twelve to twenty-four ancestors. Guests with European ethnicity, but no link to nobility or royalty, descend from very well-documented stock, and our researchers generally identify upward of two hundred ancestors for them. For anyone with links to European nobility and royalty, that list would swell to include a minimum of several hundred ancestors, with a general average being in the thousands. Finally, if any of our guests descend from one of several key European families in the 1500s, the number of identifiable ancestors can reach more than one thousand, most of whom would be born before 1400.

Then comes the culling process. Of this vast number (and during this season of *Finding Your Roots*, we explored the genealogy of twenty-nine guests in addition to my own), we aim for twelve stories to reveal to each guest in the three-and-a-half-hour interview. In the final version of the television program, we will use just three of these stories; the entire dozen or so that we have revealed in the sit-down interview appear, with the guest's prior knowledge, in the companion book to the series, which has been a staple of our research procedure since the airing of the first *African American Lives* in 2006. In fact, the chapters of each of my companion books are adapted closely and copiously from the transcripts of my full interviews with each of our guests. On rare occasions, we uncover information about a person's ancestry after their segment has aired, and in those cases, we include that new research in the companion book, as we have done in this book with the ancestry of the actor Ben Affleck.

How, then, do we decide which three of these dozen or so stories to include in that person's episode? In two ways: by the level of emotion or interest that the guest expresses when I tell him this particular story about this specific ancestor, and by that story's thematic relationship to other similar stories found on the family trees of our other guests. We aim for a diverse array of related stories across the ten episodes of the series. In one episode, we might tell the stories of three Revolutionary War veterans, and in another episode, the stories of three Civil War veterans, and in another, three descendants of enslaved female ancestors whose children were fathered by a white man, most often the man who owned them. Storytelling—really captivating storytelling—is a fine art, not a science, and sometimes our guests will contact me after the broadcast expressing the wish that we had aired the story about a particular ancestor whose saga just didn't make the cut, either because it wasn't emotive enough to us as producers, or because it didn't fit into the larger theme of an hour's documentary. I only wish that we had more time each week to share all that our research uncovers about the ancestors in the family tree of each of the guests on *Finding Your Roots*. Our cutting room floor is rich with their stories!

■ I have often joked that my grandfather, the chronicler of my family's history who started me on my lifelong quest, was so light-complexioned that my brother and I called him Casper behind his back. Of course I understood the legacy of slavery on the African American population, but when I took a DNA admixture test for the first time (this was a few years after Dr. Kittles had tested my mother's mother's genetic line through my mitochondrial DNA), I learned in cold, hard numbers that about half of my recent ancestors came from Europe. The other half came from regions in sub-Saharan Africa. And fewer than 1 percent were Native American, a fact that drives my cousins crazy. More precisely, those cold, hard numbers broke down as follows. There was variation across the three companies that tested me, but the gist was always the same. According to 23andMe, I am 50.1 percent European, 48.6 percent sub-Saharan African, and 0.9 percent Native American; AncestryDNA came back with the percentages 50 percent

African and 48 percent European; and Family Tree DNA showed slightly different percentages still, with 49 percent African, 49 percent European, and 2 percent Central/South Asian.

In other words, according to DNA analysis, in the time frame that they use as a measure, I have as many white ancestors as I have black ancestors, if we translate these geographical regions into the familiar ethnic categories that we use today. Yet I have always identified as black, and will always do so, no matter what the numbers say. The first thing I ask my guests on *Finding Your Roots* is how they identify themselves, how they describe themselves? For each participant we administer that same admixture test that yielded such startling results for me, and which determines an individual's percentages of shared genetic markers over the last five or so centuries. Geneticists conveniently group these shared genetic markers under broad rubrics such as "European," "sub-Saharan African," "East Asian," and "Native American" ancestry. As I explained earlier, three different genomics companies test the DNA of each of our guests (again, African Ancestry only tests our black guests), and we reveal the results—which are often, but not always, quite similar—during our shoots. Even for those whose results come back as 100 percent European—a reading often met with groans and refrains of "How boring!"—their DNA often reflects a great amount of ancestral genetic diversity, since these companies now subdivide broad regions such as "European" or "sub-Saharan African" into smaller geographical regions, in addition to a nongeographic category for Ashkenazi Jewish ancestry. (One company, 23andMe, also reveals one's percentage of Neanderthal ancestry.) These expansions of categories of admixture, along with the complexity of interbreeding between our modern human ancestors and Neanderthals, makes this aspect of our ancestry revelations even more intriguing to most of our guests.

In other words, a person may have a broad admixture result that is 100 percent European, but they are not necessarily 100 percent Irish or 100 percent Scandinavian; instead, they might share genetic markers with people from various parts of the continent, indicative of the mixing between humans that defies our contemporary, and genetically anachronistic, national borders. As for our participants who identify as being of (recent) African descent (after all, sixty thousand or so years ago, all of our ancestors could be thought of as "African"), the number assigned to their sub-Saharan African ancestry seems to make no difference in how they self-describe. Two of the individuals we will meet in the pages of this book made it abundantly clear that family almost always trumps genetics. In their admixture tests, they are essentially each other's polar opposite: one has a sub-Saharan African percentage of 82 percent, while the other's is a shade over 18 percent. Yet both men consider themselves black.

The numbers only tell part of the story, and for many of us, even those of us who "know" with certainty what we "are," our family histories are mysteries. There are obvious reasons for this, as was made evident in the detailed survey of how many ancestors our genealogists can find for our guests based on their ethnicity. African Americans descend from enslaved human beings who remained largely nameless in their owners' records; as property, our ancestors were cruelly stripped of their identity and individuality. Jewish people often hit a wall just two or three generations back, thanks to the massive destruction of their vital records that accompanied their vicious persecution in nineteenth-century Europe. The same is true for those of Irish ancestry, Greek ancestry—the list goes on. But what about those descended from kings and queens, whose ancestry contains intimations of power and permanence that not all of us can claim? We've traced some of our participants' ancestry all the way back to Charlemagne, and, without giving too much away, the family tree of one of our non-European guests boasts the name of an emperor who lived during years followed by the letters B.C. Yet these descendants of the "boldface names" of history, as Ken Burns aptly called them during our interview, were as in the dark about their ancestry as were the descendants of peasants.

Many of us live in a foggy state of what I can only call genealogical amnesia when it comes to our forebears, and this amnesia can't be blamed solely on a dearth of records. I see it time and again in the people who allow us the privilege of exploring their pasts. Most simply do not know how deep their roots run. They know their grandparents' names, and possibly their great-grandparents', but the line ends there. Older generations don't share, and younger generations don't ask. The tendency to hide a traumatic past is understandable, but even stories of triumph are swept under the rug. In this book alone, we will meet educators and innovators, politicians and patriots (the latter with both a lowercase and an uppercase *P*), escaped slaves, and even a conductor on the Underground Railroad—all brave men and women whose stories could have been told joyfully around the holiday dinner table year after year, but weren't.

My goal in each episode of *Finding Your Roots* is to resurrect and preserve our ancestors. Our ancestors are not meant to languish in perpetuity in an archive of a county courthouse, the all-too-fragile written records of their lives gathering dust and mildew, decaying daily and inevitably risking destruction. The names and lives of our ancestors are not meant to die with them. Today we have science and technology on our side—on the side of memory—and through DNA databases and digitized records, we can learn with great definitiveness "who we are" and whom and where we come from. Learning these things may not change the way we identify ourselves in our daily lives. But with patience, persistence, and sometimes sheer luck, we can travel back in time, walk the paths that our ancestors walked, and bring them into our present. Today, more of us than at any point in human history can find our roots, absorb them, internalize them, preserve them, and embrace them.

Henry Louis Gates Jr.
Cambridge, Mass.

CHAPTER ONE

In Search of Our Fathers

Is an ancestor's absence as powerful as his or her presence in shaping an individual's identity? The childhood memories of the novelist Stephen King and the actors Gloria Reuben and Courtney Vance are haunted by silence and loss. All three of them grew up knowing virtually nothing about their fathers' origins. When Stephen and Gloria were very young children, their fathers left their families, closing the door on half of their heritage. For Courtney, it was different. His own family was intact, but his father, who was raised in a foster home, was consumed by a desire to learn the identities of his unknown parents, which went unsatisfied in his lifetime. In sharing long-lost stories from their family trees, we would shed light on the mysteries that had surrounded their fathers' identities, as well as their own.

Stephen King (b. 1947)

From the time he was a child, Stephen King had set his sights on being a writer. "I remember being so excited by Jack London, *White Fang*, stories that I got out of the school library about Kit Carson and Wild Bill Hickok," he said. "I loved all that, and I thought to myself, I want to do this because I love it." The book-buying public has loved him for it. His first novel, *Carrie*, published in 1974, catapulted him to the top of the best-seller list and to the forefront of American fiction. His books have inspired some of Holly-

11

wood's most memorable, most horrifying films, many becoming classics in their own right. In 2003 he made history as the first author in a "popular genre" to receive the National Book Award. "That was a great thing," he said. "It had been a long struggle to respectability."

Born in Portland, Maine, on September 21, 1947, Stephen knows that many of his readers want to know where his dark stories come from, the implicit subtext of which, he says, is, "What screwed you up so badly that you would want to write those terrible things?" His childhood was, in a word, "happy." But, he said, "I was always drawn to stories of suspense and terror and the supernatural. My mother used to read *Fate* magazine, which was about the paranormal and flying saucers, and she would read the stories to me, and I was fascinated." At eleven, Stephen and his older brother, David, came across a box of books that had belonged to their father. "One of them was called *The Lurker in the Shadows*. It was a collection, an old Avon paperback, of H. P. Lovecraft stories, and it showed this green ghoul coming out from underneath a tombstone," he recalled. "There was some interior compass needle in my head that turned to that book and said, 'That's true north for you.'"

Stephen's desire to write grew out of a love of reading and storytelling that was passed down to him by his mother and, quite possibly, by his father, who left the family when Stephen was just two years old, his disappearance a mystery that remained unsolved. "I could only tell the family legend, but according to my mother, he said he was going out for cigarettes and never came back, so it must have been a hard pack to find." As an adult he was no longer tortured by his father's desertion, but as a child, hurt morphed into anger. "I can remember thinking to myself, well, if I ever meet my dad, I'm going to sock him in the mouth for leaving my mother," he said. "As I got older, I would think, well, I want to find out why he left and what he did first, and then I'll sock him in the mouth."

Although curious about his family's past, Stephen had never investigated it. "My mother had a saying: 'Peek not at a knothole lest ye be vexed.' If you look too closely, you might see something you don't like." Stephen had always described himself as Scots-Irish, "because that's what my mother said," but as he got older, he changed his answer. "I just say I'm from Maine. I'm a New Englander. In other words, I have a short leash when people talk about your past. 'Where do you come from?' Well, I come from here."

Mostly, though, Stephen describes himself as a writer. "I've said to people, if you want to call me a horror writer, you're welcome to do that. If you want to call me a suspense writer, you're welcome to do that. I see myself as an American writer, that's all. And I don't mean to put on any airs, and I'm not saying that in any way to try to elevate myself. That's not my job," he said. "My job is to write stories. It's a gift, and the gift was given to me. You just try to pass it on."

■ Who were the people who had passed this gift on to him? Stephen had no memories of his father, Donald Edwin King, and he knew little about his paternal side of the family. Once he left, Don never returned to the family or even initiated communication from afar, and Stephen's mother spoke of him infrequently. "She was very close-mouthed about Don. When we traveled around a lot, she said, 'People are going to ask you what your father does. Say that he's in the navy and that he's at sea, because that might not be a lie.'"

It was not a lie. According to his obituary, printed in 1980 in a newspaper in Eaton, Pennsylvania, Donald King was an officer in the U.S. Navy and also served as a captain in the Merchant Marines until 1956. Military records corroborated his service in the navy, from 1938 until he was discharged because of his exceptionally poor vision in January 1942.

Uncovering information about Donald King's pre-navy years, however, presented us with an unexpected challenge. His disappearance from Stephen's life was not the only factor complicating our search. There was also, it turned out, the issue of his name. According to Stephen's grandmother, and confirmed by his birth certificate, Stephen's father's original surname was Pollock. Born in Peru, Indiana, on March 11, 1914, to William Pollock and Helen Bowden, Don went by that surname until he was at least sixteen years old. In the 1930 census for Chicago, Donald Pollock was listed as living with his mother, who was by then called Helen Szczepanski, and stepfather, Victor Szczepanski (who at some point changed the spelling of their last name to Spansky). By the time he next appeared in the public record, he was twenty-three years old, and he had already changed his name to Donald King. We found no record of an official name change or any explanation of why he chose the name "King." "Well, I'm my mother's son, and if she ever said anything about that, she would have said probably because somebody was hunting for him, a husband that he had upset by visiting the wife at night, or to get out from under bills," Stephen joked. Perhaps the reason was more straightforward. "Maybe he wanted a new start."

Having Donald King's original surname allowed us to delve deeply into his roots. His biological parents, Stephen's grandparents, William Pollock and Helen Bowden, were married in 1913 in Peru, Indiana, where Donald and his younger sister, Betty, were born. By 1920, life had changed dramatically for the family. In the census for the town of Peru for that year, Helen Pollock, only twenty-three years old, was listed as a widow, living with her two children. Donald Pollock was six years old. Like his own son, Don was fatherless from an early age. An obituary published in an Indiana newspaper on October 24, 1918, filled in the sad details of the end of William Pollock's life. "William E. Pollock, a well-known engineer on Lake Erie, died last evening about seven o'clock in his home, number 232 West Seventh Street, after an illness from pneumonia."

William Edwin Pollock, born on August 3, 1888, in Peru, Indiana, died at age thirty in the massive influenza pandemic of 1918, one of the deadliest natural disasters in human history. The influenza of 1918 killed more than 50 million people, about 3 percent of the world's population at the time. More than six hundred thousand Americans—ten times the number of American soldiers who died during World War I—lost their lives to the horrific illness. "It could almost be out of a horror novel, like one I wrote called *The Stand*, where the world's population is killed by a flu strain," Stephen said. "Whatever goes around comes around. That's amazing. My grandfather died of Spanish flu."

Stephen's grandfather's life was cut tragically short, but we were able to trace Stephen's lineage all the way back into the middle of the eighteenth century, to Stephen's fourth great-grandfather, a Methodist minister born in 1762 named James Pollock. He lived in Juniata County, which was then called Mifflin County, in Pennsylvania. Described in his 1848 obituary in the *Christian Advocate and Journal* as "a lover of Methodism, mighty in prayer," James Pollock was known to have built a Methodist meetinghouse on his property, one of the first churches in the area. Religion had been a part of Stephen's childhood. "We were raised religious—not what I'd call fundamentalists. We weren't Hard-Shell Baptists or Pentecostals. We didn't roll in the aisles," Stephen said. "We were Yankees. We didn't do that kind of thing."

Stephen's fourth great-grandfather was buried in the cemetery attached to the meetinghouse on his land, and carved into his gravestone was important information about his life. By the time of James Pollock's death in 1848, he had lived in America for sixty years, immigrating to this country from Ireland around 1788, five years after the Revolutionary War. We were unable to find a birth record or any documentation of James Pollock's immigration to this country, but interviews with Stephen's relatives yielded the names of James's parents, Stephen's fifth great-grandparents Samuel and Margaret Pollock, who were born around 1740 in Ireland. James's parents would have lived through the 1741 frost, a disaster so brutal that it came to be known as the "Year of the Slaughter," *Bliain an Áir* in Irish. More than a century before the notorious potato famine of the 1840s, the great frost ravaged the land of Ireland and decimated its population. Rivers and lakes froze, and the food supply was destroyed. It's estimated that one-fifth of the Irish population perished in the ensuing famine. In the following decades, Irish immigration to America increased dramatically, and in the 1780s, the first Irish immigrants started to bring Methodism to Pennsylvania. Stephen's fourth great-grandfather was among them.

Stephen never knew he had Irish ancestors. "I can't say it really surprises me to find that I have an Irish background," he said. "I've thought to myself, you look like an Irishman; you've got the Irish imagination. I've always had an appreciation for fairies and ogres and boggarts and things of that nature."

His Irish ancestors may have passed along their "gift of the gab" to him, but another ancestor on his father's father's line, born more than 350 years ago, had a direct impact on Stephen's life and career. Wilhelm Rettinghausen, Stephen's eighth great-grandfather, was born in Germany in 1644. The family immigrated to Pennsylvania in 1688. In 1690, William Rittenhouse, as he was now known, built the first paper mill in the British North American colonies, laying the foundation for the growth of an industry that would allow the colonies to reduce their dependence on Europe. Stephen's ancestors would go on to produce paper for 150 years, and they played an important role in developing America's own publishing industry. In fact, the first poem ever printed in the mid-Atlantic colonies, "A Short Description of Pennsilvania," written in 1692 by a man named Richard Frame, was printed on Rittenhouse paper.

■ In introducing Stephen to his father's father's ancestors, we had journeyed across the Atlantic, to seventeenth-century Germany and eighteenth-century Ireland. Turning to his father's mother's ancestors, we brought Stephen to a time and place in America that he'd never imagined he was connected to. Stephen's grandmother was born Helen Bowden on February 1, 1897, in Peru, Indiana. Her paternal grandfather, Stephen's great-

great-grandfather, William T. Bowden, was thirty-two years old when the Civil War broke out. According to his military record, he was born in Camp County, Tennessee. But this was not a record from the Confederate army. Stephen's second great-grandfather, a southerner, had volunteered to fight for the Union. William was not the only southern Bolden ancestor who stood with the North. His five brothers—John F., Enoch, Elza, Raleigh, and James—all served in the Union army as well. In fact, William and his brother Elza fought side by side in Company K, 128th Regiment of the Indiana Infantry, both men part of the campaign that led up to the fall of Atlanta on September 2, 1864. Two months later, Atlanta would be the launching point of Sherman's March to the Sea.

Southerners signing up for the Union army was unusual, but not unprecedented. Their loyalty to the Union often issued from economics, feelings about slavery, or simply love of country and antisecessionist beliefs. Records for the father of the six Bowden soldiers clarified why his sons made the choice they did. Enoch Bowden, William's father and Stephen's third great-grandfather, was born on October 28, 1801, in New Bern, North Carolina. In 1836, after having settled in Tennessee, where Stephen's second great-grandfather was born, Enoch moved his family north to Indiana. Indiana was still largely unsettled by white Americans, and Enoch Bowden became the first white man to own land in Jay County, where he would serve as a judge and a leader of the Methodist Church. His obituary in Indiana's *Commercial Review* newspaper, published after his death at age eighty-four in June 1886, described him as "one of our best and earliest settlers."

What made Enoch Bowden leave his home in the South for the Indiana frontier? A book published in 1901 about the pioneers of Jay County stated the answer plainly: "Enoch Bowden and his wife, like many others, left their native state on account of slavery there." In 1830, shortly before the Bowdens moved from Tennessee, slaves comprised almost 20 percent of the state's population. Methodists in the North and the South had long been divided over the issue of slavery, and by 1845 the discord forced an acrimonious split. As a Methodist, Enoch may very well have opposed slavery on moral and religious grounds. "It's something to be proud of," Stephen said of his ancestors' choice to live according to their beliefs. "They fought on the right side."

On Stephen's grandmother's maternal line, we found an ancestor who tied Stephen to yet another defining point in American history: the Revolutionary War. Helen's mother, Stephen's great-grandmother Hattie Clear, was born in October 1870. Her second great-grandfather, Stephen's fifth great-grandfather, was a man named Johann Ludwig Clapp, born in Oley, Pennsylvania, in 1742, the child of German immigrants. A military affidavit given in Guilford County, North Carolina, on January 23, 1833, revealed that he was also a Patriot. "Ludwig Clapp was a true and faithful soldier of the Whig Party from the commencement to the end of the Revolutionary War," Stephen read. The supporting testimony of his superior officers revealed that Johann Ludwig Clapp served as a volunteer, fighting in what was primarily a guerrilla war in North Carolina, participating in some of the most brutal fighting of the Revolution. As a descendant of a Patriot, Stephen qualified for membership in the Sons of the American Revolution. He demurred. "I'll just enjoy this privately rather than join the club," he said, "because I didn't do anything. That was him. But I certainly take pleasure in knowing. It's like knowing that I had a relative who left Tennessee because of slavery. It's nice to know that I had a guy fighting on the right side of this, too."

We had restored generations of Stephen's paternal ancestors to him. He had gone from knowing almost nothing about his father to learning that he had deep roots in colonial America, in Ireland and Germany, and that he had ancestors who were veterans of both the American Revolution and the Civil War. "I'm starting to see the bigger picture, because there's very little that I know about any of these people," he explained. "There's a pretty clean snip when my father leaves." He looked at the family tree stretched out before him. "It makes them real. You see that there's a real foundation under you."

His father had closed the door on a relationship with his son when he walked out on him. Did seeing the names and learning the stories of so many of his ancestors bring Stephen any closer to his father? "I wouldn't say that it gives me a closer sense of connection. I don't think that's going to happen in my lifetime. It might have happened if I had known him or if I had re-met him." He paused. "What it gives me is a sense of closure, a feeling that, oh, yes, there is a family there. There is a texture and a history. There's fabric, and that's a great thing."

■ Stephen considered himself similar to his mother in many ways, but "if you had to boil it down to one thing," he said, "I'd say it's Yankee independence." Nellie Ruth Pillsbury, called Ruth, was born in Scarborough,

Maine, on February 3, 1913. "She was a hard worker, and she wanted to stand on her own two feet, and she didn't want other people to know what was wrong. That was something that you took care of yourself," he said.

As a single mother, Ruth's life was difficult, and she continued to wear her wedding ring to deflect questions about her marital status. "My brother and I were latchkey kids before there were latchkey kids, and she was a working woman before working women got much in the way of respect." Ruth cared for her parents and aging relatives, often paid in canned goods and coupons, and held down odd jobs to support her family. But Stephen's memories of his childhood are fond, his memories of his mother's stories priceless. "She told a story about the ragman who came once a week, and the kids were each allowed to have a piece of gum from the ragman, and they chewed it all week long," he said. "At night they would stick their chewing gum on the bedpost, just like in the song. She said one night, a moth fluttered down on her gum while it was still soft, and when she woke up in the morning, she didn't even look; she just popped the gum into her mouth and chewed. She said, 'I bit it in half, and I felt the pieces fluttering around in my mouth.'" He paused. "So you see, she had her own talent for stories."

"Ruthie Pill," as she was called as a teenager, played the piano and wrote and acted in plays in high school. Despite her own creative streak, she always tempered support for her son's literary aspirations with practical concerns. She died too early in Stephen's career to enjoy most of his phenomenal success, but she was there for the very beginning. Stephen recalled a bittersweet memory. "There were bound galleys of *Carrie*. She was dying by that point, and she was too weak to hold a book, so her sister Ethelyn read it to her, and my mother just said, 'My son wrote that.'"

What could we learn about the people who shaped this proud, independent, hardworking woman? According to their marriage license, Stephen's maternal grandparents, Guy Herbert Pillsbury and Nellie Western Fogg, were married on July 22, 1902, in Scarborough, Maine. "What I'm trying to get my head around is that my grandmother, who we called Mama, was twenty-four years old when she got married," Stephen said, "because I remember her as an old woman who was bedridden, corpulent, in her early eighties. She had chronic hypertension, and she didn't have much left. But again, you come in to the movie late." His memories of his grandfather were similarly incompatible with the young man to whom we introduced Stephen. "I remember him as an old man, coming out on his cane with his cigar, getting into the rocking chair in the kitchen in the sun where he liked to sit."

Stephen's grandparents were both born in Maine, his grandfather Guy on December 1, 1876, and his grandmother Nellie on November 9, 1877. Anything his mother had ever told him about her parents' origins was long since forgotten. "I was a kid at the time," he said, "and it rolled right over me." We traveled all the way back to the seventeenth century on his mother's father's line, to Stephen's original immigrant ancestor, who arrived in the New World just two decades after the *Mayflower*. Although we could not find a record of his birth, we knew that Stephen's seventh great-grandfather William Pillsbury was born in England and arrived in Dorchester, an early settlement of Boston, in 1640 or 1641. "Well, you can't accuse them of being Johnny-come-latelies," Stephen quipped. "It's nice to know. It fills in a lot of blanks."

At the end of his life, Stephen's seventh great-grandfather was a man of considerable wealth, a landowner in Newbury, Massachusetts. But his time in America began much differently. Stephen's ancestor had come to this country as an indentured servant, bound to a master for seven years in exchange for his passage. On July 29, 1641, a court determined that William Pillsbury and his wife, Dorothy, indentured to a different master, had behaved in a manner far outside the bounds of their Puritan society. "William Pillsbury, for defiling his master's house, was sentenced to be whipped," Stephen noted, reading the punishments. "Dorothy Pillsbury was sentenced to be whipped for her uncleanliness and defiling her master's house." Stephen laughed. "Whenever I behaved in such a way that I would not want my mother to find out, I always assumed, well, it's my father's side of the family. But we didn't find anything there. This is what we found."

Through William Pillsbury, we were able to confirm a long-held belief of Stephen's mother: that her branch of the Pillsbury family was related to the Pillsburys of baking-company fame. It was a distant relationship: Stephen King and Charles Alfred Pillsbury, the founder of the Pillsbury Company in 1872, were sixth cousins twice removed. Stephen's seventh great-grandparents William and Dorothy Pillsbury were married for forty-five years and had ten children. One of their seven sons, Joe Pillsbury, was a direct ancestor of Stephen; another of their sons, Moses Pillsbury, was a direct ancestor of Charles Alfred Pillsbury. "Wow," Stephen said, "we're related to the Pillsbury Doughboy."

■ We had one final story to share with Stephen. We had already met a pioneer of the publishing industry on his father's side of the family. Now, on Stephen's mother's side, we found a bona fide horror writer. Stephen's sixth great-grandfather was a man named Timothy Waterhouse, and he and his wife, Ruth, lived during the 1700s in a house called Pulpit Reach, just outside Portsmouth, New Hampshire. Apparently living in the home to care for the Waterhouse children was an enslaved person, not a common occurrence in New Hampshire, but not an anomaly either. When the first federal census was conducted in 1790, there were 158 slaves living in the state. Stephen's sixth great-grandparents' oldest daughter, Margaret, penned a story about that house and its inhabitants that went on to become a staple of New Hampshire folklore, a version of which appeared in a book published in 1869. The story involved boys and girls left home alone on a snowy night in 1725, a slave with "a good voice" providing the evening's entertainment, a "parental admonition to beware of raising the evil one," and, of course, a dreaded knock on the door.

Stephen relished reading every word of the story's conclusion: "Margaret, the oldest and bravest, led the way to the door, but no sooner had she opened it than she saw what she thought was Satan himself. The figure was white with a horrible black face, deep in a white lopped hat, which was hanging down over each shoulder. That the Old Scratch had now come, they all believed. Margaret fainted, and it was some time before the ugly-looking but faithful slave of Nathaniel Jackson was recognized beneath this snow covering, who had come to get Massa's shoes."

Stephen paused. He wasn't alone in his ability to send a chill up a reader's spine. His sixth great-grandaunt Margaret had done it 150 years before. "It's a little bit like having an echo from the past come back to you. It's enlightening; it's eye-opening. It's wonderful to know that that sort of thing carries through," Stephen said. "Now, maybe it's coincidence, but I don't really think it is. It's something that's as common as a family resemblance. Runs in the blood."

■ Ask Stephen King where he's from, and he'll tell you Maine. Our climb up Stephen's family tree, however, took us far afield, to the British Isles and to the southern United States, to colonial New England and Revolutionary Pennsylvania. Until now, his maternal ancestors had been lost to time, as many of our ancestors are. His paternal ancestors, however, had been simply lost. Without his father in his life, Stephen had been denied access to an entire side of his family. Through genealogy, that access had been granted. We traced Stephen's paternal line back to a man named Nicholas Clapp, who was born in Ista, Germany, in 1644. At the very top of Stephen's mother's family tree sat Charlemagne, King of the Franks, Emperor of the West, who was born in 742 and died in 814—a real king in the family. Charlemagne was Stephen's forty-second great-grandfather on his mother's side. "Boy, would she ever get a kick out of that," he said. "I'm gob-smacked."

The paper trail had already told us so much, but Stephen's DNA would tell us even more, take us back even further in time. We administered an admixture test to him, which measures a person's percentages of European, sub-Saharan African, and East Asian / Native American ancestry. This was all recent ancestry, since around the time of Columbus. Stephen laughed when he saw his results. "I'm 99 percent European, baby," he said. "My wife used to say I was the whitest white man she'd ever known. My wife was right."

We broke down Stephen's result by country. Europe West, which comprises France, Germany, the Netherlands, and some of England, registered at 68 percent. We had uncovered stories of direct ancestors from both Germany and the Netherlands, so this result was substantiated by the genealogy. We would have expected his percentage from Great Britain to be higher, as most of the ancestors we found in the paper trail traced their lineage back to England. There were smaller amounts of Scandinavia (8 percent); Iberia (3 percent); Ireland (2 percent); Europe East (1 percent); and West Asia and the Caucuses, both of which were less than 1 percent. His admixture reflected greater diversity than Stephen would have expected, given his 99 percent result.

When Stephen's Y-DNA was tested and compared against the already existing database, the matches—that is, males who had similar Y-chromosome DNA signatures—included nineteen men who carried the Pollock surname or a close variant of it. If Stephen's father had been trying to outrun his past by calling himself King instead of Pollock, as Stephen had speculated, this proves that you can change your surname, but you can't fool DNA.

■ It had been a long time since Stephen had contemplated his father's ancestry. If he asked questions, who was there to answer him? Starting from the ground up, we moved back in time and introduced Stephen to generations of ancestors who spanned the history of America. What did it feel like to have answers, after living his entire life without them? "It's a little bit like having a stage and having somebody turn on lights on different parts of it so that you can see things you never saw before."

Stephen King is the consummate writer. Entire worlds of his own invention exist between the covers of his books. In his novel *11/22/63*, he played specifically with the notion of time travel. What if he could dust off that time machine, lift it out of the pages of his novel, and aim it toward the branches of his family tree? Which of his ancestors would he point himself toward? Stephen chose "the judge, the one who left Tennessee and came to Indiana," his third great-grandfather Enoch Bowden, whose six southern sons fought for the Union in the Civil War. "I'd like to sit down and talk with him and say, 'How much of it was economic, and how much of it was Methodism?'" His second choice: the emperor Charlemagne.

The question comes up often: What do we inherit from our ancestors? Are we the sum total of their experiences and their genetics? Where did Stephen's genius and his drive come from? Could ancestors who were previously invisible to him have played a part in making him the person he is today? "I believe very firmly that nature trumps nurture in most cases," he said. "There is something genetic. We see it again and again, where some person will rise above their situation the way that some of my ancestors did to become something more than you would expect from their surroundings. You get certain equipment. You're like a car that rolls off the assembly line. Some people get the radio, and some people don't." As for his unique gift for writing, Stephen felt that maybe it was not unique after all. "It's obvious to me that I was given a gift," he said, "because this was nothing that I said at some point, 'I want to do this.' It said to me, 'You will do this because this is what you have, so develop it.'"

Finally, to borrow Stephen's metaphor, how did it feel for him to have all the parts of the stage lit? Stephen answered honestly, absorbing everything for the first time as he was: "I'm rocked back on my heels," he said. "But here's the thing. The information always leads to more questions, where you say to yourself, 'Yes, but I want to know . . .'" Long before he learned of his roots, Stephen said he had felt an inexplicable affinity for the South. "It's probably bull, but I think to myself, that's why, every time I get down here in the South, I'm happy to be here. I like it, you know? If you want me to write a scene set in Sardi's in New York City or that Four Seasons restaurant, I can do it, but I would have to strain my imagination. You want me to write a scene in Waffle House, somewhere in Asheville, North Carolina, that I can do, because I've been in those places. I love those places. That's the sort of person I am. Maybe that's my ancestors calling in my blood."

Gloria Reuben (b. 1964)

The actress Gloria Reuben is perhaps best known for her groundbreaking role as the HIV-positive nurse Jeanie Boulet on the television drama *ER*. Never before had a regular recurring character on a network program been diagnosed with HIV. Most recently, she played Mary Todd Lincoln's dressmaker and confidante, the former slave Elizabeth Keckley, in Steven Spielberg's Academy Award–winning film *Lincoln*. Even though her real-life character was born a slave, the Canadian-born Gloria didn't respond to the role in a personal way. Regarding slavery on her family tree, she said, "I didn't think there was any, frankly."

Gloria Elizabeth Reuben was born on June 9, 1964, in Toronto, Canada, to Cyril George Reuben and Pearl Avis Mills. Her father was seventy-four years old when Gloria was born, the product of his second marriage. Cyril and Pearl separated when Gloria was just five years old, and her knowledge about any relatives who came before was nearly nonexistent. "My mother wasn't able to tell me anything beyond her parents," she said. "It's just a complete blank slate, and I think it's human nature to want to know where you come from." This lifelong feeling of being disconnected from her past is one she never got used to. "It's a curious feeling when friends talk about family reunions and gatherings or holidays. Even though in my head I obviously know I come from somewhere, so I know there's lineage, in my heart, it's been a lonely kind of feeling. Without knowing, you just feel a little bit adrift."

Gloria's father, Cyril, was white and Jewish, according to Gloria's mother, and many years her mother's senior; her mother, Pearl, was a black Jamaican, at the time they met, a single mother with a young child (Gloria's half-brother) and newly relocated to Canada. Gloria had no idea what drew her parents to each other, and she speculated that their relationship must have had its share of obstacles. "This is forty-five, fifty years ago, in Canada, mixed-race couple, elderly man. Even in today's time, this would be hard."

As a child, she and her siblings lived in a predominantly white neighborhood. "We, of course, were mixed, different shades of brown and white-skinned and everything in between." When she was just seven years old, she had her first experience with blatant racism. "I remember walking to school one day and being spit on by two boys and called the N-word." This was the first time she had shared this painful memory. "In Canada, obviously the history there isn't the same as the history here," she said. "It wasn't around in a predominant, significant way, so that's also why it was completely shocking and a little confusing. I don't remember ever really thinking about it at all like that."

Her crowning as Miss Black Ontario in 1986 brought her racial identity to the forefront. "There were some people who thought I wasn't black enough because I was mixed-race," she said. "The thing that I found interesting, confusing, was that not being black enough was coming from people of color. I was experiencing racism from within. Then you really start wondering, 'Where do I belong? Where do I fit?'" Her race, or her parents' races, had never been something that dominated her thoughts growing up. "It was never part of my thinking process, not part of my psychology," she said. "I never thought of the race thing growing up unless it was pointed out to me." When she moved to the United States, it was pointed out to her, frequently. "It became so clear that you're one or the other here. That threw me into a tailspin for a while, frankly. What I had mentioned about not being black enough for Miss Black Ontario, I found that a lot in this business. I wasn't black enough."

The question of identity is a complicated one in an either-or society. After Miss Black Ontario, Gloria refused to comply. "I'm just going to be both. I'm just going to be me. One does not supersede the other. One is not better than the other." Gloria's light skin has always kept people guessing about her racial and ethnic identity. "Wherever I go, frankly, people think I'm from there," she said. She has fielded the question "What are you?" more times than she can count. "I don't like that question," she said. "I always am very snippy when I respond, 'I'm human.' But I tell them what I know, which is that I became a U.S. citizen a few years ago, so I'm Canadian American, Jamaican, Jewish." She resists the idea of labels. "That putting me into a box or a category—I'm black, I'm white. I think that it's important, especially in today's time, when there is still to this day such racial division in this country between black and white, I like to help expand the conversation in that it's not just one or the other."

■ Before we could introduce Gloria to her earlier paternal ancestors, we had to start with the one who was closest of all: her father. She knew nothing beyond the basics about him. Cyril George Reuben was born on December 1, 1890, in Falmouth, Trelawny Parish, Jamaica. Young Gloria saw her father infrequently after her parents separated when she was five, and he died when she was twelve. Gloria's mother spoke little of him, and what she said of him, as Gloria described it, was only one side of the story. "I do know that my half-siblings, whom I've never met, were not most welcoming to us and to my mother," she said. "I know there was a little discord. I expect that would play into the marriage, but beyond that, I had no idea why he wasn't there."

Broken families often lead to misinformation and misunderstandings where family histories are concerned. Gloria's knowledge of her father's family was limited by her mother's ignorance of it. Pearl Reuben never even knew the names of her in-laws. "I don't know why that's true, and frankly, at this point in my mother's life, I'm not going to ask her," Gloria said, her curiosity tempered by respect for her mother. "He was elderly. His parents were long gone. Maybe it just wasn't important to her." Gloria speculated that it might have been cultural as well. "I know some other women of my mother's age who were born and raised in Jamaica. There's part of this culture at that time where you just don't ask, or it's just not part of the conversation."

Cyril had achieved great success as an engineer after emigrating from Jamaica to Canada at the age of twenty-two. His prominence was such that his visits back to his home island were covered by the press. Therefore, we began our search into Gloria's father's past in Jamaica. We quickly hit a dead end and instead turned our focus on Canada. An obituary notice in the *Toronto Star* for a man named Percival Nathan identified Cyril Reuben of Toronto as his surviving brother. "I didn't know my father had a brother," Gloria said. "Why is his last name different?"

The answer was on Uncle Percival's marriage license, recorded in 1923 in Ontario. His parents' names, William George Nathan and Florence Gabay, indicated that Percival Nathan and Cyril Reuben were half-brothers and that Florence Gabay—Gloria's grandmother—was the mother of both men. Having his mother's name enabled us to find Cyril's birth certificate. Filed in 1890, it listed neither a father's name nor a surname for Cyril. Percival Nathan and Cyril were indeed half-siblings, and Florence Gabay was an unmarried woman. We found another birth certificate from 1898, this one filed two years before Cyril's birth. The name of the baby girl born in Montego Bay was left blank, as was the name of her father. But the mother's name was plain as day: "Florence Gabay, seamstress." That there was no name for the baby girl indicates that she died upon birth or shortly thereafter; that there was no name for the father indicates that the child was born out of wedlock, Florence's third we could trace.

Florence's was a heartbreaking story. According to her death certificate, Gloria's grandmother died on January 26, 1917, in a place identified as "Lunatic Asylum, Kingston, Jamaica." Twenty-seven years after the birth of her son Cyril, five years after he immigrated to Canada, Florence Gabay died alone in a sanatorium, her marital status—described as her "condition"—listed as "spinster." Gloria's grandmother had never married, and she gave birth to children out of wedlock. By Victorian standards, Florence would have been considered morally lax, and, in a society where respectability equaled sexual restraint, it's quite possible that she would have been deemed mentally imbalanced, unfit to live her life freely. In the Victorian mind, the two went hand in hand. "My mother would tell me stories of when she was a young woman in Jamaica in the 1940s," Gloria said, "and it was not OK. It was looked down upon even though it was happening everywhere. And this was forty years prior." Gloria was devastated to learn her grandmother's story. "They throw people away they don't know what to do with." Florence's institutionalization was possibly illustrative of the harsh punishment doled out to women who lived outside the confines of society's dictates. "I would have died fighting my way out of there." Gloria paused. "Maybe she did, too."

What more could we learn about this woman, whose life had come to such a tragic end? According to her baptismal record, dated October 17, 1869, four years after the end of the Civil War, Florence Gabay was born in the parish of St. James, Jamaica, to John Edmund Gabay, a shopkeeper, and Amelia Gabay. These were Gloria's great-grandparents. Florence was the youngest of their four children. Our research on her siblings turned up little, except for one troubling fact. The death certificate of Florence's brother, Gloria's great-uncle John Adolphus Gabay, bore an eerie similarity to his sister's: "District of Kingston, Jamaica, 1899," Gloria read. "Date and place of death: June 9, 1899, Lunatic Asylum, Kingston. John Gabay, occupation, brewer; cause of death, acute alcoholism." In a strange coincidence, Gloria was born sixty-five years to the day after her uncle died.

■ The space on Gloria's father's birth certificate that asked for his father's name had been left blank. How had he come by the last name Reuben? We continued our search through the Jamaican archives to see what we could learn. Cyril's marriage license from his first marriage, to Muriel Elfreda Bell, in 1912, told us what his birth certificate hadn't. His father's name was H. E. Reuben. According to a marriage certificate dated 1884 that we discovered for H. E. himself, his full name was Henry Emanuel Reuben, and he was born in 1848. H. E. Reuben was Gloria's grandfather, and he was married three times, but never to Gloria's grandmother, Florence Gabay. Gloria found Cyril's use of his father's initials, H. E., instead of his name, curious. "I think this really ties into my own questions about my father," she said. "Did my father know his father?" There was no way to tell, but there was much to learn about H. E. Reuben from the paper trail he left behind.

A subsequent marriage license showed Henry Emanuel Reuben marrying a woman named Rose Annie Ansell on March 13, 1890. Gloria's father, Cyril Reuben, was born on December 1, 1890, to Florence Gabay. In other words, Cyril was most likely conceived in March 1890, when his father was entering into a marriage with a woman other than his mother. While this marriage certificate led us to ask a host of questions about the complexities of human relationships that we could never answer, it contained the name of Gloria's great-grandfather Isaac Reuben, born in 1805 in Jamaica, which ultimately led us to birth records for all of Gloria's grandfather's siblings. With the discovery of these long-lost relatives, we were able to confirm for Gloria something about her heritage she had long suspected. The names of Henry's siblings, all born between 1833 and 1837, were transcribed in the Registered Book of Births in Kingston's English and German Synagogue. At long last, Gloria had proof of her Jewish heritage.

The history of the Jewish people in Jamaica is little known but centuries old. The story actually began in Spain in 1492, the same year Columbus discovered the New World, when Queen Isabella and King Ferdinand ordered all their subjects to affirm their belief in the Roman Catholic Church. Spain's Jews were given three choices: conversion, expulsion, or execution. In an effort to preserve their identities and maintain a semblance of religious freedom, a small number of Jews fled to the Spanish New World outpost of Santiago, known today as Jamaica. There the Jewish population would remain a tiny minority. By 1880, ten years before Gloria's father was born, Jamaica's total population was about 580,000; within the island's white population, which was less than 15,000, only about 2,500 were Jews.

From the time of their arrival in Jamaica, Jews were treated as second-class citizens on the island, unable to vote or hold public office. After nearly three hundred years, that would begin to change. Gloria's great-grandparents, it turned out, were part of a remarkable generation in Jamaica that fought and ultimately dealt a major blow to legalized anti-Semitism. On December 19, 1831, Jewish people in Jamaica were finally granted full rights under the law. The marriage license of Henry Emanuel Reuben's parents brought us back to this triumphant time in Jamaican Jewish history. On August 15, 1832, Gloria's great-grandparents, Isaac Reuben and a woman named Judith, last name unknown, were married in Kingston, full citizens under Jamaican law.

We could go back only one more generation on Gloria's father's family tree. Isaac and Judith's marriage certificate allowed us to identify two of Gloria's great-great-grandfathers: Isaac's father, Jacob Reuben, and Judith's father, Samuel, last name unknown. Jewish records in Jamaica are limited, and at this point, the paper trail for Gloria's Jewish ancestors ran out. For years, Gloria had been led to believe that her grandparents were not born in Jamaica, but now she learned that she had a family tree going back more than two hundred years on the island. She contemplated her long-suspected, now-confirmed Jewish heritage. "It's really overwhelming, all of this information," she said. "The whole fighting for basic human rights that the Jewish community was doing in Jamaica in 1831, I can relate to that fighting spirit. There's something about that that rings true to me."

■ Gloria's black relatives on her mother's side were as much of a mystery to her as her white Jewish relatives on her father's had been. Her mother, Pearl Avis Mills, was born in Runaway Bay, Jamaica, on October 28, 1925. "She's really smart, strong, and very brave in a lot of ways," Gloria said. Looking at her own life, Gloria felt that she inherited her mother's intellect and willingness to take chances. To cope with some of the trauma she experienced as a married woman, Pearl Mills leaned on her faith. "Even in her childhood, music and church were always intertwined." Pearl was noted in the Jamaican press for her singing. "She loved to sing," Gloria said. "Everybody knew my mother in Jamaica as being one of the best singers. She was the best." But acclaim as a singer wasn't enough to keep Pearl in Jamaica, and as a young woman, she left her home country for Canada. Before emigrating, Pearl had given birth to Gloria's half-brother Dennis. "My mother wanted to create a new life for herself and for her son. It took a lot of courage to do that."

Gloria was surprised to learn that her mother knew neither the birth dates nor the birthplaces of her own parents, Gloria's grandparents, Thomas Leopold Mills and Myra Gertrude Samuels. Fortunately, we were able to find Myra Samuels's birth certificate, and it was the start of an amazing journey. It contained two generations of Gloria's family: her grandmother herself, Myra Gertrude Samuels, who was born in St. Ann Parish, Jamaica, on February 19, 1903, and her great-grandparents, Hezekiah Samuels, born on March 12, 1861, also in St. Ann Parish, and Rebecca Higgin, born on August 28, 1879, in Orange Valley. Through the name Higgin, we would travel further back on a black person's family tree than we ever had before.

Rebecca Higgin's father, Gloria's great-great-grandfather, was named Isaac Higgin. He was born on October 22, 1846, in St. Ann Parish, Jamaica, to Thomas Higgins, as the name appeared on his son's birth certificate, and Elizabeth Martin. Thomas and Elizabeth were Gloria's third great-grandparents, and they were born in slavery.

As in the United States, slaves' names in Jamaica were almost never recorded. Unbelievably, we found Gloria's third great-grandfather's name listed in the Slave Register from 1829, alongside the name of the white man who owned him: Isaac Higgins. (Thomas's son, Gloria's great-great-grandfather Isaac, born just twelve years after slavery was abolished in Jamaica and throughout the British Empire, bore the same name as his father's master.) In that same register from 1829, we found a record of Thomas's birth. "Thomas, Negro," Gloria read, "born on September 22, 1826, son of Christmas." Not only had we found an actual birth date for a slave ancestor, but also the name of his mother, Gloria's fourth great-grandmother Christmas. The discoveries were astounding. We could now follow Christmas, a slave in early-nineteenth-century Jamaica, back through the paper trail.

Isaac Higgins's notes that accompanied Christmas's name in the Slave Register from 1817 provided a clue about her birth. As part of a list of his female slaves, he wrote: "Christmas, 10 years old, creole." At this time, the term "creole" described persons born in the New World as opposed to their country of ancestral origin. In other words, Christmas was not imported from Africa in the slave trade; she was born on Jamaican soil. Miraculously, this Slave Register brought us back another generation still, to Christmas's mother, Gloria's fifth great-grandmother. Gloria read the entry aloud: "Leonorah, negro, 50 years old, African."

Isaac Higgins's meticulous record keeping had inadvertently given Leonorah's descendants a tremendous gift, something most black people only dream of finding: their link to the mother continent. Leonorah was Gloria's original African ancestor, and we knew her name, her age, and the year of her birth. Born around 1767, in Africa, she was brought to the New World by force. A million and a half Africans died in the Middle Passage, but Leonorah survived the harrowing voyage, to be deposited on a Jamaican sugar plantation and held in bondage for what would be the rest of her life. Gloria went from having essentially no family tree to the richest one we had ever raised for a black person. "I would never have thought that it would be possible to go back this far," Gloria marveled, "into the heart of slavery."

■ Gloria was the product of two diasporas, two exiled peoples. Her Jewish ancestors were dispersed forcibly from Spain, her black ancestors from Africa. The paper trail had taken us further back than we had ever expected to go, and now we would use DNA to continue our journey into Gloria's ancestry. On her father's side her oldest named ancestor was Jacob Reuben, born in Jamaica around 1780. On her mother's side, we had hit the genealogical jackpot and found Leonorah, who was born somewhere in Africa around 1767. Gloria herself took two different DNA tests: one that determined her admixture, which is the breakdown by percentage of European, sub-Saharan African, and East Asian / Native American ancestry over the past five hundred years or so; and one that evaluated her mitochondrial DNA, which she got from her mother. Her brother Lennox took a test to determine his Y-DNA, which comes from the father and is passed down only to sons.

The results of Gloria's admixture were 59.3 percent European, 38.7 percent sub-Saharan African, and 0.3 percent East Asian / Native American. Genetically, Miss Black Ontario was far more European than African. Although we were not able to find a white ancestor by name on Gloria's mother's line, the numbers proved that there was mixing, the expected by-product of slavery.

We broke down the results of both Gloria's European DNA and her African DNA to reveal specifics about her origins. Her European ancestry registered at 28 percent northern European, 10.4 percent southern European, and 12.3 percent Ashkenazi Jewish. Ashkenazi, or eastern European, Jews comprise 80 percent of the world's Jewish population; the remaining 20 percent are Sephardic, originating in Spain, Portugal, and North Africa. We were not able to trace Gloria's Jewish ancestors back to Europe, but remember that Jamaica's original Jewish immigrants fled Spain to escape the Inquisition. Her large percentage of southern European DNA hints that Gloria may have significant Sephardic Jewish ancestry as well as Ashkenazi. Gloria laughed. "Basically I'm a Jewish girl in a black body!"

Her African results were indicative of descent from enslaved people. Her largest percentage of African DNA came from Nigeria, at 23 percent, followed by Mali, at 8 percent, and the Ivory Coast and Ghana, at 7 percent. At the time that Gloria's original slave ancestor, Leonorah, made the crossing sometime during the late eighteenth century, 40 percent of the slaves arriving in Jamaica were from what is now eastern Nigeria, mostly the Igbo people; 30 percent came from what is now Ghana; and 15 percent came from the Congo-Angola region. While we couldn't determine Leonorah's country of birth definitively, Gloria's DNA confirmed West African origins. Through further analysis of Gloria's DNA, we determined that she had African ancestry on her father's side as well, and that it came from a relatively recent ancestor on his mother's line. "It was Florence," she said. "I knew it was Florence."

We also analyzed Gloria's mitochondrial DNA, an identical genetic fingerprint passed down from mother to child, generation to generation. Gloria's oldest direct maternal ancestor was Elizabeth Martin, her third great-grandmother who was born in slavery. Gloria's direct maternal line connects her to Cameroon.

To test Gloria's father's line, we administered a test to her brother Lennox. Y-DNA is passed from father to son and tells an individual's haplogroup, a genetic population group that shares a common ancestor. The results would lead us to another surprise in Gloria's ancestry. Lennox and their father's Y-DNA is most common in North Africa and southern Europe, sometimes found in males of Sephardic Jewish ancestry, so this further supports the conclusion that Gloria has Sephardic Jewish ancestry. We discovered that Lennox's Y-DNA closely matches that of a Lindo family, a Sephardic Jewish family living in Jamaica since sometime before 1765, according to a 1904 study of Jewish families living in the Caribbean. Because her brother's Y-DNA signature is extremely rare, there is no doubt that Gloria and her brother share a common ancestor with the Lindos.

In uncovering the history of the Lindos, we discovered what might be the most shocking plot twist in Gloria's family story yet. We couldn't establish precisely when the Lindos entered Gloria's family tree, but because of the very close autosomal DNA cousin matches in the DNA databases between the Reubens and the Lindos, we can say with certainty that the connection is definite and recent. The enormous amount of autosomal DNA, which an individual inherits from her parents and from all of those on her ancestral lines, that Gloria and her brother share with multiple Lindo families indicates, in fact, that Gloria's paternal grandfather was a Lindo.

We know that Gloria's grandmother, Florence Gabay, had children by a number of men, none of whom she married. Now the DNA evidence was pointing to the fact that Gloria's father's biological father wasn't H. E. Reuben at all, as Cyril Reuben claimed on his marriage license, but a Lindo instead. This stopped Gloria in her tracks. "Are you saying that my last name should be Lindo?" The answer to that question depended on Gloria's definition of family, whether it was blood or otherwise.

■ Gloria's ancestry was among the most complicated that we had ever seen. She had experienced a flood of emotions and learned a wealth of new information. "Sephardic and Ashkenazi are new words for me," she said. "I've believed or was told that there was a Jewish part. It was surprising and validating to find out that it's such a large, high percentage." Of her African ancestry, she said proudly, "It can't get any deeper than that. It's definitely enhanced a greater understanding of things, and the broader possibilities and broader known scope of my ancestry, going back to Leonorah. That's really extraordinary."

It had taken copious amounts of research to discover the identity of Gloria's father's father, H. E. Reuben, a name that had been unknown to Gloria before her journey. Then that research was in a sense upended by DNA, which revealed that her biological grandfather was actually a man with the last name Lindo. The news was disconcerting to Gloria, and she was unsure how to react. "If the truth is that H. E. Reuben was not my grandfather, then I should not be named Reuben. I didn't know my father. So now I feel like maybe I don't know even more."

Despite her mixed emotions, Gloria's overriding feeling on meeting her ancestors was one of joy. And whether they were connected to her by blood or by name, if she could meet just one, "in a heartbeat," she said, it would be Leonorah, her fifth great-grandmother, her original slave ancestor. "I want to know her parents and how she grew up and what village she came from. What was that journey like? I would like to be with her for the majority of her life." Gloria's own amazing journey had led her to discover a complicated, complex ancestry, marvelously detailed, with many twists and turns.

The Tony Award–winning actor and TV star Courtney Vance lives in Los Angeles with his wife, the actress Angela Bassett, and their twins. But in his heart, he will tell you, home is Detroit, the troubled city in which he was born on March 12, 1960, and in which he spent what he calls an idyllic childhood. After several moves, Courtney, his parents, and his sister, Cecilie, moved into a home on West Grand Boulevard, just down the street from the legendary Motown Studios. Even in the cocoon provided by his protective parents, Courtney learned quickly that history was happening around him. When he was seven years old, the 1967 race riots tore Detroit apart. Forty-three people were killed, and more than a thousand were injured. Property damage skyrocketed into the millions. Courtney's family wasn't left untouched. The grocery store that his father managed was burned to the ground. Unable to comprehend the scene unfolding around him, young Courtney had a terrifying experience. "GI Joe was big at that time, and I had all the dolls and stuff," Courtney recalled. Though he would often sit on the steps outside his home and watch Motown's biggest stars arrive— "We didn't know who was coming in, but it was probably Smokey"—he now saw soldiers on his street. "All I thought of was GI Joe. I went up to one of the soldiers and said hi. He turned his bayonet on me, and it was just a frightening time." As a child, he ran to his mother for comfort. As an adult, he realizes the extent of the damage to the city and its people. "The city took a turn that it's still recovering from now."

In big cities across the country, demographics were changing, and Courtney's family witnessed the phenomenon of "white flight" happening around them. "My dad said that when we moved into our house, it was all white with a sprinkling of blacks. I guess we moved in June," Courtney recalled. "By the time we went to school in September, the neighborhood flipped." As white people left the city for the suburbs, resources went with them, and the urban landscape experienced tremendous decline. The environment was a negative one for Courtney and his sister. "Slowly but surely, we started having trouble," he said. "We were A students, but the focus went off being about schoolwork and on what you're wearing, how fast you were." Their parents wouldn't stand for it, and in what Courtney called "a clandestine operation, over one night," they switched their children to an all-white Catholic school. To ease his transition, Courtney's mother sent him to the Boys' Club, where a counselor took Courtney under his wing, encouraging him to apply for a scholarship at the suburban private school where he worked. "That changed my life," Courtney said. "The trajectory just went from there."

The trajectory that Courtney referred to brought him to Harvard University and the Yale School of Drama, where he met his wife, Angela. After graduating from Yale in 1986, he appeared in August Wilson's Pulitzer Prize–winning play *Fences*, starring alongside his stage parents, James Earl Jones and Mary Alice. "I got my MFA at Yale," Courtney said, "but I got my PhD from watching the two of them for six hundred performances." On the stage, playing the character of Cory, a young man who loses his father to an untimely death, Courtney acknowledged that he was standing on the shoulders of giants.

Off the stage, his praise and admiration for his own parents knew no end, but he could never be sure on whose shoulders he was standing. His father, who tragically committed suicide in 1990 when Courtney was thirty years old, was raised by foster parents. He never met his real parents or knew their names. Courtney believed that his father's unfulfilled desire to know who his parents were left him feeling untethered and isolated, and ultimately consumed him. Really, it consumed Courtney's whole family. "That's why I think our family was so close, because we knew that we were all we had," Courtney said. "My mother just weeps with the idea of knowing who her husband was and where he came from."

Courtney has written that his father's death left him without a connection to part of his past. "There was an area that we went, and we just didn't go any farther, so we just got used to going that far," Courtney said. "That's something we learned in our family, not to ask him about what had happened." Courtney had a lifetime's worth of unasked questions. We hoped we could give him the answers.

■ Courtney's father, Conroy Vance, was born in Chicago on February 6, 1933. Although Conroy passed away many years ago, his son's emotions were still close to the surface when he talked about him. "He asked me shortly before he died who were my heroes. I said, 'You are, Daddy.' I know that meant the world to him, but it was absolutely true." Conroy was a devoted father, a tinkerer and reader who "was there for everything." "He liked to fix everything himself. He wouldn't let me actually get in there and tell me what he was doing. He would just go, 'Hand me this.' My dad loved to go to Sears, to the tool department, and just poke around. He'd say, 'Come on, Court. Let's go take a run.' So I used to just take runs with him." Looking back, Courtney wondered if those runs were lost opportunities to reach out to his father. "Maybe during one of those runs, we could have talked about it"—"it," of course, referred to his father's unabating sense of loss for the mother and father he never knew.

Shortly after Courtney's father was born, he was taken in by John B. and Lucille Cooper. By the time Courtney met John B. Cooper, Lucille had passed away, and John was remarried to Bertha. Courtney and his family visited the Coopers at their home in Vandalia, which he described as halfway between Detroit and Chicago, for Thanksgiving and summer vacations. "It was a magical place for us," Courtney said. The Coopers were all Courtney knew of his father's childhood.

Finding Conroy Vance's birth certificate opened a window onto his father's past that Courtney had believed was sealed shut. For the first time, Courtney learned the name of his grandmother, Conroy's biological mother: Ardella Vance. Born in Brinkley, Arkansas, on March 16, 1915, Ardella was only seventeen years old at the time of her son's birth. On the birth certificate, the space for the father's name was left blank, indicating that Conroy was born out of wedlock. Given that she was unmarried, her reasons for putting her baby up for adoption seemed clear.

An article published in the *Chicago Defender* on October 1, 1932, revealed that there was considerably more to the story of Ardella Vance than simply that of a young unwed mother. "Girl accuses pastor as child's father," read the headline. "A seventeen-year-old schoolgirl who expects to become a mother sometime in December accused a minister of being responsible for her delicate condition Tuesday morning." The minister was the Reverend Richard W. Warren, the pastor of Mount Zion Baptist Church on Chicago's South Side and a prominent member of the Chicago community. Nearly four decades her senior, he was also a husband and a father. Ardella, who sang in his choir, testified that he brought her to an apartment several times and had sex with her.

The *Baltimore Afro-American*—along with the *Chicago Defender* and the *Amsterdam News* one of the three most prestigious black newspapers in the country—followed up on the sordid story on March 25, 1933, six weeks after Ardella had given birth to Courtney's father: "Pastor freed on paternity charges." The article detailed the outcome of the case. "A ruling that it is a scientific impossibility for a man to be the father of an eleven-month-old baby freed the Reverend Richard Warren, fifty-four-year-old pastor of the Mount Zion Baptist Church, 5512 Lafayette Avenue, last week of charges made by Miss Ardella Vance, seventeen-year-old choir singer, that he was the father of her child," Courtney read. "Testimony disclosed that the girl had known the pastor for two years and that her intimate relationship with him took place between the latter part of March 1932 and April of the same year. The girl stated that she had been with the pastor every week during the period. The baby was born February 6 past." The article went on to state, "Questioning by defense counsel revealed that the girl had a sweetheart, Solomon Green, with whom she had had prior relations." The Reverend Warren was set free, and Ardella was, in the words of her grandson, "cast as a loose woman." The case was closed in the courts, but we would reopen it later using DNA science.

Although the press focused on the unknown identity of Conroy's father, for Conroy's whole life, and for Courtney's too, Ardella's identity had also been a mystery. Now that we had her name, we discovered there was much to learn about her. "I want to know everything about her," Courtney said. Her paper trail would lead us back home to rural Arkansas, but for now we stayed with her in Chicago, where, according to the first newspaper article that investigated the paternity case in 1932, she was living with "relatives"; her uncle, a man named James Holman, was referenced by name. What had brought her to the city in the first place? A second birth certificate from the Illinois State Archives answered our question: "Larry Franklin Vance. Legitimate? No. Birth date, September 5, 1930. Mother's maiden name, Ardella Vance. Age at birth date, 15." Her birthplace was listed as Brinkley, her occupation as "school girl." Larry Franklin Vance was Courtney's biological uncle, his father's brother or half-brother. We suspect that he was put into foster care like his younger brother was; no documents proved that he ever lived with Ardella or any other member of her family.

On a Social Security application that Courtney's uncle Larry filled out sometime before his death in 2007, he provided information that Courtney's father never appeared to have. In the space for his mother's name, Larry had written "Ardella Holman"; "Vance" had been crossed out and scrawled, with an illegible first name, in the space for the name of his father. We knew that the name Vance had passed to Larry through his mother; whether or not Larry knew is unclear. It was guesswork on our part, but we believed the names Larry provided indicated that he had some knowledge of his parentage, if not a relationship. We wondered if there had ever been any similar connection between Ardella and her younger son, Conroy.

A map of Courtney's father's neighborhood suggested that it was possible. The house in which Ardella lived when she gave birth to Conroy was just around the corner, on State Street and Indiana Avenue, from the home of Conroy's foster parents, the Coopers. Courtney remembered the address. His father had once pointed it out to his mother. "They were driving in Chicago, and he said, 'That house, that house.' She said, 'Well, let's stop in.' No, he said, 'Let's keep going.' We don't know why he was so adamant about not finding out about it, but we know there's a whole side of us that we know nothing about." Courtney considered his father's childhood, and his proximity to his birth mother. "I wonder if he knew her," he said.

No matter how nurturing Courtney's father's foster parents may have been, Conroy harbored feelings of confusion and abandonment throughout his life. Ardella Vance, it seemed, also had a complicated childhood. A Social Security application that she submitted in 1940 included the full names of both of her parents: Todd Vance, born in March 1883, and Katie Holman, born in March 1890. Both of them were born in Brinkley, Arkansas, like their daughter, and a marriage certificate filed in Monroe County, Arkansas, confirmed that they were married at the time of her birth. In the 1920 federal census, we found Ardella, then called Victoria, living in Monroe County and leading a peripatetic life, claimed as part of two different households, that of her father, Todd Vance, and her stepmother, Hattie Bunch, and also of her grandparents, John and Pollie Holman. Ardella's mother, Katie, had died when Ardella was not even two years old. After her mother's death, the little girl moved back and forth between the two homes. "That poor baby," Courtney said sadly. "She bounced around."

From a contemporary perspective, Ardella's young life appeared chaotic, but that was not necessarily the case. In fact, the paper trail for Courtney's ancestors actually spoke to a level of stability that gave Courtney a sense of rootedness that was new to him. Arkansas, we learned, had been home to Ardella's family for a long time. Her grandparents, Courtney's great-great-grandparents John and Pollie Holman, had migrated to Arkansas sometime before 1880. From Pollie's death certificate, we learned that John and Pollie were both born in Tennessee, John two years before the Civil War ended and Pollie two years after. They moved to Arkansas, either separately or together, as part of a postwar mass migration of African Americans, the vast majority of whom were newly freed slaves. By 1870, more than half the black population in the state had once been held in slavery elsewhere in the South. Laws would become more restrictive after

1870, but in those first years after the war ended, Arkansas, with its cheap farmland and plentiful work on the railroads, gained a reputation as one of the most hospitable southern states for African Americans. Courtney's great-great-grandparents took advantage of the abundant opportunities their new home offered and purchased the land and the small farm on which they would raise their daughter and later their granddaughter.

Just as her granddaughter would leave Brinkley, Arkansas, for the big city of Chicago, Courtney's great-great-grandmother did, too. Around 1935, a widow for twelve years, Pollie Holman made her way north, for the second time in her life part of a mass movement of African Americans, the Great Migration, which saw more than 6 million black people move from the rural South to the urban North, Midwest, and West between 1910 and 1970. The 1940 census from Cook County, Illinois, found Courtney's great-great-grandmother living in the household of her daughter Louise Quinn and her son Joseph Holman. During the 1930s, Chicago appeared to have become the magnet for Courtney's family that Arkansas had once been. Ardella had given birth to both of her sons in Chicago, in 1930 and 1932, and she lived there for much of her life. After marrying a man named Andrew Burnett Jackson in 1935, Ardella worked as a live-in domestic with a white family in Chicago, and she had one more son. Conroy Vance's mother died in 1995 at the age of eighty.

We had dug deep into the history of Courtney's father's family. Pain and trauma colored many of the stories we had shared with him. We had uncovered the names of many people related to Courtney and his father by blood, but no amount of research could ever prove what Conroy Vance knew of the circumstances surrounding his birth or of his mother's life. "That's a question my sister and I wondered," he answered. "How much did Conroy Vance know of what his mother went through? That was something he may not have wanted, and he had to reinvent himself, as she did."

■ Courtney had gone from knowing nothing about his father's ancestors to seeing a full family tree with multiple branches spread out in front of him. Now we turned to his mother's side. Leslie Anita Daniels was born on October 22, 1934, in Boston, Massachusetts. She worked as a librarian for thirty years in Detroit. "We grew up with a love of books because we always used to go to the library and bug my mother and do our homework there," he recalled. "You had to go to the library and do all your research, because your family couldn't afford the *Encyclopaedia Britannica*." Unlike Courtney's father, his mother came from a large, close-knit family. "Mom was the connector," Courtney said. "She taught us that you call your grandmother, and you speak to your grandfather and your grandmother and your relatives at least two or three times a week." To this day, Courtney remains bound by some of his mother's rules. "When we travel, before we go and when we land, we have to touch base with my mother just to make sure. 'Yeah, we're about to take off. OK, we've landed.' Otherwise, she'll say, 'You didn't call me.'"

Courtney's mother's parents were Lloyd Abbott Daniels, born on October 6, 1912, in Lincoln County, Oklahoma, and Virginia Naomi Harris, born on April 6, 1915, in Washington, D.C. We traced Lloyd's lineage far back into slavery, to Courtney's third great-grandparents—incredibly, three sets of them: Frank Sales, born in 1826 in Alabama, and his wife, Lucinda, born around 1836 in Kentucky; Carl Lane, born in 1826 in Alabama, and his wife, Ann McClean, also born in Alabama, around 1860; and Wesey Daniels and Maryann Eutsey, for whom we were unable to locate birth years or birthplaces. To identify this many slave ancestors by name is exceedingly rare.

Little other documentation existed for Courtney's grandfather's family, and beyond this Lloyd Daniels's ancestors proved difficult to research. We had considerably better luck uncovering Courtney's grandmother's roots. A marriage record filed by his great-great-grandparents John Janey and Carrie Skinner on November 28, 1887, opened the door to a truly amazing story. John T. Janey was born in Bladensburg, Maryland, in 1842, and Caroline Skinner was born in Prince George's County, Maryland, in 1869.

At the time Courtney's great-great-grandfather was born, almost two decades before the start of the Civil War, the black population of Maryland was split almost evenly: 60 percent slave and 40 percent free. When war broke out, President Lincoln strategically allowed Maryland, bordering the nation's capital, to keep its slaves in return for being part of the Union. Slavery wouldn't be abolished in Maryland until 1864. Had Courtney's ancestor lived through those turbulent decades as a slave or as a free man? His name didn't appear in the 1860 census, as it would have were he free, but neither did we find the records of any slave owner to prove that he was held in bondage.

An advertisement printed in the *Baltimore Sun* on September 23, 1858, furnished the proof we needed. "John Janey, age 22, light brown color, five feet six or seven inches high, broad across the shoulders, has one of his front upper teeth broken, has a scar upon one of his great toes from a cut of an ax. For their recovery, if taken in a slave state, I will give two hundred dollars each. For their recovery from a free state, I will give half their value. Joseph Griffiss." Courtney's great-great-grandfather was a runaway slave, a wanted man. In the first half of the nineteenth century, runaway slaves were presumed safe if they crossed the Mason-Dixon Line and made it to the North. That changed with the passage of the Fugitive Slave Act of 1850, which required northern citizens to return runaways.

The printed word had allowed us to prove conclusively that Courtney's great-great-grandfather was a slave—and also that he evaded capture. In 1871, a book called *The Underground Railroad* was published. The author, William Still, was a free black man in Philadelphia who had risked his own freedom in the years before emancipation to shepherd hundreds of escaped slaves to safety in the North. Still's book contained profiles of every runaway slave who had passed through his network, Courtney's ancestor John Janey among them. Courtney read Still's evocative description: "Five feet eight or nine, bad teeth. September 10, 1858, John Janney [*sic*] is a fine specimen of the peculiar institution, color brown, well formed, self-possessed and intelligent." Courtney paused. "He says that he fled from Master Joseph Griffiss of Culbert [Calvert] County, Maryland. . . . His reason for leaving was partly 'bad treatment' and partly because he could 'get along better in freedom than in slavery.' He found fault with his master for not permitting him to 'learn to read,' etc. He referred to his master as a man of 'fifty years of age, with a wife and three children.' John said that 'she was a large, portly woman with an evil disposition.' . . . Thirty head of slaves belonged on the place."

With his owner's name and location, we were able to trace John Janey back into slavery, to the plantation from which he had made his brave escape. The Slave Schedule of 1850 was an addendum to the federal census that listed all the slave owners in the nation by name; their slaves were reported anonymously, described by age, gender, and color. Since John Janey was twenty-two years old when he ran away in 1858, we scoured the Slave Schedule for Calvert County, Maryland, for a boy of about fourteen on the plantation of Joseph Griffiss. We found in Griffiss's possession, among the "thirty head of slaves [that] belonged on the place," one thirteen-year-old and three seventeen-year-old males. The ages were close enough for us to feel confident that one of these nameless teenage boys was Courtney's ancestor.

Three years after John Janey's escape from slavery, the Civil War erupted.

The war raged for nearly two years before the Emancipation Proclamation officially gave black soldiers, including former slaves, the right to fight for the Union and to bear arms in combat against white Confederate soldiers. John Janey exercised that right. On October 3, 1864, Courtney's great-great-grandfather was drafted into the U.S. Colored Troops, one of nearly nine thousand black men from Maryland who served. In the year that he served, John Janey found himself at the heart of two key events of the war. Shortly after he was drafted, his regiment, the Twenty-Second, was one of the first to occupy Richmond, Virginia, when the Union army besieged the capital of the Confederacy in 1864. This battle saw some of the war's most brutal fighting. A year later, John Janey's regiment marched in the funeral procession of Abraham Lincoln. Courtney marveled at his ancestor's proximity to history. "I'm very, very proud. I'm always watching programs that deal with the Civil War and the black troops there, and to actually know that my great-great-grandfather was in the Colored Troops, was drafted and accepted, it was a big thing for black men to feel that they were helping free the slaves," Courtney said. "That you go from, in the same breath, seeing that he was a slave, that he ran away and that he participated in the Union army, and then that his regiment walked in the processional for Lincoln's funeral, the swing is so huge. My head is spinning." He paused. "I wonder if my mother knew."

■ We could trace John Janey's amazing life no further, so we turned to the family of his wife, Caroline Skinner. Caroline's father was a man named Hensen Skinner, born around 1830 in Maryland. A document called "Slave Statistics from Prince George's County," authorized by the Maryland General Assembly in 1867, contained the claims of Maryland slave owners who had sent their slaves to serve in the Union army and believed they were due compensation from the government for the loss of their slaves to the war effort. One such claim was filed by a man named H. S. Wright, whose son Henry S. Wright Jr. was drafted in 1863. There was absolutely no record of Henry S. Wright Jr.'s service. In Maryland, it was common practice for white men to send their slaves to war in their own place or in place of their sons. Although Maryland was nominally part of the Union, Prince George's County was deeply sympathetic to the South. It had a plantation economy, and more than half of the people who lived in the county were slaves. In the presidential election of 1860, Abraham Lincoln received only one vote in all of Prince George's County.

Henry S. Wright Sr., it seemed, had sent his slave Hensen Skinner to war in his son's stead. Courtney's third great-grandfather's name was among those listed in "Slave Statistics": "Skinner, Hensen, age 33, drafted in 1864 at Ellicott's Mills, Maryland, left owner to report, but is supposed to have absconded, no compensation." According to the 1860 Slave Schedule for Prince George's County, Maryland, Wright owned a twenty-eight-year-old male slave, almost certainly Courtney's third great-grandfather. "Part of me is not so amazed, because ultimately all of us came here this way," Courtney said, "but it's amazing to see that this is me."

Courtney's third great-grandfather Hensen Skinner defied orders and refused to serve. Either choice—to serve or to flee—could have spelled death for Hensen. The Confederates had pledged that they would either kill or impress back into slavery any black prisoner of war, and chances of surviving the Civil War alive as a soldier were grim: the war had a death toll of nearly three-quarters of a million. Two hundred thousand African Americans served in the United States Colored Troops. Courtney's second great-grandfather John Janey was one of them; his third great-grandfather Hensen Skinner, John Janey's father-in-law, was not.

Hensen Skinner disappeared from the record until the federal census of 1870, the first census in which African Americans appeared by name. In that census we found him living in the very place he had fled, Prince George's County, Maryland. Courtney's third great-grandparents Hensen Skinner, a forty-year-old farmhand, and Margaret Skinner, a homemaker, now lived in freedom with their four children, including Courtney's great-great-grandmother Caroline, then eleven. We have no idea what Hensen did in the intervening years between 1864 and 1870, but the census made clear that in freedom he reunited with his family.

It was rare enough that we had met Courtney's slave ancestors by name, but to learn the details of their experiences during the Civil War was astonishing. "If I was told to go fight for somebody's son, I wouldn't want to do it. At the same time," Courtney continued, "I understand Janey running away and wanting to serve. You had two ends of the spectrum, and they both end up surviving." Courtney's ancestors' paths were different, but their dreams were the same: "Everybody wants to be able to start a family and have a life."

■ Courtney's was a truly storied past. Although he had heard names from his mother's family tree, the details of their lives had been lost to time. His father's family tree had been a complete blank for him. Now we had taken Courtney back several generations and centuries, to slavery and the South, on both sides of the family. On his father's side, his earliest traceable ancestors were his fourth great-grandparents Gabriel Wilburn and Minervia Hall, born in slavery in Mississippi around 1839. On his mother's side, the earliest ancestor we identified was a woman named Jane, who was born in slavery around 1813, possibly in Alabama. We could go even further back into Courtney's ancestral past by turning to DNA science. We administered three tests to Courtney, one for his father's direct line, one for his mother's direct line, and one for his admixture, which measures an individual's percentages of European, sub-Saharan African, and East Asian / Native American ancestry over the past five hundred years or so. Courtney's African result was significantly higher than average for an African American, at 85.8 percent. His European result was only 11.8, his Native American less than 1 percent.

More than a third of Courtney's African ancestry came from Nigeria, at 38 percent. Reflected in his DNA were the regions most heavily mined for the transatlantic slave trade. Out of a total 388,000 Africans brought to America as slaves, about 72,000 came from Nigeria. Significant amounts of his African ancestry also come from Ivory Coast and Ghana (19 percent), Cameroon and Congo (10 percent), and Senegal (9 percent).

The results of Courtney's mitochondrial DNA test and his Y-DNA test held few surprises. Every human being, man or woman, gets his or her mitochondrial DNA, their maternal genetic signature, from their mother. It is identical from one generation to the next, a direct line for thousands of years, mother to child. In a test we did on his mother's line, we learned that his maternal haplogroup is very common among African Americans, reaching about 20 percent. It goes straight back to West Africa; in other words, there is no question that Courtney descends from an African female slave who came to this country during the time of the slave trade. Next we looked at his father's line. Fathers pass their Y-DNA to their sons, and his paternal haplogroup is very prominent in West Africa. Not surprisingly, Courtney's Y-DNA traces back to Africa as well. On both sides, he is a descendant of Africa.

Courtney could now pinpoint the African countries in which his ancestors originated, but the abiding mystery of his life remained unsolved. His grandmother Ardella's paternity case had indeed been closed, but Courtney remained dubious about the minister's acquittal. Now, some eighty years later, with the advances of DNA science, we could help him conclusively answer the question that had always haunted him about his father's paternity. We located a descendant of the Reverend Warren, his great-grandchild, who agreed to take the test. There was not a single segment of shared DNA between Courtney and the descendant. The court had ruled correctly. We also tested a descendant of Ardella's boyfriend Solomon Green, whom we had discovered in the 1930 census living just a few miles away from Ardella. Again, there were no overlaps between Courtney's DNA and that of Solomon Green's descendant.

We wanted to give Courtney the closure he so desperately desired, and we had one more test at our disposal. We ran a very specific test of his Y-DNA, an identical genetic fingerprint passed down from father to son, in a direct paternal line, for hundreds, even thousands of years. In other words, if there is a man alive on this earth with a Y-chromosome identical to Courtney's, this means the two of them have a shared direct male ancestor.

In yet another amazing twist in Courtney's journey, we found a match. A company specializing in genetic genealogy ran Courtney's own Y-DNA results through a vast Y-DNA database, comparing it to the Y-DNA of more than five hundred thousand men. The computer doesn't require an exact match for two men to be considered genetically linked. A "match" may have up to several mutational differences in his Y-DNA signature. In Courtney's case, we found a perfect match: a doctor in Lewisville, Arkansas, named James Arrington. Courtney and this stranger's Y-DNA results were identical. This is not random: it means they share a common male ancestor on Courtney's father's father's line, so it's possible that Courtney's father's father was also an Arrington. It was determined that there were several Arrington men in the vicinity of Ardella's residence at the time of Courtney's father's conception, so this is a very real possibility. The Y-DNA changes very slowly, so there's no way to pinpoint exactly when the shared ancestor lived or whether he unequivocally carried the Arrington surname (which was inherited from a slave owner), but the relationship itself is definite. "I've got to talk to him!" Courtney exclaimed. His excitement and relief, however, were tinged with sadness. "I wish my dad could have hung around so he could have seen this day," Courtney said. "But my mother's going to see it, and my sister's going to see it, and my children. It's a big dream."

■ We had gone back a long way on Courtney's family tree, deep into slavery and into the fight for freedom. Everything he had learned about his past was new, and in uncovering that past, he had learned the names of those, both living and dead, who shared his history. For Courtney, who had spent so much of his life unable to ask questions, having so many answers gave him great joy. Knowing names and places was different from knowing what was going on in someone's heart and head, though, and if he could go back in time to continue to piece together the story of his family, which ancestor would he choose to talk to? He answered without hesitation. "Ardella," he said. "I want to talk to Ardella." He had tremendous sympathy for his grandmother. "Poor baby. She had to have two children before she found her way. Just let me know the importance of those foundational years. No telling what she had to endure." Understandably, Courtney couldn't separate his imaginary meeting with Ardella from one with his father. "Did he just not know and he was an innocent, or he knew and didn't want to know? That's the question, because if he knew and didn't want to know, there was that pain threshold, and he just got to the place where he said, 'That's enough. I can't.'"

For Courtney, the experience of meeting his ancestors was a "journey of dead end to hope." He felt that his ancestors' own experiences contributed to the person he was as much as his DNA did. "Everybody has to know where you're from, who you're from, and where you're going. You've got to know. Why reinvent the wheel? The wheel doesn't need to be reinvented. You're somebody. You're great. Your people are great. In other words, they survived in order for you to be here and do something. My back is a little straighter now."

So is his path. Courtney once said that he'd love to get in a car and travel around the country, with one final destination: family. "I'd like to be able to say that we're going to go to our family reunion. 'I'm going to drive to our family reunion.' I haven't been able to say that," he said. "There's all these family members that are just waiting for us: 'Finally we found you guys,' or, 'You found us.'" We had given him the roadmap; now it was up to him to continue the journey on his own.

Stephen King creates characters, and Gloria Reuben and Courtney Vance interpret them. All three know the value of creating mystery and suspense, of keeping people on the edge of their seats until secrets revealed give the audience clarity and understanding. But living with mystery and suspense in one's life is another story. Stephen, Gloria, and Courtney had all begun their journeys into their roots with blanks about their fathers that needed to be filled in. The power of genealogy and DNA science allowed us to do just that, giving each one a much fuller sense of the ancestors from whom they descended. To borrow a metaphor from Stephen, for all three, the stage had been brought from darkness into light, the players now visible for all to see.

CHAPTER TWO

Born Champions

Tennis legend Billie Jean King, Yankees all-star Derek Jeter, and women's basketball pioneer Rebecca Lobo are among the greatest American athletes of all time. They each acknowledge their devoted families as the source of their strength and their success. Their parents and siblings, after all, were their earliest coaches, their earliest teammates, their earliest opponents. But what exactly goes into the making of a champion? Billie Jean, Derek, and Rebecca all come from immediate families who put a premium on involvement in their children's lives, but they knew little of their ancestry beyond their closest relatives. Did these tremendous athletes come to greatness through hard work and individual effort, or is their talent simply encoded in their genes, a gift of their hidden histories?

Billie Jean King (b. 1943)

She is one of America's most iconic sports figures. Born Billie Jean Moffitt on November 22, 1943, in Long Beach, California, she has won countless Grand Slam titles, including a record twenty Wimbledon championships, making her one of the most dominant players in the history of professional tennis. One victory stands out above all the rest: on September 20, 1973, the entire nation tuned in to watch Billie Jean King face off against Bobby Riggs. The contest was held only a year after the passage of Title IX, the federal law banning discrimination on the basis of sex in any federally funded program or activity, and Billie Jean saw it as an opportunity "to start getting the hearts and minds of people to match Title IX. I wanted to bring people together," she said, "because that's how you learn to have dialogue. That's how you learn from each other. That's the way things evolve." The match was a watershed moment in the fight for women's rights, known as the Battle of the Sexes. Bobby Riggs, who claimed that a woman could never beat him at his own game, was beaten—badly, in straight sets. Billie Jean's victory reverberated far off the tennis courts. "I knew this match was about social change. Tennis became a platform for me to try to change things," she said. "What it did for women, it helped their self-esteem." When President Obama presented her with the Presidential Medal of Freedom in 2009, he mentioned the impact Billie Jean has had on all women, athletes and nonathletes alike, including his own daughters. Billie Jean said it had meaning for men as well. "Men have come up to me with tears in their eyes, and they'll say to me, 'That match changed my life. Now I have a daughter, and I want my sons and daughters to have equal opportunity.'"

Billie Jean helped countless women rethink their identities, but she had questions about who had shaped hers. Both sides of her family kept their ancestry in the shadows. Billie Jean's father had always taught her that what mattered was the present, not the past. "He wouldn't let me read my press clippings," she said. "The first time I made the front page is when I lost. I said, 'Dad, how can they put me on the front page? I lost.' He says, 'When was it?' I said, 'Yesterday.' He says, 'Does that really matter today?'" Her family adopted the same attitude toward ancestry. Billie Jean accepted her father's lesson in terms of tennis, but not in terms of her own personal history. She wanted to learn everything we could tell her, even if it meant upending the few stories that had been passed down to her over the years. "I just love history, because it's not about the past; it's really about change," she said. "The more you know about history, the more you know about yourself."

■ On Billie Jean's father's side of the family, divorce and adoption in earlier generations had led to a complicated, cut-off family tree. Billie Jean drew no distinction between adoptive relatives and those who were biologically related to her. "That doesn't count to me at all," she said. "Family's family, and I go by the person." But in America at the turn of the twentieth century, both were still stigmatized and little spoken of. Billie Jean's father grew up in silence and passed that on to his daughter. William Jefferson Moffitt, who went by Bill, was born on April 8, 1918, in Livingston, Montana. An athlete himself, Bill was a basketball star at Polytechnic High School in Long Beach City, California. "Dad didn't miss a free throw in high school for three years, not once," Billie Jean boasted. He went on to play for the U.S. Navy and worked as a firefighter throughout Billie Jean's childhood. "He was outwardly fiery, but he was also a softie," she recalled. "If he saw the flag, he used to cry every time."

Billie Jean described her own upbringing as a *Leave It to Beaver* sort of childhood, with her homemaker mother and her firefighter father, both of whom worked hard for their children and were ever present in their lives. "Without Avon and Tupperware," Billie Jean said of her mother's part-time income, "I probably wouldn't have made it; they had to buy tennis shoes." Billie Jean's father, however, had an entirely different experience growing up. Billie Jean's paternal grandfather, William D. Moffitt Jr., was born in 1891 in Minneapolis and worked as a brakeman on the Northern Pacific Railway. Her grandmother, Blanche Leighton, called Gammie by Billie Jean and the family, was born in 1897 in Massachusetts. After years of what Billie Jean understood to be a tumultuous relationship, Bill's parents divorced when he was thirteen years old. Bill Moffitt Jr. paid child support for his son, but his involvement went no further than the monthly check.

Gammie was a different story. "I loved to go listen to her. Sometimes she'd play the piano," Billie Jean recalled. "She was interested in politics, sports. She used to smoke, which I hated. She had a temper." She also had a secret. "It's like the two-thousand-pound elephant in the room," Billie Jean said. "I think she was considered illegitimate. I kept trying to find out her maiden name, and I'm hearing all these things, but nobody had any facts. She wouldn't talk too much. I always felt like I had to drag any little itsy-bitsy piece of information out." Only once did Gammie reveal to her granddaughter the secret she had concealed for most of her life. "She said her real last name was Campbell, and I think adoption may have been mentioned once. But boy, I think she felt ashamed of her birth."

Before we began our search for Gammie's birth parents, we traced the roots of the people who had raised her. Gammie's adoptive father was named Jefferson Jerome Leighton, born on December 31, 1872, in Albion, Maine, and her adoptive mother was named Georgia Wright, born on October 18, 1874, in Ditton, Canada. Jefferson, which is Billie Jean's father's middle name, was a carpenter, first in Massachusetts and later in Montana, and Georgia worked in a candy factory. Billie Jean had never heard the names of her great-grandparents before. By tracking the family through census documents, we were able to go back another generation. In the 1880 federal census for Albion, Maine, we found Billie Jean's adoptive great-great-grandparents, James Leighton and Viola James. Both were born in Maine, James in 1840 and Viola in 1842.

James Leighton was born twenty-one years before the Civil War started, and almost 25 percent of adult men fought in the Civil War. A muster roll for Maine's Twentieth Regiment told us that Billie Jean's ancestor was among them: "Joined for duty and enrolled August 23, 1862, age 22, James Leighton." Less than a year later, Billie Jean's great-great-grandfather found himself fighting to the death in the bloodiest battle of the Civil War: Gettysburg.

In the spring of 1863, Robert E. Lee led the Confederate army on its most successful offensive in the North, and the Union was eager to block his momentum. They deployed tens of thousands of troops to stop him. Just outside Gettysburg, Pennsylvania, the two armies collided on July 1, 1863, and the Confederates easily won the first day of fighting. On July 2, the Twentieth Maine, including Billie Jean's great-great-grandfather James, were charged with holding the hill Little Round Top, one of the most important strategic points for the Union defense. A man named Howard Prince, the quartermaster in Maine's Twentieth, delivered a speech describing the events. "The front surged backward and forward like a wave," Billie Jean read. "Already, nearly half of the little force is prostrate. The dead and the wounded clog the footsteps of the living." A Union loss at Little Round Top could spell defeat for the whole war effort, and after several hours, the Union was flagging. "Ammunition is rapidly exhausted," Prince wrote. "The one word, 'Bayonets,' rings from Chamberlain's lips. Pistols are leveled, swords flash, and bayonets clash." The Twentieth had their backs against the wall, and Colonel Joshua Chamberlain ordered his men into hand-to-hand combat against the Confederates, bayonets pitted against firearms. Little Round Top would be one of the most critical moments in the entire war, and it was brutal. Fifty thousand men died during the three days of fighting at Gettysburg. One of every four soldiers in Maine's Twentieth Regiment died during the battle of Little Round Top. Amazingly, the Twentieth pushed the Confederates back off the hill and held their ground. The Union claimed victory. Billie Jean's great-great-grandfather survived a hail of bullets armed only with a bayonet. "I just don't know what would go through somebody's mind," Billie Jean said. "You go because you want to save the Union, yourself, and of course your fellow soldier. I don't think, unless you've really lived it, you would know. But this is beautiful. You took the order, and that's your job, and you're going to do it, and that's it. You want to protect."

Billie Jean had had no idea that she had an ancestor who fought in the Civil War, which claimed the lives of nearly 750,000 men, or that he played a key role in its most legendary battle. "These are the stories I wish my parents could have told me," she said wistfully. "But they didn't know them either." Genealogy is sometimes like a magnet, and we don't know why. "I've been drawn to New England; I've been drawn to Pennsylvania," she said. "Now this is clarifying. I love to understand things. When I understand things, I can relax. Knowing is so important."

The Leighton line didn't end here. We were able to trace this line, incredibly, back eight more generations to Henry Woodward, born on May 22, 1607, in England. His wife, Elizabeth Mather, was also born in England, in 1625. Henry and Elizabeth were Billie Jean's tenth great-grandparents, her original immigrant ancestors. They sailed to North America on a ship called the *James* in 1635, fifteen years after the *Mayflower* landed at Plymouth Rock. Unfortunately, the manifest for the ship burned, but we were able to learn quite a lot about Henry Woodward regardless. Trained as a doctor in England, he continued to practice medicine in the New World. He died in 1683 in Northampton, Massachusetts, according to family lore, struck dead by lightning.

Through Dr. Henry Woodward, Billie Jean had a very famous distant cousin, a fixture at Wimbledon throughout the 1980s: the late Diana, Princess of Wales. Billie Jean was delighted. "I sat with her son and Kate in the Royal box two years ago at Wimbledon, and we talked for four hours, and he was adorable!" she exclaimed. Henry Woodward, Billie Jean's tenth great-grandfather, was Princess Di's ninth great-grandfather, making Billie Jean and Princess Diana tenth cousins once removed through her adoptive great-grandparents.

■ We had gone on an amazing journey with Gammie's adoptive parents, all the way back to the early seventeenth century. Uncovering her biological parents was going to be a challenge. The name that Gammie went by as a child, Blanche Leighton, was not her birth name, and adoptions are rarely preserved in the public records that genealogists rely on. Almost immediately, we hit a wall. With no public records available to us, we turned to oral history and learned from Billie Jean's aunt Patty, the family historian, that there was an old family Bible, inside which was a carefully recorded genealogy. "We have a family Bible? That I didn't even know," Billie Jean said. The notes recorded in the Bible contained three vital pieces of information about Billie Jean's grandmother's origins: first, her birth name, Hazel Campbell; second, her birth mother's name, Elizabeth Durkee; and third, her birth mother's place of residence, Brockton, Massachusetts.

Armed with this key information, we pored over birth records for 1897, the year Gammie was born, and found a baby born in Boston with no first name but two last names: Campbell and Leighton. We had found Billie Jean's grandmother's birth record, and indeed, her birth mother's name was recorded as Elizabeth. Elizabeth was Billie Jean's great-grandmother. As we looked closely at the record, more details about Gammie's birth began to emerge. The column where the name of Gammie's father should have been was left blank. She was one of dozens of babies born at the same address, 206 West Brookline Street in Boston, that year. Baby name after baby name appeared, the column providing space for the fathers' names almost entirely blank. An advertisement in the *Boston Evening Transcript* for the home on West Brookline Street from 1912 clarified what Billie Jean had long suspected. "Talitha Cumi Maternity Home," Billie Jean read, "a home and hospital with a message of compassion and hope for girls who are facing unmarried motherhood." Talitha Cumi, Aramaic for "Arise, young woman," was a home for unwed mothers, a part of the New England Moral Reform Society. Billie Jean recalled the pain with which her grandmother had shared the scantest bit of information about her childhood. "I can feel my grandmother not wanting to say, 'Well, I was born out of wedlock.' She couldn't say it. Personally, I wouldn't have cared, but her generation would have cared. She felt a lot of shame."

Now that we had solved the mystery of Gammie's birth, we wanted to learn more about her birth mother. Elizabeth was young and unmarried when Gammie was born. The stigma was harsh, and census records revealed that after she gave her baby up for adoption, Billie Jean's great-grandmother lived with her parents in Lowell, Massachusetts, until she was in her early thirties. In addition to providing us with the name recorded in the family Bible, Billie Jean's aunt Patty told us that Elizabeth Durkee had married a man named Jim who was not the father of her child. Their union was confirmed by a marriage certificate filed in Brockton, Massachusetts, on December 16, 1914. According to the document, Elizabeth Campbell was thirty-one years old at the time of her wedding, and her husband, James Durkee, was thirty-three. Following her through the years, we learned from the 1940 census for Randolph, Massachusetts, a town about ten miles away from Brockton, that Elizabeth Durkee, age sixty-one, lived out the rest of her life as a homemaker. Her husband was a gas station attendant, and she never had another child. (There was an inconsistency between their marriage license and the 1940 census record. According to the census, Elizabeth was sixty-one in 1940, which meant that she was born in 1879 and eighteen when she gave birth to Billie Jean's grandmother. But the marriage license said she was thirty-one in 1914, which would place her birth year at 1882 or 1883. If the age on her marriage license was accurate, Elizabeth would have been just fourteen or fifteen years old when Billie Jean's grandmother was born. We were never able to resolve this discrepancy, but, based on additional census data, our genealogists believe that Elizabeth was most likely born in 1882.)

We filled in the final blank for Billie Jean by showing her a picture of her great-grandmother, so long the mystery person on her family tree. "It feels good. It feels connective," she said. "It's great to see her face, her expression. She's got good hair. We have good hair on my Gammie's side."

From here we could introduce Billie Jean to an entirely unknown branch of her family. According to her marriage certificate, Elizabeth Campbell's parents, Billie Jean's biological great-great-grandparents, were named Duncan Campbell and Ellen McCann. The 1860 census for Lewiston, Maine, was a pivotal document for our research. In it, we found Duncan Campbell living at home with his father. "This is Duncan Campbell, age 46, dyer, and then Duncan Campbell, Jr., age 18, dyer." The elder Duncan was Billie Jean's third great-grandfather. Father and son worked side by side in Lewiston's textile mills, spending twelve hours a day churning out the wool coats needed to clothe America's expanding population. Lewiston was a boomtown, and thousands of immigrants were drawn to the abundant jobs in the city's factories. It turned out that the Campbells were two of these many immigrants; the census reported their place of birth as Scotland.

Duncan Campbell Jr. and Duncan Campbell Sr., Billie Jean's second and third great-grandfathers, were her original immigrant ancestors on her grandmother's biological line. A naturalization card from that same year, dated October 1, 1860, put Billie Jean on the ship that carried her ancestors to this country. "Oh, here we go!" she exclaimed. "Name, Duncan Campbell.

Country of birth or allegiance, Killbride, Scotland. Date and port of arrival in the U.S., August 22, 1854, New York, New York." Duncan was born in 1813, in the town of Killbride, a center of weaving and dyeing just southeast of Glasgow. Her family had always talked of Scottish ancestry, and here was the proof. Now we knew where her ancestors came from, but she still wondered why they came. "It's like coming back to where everything started. I'm an American because of these beauties, coming over here and making the effort," she said. "I always wonder how people get here. What makes people want to go from point A to point B? There's got to be reasons that life wasn't right at home, or they thought it would be better someplace else. What motivates somebody to make that change, to have the courage or stupidity, whatever way it works out, to go for it?"

Billie Jean has traveled all over the world. In all of her trips to England—"Since '61, I haven't missed a year," she said—she had only been to Scotland once. "That was one of my bucket lists. When I was there, I was thinking, I've got some of my blood here. It's got to be here someplace, because I look too much like them. Now I can go look at where they're from," she said. "I've got places to go and things to do here. I've got some direction." Billie Jean couldn't help but wonder how her grandmother would have felt being handed her lost heritage. "She's been gone a long time," she said. "I hope she would have been interested and not felt ashamed."

■ Our journey through Billie Jean's father's family tree had taken us back to the early seventeenth century, revealed secrets that were recorded quietly in a family Bible without ever being uttered in public. Where would our journey through her mother's family tree take us? Billie Jean's mother, Mildred Rose Jerman, known as Betty, was born on May 26, 1922, in Taft, California. There were so many mysteries on her mother's side of the family that Billie Jean wasn't sure what to believe. "We keep hearing we have Seminole Indians in our blood. I'm thinking we're probably not Seminole. We're probably just British or something, although my grandmother on her side had pretty high cheekbones," Billie Jean laughed. Betty loved to think of herself as a descendant of Seminoles, producing Native American–style art and instilling the idea in her children. "It's been very important to my mother's identity." Despite her skepticism, Billie Jean had written of her Seminole ancestry in her memoir.

The Seminole piece was about the only thing her mother seemed to discuss openly. "My grandmother I think got married five or six times, which my mother didn't want to talk about in those days. I remember my mother saying she and my grandmother had to jump out the window, because I guess one of her husbands wasn't very nice." There were so many half-told stories. "It's hard to get a lot out of them."

Billie Jean's mother even kept her own athletic ability hidden from her daughter. "She never bragged about how good an athlete she was. She only told me a few years ago. She said, 'Oh, by the way, I was a good athlete, too.' I said, 'Why didn't you tell me?' 'Well, you know, your dad, he liked to be the one.' You know how women would defer." Billie Jean attributed her mother's reluctance to steal the spotlight from her father to her generation. "My mom finally opened up to me a few years ago about how she could run. She could beat the boys in running. She loved to fly kites. She was a really great swimmer."

What else might have been hidden? We started with Billie Jean's grandparents. Billie Jean's grandmother Doris Holliday, called Dot, was born on April 4, 1899, in St. Augustine, Florida. Her grandfather Roscoe William Jerman was born on May 14, 1901, in Mount Jewett, Pennsylvania. He was absent from both his daughter's and granddaughter's life, and it was a nonblood relation that Billie Jean preferred to call "Grandfather." "My grandfather Kehoe, who was probably my grandmother's sixth husband, was really my grandfather to me. He was adorable. I used to comb his three hairs on his head, and he was the best."

St. Augustine seemed to be at the heart of the question surrounding Billie Jean's grandmother's purported Seminole ancestry, so we began our investigation there. In the 1910 census for St. Johns County, Florida, of which St. Augustine is the county seat, Billie Jean's grandmother Dot was referred to as Ida, and she was living with her older sister and their parents, Charles G. Holliday and Vianna Crawford. Charles and Vianna were Billie Jean's great-grandparents. "Here's what I was told," Billie Jean started. "He was a black sheep from England, and he married a Seminole Indian. I'm like, uh-huh, sure." So far, half of what Billie Jean had learned about her great-grandparents was untrue. Her great-grandfather had been born on American soil, in 1875, in New York City. Vianna Crawford was born in 1879 in Volusia County, Florida. The truth about her great-grandmother remained to be seen. A number of our subjects over the years have heard family stories about Native American ancestors that turned out to be untrue. Why did this myth persist? Why do so many Americans, both black and white, aspire to Native American roots? "I think because they're the people who were really here," Billie Jean responded. "I know that a lot of people feel bad about the way we've treated them. But I really don't know."

Billie Jean had grown up in a home where their avowed Native American ancestry was a source of pride. Even her brother Randy collected arrowheads and Native American pottery and jewelry. Could the census shine any light on Vianna's birth, and therefore on Billie Jean's heritage? "Vianna, wife, 30 years old, white." She laughed. "White. I love it. This is perfect." She paused. "Oh, God, I'm not going to tell my mother!" In all fairness, race was in the eye of the beholder when it came to the census, so the "white" label wasn't necessarily accurate. We could assume that whatever her background, Vianna's skin was light enough to warrant such a description. Billie Jean would have to wait for her DNA results to learn the truth.

■ Billie Jean's grandfather, Roscoe Jerman, was a shadowy presence in the lives of his daughter and grandchildren, but his family roots were solidly planted in America. We traced his family far, far back, to the middle of the 1700s. In Colt's Station, Pennsylvania, a headstone had been erected for a man named Shubael Luce, born in 1734 and died in 1800. Shubael and his wife, Eleanor Swayze, who was born in 1732, were Billie Jean's sixth great-grandparents.

Shubael was born in Southold, Long Island, New York, in the British colonies. Already forty-one years old when the American Revolution broke out in 1775, was he too old to fight for the colonies' freedom? We found the answer in the pension file of a man named Jesse Losey. Billie Jean's sixth great-grandfather Private Shubael Luce fought in Captain Joseph Harker's company, in the Second Regiment of the Sussex County Militia. "I've got a lot of warriors here. I love it!" Billie Jean shouted. "He fought for our country to become what it is." Descended from a Patriot, Billie Jean was now eligible for membership in the Daughters of the American Revolution.

Shubael Luce, the son of David Luce and Jemima Corwin, Billie Jean's seventh great-grandparents, both born in 1705 in New York, was one of thirteen children. Through Shubael's sister, Billie Jean's sixth great-grandaunt Bethia, we uncovered another amazing story, this one about Bethia's husband and the vagaries of life during wartime for the Luce family.

In 1775, the year the Revolutionary War began, Bethia Luce married a man named Isaac Swayze (also appearing in documentation as Sweezey and Swayzie). We wondered: did the brothers-in-law Isaac Swayze and Shubael Luce serve together in the Patriot army? We combed the Continental army records and turned up nothing, but we did find Isaac's name in an article from a newspaper called the *Niagara Guardian*, dated October 26, 1811. "Isaac Swayze," Billie Jean read, "belonged to a family of that name in New Jersey, where their efforts in aid of the British cause rendered them notorious. The savage temper exhibited by Swayze in the affair affords a pretty fair specimen of the disputation of the whole gang of Revolutionary Tories." Billie Jean was shocked—a Civil War veteran, a Patriot, and now this. "I've got everything going on in this family!"

Tories, or Loyalists, were colonists who remained loyal to the British Crown during the Revolutionary War. Billie Jean's sixth great-grandfather Shubael Luce the Patriot had a Loyalist brother-in-law, notorious not only for his savage temper but also for criminal activity. "While New York remained in possession of His Majesty's troops," an article from the *Liberty Herald*, published in 1799, explained, "the Swayzes found a safe refuge there from when they made frequent excursions into the neighboring counties of Essex, Bergen, Morris for the purpose of stealing horses and other property." The family was torn in two. "This happened a lot," Billie Jean said. "Families became divided. Families had resentments forever from these occasions."

Isaac, it seemed, was quite a character. According to oral history, he was a counterfeiter and a secret agent for the British. Billie Jean was floored. "Oh, my God. Isaac, you go!" she laughed. "You're amazing. I don't think you're on the right side, but you're amazing." He was arrested for his wartime behavior, and, again, according to oral history, Isaac's wife—Billie Jean's sixth great-grandaunt Bethia Luce—helped him break out of jail. Like many other Tories, Isaac Swayze fled to the safety of Canada after the war. He died in 1828 at age seventy-seven, and his obituary was published in a history of Niagara, Canada. "He suffered imprisonment for being loyal to his king and country, escaped to the British line and has been the representative in Parliament for several years," Billie Jean read. "Isaac served during the Revolutionary War with the British army. For his services, he was granted twelve hundred acres of land in Pelham Township and Niagara Township." For his loyalty to the Crown, the British government rewarded Isaac Swayze with land; his fellow citizens rewarded him too, with election to Parliament.

Billie Jean had heard bits and pieces of some of the stories we'd told her today, but the details were always slightly off. "My mom was close. She thought the name was Lucey, that it was French, but it's not," Billie Jean said. "It's Luce, and it's Canada. They got the Canada right. It's funny.

That's just what happens with oral history. You get half right, and as you pass it down, it doesn't quite come out right." We were glad to set the record straight for Billie Jean.

We had one more story for Billie Jean attached to the Luce name. On her father's side we discovered that Billie Jean is related to perhaps the most celebrated tennis watcher in history, Diana, Princess of Wales. On her mother's side she had another famous relative whose path she had crossed many times during her tennis career. She and Henry Luce—the founder of the magazines *Time, Life, Fortune*, and *Sports Illustrated*—were seventh cousins three times removed, descended from the same Henry Luce, who was born in 1650 in England. She had appeared on the cover of her cousin's magazines many, many times, never realizing she appeared on his family tree as well.

■ Billie Jean approached her DNA tests with her characteristic enthusiasm, and it was a family affair. "My brother and I did our DNA at the same time, and we did it in the kitchen at my mom's." We administered three DNA tests to Billie Jean and her brother, Randy: a Y-DNA test to establish their direct paternal line; a mitochondrial DNA test to determine their direct maternal line; and an admixture text, which reveals percentages of European, sub-Saharan African, and East Asian / Native American ancestry since around the time of Columbus. First we looked at the results of the mitochondrial and Y-DNA results. Both Billie Jean's maternal haplogroup, a genetic population group that shares a common ancestor, and her brother's paternal haplogroup take us back to Europe. Her distant direct maternal ancestors were from the Caucuses, along the shores of the Caspian Sea, and her distant direct paternal ancestors were concentrated entirely in the British Isles. She shares a paternal haplogroup with a guest from a previous series, Stephen Colbert, as well as former president of the NAACP Ben Jealous, who is descended from many white ancestors.

Most important to Billie Jean in her quest were her admixture results. Once and for all, she would learn whether the story of her Seminole ancestor was fact or fiction. If her great-grandmother had been fully Native American, Billie Jean's admixture would be one-eighth, about 12.5 percent, Native American. She knew that she was "pretty white," but she didn't realize how white. "One hundred percent!" she shouted. "That is so boring. I didn't want to be 100 percent European." Now Billie Jean knew for sure— and worst of all, she had to break the news to her mother: there were no

Native American ancestors on the Holliday line or anywhere else on her entire family tree, at least not in recent centuries. "I would love to have Seminole," she said. "But I'm happy, because I like to know. I just think, wow, I've got to adjust here. Champions adjust." She laughed.

In terms of her European ancestry, Billie Jean's DNA underscored what we'd learned through her genealogy: she was overwhelmingly British and Irish, with a smattering of Scandinavian, French and German, and eastern European. Her result also showed 0.1 percent Ashkenazi Jewish ancestry. This Jewish ancestry, albeit a low percentage, came as a welcome relief. "Finally, a little different!" Her brother's admixture told the same story, and although the European breakdowns were slightly different, the Ashkenazi Jewish percentage was exactly the same. How did Billie Jean think her brother would react to being a full-blown white man? "He and I are going to laugh so hard," she said. "The only thing I was really concerned about was that we didn't own slaves." Her brother, though, like her mother, had identified strongly with what they believed to be their Native American heritage. "We both wanted to have the Seminole Indian part," she explained. The "goose egg" of Native American ancestry in her admixture was the most surprising finding to Billie Jean, and also the most upsetting. "I cannot tell you how this is talked about all the time and how important it is to my mom."

◾ Billie Jean's family may not have the diversity of North America in their blood—diversity they desperately wanted—but the diversity of Europe was part of them more than they realized. She had met many ancestors, learned many stories from her adoptive and biological family trees both: was there one person in particular she'd like to meet if she could go back in time? There were two; she simply couldn't separate the brothers-in-law Shubael Luce and Isaac Swayze, divided as they were in life. "I would love to meet the two soldiers who fought against each other in the Revolutionary War," she responded, "just to hear their stories and learn why one went with the Tories and one didn't. I just like to know why people decide things."

Billie Jean firmly believed that we are a combination of all those who came before us, related to us by blood or otherwise. Yes, she does feel that there's an "athletic gene" and a "gay gene," and our experiences and our upbringings have as much bearing on who we are as our genetic material does. "I think it's everything," she said. "It's DNA because God gives us certain abilities. Our brains are connected a certain way, our bodies. It's both nature and nurture." The connections, however we come by them, she said, are essential to who we are and who we become. "There's influence, and it may not be your DNA, but it's still legacy, and legacy adds up to a lot. We copy people a lot with our legacies," she said. "Each person in your life influences you. Each generation influences the next generation. All these people influenced my ancestors, whoever they are, so I'm a part of them." Billie Jean recalled the pleasurable hours she spent as a little girl getting lost in "little orange biographies" from the library. Even then, she was eager to know the history behind the names. "It helps to know about your family because you understand why you are the way you are, why I am the way I am. It makes me feel more connected."

Derek Jeter (b. 1974)

When Derek Jeter announced his retirement from baseball in 2014, it seemed impossible that he had left any dream unfulfilled. As a child he wanted to play shortstop for the New York Yankees; as an adult he did. A thirteen-time all-star, he won five World Series titles and five Golden Gloves. To date he is the Yankees' all-time hit leader by far, having accumulated more than three thousand hits. The name Derek Jeter is synonymous with winning, and he is one of the greatest players in all of baseball history.

Derek dreamed big for our exploration of his family tree, too. "I'm hoping to learn everything," he said. "Shamefully I say, but besides the closest relatives, immediate family, I don't know much. My father's black. My mother's Irish and a little bit of German. That's all I know." His parents had tried to put together their family trees, with little luck. We hoped we could untangle Derek's complex roots for him.

Derek Sanderson Jeter was born on June 26, 1974, in Pequannock, New Jersey. His parents, Sanderson Jeter and Dorothy Connors, met and fell in love in 1973, both privates in the U.S. Army stationed in Germany. Derek suspected that his parents' early years together were difficult. "I'm sure they sheltered us from a lot of the troubles they went through," he said. "They tried to explain to us that we were going to get looks. 'It's just people's ignorance; they're not used to seeing it. Don't let it bother you.'" At the time that Derek's parents married, in 1974, interracial marriage was a controversial issue: it had been illegal in many states until 1967, when the Supreme Court issued its famous decision in the landmark civil rights case *Loving v. Virginia* and finally overturned the antimiscegenation laws that had been on the books in one form or another since colonial times.

When Derek was about four his family moved to Kalamazoo, Michigan, where his father earned a master's and PhD in social work at Western Michigan University. A mixed-race family in the Midwest raised eyebrows. "Nowadays you see couples of mixed race, people don't really pay much mind to it," Derek said. "But back in the day, especially if I was going somewhere with just one of my parents, you'd get second glances, people trying to figure out what the dynamic is there. If you'd go somewhere with both of them, obviously you'd get some stares. It was a different time."

Derek and his sister, Sharlee, spent the school year in Kalamazoo, but summers they were back in New Jersey, surrounded by their maternal grandparents, cousins, and Yankees baseball. "Every night my grandmother would watch the Yankees game, so I'd sit there next to her and watch," he recalled. "That was the first thing I wanted to do. I wanted to play shortstop because my dad was a shortstop, and I wanted to play for the Yankees. I was brought up in Michigan, but I'm from Jersey. That was my first love, the New York Yankees."

Tossing the ball in his backyard as a kid, Derek couldn't imagine the heights he would reach in his career. He said that that's not part of the dream for anyone. "The dream for a lot of kids is to make it to the Major Leagues. Everyone's in the backyard pretending that they're hitting in game seven of the World Series, but that's about it," he said. "The dream never extends beyond getting there and maybe winning the World Series. You don't ever sit down and say, 'Hey, I'm going to do this for twenty years.' That's not part of the dream at all. This is all icing on the cake." Derek's love of baseball was passed down to him, and so, it seemed, was his talent, but what about all the other traits that had gotten him to the top? Fortitude, focus, drive—we would find all in large supply on his family tree.

■ Derek Jeter's father played shortstop for Fisk University in Nashville, Tennessee, one of the nation's historically black colleges. "My dad claims he was a great athlete," Derek laughed. "I remember sitting down with him, and he had this little book where he had his newspaper clippings, and he said, 'One day, if you work real hard, you're going to have a book just like this. We'll be able to compare.'" Derek's success as a professional ballplayer was never a bone of contention in their relationship. "He's never said that I'm living his dream. He told me he was good. He told me he was at a disadvantage. My dad is always at a disadvantage, no matter what. He's riding a bicycle with no tires. He's swinging a bat, and the bat's broken; they put nails in it. He said he didn't hit much, but it wasn't his fault." The affectionate bond between father and son was clear. "He's always been very proud of me, very supportive, always there for advice if I ask."

Born on November 12, 1948, in Montgomery, Alabama, Sanderson Charles Jeter never shared this bond with his father. He didn't even know his name. Sanderson's mother, Lugenia Jeter, was born in Wetumpka, Alabama, on November 2, 1914, during World War I. She died on March 8, 1979, when Derek was four years old. A single mother and a housekeeper, she had five children, all of whom bore her last name, not their fathers'. Lugenia kept Sanderson's father's name a secret; she just told him that he had a different father from his four older sisters. According to Derek, Sanderson wasn't troubled by his father's absence. "He never spoke of him, never brought it up. We just didn't talk about him." Derek, however, had a harder time fathoming it. "I always had at least one of my parents at all of my events, even though they worked and they had multiple jobs. Just knowing that they're there makes you feel good. Even today, when they come to the games, I try to find them before we start. I don't know if it's a comfort thing. It's just something I'm used to, but I always know where my parents are." Derek guessed that Sanderson may have "wanted to be the complete opposite" of his father. "It is odd to think about how close we are, and how much he was around for us. Maybe that's part of the reason why he was always there for us, because his father wasn't around."

Sanderson loved his mother deeply. "He was extremely happy with how she raised them," Derek said. "When you meet him, it shows. He's very strong like her." Like her son, Lugenia also grew up without her father. Derek's great-grandfather, John B. Jeter, known by his middle name, Busstee, was born in Elmore County, Alabama, in June 1873. In 1904 he married Minnie Palmore, Derek's great-grandmother, who was also born in Alabama, on December 20, 1884. When Minnie was just thirty-two years old, she died of tuberculosis, leaving her husband to raise their nine children. Derek's grandmother Lugenia, the youngest, was three.

By the time the 1920 census for Macon County, Alabama, was conducted, Busstee no longer lived with his family. Instead, his mother, Derek's great-great-grandmother Jane Jeter, age sixty-five, was listed as the head of household. Old census records are often riddled with spelling errors, and the census taker recorded the family's name with a "G." Derek's grandmother "Lugene Geter" was listed as seven years old, living in a household of twelve inhabitants, all of whom were Jane Jeter's grandchildren. Busstee had remarried about ten years after his first wife, Minnie, died. He was fifty-five years old. For the second time, with a second Minnie—Minnie Dabney, known as "Ma Minnie" in the family—Derek's great-grandfather became a father of nine. In fact, by the time he died on February 23, 1942, Busstee had fathered twenty-three children, fourteen of them born after he was fifty-five.

In piecing together the Jeter family tree on his own, Derek's father had come across the name of Busstee's father and Derek's great-great-grandfather, Green W. Jeter. According to family legend, Green was a prominent person in his hometown in Alabama. We hoped to go beyond the legend to get at the truth. Born in Coosa County, Alabama, in May 1844, Green Jeter spent the first twenty-one years of his life in slavery. In 1872, seven years after emancipation, Derek's great-great-grandfather founded the Mount Zion Baptist Church, one of the first black houses of worship in Wetumpka, Alabama. It was a gathering place for African Americans who had been recently released from slavery following the Civil War and who were now struggling to build their lives as free men and women. Green Jeter's legacy is still recognized in Wetumpka today. Although the original building no longer stands, the church bears a plaque that memorializes his contribution: "Mount Zion Baptist Church, organized 1872, Reverend Green Geeter, rebuilt in 1957." Furthermore, he appeared to have some standing among white community members. On October 23, 1890, the Elmore County, Alabama, *Times Democrat* described him as "the most respectable colored citizen of our community" and "a colored gentleman whom we all like." This was 1890, the year that the passage of the Separate Car Act in Louisiana opened the door to the establishment of the doctrine of "separate but equal" and legalized segregation. Even though the time known as the nadir of race relations in this country was beginning, in this paper ex-Confederates wrote openly of their affection for a black man in Alabama. This was by no means typical of the African American experience. Although the content is patronizing to our modern ears, implying that a "respectable colored citizen" was an anomaly, at the time the words were written they spoke volumes about Green Jeter's stature. In those difficult first years of freedom, how had Derek's great-great-grandfather attained such lofty status?

We were unable to track Green Jeter's whereabouts prior to the founding of the Mount Zion Baptist Church in Wetumpka in 1872. If we couldn't find him during those first seven years after emancipation, when he was a free man, it seemed unlikely we would be able to find him in slavery. Slaves had no legal standing, and their names were not recorded in census documents or other public records. Often, the only chance of finding an African American slave by name was to first find the name of his or her white owner.

Because slaves commonly took the names of their former owners, we began our search with the Jeter surname. Not only did we find a slave owner named James W. Jeter in the right part of Alabama, we also, incredibly, found his will, in which he listed the names of his slaves. "It is my will and desire," Derek read, "that the following named Negro slaves—Charity, a woman, and her six children, Green, Lewis, Laura, Hilliard, Maria, and Frances—and Pheby, a woman and her four children—Neal, Jasper, Harriet, and Alfred—and their increase be equally divided between my children by my first wife." With this document, through the words of James W. Jeter himself, we established definitively the master-slave relationship between James and Green, and also Green's mother. James W. Jeter died in 1861, the year the Civil War broke out, and in his will he bequeathed not only two generations of Derek's then-living ancestors (his great-great-grandfather Green and Green's mother, Derek's third great-grandmother Charity), but as-yet-unborn generations, their "increase," as well. "So that's how he got the name," Derek said. "I thought it was French. I was told it means 'to throw' in French." *Jeter* does indeed mean "to throw" in French, but the name was not passed down through French ancestors. None existed on Derek's family tree. James W. Jeter was the point of origin of Derek's last name.

Having his owner's name allowed us to dig even deeper into Green's roots. With no male adult named in James W. Jeter's will, we could not yet determine the identity of Green's father. We consulted the 1850 Slave Schedule from Coosa County, which contained a list of all the slaves James Jeter owned, recorded not by name but by age, gender, and color. Born in 1844, Green would have been six years old at the time the Slave Schedule was compiled. On this particular schedule, the slaves seemed to be listed by family units, because their ages were randomly grouped together. We found an entry for a six-year-old male, and immediately above it one for a twenty-one-year-old female. These were the slaves we assumed to be Charity and her son Green, listed together, with no accompanying adult males in the reckoning. Once again, this didn't help us address the question of Derek's great-great-grandfather's paternity. The anonymity of the record troubled Derek. "It's just like the cattle," Derek said. "It's just hard to believe that people are just nameless."

We moved forward in time, to the federal census of 1870, the first census in which African Americans appeared by name. Next to Green Jeter's age and occupation in the column indicating gender and color—"22, farmer, laborer"—were two letters, one of which gave us a very important clue: "M, M." The first "M," of course, stood for "male," the second for "mulatto." Derek Jeter was not the first mixed-race person in his family; his great-great-grandfather Green Jeter was mixed-race as well. While the designation "mulatto" didn't provide us with the identity of Green's father, it brought us a step closer. The fact that Green was described as mulatto suggested white ancestry, although when that white ancestry entered his family tree was impossible to say at this point.

The census contained yet another crucial piece of information. Green's personal property was valued at $250, the equivalent of about $4,000 today—a huge sum for a black man five years out of slavery to possess. By 1871, within one year of the census, another record revealed that Green had purchased 113 acres of land. Perhaps the most telling detail of all was that Green built his Mount Zion church on Jeter family land that had been given to him. Incidentally, Green's owner, James W. Jeter, who died when Green was about seventeen years old, had become an ordained minister near the end of his life. Less than a decade after the end of slavery, Derek's great-great-grandfather had become a very prosperous man in a very short time—a minister, a church founder, a property owner. He was advantaged in a way that was extraordinarily rare for newly freed slaves. The circumstantial evidence was mounting, and it was pointing toward the conclusion that Derek's great-great-grandfather was the son of his master. "So actually the name that I thought before was the name just coming from the slave owner, with really no ties, might have come from James and Charity," Derek said.

Many slave owners fathered children with their female slaves. In fact, every African American series participant we had ever tested over the years displayed some European ancestry. It's almost impossible to know the circumstances under which these children were conceived, but rape was common. As Derek put it, "Anytime you talk about slave owners and slaves, I'm sure they weren't buddy-buddy. It was not a consensual relationship, I would guess." But if James W. Jeter was indeed Green's father, there was compelling evidence that he honored his obligation and responsibility to his child, which perhaps hinted at a more loving relationship with the mother, albeit one founded in abject inequality. Derek reconsidered the different scenarios we constructed. There was hope that "it was a good relationship," he said tentatively, "or as good it could be." We could never learn what the emotional component of such a relationship was, but DNA would tell us conclusively if the relationship existed at all. For now, the paper trail on Derek's father's mother's line ended with a question mark.

■ Derek's ancestors on his father's side of the family had been brought to this country by force. He believed that his mother's family had emigrated from Ireland, but he never knew when. His mother, Dorothy Connors, was born on September 5, 1952, in Jersey City, New Jersey. She imbued him with a strong sense of self-confidence. "She believes that you can achieve anything if you set your mind to it," Derek said. "Growing up, she never allowed us to use the word 'can't,' because she really felt as though if you put your mind to it, you could accomplish it." Dorothy Connors came from a "huge" family, according to Derek—thirteen brothers and sisters, many of whom were involved in church life.

Although summers were spent with his grandparents and extended family, Derek knew little about his mother's ancestors. Like their daughter, his mother's parents were both also born in Jersey City, his grandfather William "Sonny" Connors Jr. on February 4, 1930, and his grandmother Dorothy "Dot" Tiedemann on November 18 of that same year. It was his grandmother who turned him into a Yankees fan. He spent long hours with her, but his grandfather was not as present. "They were close," he said of his grandparents, "but my grandfather was always at work. He worked at the church, so when I was there, he'd be gone before I woke up, and he'd get back pretty late. She did a lot of raising of the kids while he worked, but you could tell there was a mutual respect."

Derek's grandfather's own foundations hadn't been as solid. In fact, Derek had always been told that his grandfather had run away from home. "He was taken in by the church," Derek explained. "That's why I think he pretty much devoted his whole entire life to the church."

A look at Sonny's parents' death certificates reveals the sad truth about their difficult lives. It wasn't hard to see how their early deaths could have had a negative impact on their son. Derek's great-grandparents were also born in Jersey City, his great-grandfather William Connors Sr. on November 29, 1900, and his great-grandmother Mary Purtell on May 11, 1907. William Sr. died of pulmonary tuberculosis when Sonny was just thirteen years old. According to the family, Sonny's father was a chronic alcoholic, which likely weakened his immune system and hastened his death. Unemployed and a widow at thirty-five, Derek's great-grandmother received help from the church to feed her family. She outlived her husband by less than two years, dying of a heart attack just a few days after Sonny's fifteenth birthday. In the span of two years, Derek's grandfather lost both his parents. He was sent along with his two sisters to live with relatives, but he wouldn't stay put. Family lore said that the home he was sent to was as unstable as the one he'd left and that Sonny, too young to work and considered a burden by his new caregivers, was abused. He often sought refuge in the local Catholic church, St. Michael's in Jersey City, the same one that had given his widowed mother family assistance during desperate times.

At St. Michael's, Derek's grandfather met John Tiedemann. John and his wife, Julia, had nine children when they met Sonny. They took him in and raised him as their tenth child. Although he was never officially adopted, he became part of their family. John and Julia were Dot Tiedemann's aunt and uncle; Dot Tiedemann would become Sonny Connors's wife, and Derek's grandmother. Derek started to put together the pieces of his mother's large family. "My mother has thirteen brothers and sisters. Four are adopted. My grandmother and grandfather just had kids come in all the time," Derek said. "So that explains it." Derek's grandparents emulated the family life into which Sonny had been welcomed.

Eager to explore Derek's Irish heritage, we went back on his mother's father's line to the mid-1800s, to Derek's third great-grandfather William Charles Pierce, only to learn that Derek's ancestor wasn't Irish at all. His application for U.S. citizenship, dated October 7, 1876, listed his place of birth as Manchester, England. "England?" Derek marveled. "I can't wait to show her this!" We weren't able to pinpoint when Derek's third great-grandfather arrived in America, but we believe it was sometime during the 1860s, probably during the Civil War, when he was a young man in his twenties.

Like many poor immigrants who came to America in the middle of the nineteenth century, William Pierce was forced to settle in the notorious slums of Lower Manhattan, where immigrants crammed into dilapidated tenements and struggled daily. Derek's third great-grandfather did what he could to survive, and in 1868 he found himself defending his livelihood in a court of law. One of New York's major newspapers reported on the charge brought against Derek's ancestor. "William C. Pierce," Derek read, "the oyster saloon keeper of Number 2 Renwick Street, was tried before the Court of Special Session on a charge of keeping of a disorderly house. The complaining witness testified that the person's place was frequented by dissolute persons who were continually quarreling and fighting." Derek's ancestor ran a rough and rowdy New York City bar—not a brothel—located downtown in what was known as the Gashouse District. The complaint was eventually dismissed, but William ultimately abandoned his saloon anyway and moved to Jersey City, where he opened a furniture store. Although he started out under a cloud of disrepute, Derek's third great-grandfather's life became a classic immigrant success story. His earnings allowed him to buy a house on a quiet street in Jersey City, where he would marry and have children, laying the foundation for Derek's mother's side of the family tree.

■ The paper trail had come to an end on both sides of Derek's family. But on his father's side a mystery still lingered that could only be proven through DNA. Were the white slave owner James W. Jeter and Derek's second great-grandfather Green W. Jeter father and son? Based on the paper trail we had reason to believe this was true, but to know for sure we had to compare the Y-DNA of a direct male descendant of Green Jeter to that of one of James Jeter's white descendants. If James Jeter was Green Jeter's father, this descendant would have inherited James Jeter's Y-DNA. We found descendants on both sides who agreed to the test, and the results were definitive. It was, to borrow a metaphor from the wrong sport, a slam dunk. (This was complicated. Why couldn't Derek's own Y-DNA be used to determine paternity in this case? Testing a descendant of Green Jeter, and not testing Derek himself, was essential, because Derek's surname was inherited through a female line; in other words, Derek would not share Y-DNA with James Jeter. However, because Derek's relationship with the descendant of Green Jeter was established through the paper trail and verified through shared autosomal DNA, which is inherited from our parents and all our ancestral lines, testing in what may seem like a roundabout way solved the mystery of Green Jeter's father's identity conclusively.)

The definitive DNA evidence that Green Jeter's master was his father opened up yet another branch of Derek's family tree, and this one went all the way back to seventeenth-century England, to Derek's fifth great-grandfather William Jeter, who was born around 1717 in Lunenberg

County, Virginia. Another fifth great-grandfather, a man named Robert Moseley, fought in the American Revolution, enlisting in the Continental army on March 30, 1776, just a few months before the Declaration of Independence was signed. A private in the South Carolina regiment of Colonel LeRoy Hammond, Derek's fifth great-grandfather took part in the "reduction of Charleston," or the British invasion of Charleston, South Carolina, in 1780. The slave owner James W. Jeter's family tree was Derek's family tree, and as a result Derek now qualified for membership in the Sons of the American Revolution, as the descendant of a man who had risked his life to fight for the freedom of our country.

■ For the first time, thanks to DNA science, Derek learned that he had British ancestors with deep roots in the founding years of this country; that his roots in the South came not only from his enslaved ancestors, but also from the man who had enslaved them. Once we had the DNA evidence, we were able to trace Derek's Jeter line back to seventeenth-century England, to Derek's ninth great-grandfather William Moseley, who was born around 1605. On his mother's side, we could go back as far as Derek's fourth great-grandfather Johann Heinrich Tiedemann, who was born in Germany in the early nineteenth century.

Incredibly, DNA could tell Derek still more about his ancestry. He took three DNA tests: one to test his Y-DNA, which came from his father; one to test his mitochondrial DNA, which came from his mother; and one to test his admixture, which would measure his percentages of European, sub-Saharan African, and East Asian / Native American ancestry from roughly the last five centuries. Derek had never been able to identify his paternal grandfather by name, but testing Derek's Y-DNA proved that this unknown man carried an African Y-chromosome, which had been passed to Derek. In other words, we were able to determine conclusively that Derek's father's father was black, at least on *his* father's side. Derek's mitochondrial DNA, an identical genetic fingerprint passed from mother to child, would tell us where his maternal ancestors came from. His maternal haplogroup, a genetic population group of people who share a common ancestor, took us back to northern Europe, where it is particularly prevalent in England and Germany and Ireland. This is consistent with the paper trail.

In the admixture test, Derek's European and African results dovetailed with his genealogy—59.4 percent and 39.4 percent, respectively. His African results, when broken down, correlated with the regions most affected by the transatlantic slave trade. The largest portion of Derek's African ancestry came from Nigeria, at about 15 percent, with smaller but still significant amounts coming from Benin and Togo, Senegal, and Angola.

■ Derek told us that on census forms, he checks neither black nor white. He has always embraced both sides of his family equally, and he approached his new ancestors in that same spirit. Meeting his ancestors, black and white, didn't change his feelings about himself and his identity, but it did give him a new perspective on this country's history. After all, Derek's journey through his roots was a journey through American history, from the Revolutionary to the Civil War eras. Some ancestors were on the right side of history, and some weren't, but they had all contributed to the person Derek was today. "It just lets you know that everyone comes from someplace, and good and bad, whether it's good experiences that your ancestors had or bad experiences, this is what it's come to," he said. "I'm just glad I know it."

In Derek's long line of ancestors we'd introduced him to a Patriot, a slave who became a pillar of the community, a slave owner who turned out to be a forebear, and a saloon owner, among others. If Derek could charter a time machine to take him anywhere, which ancestor would he talk to, and what questions would he ask? The relationship between his third great-grandparents, the white James W. Jeter and his black slave Charity, continued to perplex Derek, and he wanted to ask his third great-grandfather to clarify it. "I have in my mind how I assume the relationship with Charity was, but it would be interesting to see what he was like, to see how that dynamic was," Derek said. After all, a large part of Derek's identity came out of that complicated coupling. "That's where the name started, with the slave owner." He paused. "He'd be the one. That's my name."

Rebecca Lobo (b. 1973)

Rebecca Lobo is one of the greatest players in the history of women's basketball. Born on October 6, 1973, in Hartford, Connecticut, she was the baby of the family, the youngest of three siblings. A self-described tomboy, as a little girl she followed in the footsteps of her big brother and sister onto the soccer and softball fields in the small town of Southwick, Massachusetts. But she needed go no further than the driveway of her family home to find her calling. "I loved sports," she said, "but basketball was the one that I did the most. It gave me a reason to like being tall. It was hard going to school dances. No boy's going to ask the really tall girl to dance. But on the basketball court, being tall gave me an advantage, and it made me better, and it gave me a lot of confidence." At Southwick-Tolland Regional High School, Rebecca scored 2,740 points, a state scoring record for girls and for boys until it was broken in 2009—by another girl. From the time she was a young girl she knew she wanted to play basketball professionally—a tall order for an American woman at the time, before there was a WNBA.

Preconceived notions about what girls should and shouldn't do dogged Rebecca throughout childhood. In fifth grade, her teacher pulled her aside and told her, "You need to dress more like a girl, and you need to act more like a girl. You're the only girl playing with all the boys at recess; you're the only girl sitting at the boys' table at lunch." With Rebecca in tow, her mother went to the school and laid down the law. "She was all about supporting me in what I loved to do. She made it very clear to me that it didn't matter what I wore, it didn't matter if it was boys or girls I was playing with. My mom was never the person who said, 'Why don't you wear more dresses? Why don't you do more girl things?' That wasn't what was important in life, and thank goodness, or else who knows how I would have turned out?"

A political science major at the University of Connecticut, she excelled in both academics and basketball. She led the Huskies to their first national championship in 1995 and was named NCAA Women's Basketball Player of the Year. With no professional women's basketball league in the United States yet, she planned to play overseas but instead went to the 1996 Summer Olympics, winning a gold medal as the youngest member of the U.S. women's basketball team. The WNBA formed the following year, and during her six-year career, she played for the New York Liberty, the Houston Comets, and the Connecticut Sun. "It was almost like there was a higher power rolling out this red carpet for me to walk down." She retired from professional basketball in 2003—although she still spends time on the court as her daughters' coach—and became a basketball commentator on ESPN. That same year, on April 12, she married the *Sports Illustrated* writer Steve Rushin at the Basketball Hall of Fame in Springfield, Massachusetts.

Rebecca has achieved great success through both hard work and natural talent. She grew up in a fiercely competitive family. "My grandmother, my mom's mom, would cheat at cards if she had to to win," Rebecca laughed.

"Our competitive nature definitely came from within the family, and I think the sense of teamwork did as well." And the athletic ability? "I have wondered where the height came from, but especially when I watched my mom try to play basketball with us, I realized, 'Oh, I did not inherit my athletic ability from her!'" Wherever it came from, we were determined to find it.

■ Rebecca's family was a true European melting pot. Her father traces his roots back to Spain and Poland, and her mother comes from Irish and German stock. It was those Hispanic roots on her father's side that Rebecca always identified with first and foremost. Her father, Dennis Joseph Lobo, was born on December 30, 1942, in New Britain, Connecticut. He played basketball while he was a student at UConn and went on to become a high school history teacher. "I never saw my dad play pickup. He was better than my mother when we would shoot around in the yard," Rebecca recalled, laughing. "I like to think that he was a decent basketball player." She hoped she inherited more than just athletic ability from him. "He's a tremendously caring father who was very supportive, and hopefully I am those things to my children."

Dennis's parents, Rebecca's grandparents, were Joseph María Lobo, born on December 11, 1912, in New York City, and Catherine Wade, born on August 8, 1915, also in New York. They had lived nearby, and she visited them frequently as a child, but she knew little about their origins other than that her grandfather Joseph's father, Rebecca's great-grandfather José María Lobo, was born in Cuba and was somehow involved in cigar making. The paper trail would corroborate this and tell us much, much more. On the ship manifest for the USS *Gussie*, dated June 26, 1905, we found Rebecca's great-grandfather's name among the steerage passengers journeying from Havana to Key West, Florida. He was eighteen years old, and his occupation was listed as "cigar maker." From Key West, José Lobo made his way to Tampa, to the now-famous neighborhood of Ybor City, in the midst of a tremendous population explosion of Cuban immigrants. First settled by a Spanish cigar maker from Havana in the year 1885, Ybor City had become the epicenter of American cigar manufacturing by 1900. Thousands of Hispanic immigrants flocked there to find plentiful work, churning out hundreds of millions of cigars a year. Between 1900 and 1910, the population of Tampa increased from sixteen thousand to thirty-eight thousand. By the end of that decade of intense immigration, more than ten thousand residents of the city—a quarter of its population—were foreign-born, including Rebecca's great-grandfather, José María Lobo. He would live there almost continuously for the next forty-seven years.

When he first arrived in Tampa, Rebecca's great-grandfather worked as a laborer, rolling cigars in someone else's Ybor City factory. His naturalization record, however, dated 1936, showed that he had achieved great success in his new home. On the document, he described himself as a cigar manufacturer. He now ran his own business alongside his wife, Emilia, producing boxes of cigars out of their tiny home in Tampa Heights, Florida. Despite tremendous competition in Tampa, where in 1935 nearly one hundred cigar manufacturers had set up shop in that city alone, about half run by people of Hispanic origin, José did well, and this modest business launched the Lobo family into the middle class.

Rebecca's great-grandfather became an American citizen three decades after he arrived in this country. His naturalization certificate not only provided a glimpse into his life at the time, but also painted a vivid picture of him physically. "I, José María Lobo," the document read, "cigar manufacturer, aged forty-eight years, do declare on oath that my physical description is male, white, or light complexion, brown eyes, brown hair, 5'7" tall, and weigh 120 pounds. Nationality, Cuban." "Sometimes," Rebecca said, "when you talk about your ancestors, you might have a picture of them in your brain if you've seen a photograph, but you don't think about their journey and how they got here."

What inspired his journey in the first place involved a bit more searching. José and his family lived in a town called Paso Viejo, in Cuba's westernmost province, Pinar del Río. About one hundred miles west of Havana, Pinar del Río was one of Cuba's richest provinces, producing 70 percent of Cuba's entire tobacco crop. Labor unrest among Cubans in the 1870s precipitated a division between the production of tobacco itself, which was largely dependent on the island's vast slave labor force, and the cigar production trade, which began to migrate to Florida. Cuba did not abolish slavery until 1886; in the Western Hemisphere, only Brazil held on to its slaves longer, resisting emancipation until 1888. By 1905, when Rebecca's great-grandfather immigrated to Florida, this system had been in place for about thirty years, and José would have known that he would easily find a job in the United States.

His reasons for leaving Cuba may not have been purely economic. The Cuban War for Independence, which lasted from 1895 to 1898, was tearing his homeland apart and making life unlivable. A headline in the *San*

Francisco Chronicle, dated April 28, 1896, trumpeted the horrors: "Suffering in Pinar del Rio. Plantations laid waste by rebels, cruelty of the Spaniards." The scene the article described was one of utter destruction. "The general health is bad there, and many poor people from the fields who are without homes are dying. No business is done, and there is great suffering. Many plantations, including three hundred buildings, have been deserted, and there is nothing left to support life." Ever since Christopher Columbus landed in Cuba in 1492, the island nation had been ruled by Spain, but by the middle of the nineteenth century, Cuban rebels determined to end Spanish domination waged a series of wars, culminating in this bitter struggle.

The war would eventually spread to other parts of the island, but at the outset Pinar del Río was at the center of the conflict, buffeted between the rebels and the Spaniards, and it suffered terribly. At first, the Cuban freedom fighters sought to deprive the Spanish of Pinar del Río's abundant resources, so they torched farms and houses across the province. They even destroyed fences, allowing livestock to escape. It was guerrilla warfare. Near the end of 1896, conditions in Pinar del Río took a dramatic turn for the worse when the Spanish began to employ a ruthless tactic so novel that they had to invent a name for it: "reconcentration." It is a well-kept secret that concentration camps were the brainchild of the Spanish. Moving to stamp out the rebellion in the rural areas, Spanish troops herded the residents of Pinar del Río and Havana into camps, where prisoners were forced to live in dangerously dilapidated structures, exposed to the elements and underfed. Famine and disease spread through the camps like wildfire. More than four hundred thousand Cubans are estimated to have died as a result of this inhumane Spanish policy.

In 1898, the United States entered the conflict, and Teddy Roosevelt's Rough Riders gained acclaim for their ultimate vanquishing of the Spanish troops. In American history books, what Cubans call the Cuban War for Independence, we call the Spanish-American War. America's involvement finally set Cuba on the road to independence, but Rebecca's ancestors' homeland of Pinar del Río lay in ruins. Only five significant towns in the province escaped total incineration. Her great-grandfather José was just eleven years old when all this was happening. He would stay in Cuba for another seven years, setting sail for America when he was eighteen.

In researching Rebecca's great-grandfather, we learned that his family had been loyal to Spain rather than to the Cuban rebels during the War of

Independence, and in fact did not take part in the fighting. Gaining access to Cuban records was extremely difficult, but fortunately Rebecca's great-grandfather's baptismal record had survived, and inscribed on it was the reason for the Lobos' loyalty. Baptized as the "legitimate son" of José María Lobo and Vincenta Perez, Rebecca's great-great-grandparents, in 1887 in the church of San Rosendo in the city of Pinar del Río, Rebecca's great-grandfather was Cuban-born. On this one document, where we found three generations of family names—her great-grandfather's, her great-great-grandparents', and their parents' or Rebecca's third great-grandparents', Vicente Lobo and María Montoto and Nicholas Perez and Josefa Blanco—we learned that the generations preceding her great-grandfather were born not in Cuba but in the Asturias province of northern Spain. José's parents had been in Cuba for just one generation, and in the war they stood on the side of their homeland. Rebecca had had no idea that her family's time in Cuba was so short. What did she make of this revelation? Did she now consider that branch of the family Cuban or Spanish? "I've always felt like they were Cuban. I'm not sure how to think of them, especially since they were loyal to Spain in the war," she said.

Rebecca's great-great-grandfather José Lobo had immigrated to Cuba from Cádiz, Spain, in 1872, fifteen years before her great-grandfather was born in Pinar del Río. He traveled aboard a mail-carrying steamship called the *Antonio Lopez*, leaving established Spain for the Wild West of Cuba. Through additional meticulously kept church records, we were able to learn the names of the ancestors whom Rebecca's great-great-grandparents left behind. Her great-great-grandfather's baptismal record, from June 7, 1842, describes him as the "legitimate child of a legitimate marriage" of Vicente Lobo and María Montoto, Rebecca's third great-grandparents, already identified on her great-grandfather's baptismal record. Like the Cuban baptismal record, this one also contains the names of the paternal and maternal grandparents—Rebecca's fourth great-grandparents—Manuel Lobo and Gertrudis de Pedro, and José Montoto and María Espina. For both the maternal and paternal sides of her great-grandfather's family, Asturias, a province in northern Spain, was home. Rebecca's family, it turned out, has deep roots in northern Spain.

■ It was time now to turn to another line of Rebecca's father's family, that of José María Lobo's wife, Rebecca's great-grandmother Emilia Gutiérrez. Emilia died before Rebecca was born, and Rebecca knew little about her.

"I remember being told that she was tall," Rebecca laughed. "But in terms of her origins, I don't remember hearing very much." Emilia and José met and married in Florida, but where did her family come from? Her naturalization record, filed in Florida on June 10, 1936, gave us our answer. "I, María Emilia Lobo, housewife, aged forty-four years," Rebecca read, "do declare on oath that my physical description is female, white, of light complexion, brown eyes, gray hair, am 5'9" and weigh 250 pounds, and I am Spanish."

This document confirmed that Emilia was indeed a tall, imposing woman, in fact weighing twice as much as her husband, but much more importantly, we now knew definitively that Emilia was Spanish. Yet according to family lore, Emilia had been born in Tangier, Morocco. Fortunately Emilia's baptismal record had survived, dated February 6, 1891—from the Catholic Church of the First Conception in Tangier. Given the name María Emilia at birth, she was "a legitimate daughter" of Antonio Gutiérrez of Puerto Real in Cádiz and of Catalina Roca of Gibraltar. The family stories were true. Emilia was born in Tangier, but her parents, Rebecca's great-great-grandparents, were born in Spain. What brought the Gutiérrez family to Morocco?

In the late nineteenth century, Tangier was not an unusual place for a Spanish family to settle. It was an international crossroads where open-air markets overflowed with Arabs, French, and Spaniards. Despite an exhaustive search, we could learn nothing about Rebecca's great-great-grandfather Antonio's life in Cádiz. All the official records had been destroyed, but something very precious remained in Rebecca's family. One of her cousins showed us a handwritten diary that Rebecca's great-grandmother herself had kept more than a century ago. "When you see handwriting versus typewritten things, it just feels more alive," Rebecca said. In it, Emilia had written pages and pages about her father's life back in Spain that brought the family's first migration to life and revealed that their move was tied up in the politics of the day. "Father was a free-loving one," Rebecca's great-grandmother had written. "He had done his share of giving Spain its First Republic, which lasted but six months. He had to leave his native country because of his way of thinking."

Spain's First Republic represented a dramatic, albeit short-lived, moment in Spanish history. In 1873, when Rebecca's great-great-grandfather Antonio was twenty-four years old, democratic revolutionaries briefly overthrew the Spanish monarchy. The hard-won republic would last for less than two years. According to Emilia's diary, her father fought with the rebels and was very friendly with a brash, charismatic figure named Fermín Salvochea, the leader of the revolution in Antonio's home province of Cádiz. Although obscure today, during the 1860s and 1870s Salvochea was a notorious revolutionary. When the First Republic fell in December 1874, Salvochea was arrested and sentenced to life in prison. In 1883, he escaped and fled to Morocco. From Emilia's diary, we would learn that Antonio's fate was intricately intertwined with Salvochea's.

In an undated letter that Emilia wrote to her son, Rebecca's grandfather, Joseph Lobo, she told the spectacular story of her father's departure from Spain. "Your grandfather, Antonio, and his friend had to leave in a little sailboat dressed as priests. This man, Mr. Salvochea, put me to sleep in his arms many times when I was a baby," she wrote. "Remember, you are a seed of that republic." Rebecca admired her grandmother for passing the story down, ensuring that the family history was not lost. She had many times told her own children the same thing: "Don't forget where you come from."

Now that we understood the first leg of the Gutiérrez family's journey, from Spain to Morocco, what about the second leg, from Morocco to the United States? On October 12, 1896, Rebecca's great-grandmother Emilia, just five years old, arrived at the Port of New York from Gibraltar with her parents, sister, and brother. At the turn of the twentieth century, the time of the Gutiérrezes' migration, the United States was flooded by a wave of immigrants in numbers almost unparalleled in modern human history. Some 10 million people sought safe haven on these shores, drawn to the United States and its promise of freedom and opportunity.

Emilia's family, however, never intended to be among them. In her diary, Emilia chronicled her family's exodus from Morocco. "After twenty years in Tangier," she wrote, "my parents made a decision to leave for South America, but when we arrived at Gibraltar, the steamer we were supposed to leave on had left. So right then, they decided to take the steamer that was going to leave in a few hours for North America." Rebecca laughed as she continued reading. "Father said to Mother, 'Kitty, we are going to the country we do not know, but I have heard it is the land of opportunity.'" Her Argentina-bound great-great-grandparents had literally missed the boat, and in a split second Rebecca's great-great-grandfather changed the course of his and his descendants' lives. "It's amazing," Rebecca said. "Any little misstep along the way, and I wouldn't be here."

■ We had gone back generations on the Lobo branch of the family tree. Rebecca was less hopeful about tracing her ancestors on her paternal grandmother Catherine Wade's side. "I'm thinking this one is going to be a lot more difficult to document," Rebecca said. Her grandmother's childhood had been one of tremendous hardship, and Rebecca knew little beyond that. We would see what we could add to the story of her life. We started our search in the 1930 federal census for Brooklyn, Kings County, New York, and found the large Wade family, headed by Rebecca's great-grandfather Joseph Wade, living in a home he and his wife, Mary, Rebecca's great-grandmother, rented for twenty-three dollars a month. Catherine, at age fourteen, was the eldest of four children. Although Catherine and her father shared the same last name, Rebecca said that he was not her biological father. "My understanding is that Pop Wade was not a kind man to her. In terms of her family, that's about what I know."

Rebecca's great-uncle Joe, the youngest of the Wade children, told us that the family struggled financially. During the height of the Great Depression, they came home one day to discover their furniture on the street because they hadn't paid their rent. They ended up sleeping in the park for several nights. "I know that they didn't have an easy life," Rebecca said. "But when my grandmother spoke of New York, it wasn't in unfavorable ways. Most of the stories she would tell me would be about walking down the street with my grandfather when they were dating or those type of things." We saw painful memories suppressed like this time and again in our searches for people's roots.

According to their marriage license, Rebecca's great-grandparents Joseph Wade and Maria Olech, called Mary in the census, were married on July 3, 1917. Mary's daughter Catherine, Rebecca's grandmother, was born on August 8, 1915, lending credence to the idea that she was not raised by her biological father. What more could we learn about Rebecca's great-grandmother to get us to the heart of the matter? Both the census and her marriage license told us that she had emigrated from Austria to the United States in 1913. We confirmed this on a passenger list for the SS *Prinz Friedrich Wilhelm*, which arrived at the Port of New York on October 6—Rebecca's birthday. Nineteen-year-old Maryanna Olech had come to this country, in steerage, with twenty-five dollars in her pocket, her occupation listed as "servant" and her race listed as "Polish," from the town of Brzezany. Today Brzezany is in Ukraine, but Rebecca's great-grandmother's hometown changed hands many times. It was part of a region of eastern Europe called Galicia, which was under Austrian rule until the end of World War I. With the war's end Galicia reverted to Poland, to which it had belonged during the sixteenth century.

At the time of Mary's birth, Galicia was the poorest province in the Austro-Hungarian Empire. Indeed, it was one of the poorest provinces in all of Europe. Not surprisingly, that region soon became a major source of immigration for the United States. In 1913, the year that Rebecca's great-grandmother emigrated, another four hundred thousand people left Galicia—nearly a half million people from one province in one year alone. Unfortunately, despite our best efforts, we found no records to tell us more about Mary's origins in Galicia. Her family was most likely very, very poor, and, like so many others, she came to America looking for a better life.

A photograph of Rebecca's great-grandmother Mary, taken in New York City in 1916, indicated that perhaps she had found it. She was dressed in the height of fashion, wearing a fur coat and a muff. Fabric experts analyzed the photograph and determined that the coat was probably fox and, together with the muff, would have sold for just under three hundred dollars—the equivalent of six thousand dollars today. We learned that after her arrival in New York, Rebecca's great-grandmother found work as a maid in the home of a wealthy family in the city. Relatives told us that she had an illicit affair with a man of that house and became pregnant. That man would thus have been Catherine's biological father. It was a tantalizing story, one that might explain the upscale clothes worn by this recently downtrodden woman, but the evidence was merely circumstantial. The identity of Catherine's father would for now remain a mystery.

■ In 1996, the year the WNBA formed, Rebecca and her mother, RuthAnn McLaughlin Lobo, coauthored the book *Home Team: Of Mothers, Daughters, and American Champions*. Rebecca never looked any further than her own home to find her heroes. "People ask me 'Who was your role model when you were a kid?' and they think I'm going to mention a basketball player," Rebecca said. "But it was my parents." Her mother championed her at every turn. "When I was in third or fourth grade, I was the only girl on the first basketball team I played on, because only two girls had signed up to play," Rebecca recalled. "The team called and said, 'We're sorry; there's not a girls' team.' My mom said, 'Well, let Rebecca play on the boys' team. Treat her exactly the way you treat all the boys, except when you go shirts and skins, she's on the shirts team.'"

RuthAnn McLaughlin was born on January 5, 1944, in Wilkes-Barre, Pennsylvania, to a young widow named Ruth Sauer. RuthAnn's father, James McLaughlin, a tail gunner on an airship during World War II, was killed in action seven months before his daughter was born. He was only twenty-one years old. Rebecca's grandparents had been married on March 28, 1943, shortly before James shipped out and just shy of three months before he was killed. They were together as husband and wife only for a few weeks. Rebecca admired their wedding photo, noting that she and her mother had both inherited their height from the young soldier. Rebecca's grandfather served in the 379th Bombardment Group of the Army Air Corps. The 379th's achievements ranked among the best in the European theater of operations during the entire war, but these achievements came at a great cost to Rebecca's family. "My mom talked about the fact that she never got to meet her dad, but she had such a wonderful stepfather, who was just her father to her, that I don't think she ever felt a void in her life," Rebecca said. "But the area where it really touched her was to think of her mom as a bride, a widow, and a mother all in the span of a year. That's the part that really got to my mom. I know very, very little about my mom's dad's side of the family."

Rebecca's grandparents' marriage certificate allowed us to go back a generation on the McLaughlin line. James McLaughlin's parents, Rebecca's great-grandparents, were Peter McLaughlin and Jule Ayers, and they lived in Wilkes-Barre, Pennsylvania, with their four children, James and his three sisters. Peter McLaughlin was born on January 19, 1896, and Jule— also called Julia—was born on February 15, 1899, both in the town of Plymouth in Luzerne County, Pennsylvania. This was coal-mining country, and Rebecca's great-grandfather was a coal miner. At the time, 99 percent of all the anthracite coal that was mined in the entire United States came from a narrow strip in northern Pennsylvania. It was only twenty-five miles long and thirty-five miles wide, and Rebecca's ancestors lived right in the middle of that strip. Every word of this was new to Rebecca. "I didn't know that," Rebecca said. "I didn't even know my grandfather had three sisters."

Rebecca's great-grandfather's employment record from the year 1929 with a company called the Glen Alden Coal Company not only revealed facts about his life in present-day Luzerne County, Pennsylvania, but also opened wide a window onto Rebecca's family's past. According to the record, by 1929, Peter Vincent McLaughlin, of Irish descent on his father's side and Welsh descent on his mother's, was earning $220 a month after twenty years in the anthracite industry, seventeen years with this company in particular. The highest level of education he had completed was sixth grade, and three other relatives were employed by the same company: his father, James, Rebecca's great-great-grandfather, was a pulleyman; his brother James was a timberman; and another brother, Edward, was called an "outside laborer."

Four of Rebecca's McLaughlin ancestors were working for the same company, leading the same dangerous, difficult life. A clipping from the local Wilkes-Barre newspaper from 1915 underscored just how dangerous and difficult it was, on a very personal level. "John Ayers killed in Parrish Mine," Rebecca read. "The unfortunate man was employed as a timberman and was at work assisting in unloading a large collar from a mine cart when it rolled over upon him and crushed his body badly, causing instant death. The deceased was twenty-nine years of age." John Ayers was the older brother of Rebecca's great-grandmother. She was sixteen years old when this accident occurred. The Pennsylvania coal-mining industry's history is rife with such disasters. In 1919, the year that Peter McLaughlin and Julia Ayers were married, a massive explosion, which became known as the Slavic Inferno, rocked Wilkes-Barre's Baltimore tunnel, killing ninety-two men, most of whom were immigrants. That was just a fraction of the more than six hundred men who died that year alone in these mines.

The death certificate of William Ayers, Julia's father and Rebecca's great-great-grandfather, dated March 30, 1911, revealed another deadly hazard associated with coal mining. At age forty-two, Rebecca's great-great-grandfather succumbed to what his death certificate termed "anthracosis," or black lung disease. The Ayers family's suffering was not out of the ordinary for the region's many coal-mining families.

Like so many other immigrants, Rebecca's Ayers ancestors had come to this country seeking a better life. Rebecca's third great-grandfather John Ayer made the crossing in 1846. (The next generation added the "s" to the surname.) A petition he filed with Luzerne County in 1859, two years before the Civil War started, brought us back to the moment he first landed on American soil. "The petition of John Ayer, a native of Ireland, respectfully showeth that your petitioner arrived in the United States of America, to wit, at the Port of New York on the 22nd day of June in the year 1846." John Ayer was the first Irishman in Rebecca's bloodline to become an American. In an interesting coincidence, June 22 was the date on which Rebecca's grandfather died defending this country during World War II.

The same summer day marked a triumphant arrival and a tragic loss in Rebecca's mother's family.

We don't know from where in Ireland John Ayer came or who his parents were. Irish genealogy is notoriously difficult to trace because of the widespread destruction of genealogical files and church records. We knew, though, that the year of Rebecca's third great-grandfather's arrival in this country, 1846, was a devastating one for Ireland. The Irish potato famine had begun the year before. With the failure of the potato crop, Ireland's Roman Catholics, among them Rebecca's Ayer ancestors, were starving, but the British demanded that they continue to export wheat, barley, and oats to England. Approximately 1 million Irish died of starvation and disease between 1845 and 1851, and another million, about 25 percent of the population, fled their homeland. Rebecca's third great-grandfather John Ayer was part of that mass exodus. In the same year that the potato famine finally ended, Rebecca's third great-grandfather filed a declaration of intention in Schuykill County, on September 8, 1851. "John Ayer, upon his solemn oath, declares his bona fide intention to become a citizen of the United States and renounce forever all allegiance and fidelity to the queen of Great Britain and Ireland, of whom he was before a subject." The document bore Rebecca's ancestor's signature. "The handwriting gets me more than anything," she said. "It brings him to life."

John Ayer came to America, settled in Pennsylvania coal-mining country, and started this line of Rebecca's family, which led all the way down to her own mother, RuthAnn. Amazingly, her mother either didn't know or didn't share any of this with her daughter. "She said she knew that they were Irish, but did not tell me about their working in the coal mines or anything like that. I don't know if she knew that." She paused. "But she did know she came from very, very hardworking people."

■ When we first met Rebecca, she told us she had always described herself as German, Irish, Spanish, and Polish. We had given her names and places and facts to support her most basic knowledge of her ancestry. We were able to trace her paternal side all the way back to her fourth great-grandfather Manuel Lobo, who was born in Berbio, Spain, in about 1770, five years before the Battles of Lexington and Concord. The oldest ancestor we identified on her mother's side was also a fourth great-grandfather, Georg Jacob Gorlitz, born around 1771, at about the same time as Manuel Lobo, in Germany. Georg's son Nicholas had arrived at the Port of New

York in 1852 and then moved to Wilkes-Barre, Pennsylvania, a town that figured prominently in Rebecca's mother's family history.

Our genealogical research on Rebecca had taken us to the time before the American Revolution. We could go back even further into Rebecca's past with DNA. We administered three different tests to her, one of which was an admixture test, which shows an individual's percentages of European, sub-Saharan African, and East Asian / Native American ancestry since the time of Columbus. "Holy smokes," she laughed, looking at the results on the chart in front of her, "there's a lot of European in here." Rebecca's European result was 99.3 percent. "Don't most people tend to have a little more of a mixture?" Rebecca asked. "It surprises me a little bit, because I would just think that there might have been something else that found its way in there."

The breakdown of Rebecca's European DNA was largely consistent with her genealogical history, with large percentages from both northern and southern Europe and the British Isles. One result, however, didn't corroborate any ancestry we'd uncovered in the paper trail. Rebecca has 10.7 percent eastern European ancestry and 10.2 percent Ashkenazi Jewish ancestry. Since we all inherit roughly 12.5 percent of our DNA from each of our great-grandparents, Rebecca's results strongly suggested that one of her great-grandparents was Jewish. She recalled the central mystery of her grandmother's life. "I think it would be the mystery great-grandfather," she said, "my grandmother's father that we don't know anything about." Chromosome analysis revealed that Rebecca's Jewish DNA came from her grandmother Catherine, meaning that one of Catherine's parents actually was Jewish. When we had researched the genealogy of her mother, Rebecca's great-grandmother Mary Olech, we found no evidence of Jewish heritage. Catherine's mysterious father, beyond a shadow of a doubt, was Jewish. "Finally, finally we know something about him," Rebecca said. "We finally know part of the story we didn't know before. This whole thing is a gift being given to me."

There was one more set of test results to share with Rebecca. An autosomal DNA test, which evaluates DNA received from both an individual's parents and all of his or her ancestral lines, can locate living genetic cousins, people who share common ancestors. Rebecca, it turned out, had a very large Jewish family. Of previous participants in our series, she was genetically related to Harry Connick Jr. and Barbara Walters. Her father found genetic cousins in Rabbi Angela Buchdahl and Carole King. Their distant common ancestor has to be linked to each of them through the nameless Jewish man who fathered Rebecca's grandmother. If we had ideal family trees for any of these individuals, with sixty-four fourth great-grandparents, thirty-two third great-grandparents, and so on, the same man would appear on both of their trees. "It's like the NCAA brackets," Rebecca joked, "going from sixty-four down to one."

■ We had come to the end of our journey with Rebecca, and it was a fascinating one. When asked which of her many ancestors she could meet if she had the opportunity to travel back through time, she didn't look further than the twentieth century. "It would probably be my mom's dad," she said. That was James McLaughlin, who died tragically young in the service of his country and whose daughter was born seven months after his fatal plane crash. "There's a very incomplete picture there, because my grandmother wasn't married to him for that long, and my mom never met him. I just know how much she loved him. It's not that far back, but it's somebody I would like to know."

She had met countless other forebears in our time together, learning names of ancestors born before the American Revolution. What was their impact on her? Is it the DNA we share with our ancestors that makes us who we are? Is it the lives we lead, or even the lives they led? For Rebecca, nature and nurture were inextricable. "There are some strong lines in my history, whether it's from Spain or the Ukraine or wherever. There seems to be that common notion of people working really hard to make a better life for their children, and a legitimate one," she said, recalling the number of times the word "legitimate" appeared on her Spanish ancestors' birth records. "A big part of it is our DNA and where we come from, but I don't think it's necessarily the geography of it as much as it is the backgrounds in terms of the struggles that people have had to forge through, that have cultivated who they become as people in terms of how hard they were going to work, what faith they were going to be, and how they were going to raise their children."

Many of the stories on Rebecca's family tree came as a complete surprise to her. Only three generations stood between her and her Spanish ancestry, and she had significant Jewish ancestry that had been entirely unknown before now. Did this new knowledge change the way she saw herself? "I don't think it changes how I see myself, but it definitely makes me appreciate how I got here. There's a fascinating narrative for each one of these journeys that my ancestors took to get here." She recalled the theme of fortitude that ran through her family stories. "Now I know the hardworking background that my family comes from was established a long time ago. Now I know where that started, and it's really amazing."

Some scientists believe that athletic greatness is largely genetic, that athletes inherit biological traits that are the secret to their success. But in a crowded field of great athletes, Billie Jean King, Derek Jeter, and Rebecca Lobo stand out above the rest, their athletic abilities matched only by their capacity for focus and determination. We had discovered long lines of individuals on their family trees who exhibited resolve, endurance, and strength under pressure. The source of these athletes' greatness, it seemed, was not simply in their DNA, but also in the values that their ancestors had passed down to them, in ways they had never known.

CHAPTER THREE

Our American Storytellers

Throughout their careers, the documentary filmmaker Ken Burns, the journalist Anderson Cooper, and the playwright Anna Deavere Smith have been compelled to chronicle the lives of others. Their singular approaches to presentation and performance have changed the way we view history and the individual's role in it. For Ken, a faded photograph of a bedraggled Confederate soldier leads to a probing and personal exploration of the Civil War. For Anderson, a report on war-torn Somalia in 1992 is not a broad overview of monolithic "refugees," but an intimate portrayal of an individual with a specific name and a specific story of suffering to tell. For Anna, pitch-perfect impressions gleaned from her interviews with thousands and thousands of people result in stage plays that confront and clarify issues of race and identity, unique in their intimacy and insight. Ken, Anderson, and Anna had always known they had stories to tell, but those stories belonged to others. In looking outward, they had neglected to look inward to discover their own.

Ken Burns (b. 1953)

Ken Burns is one of the country's most celebrated documentary filmmakers. His films on the Civil War and the history of jazz and baseball are etched into our national consciousness, not just for their scope but for their signature style as well. "Nobody pressured me to be an anthropologist or a doctor or a lawyer or an Indian chief," Ken said. "I was allowed to be what I wanted, and I wanted to be a filmmaker." Kenneth Lauren Burns was born on July 29, 1953, in Brooklyn, New York, to Robert Burns, a cultural anthropologist, and Lyla Smith Tupper, a biotechnician. His was a nomadic childhood. He and his brother Ric, also a filmmaker, were uprooted frequently by their academic parents. At different points in his life, Ken called home Brooklyn; France; Baltimore; Newark, Delaware; and Ann Arbor, Michigan.

His mother's death, as well as the anticipation of it, loomed over his entire childhood. "My mother died when I was eleven of a cancer that began when I was two. There was never a moment in my childhood where she wasn't dying and where there wasn't the apprehension of a very small boy that something really terrible was going to happen." He was well into adulthood before he realized that his mother's death was present in every film he made and was the driving force behind the direction that his career took. "It took me into my forties to put it all together. I had a really close friend who, when I was having some trauma, I just said, 'I seem to be keeping my mother alive.' He said, 'I'll bet as a kid, you blew out your candles, wishing she'd come back.' And I said, 'What do you mean?' 'Look at what you do for a living: you wake the dead. You make Abraham Lincoln and Frederick Douglass and Jackie Robinson and Louis Armstrong come alive. Who do you think you're really trying to wake?'" Ken thought about the career path he'd chosen as compared to his father's. "I sort of felt I had done something different, and yet, when I look back, there's no gap between him and me. Cultural anthropologist."

American history has always figured into Ken's worldview. The town of Burnsville, Virginia, was named for an ancestor. His grandparents visited Civil War battle sites on their honeymoon. "History may have been the seed," he said. "I was always interested in it, always interested." He describes his storytelling and editing technique, which has been dubbed the "Burns effect," as a way of looking at the past and bringing that past into our lives. "What I was doing in my own films was to trust that that arrested moment had a past to it and a future, and that you could bring that photo alive." Ken Burns has left his stamp on many families, not just those who have watched his series. "I know I've saved lots of bar mitzvahs and weddings and vacations by being able to organize people's stuff into a nicely moving series of still photographs." Family slideshows, he concedes, aren't entirely different from his films. "Whatever we're doing, whether it's making that 'This is what I did on my summer vacation' or struggling to understand the Civil War, we tell ourselves stories."

Ken had explored some of his own family history, but there were mysteries in his background that remained just that, and he hoped that we could solve them. "I've spent my entire professional life as a filmmaker inexorably drawn to race and assumed that somewhere there must have been some African American blood. Earlier genealogical investigations had proved not. They had given me the idea that I was the sixth cousin of Abraham Lincoln, which was tremendous solace for not having even one drop of African American blood, which was still a bitter disappointment to me." Then there was the matter of his last name. "Through my upbringing, we were told by relatives who weren't in the business of making things up, professionals with PhDs, scholars, scientists, that we were somehow tangentially related to the poet Robert Burns. Every bookcase of every Burns family in my family has Burns's volumes, and mine is no exception." A trip to Scotland seemed to confirm the connection. "When I visited Alloway in Ayrshire where he was born and went to his cottage, we stumbled across a color portrait, and we just stopped, and the women in the gift shop fainted dead away, and I produced my American license, and from then on there was nothing we could do. I was Kenneth Lauren Burns, son of Robert Burns, and therefore directly related to Bobby Burns, the poet." Physical resemblance aside, no genealogical link had ever been established. Maybe this time the story would have a different ending.

■ Ken's father, Robert Kyle Burns Jr., born on June 8, 1925, in Cincinnati, Ohio, shared with his son a love of photography and a love of film. Both were a release for the emotionally distant man. A cultural anthropologist, he descended from a long line of scientists. His parents, Ken's paternal grandparents, Robert Kyle Burns Sr. and Emily Lucille Moore, were married on June 21, 1924, after having met at Yale, where Emily received a PhD in 1921 in zoology, a rare accomplishment for a woman of her day. Ken's petite grandmother had an outsize hold on his heart. "My under-five-foot Lucille Moore Burns, who is just one of the most extraordinary people I've ever met," he said. "It's my grandmother who I just loved. There is nothing she didn't do." He knew he carried parts of her in himself. "I can remember the way she'd clear her throat, the way my dad clears his throat, the way I clear my throat," he reminisced. He described his grandfather Robert, who became a developmental biologist and in 1955 was elected to the exclusive National Academy of Sciences, as "kind of opaque and difficult." Yet there was a connection regardless. "I can recall having my grandfather sing to me and read me a book called *The Bears of Blue River*, which is stories of the frontier of the country folk in Appalachia, our people, fighting bears and surviving attacks."

Ken's grandfather cherished his deep southern roots. During the making of his *Civil War* series, Ken was shocked to learn that he had ancestors who fought on the side of the Confederacy, his great-great-grandfather Abraham Burns among them. Born in 1833, Abraham Burns was twenty-nine when he enlisted in John McClanahan's Horse Artillery Company. He served the Confederacy from 1862 through 1865, protecting General Lee's army at Gettysburg and fighting valiantly in several other major battles, including the Battle of Piedmont in Augusta County, Georgia. Buried deep in a Civil War archive, we discovered a detail about his service that we didn't expect. Ken's great-great-grandfather, Private Abraham Burns, was one of more than two hundred thousand Confederate soldiers imprisoned during the course of the war. Abraham was captured not in a skirmish, but by Union soldiers dressed up in Confederate uniforms who attacked his regiment's camp from within before dawn on August 7, 1864. In the ensuing melee, Abraham was captured and held at Athenaeum Prison in Wheeling, West Virginia.

Ken's great-great-grandfather was also among those given the opportunity to win back his freedom—and he seized it. "Roll of prisoners of war, who have applied for the oath of allegiance from December 1 to 15, 1864," Ken read from his ancestor's service record. "A remark states that he was conscripted and forced to join the Rebels." To secure his release, Abraham Burns swore an oath of allegiance to the Union. Ken had no doubt about his ancestor's insincerity. "A likely story. 'They forced me to do this,'" he quipped. "'I love Abraham Lincoln, my namesake.'" Abraham Burns was freed, transferred from Camp Chase, and eventually released from City Point, Virginia's wharves on the James River, on March 11, 1865, exactly a month before the Confederate surrender at Appomattox.

After the war was over, Abraham Burns returned home to his wife, Margaret, and their three children, Emma, Robert, and Agnes. Affectionately called Uncle Abe by friends and family, Abraham lived for another forty-six years, dying on December 31, 1911. Ken believed it was important to hear a story like Abraham's. "I think we can find, as the poet William Blake said, the world in a grain of sand. For me, Abraham Burns is a grain of sand. His story permits us to personalize something that inevitably gets depersonalized by numbers."

Ken has said that he has "no sentimentality about the cause" that the South was fighting for, yet he has defended Confederate soldiers as young men who "didn't fully understand the cause." "I'm not sure 'defend' is the right word," Ken explained. "You just have to accept your family. You can't undo it. You don't look at that old photo album of you with that paisley shirt and wide collars from the seventies and rip that out." To Ken, Abraham Burns wasn't a remote symbol of a system he despised. "He's in that direct eyesight of my life. He is my grandfather's—who I knew—grandfather. This is a big deal."

From the Civil War, we continued our journey up Ken's Burns family tree to an ancestor who was born before the American Revolution. Ken's fifth great-grandfather was named John Burns, and he was born in about 1750 in Pennsylvania. A land grant dated 1792 from a rural area in Virginia called Bath County brought us to the very moment that Ken's ancestor became one of a small number of people who owned property in this very remote area, about eighty-five miles north of Roanoke. "The said David and Elizabeth Frost have bargained and sold . . . unto the said John Burns and to his heirs and assigns, forever, a certain tract and parcel of land containing one homestead and eighty-six acres, more or less." In 1836, Ken's fourth great-grandfather John Burns Jr., born on the Fourth of July in 1791, added to his father's homestead. Within just two generations, Ken's ancestors accrued more than four hundred acres of land. For Ken, the area of Bath County was something of an ancestral home, the land his forebears had lived on and worked generations before. "I have driven the road up to the very remote crossroads that is still Burnsville," he said. "We photographed all the graves and the graveyard and got to meet all the Burnses that I was related to." Meeting a conservative congressman from the area had given him an interesting perspective on the land and, by extension, on family. "We've met many times and understood that we had perhaps differing sensibilities, but we shared kinship of the area." He paused. "That goes to something else about family, which is when we try to make distinctions, we forget that the good part about rising up, as well as the bad part, you lose the detail, but you also realize you are one, and so you keep a family connection to one another." We would meet Ken's fifth great-grandfather John Burns again, for it was he who would be a key player in determining whether the Scottish poet Robert Burns was part of Ken's family tree or not.

■ Ken's father's mother's family tree also brought us back to the eighteenth century, to an ancestor who played a unique role in the American Revolution. Ken's family had been in America since colonial times, yet he never felt the period was an easy fit for his work. "The absence of photography makes us fall back on re-creation," he explained, "and if you use too many paintings in a row, you lose a thread, and the whole thing about this storytelling is that connection."

Ken's fifth great-grandfather Gerardus Clarkson, baptized in New York on December 26, 1738, was a surgeon for the Board of War in 1776 and 1777. His name appeared in excerpts from the minutes of the Patriot organization the Council of Safety in New York, recorded on September 16, 1776. "Resolved, that a house be taken for a hospital and that a matron be hired to nurse sick soldiers of this state," Ken read. "Resolved, that Dr. Gerardus Clarkson be appointed to attend the sick in the said hospital." During the Revolution, designated military hospitals were few and far between, and homes were often commandeered to house the sick. Medical practices were ghastly. Surgeons performed amputations without any anesthesia or proper sterilization. Officers received rum or brandy when it was available, but enlisted men got a wooden stick on which to bite down. A competent surgeon could saw through bone in less than forty-five seconds. Only 35 percent of those who underwent such surgery survived.

Ken's fifth great-grandfather's experience with the crude, often barbarous surgical techniques used during the Revolutionary War made him a leading advocate for modernizing medicine after the war ended. We found Dr. Clarkson's signature on a document dated January 2, 1787, that revealed the role he played in the founding of the College of Physicians in Philadelphia, an institution known as "the birthplace of American medicine." His was the sixth signature down. The signature immediately above belonged to Benjamin Rush, a signer of the Declaration of Independence and, in Ken's words, "the most famous physician of the time." Clarkson's signature on this oath placed him in the orbit of the Founding Fathers. As one of the founders and the first treasurer of the College of Physicians in Philadelphia, he helped the medical profession progress beyond its atrocious practices of the war and encouraged the advancement of modern medicine.

■ Based on his presumed shared ancestry with Robert Burns, Ken had always imagined his roots on his father's side lay in Scotland. Instead, we found them next door, in England. Ken's ninth great-grandfather John Claypoole Sr. was baptized at Maxey in Lincolnshire, in England, on April 13, 1595, in the same year Shakespeare wrote *Richard II* and *A Midsummer Night's Dream*. John Claypoole was an outspoken antimonarchist during the time of the English Civil Wars, which were fought between 1642 and 1651 and found a radical group of Parliamentarians known as Roundheads, led by Oliver Cromwell, advocating the implementation of an all-powerful Parliament and the overthrow of King Charles I. A few years earlier, in 1637, Ken's ninth great-grandfather stood trial for having openly opposed the king's taxation policies. He was brought before the fearsome Star Chamber, a clandestine court of law in Westminster notorious for abusing its power to suppress opposition and prosecute dissenters. We could not confirm the outcome of the trial, as the relevant documents were destroyed by fire, but we know that John Claypoole held firm to his opposition and stood behind the Roundheads in the next decade.

The war culminated in the execution of Charles I in 1649, the overthrow of the English monarchy, and the establishment of the Commonwealth of England. In 1653, Oliver Cromwell, the most prominent military and political leader of the rebellion (and an extremely divisive figure in British history, largely remembered for his enactment of the Penal Laws in Ireland, which set the tone for suppression of Irish Catholics for centuries to come), would become lord protector of England. With Cromwell's ascension, Ken's ninth great-grandfather's fortunes rose. In 1654 he was elected a member of Parliament for the House of Commons, and on July 16, 1657, Oliver Cromwell ordered Ken's ninth great-grandfather knighted. Ken applauded his ancestor's stance against the monarchy and his service of the people. "We've just got democracy running through our blood," he said, "connections to the overthrow of the monarchy and the pretensions of people who have boldface names." Ken reconsidered his knighted ancestor for a moment. "I guess he's now a boldface name himself. But he was in the House of Commons. I like that part."

In the latter half of the seventeenth century, John Claypoole's son's name appeared on a travel document dated February 22, 1678, which included a list of "persons of quality," emigrants from Barbados who were given tickets to places including New York, New England, Carolina, Virginia, Antigua, Jamaica, and Newfoundland during 1678 and 1679. Ken's eighth great-grandfather Norton Claypoole was the sole passenger on the ship *Bachelor's Delight* as it set sail for New York. Having spent the previous three years in Barbados with his brother, Edward Claypoole, Norton, at age thirty-eight, embarked on the voyage that took him to Delaware, where he developed a plantation of more than two thousand acres. The son of an opponent of the British monarchy was Ken's first immigrant ancestor to this country.

We followed Ken's illustrious British ancestry further. He had an outspoken anti-Royalist in his blood and also, it turned out, a princess. Ken shared a common ancestor with the late Diana, Princess of Wales, his thirteenth cousin once removed. We exhausted the paper trail for Ken's father's side of the family on a strangely regal note.

■ Now we turned to Ken's beloved mother's side of the family. Lyla Smith Tupper was born on November 26, 1922, in Clarksburg, West Virginia. She died after a long struggle with cancer when Ken was only eleven years old. He once said, "I've been able to understand that all my films stem from that tragedy." When she was a girl, she moved with her parents from Clarksburg to Chicago, where she would attend Northwestern University and study biology. Ken believed that his ambitious mother was "very different" from her parents, George Bancroft Tupper, born on October 4, 1890, in New York City, and Lyla Morris Smith, born on August 14, 1895, in Cumberland, Maryland. Ken's mother was their only child. "Her mother was a kind of hysteric. She was a great beauty. I believe she had two sisters, one sort of sane one, Mary, and then an unmarried sister, Jacqueline. The legend goes that there was a gunfight in a saloon over who was more beautiful, Jackie Smith or Lyla Smith." Ken's memories of her were equally cinematic. "I remember her in housecoats with Siamese cats, smoking like a chimney and being extraordinarily dramatic." He recalled his grandfather with comparable vividness. "My grandfather, who died with spectacles and an almost completely bald head at age sixty, my age, of a heart attack, was a traveling salesman of cutlery, but a very high-level salesman, enough that he could replace his car every year and belong to clubs." Ken had always wondered how his mother came by her determination. "The question I've always had is, where did this come from, other than just that classic American thing, which is, 'I want my kids to do better,' period, full stop?"

We started our journey into Ken's mother's roots on her mother's mother's line, and we uncovered many rich stories that were new to Ken. On

May 22, 1894, Ken's great-great-grandfather Jacob B. Humbird was elected mayor of Cumberland, Maryland, the second biggest city in the state behind Baltimore throughout much of the nineteenth century. Jacob B. Humbird's path to politics, it seemed, was preordained. On May 16, 1860, less than a year before the Civil War began, his father, Ken's third great-grandfather John Humbird, had been elected to the same post. The family, we learned, had distinguished itself outside the political arena in the years prior. John Humbird, Jacob's father and Ken's third great-grandfather, was born on April 23, 1810, in Pennsylvania, and had moved to Cumberland in the 1830s. In 1837 John and his younger brother formed the construction company Humbird and Company in Cumberland. Their work spanned decades and was a fundamental part of the nation's movement west.

Ken's third great-grandfather's political career was part of a much larger career as a builder of public works. Among other major projects, John Humbird and his brother helped build the B&O, the Baltimore & Ohio Railroad, the first railroad to connect the Eastern Seaboard with the Ohio River and one of the largest railroad projects in American history. Construction began in 1828, and the railroad reached St. Louis in 1857. During the Civil War, it moved Union troops and supplies. By the end of the nineteenth century, the B&O had 5,800 miles of track and connected with Chicago, Philadelphia, and even New York City. An 1874 article in the Fort Wayne, Indiana, *Daily Sentinel* on "the remarkable success" of a road-building project in the region described John Humbird's management style: "He has had the active superintendence of the work, has camped on the line, and pushed the work with an energy seldom witnessed." His mother's descent from these men made sense to Ken. "That's where it comes from," he said.

In the 1850s, while the Humbird brothers were pushing westward, another third great-grandfather—and another Abraham—was deeply settled in the South, living in Taylor County, Virginia. Abraham Smith was born on June 21, 1790, in Clarksburg, Virginia, which today is Clarksburg, West Virginia, the birthplace of Ken's mother. In the 1860 Slave Schedule, which listed all the slave owners in the country by name and their slaves only by age, gender, and color, we found the name Abraham Smith. The year before the Civil War broke out, Abraham Smith owned six slaves ranging in age from eleven to sixty-two. "This hurts," Ken said. "I assumed and questioned within the Burns lineage, the paternal side, and assumed that, because of the poverty and because of the hill country, that they didn't have any slaves, and apparently they didn't. But I never thought the more northern maternal side would have that." African American history has been a leitmotif throughout Ken's work. Perhaps, unbeknownst to him, his family history was what drew him to it. "It's nothing that I go looking for particularly," he said. "It makes this quest for African American blood perhaps redemptive."

Ken's reaction to having a slave owner in the family was understandably complex. "I don't feel guilty, but there's a kind of sadness. I now have a personal connection to this thing that I find so repugnant and so un-American, and yet such a particularly American institution, and all the things that go with it." One of the things that goes with it, as Ken said, is secrecy. "My mother never mentioned that. My grandmother would not have mentioned that," he said. "Unless you're willing to lift up that tapestry and show all the things, then we're not going to talk about it. And if you don't talk about it, then the next generation forgets it, and they don't talk about it." As ugly a piece of history as this was, Ken preferred it to be out in the open.

■ Ken's ancestors on both sides of his family had taken part in the most pivotal events in our nation's history. On his father's side he had a Confederate soldier, on his mother's a slave owner. Dr. Gerardus Clarkson had been a nonmilitary Revolutionary War hero on his father's family tree, and now we were about to introduce Ken to an ancestor on his mother's side who also played a part in this country's battle against colonial rule. This was Ken's mother's mother's line, the Tuppers, and they had deep roots in Massachusetts. Ken's fifth great-grandfather Eldad Tupper was born in 1754 in the town of Sandwich. A military muster roll from 1778, during the height of the American Revolution, revealed Eldad Tupper's rank, lieutenant. At this time, Massachusetts was a Patriot stronghold, yet there was no Massachusetts brigade or state infantry number shown anywhere on Eldad's record.

This was no transcription error; there were no state infantry numbers because this chart did not belong to the Continental army. Ken's fifth great-grandfather was a Loyalist—he fought for the British. Ken was floored. "Oh, no! A Tory!" he laughed. "God help me. I was thinking that with Claypoole in England being with Cromwell, we were sort of set with this." After serving aboard a British ship for more than a year, Ken's fifth great-grandfather was honorably discharged, moving to Elizabethtown Township in Canada after the war to live out his days. He would die in Brockville, Ontario, Canada, in 1832. Going back another generation to Eldad's father, Prince Tupper, Ken's sixth great-grandfather, we learned that Prince was arrested in Sandwich and imprisoned for his Loyalist allegiance in 1779. Although good-natured about the revelation, the news of his Loyalist ancestors was hard for Ken to swallow. "This is the thing I'm most ashamed of. I am humiliated by this part, because I bleed red, white, and blue, and this is not the Union Jack. I'm hugely disappointed."

Even stories that seem black and white have their complexities, and the Tuppers' was no exception. The first-ever federal census was taken in 1790, and the census for Sandwich, Massachusetts, indicated that Ken's sixth great-grandfather Prince returned to live in Massachusetts with his family, while his son Eldad stayed in Canada. Prince had been found guilty of treason, so how was it possible for him to make a home here? Ken read from a petition filed by his sixth great-grandfather in 1779, the year of his arrest. "Whereas Prince Tupper and John Jennings, inhabitants of the Town of Sandwich, in the County of Barnstable, who were committed to the gaol in said County for refusing to take the Oath of Fidelity and Allegiance to the State, have made an application to the Court, confessing their error in that refusal, acknowledging their obligation to take said Oath and praying liberty therefor." Ken's sixth great-grandfather was permitted to rejoin the commonwealth of Massachusetts on the condition that he pledge allegiance to the United States and pay a fine of one thousand pounds—the equivalent of $187,300 today. "The price of liberty," Ken said. This sum, however, might have seemed like a pittance compared to the other condition of his freedom: he could not associate himself "with any persons inimical to this country." In other words, he could no longer see his son without the threat of reimprisonment. Ken thought of his own four daughters and was hard-pressed to imagine his ancestor's mind-set. "What's the tug? What's he willing to do?" Ken wondered. "To give a fortune in money to come back because he loves the land, because he loves somebody, because he loves maybe the idea of liberty now? I don't know. Maybe there's something there, but to forgo the family connection is huge. That's a great mystery."

And a mystery that we would never be able to solve. The severing of immediate family ties notwithstanding, the Tupper line was long and well documented. We went further up the Tupper line to Prince's grandfather, Ken's eighth great-grandfather Captain Thomas Tupper. Captain Thomas Tupper was born on January 16, 1637, in Sandwich, Massachusetts, only seventeen years after the Pilgrims famously landed on Plymouth Rock. Ken's family went back nearly four centuries on Cape Cod. Captain Tupper was one of the colony's largest landowners and a prominent citizen. He served as town clerk, selectman, and deputy to the Court of Plymouth, and in 1690, he was appointed captain of the military company of Sandwich.

Captain Thomas Tupper topped off a distinguished career as a civil servant in 1694 when he was appointed commissioner to the Indians in the commonwealth, acting as constable and justice of the peace and presiding over the Herring River tribe "in all matters, civil and criminal." Ken was dubious about his ancestor's role as an overseer of Indians. "He obviously had great civic responsibility. He's been a selectman, and he's been a delegate to Plymouth, so I imagine that this was a spoil that was given to him," Ken said.

Maybe this was in part true, but Ken's eighth great-grandfather was committed to what he believed was in the Native Americans' best interest, as was evident in this document from 1680. "Through his efforts, a meetinghouse for the Praying Indians, under his instructions, was erected at Herring River, on land donated by him, completed in 1688, which was maintained partly at his own expense." His mission was to convert the Indians to Christianity, which doesn't sit well with our modern sensibilities, but in the process he was also willing to educate and provide care for them. "It does mitigate that a bit," Ken said. "It doesn't feel so much like a spoils position or patronage. Although we are imposing on their cultures what we think is the dominant one, he was a minister unto them, and that's a good thing." Thomas Tupper's son Eldad, Ken's seventh great-grandfather and likely the namesake of his Loyalist ancestor, was ordained and preached in the church, too. Missionary work was a Tupper family tradition.

Ken's mother's family was fascinating. We had already found connections to both the Revolutionary War and the Civil War in her lineage, and now we found an ancestor involved in a lesser-known war of the colonial period, King Philip's War. We stepped further back into her family history, to Ken's ninth great-grandfather John Tisdale, Ken's earliest ancestor that we can place in the New World. He was baptized in Ripon, Yorkshire, England, on November 7, 1614—exactly four hundred years before our meeting with Ken. When he was around twenty years old, John Tisdale (whose name was also spelled Tisdall in records of the time) sailed for America, arriving at Plymouth Plantation in 1634. He eventually bought a plot of land from the chief of the Wampanoags whose name was Metacom. The English called him King Philip. Ken was flabbergasted. "This is amazing. All I can think about is my brother, who is a filmmaker, too, who's really concentrated on New England history, and particularly the Pilgrims and particularly the Native American aspect of it, and how much he knows about King Philip." On the land John Tisdale bought from Metacom, he built a home on the east side of the Assonet River near Mount Hope, Rhode Island, King Philip's home, and was settled in the area by the early 1670s. At this time, King Philip, previously considered "friendly," began to complain bitterly about encroaching colonial settlements. The British anticipated trouble and prepared for battle.

A transcription of the minutes from a council meeting held in Plymouth on July 8, 1671, shed some light on the situation. Ken read it aloud. "The towns of Taunton, Rehoboth, Bridgewater, and Swansea are to cause their soldiers that are to be sent forth to give meeting to the major and the rest of the company at or near Assonet, about John Tisdale's farm." In other words, Ken's ancestor's farm was the launching pad for an attack on King Philip in 1671. Ken put it more bluntly: "It means that King Philip's War is happening on my ancestor's land."

King Philip, hearing of the impending attacks, agreed to talks with the colonists, but the peace didn't last. A document from Plymouth Colony Court dated March 6, 1676/77 (the year is rendered both ways in different sources, reflecting the change from the Julian calendar to the Gregorian calendar that took place in 1582), proved how bloody the battle became. Ken's ninth great-grandfather and two other colonists were killed, allegedly by three Native Americans who attacked John Tisdale's farm and burned his house down. Their names were Timothy Jacked (alias Canjuncke), Nassamaquat, and Pompacanshe, and they were apprehended in the nearby town of Rehoboth on August 1, 1675, with Ken's ancestor's musket in their possession. The three "had due processe in law, according to the English manor, by a jury of twelve men," the court record noted. While the verdicts were not the same for all three men, the penalty was. The jury found Canjuncke and Nassamaquat to be "very suspicious of the murder charged on them," but "in reference unto Pompacanshe, wee find nothing against him. There not appearing further evidence against them to cleare up the case," the statement continued, "the centance of the Court was, that the two former were to be sent out of the country speedily, and the other likewise, as hee is prisoner taken in warr." They were not hanged, as Ken had supposed. Instead, we suspect that Canjuncke, Nassamaquat, and Pompacanshe were sold into slavery and shipped to the West Indies, since this was the common fate of Native American convicts and captives during this period. Ken's ninth great-grandfather John Tisdale, his first immigrant ancestor on his mother's mother's side, was one of the first white casualties in what became known as King Philip's War, but both sides in the conflict paid dearly.

◼ On both sides of Ken's family, we had found ancestors in America since the colonial period. DNA, however, would bring us even further back in time. On his maternal side, we went all the way back to Robert Baldwin, who was born in 1475 in England; on his paternal side, we found royalty once again: Charlemagne, King of the Franks and Emperor of the West, who was born in 742 and died in 814. The paper trail on both sides repeatedly went back to England. Would Ken's DNA follow suit? The admixture tests we administered would measure his percentages of European, sub-Saharan African, and East Asian / Native American ancestry over the past five hundred years or so. His results came back as 100 percent European— "Lily white," he laughed. Breaking down his admixture results, we found more diversity in Ken's DNA than that overall number indicated. Although the ancestors in the paper trail had come from England, 26 percent of his European DNA actually came from Ireland, with only 10 percent from Great Britain. Even more surprising was the 6 percent Iberian Peninsula result. Different companies can uncover different findings, and the results of a second test found that drop of African blood that Ken felt certain he had. This time, his results were roughly 99.6 percent European, 0.4 percent sub-Saharan African, and 0.1 Native American. Whatever the circumstance of its entry, Ken's DNA contained a remnant of African ancestry.

◼ Of all the incredible information we had shared with Ken today, he was still left wanting. The mystery that was so central to his life—whether there was truly an ancestral relation to Robert Burns—had not yet been solved. Before we got to that, though, we had one more ancestor we wanted him to meet, someone he already knew well through a lifetime dedicated to the pursuit of understanding, and helping others to understand, the American Civil War. Rumors had lingered that Ken was a distant cousin of Abraham Lincoln, and we were able to prove, definitively, that that was true. Dr. Gerardus Clarkson, the Revolutionary War surgeon, connected Ken to the president who helped heal the nation's wounds. Through Gerardus Clarkson's wife, Mary Flower, Abraham Lincoln was Ken's fifth cousin four times removed. Ken had two Abrahams on his paternal family tree already, one a soldier and the other a slave owner on the side of the Confederacy, and he was overjoyed to see this third one from the Union enter. "This is the guy that I have in my soul."

And now to Robert Burns. "There's just been a sense of kinship with him," Ken said. "This is an extraordinary artist. This is somebody whose work has been handed down to me, so he feels like family." But was he? Ken's fifth great-grandfather John Burns was born around 1750 in Pennsylvania. Robert Burns was born Robert Burnes on January 25, 1759, in Ayrshire, Scotland. Robert didn't adopt the spelling Burns until 1786, at which point Ken's Burns ancestors had already been living in the colonies for more than thirty years. This made a direct link seem unlikely, but only DNA could tell us for sure. First we looked for someone on Robert Burns's direct paternal line. Only one of Robert Burns's sons had children of his own, and of those three children, just one, Sarah, survived. Our researchers tracked down Sarah's descendants. Some lived in Canada, others in the United States, but unfortunately there were none on the direct paternal line to test. This meant we had to go back further in his direct paternal tree.

The earliest known ancestor of Robert Burns is Walter Burness, born about 1615, in Scotland. If Ken descended from Walter Burness on his direct paternal line, like Robert Burns, we would expect for his Y-DNA to match his. But there was no match. Now we had definitive proof that he and Robert Burns weren't related on Ken's direct paternal Burns line.

There was one more test that we could administer to Ken to test his autosomal DNA, which is inherited from both of an individual's parents and all of his or her ancestral lines. On Robert Burns's paternal family tree, in addition to the Burness line, there were two other families of particular interest: the Keith family (Robert's grandmother's family) and the Falconer family (Robert's great-grandmother's family). All three families were from the area around a place called Kincardineshire in Scotland, and Ken's autosomal DNA showed scores of significant connections to this exact area. Many of his matches in the DNA databases traced back to these very families. Ken wasn't directly descended from the poet, but at long last we could prove that they were related through Robert's mother. Ken was thrilled to finally have proof. "I just somehow knew, maybe it's tangential," he said, "but there's got to be some DNA somewhere." It was a privilege to tell him there was. "So in the end," he said, "my grandmother, who was a scientist, didn't lie or mythologize."

■ How to sum up such a wide-ranging and eye-opening experience as Ken's journey into finding his roots had been? He was once told that he had spent his career trying to bring the dead back to life. His camera was, in a sense, his time machine. Which of his ancestors would he bring into focus if he could? It was impossible for him choose one person. "The quick thing would be Robert Burns, but this is so tangential," he said. "I'm drawn a little bit to the slave owner, Smith, the great-grandfather of my grandmother Lyla Smith. I would certainly like to talk to Abraham Burns, who was in the Civil War, something I purport to know about. I'm interested in Clarkson, the physician, the healer. Those are the ones that catch my attention." He continued to scroll through his family tree. "But the builder of the B&O Railroad, and the mayors in two different generations—I like there's ambition, there's politics, there's engagement. That's what I like in life."

Those were certainly some of the traits that governed his life. So what is it that makes us who we are? Was it our DNA or the ancestors from whom we inherited it? Their experiences or our own? "My experience is family," Ken said. "That has a kind of complicated determinant to it, the most joys, the deepest sorrows. I think it's the interrelationship of family in geography that suggests community but also politics, that suggests country and allegiance, that suggests faith, if it's there. The family unit seems to be above all." Exactly how did Ken define that family unit? "I felt that my family was this little group here." But this experience, he said, "just spread it out."

For many years Ken had longed to know whether he and Robert Burns were related. The long-awaited answer to that question seemed to be more of a confirmation than a surprise. In his heart and in his mind, Ken felt he always knew. But on a journey like this one, there were bound to be true surprises, and for Ken it was the unforeseen variety in his own DNA. "I'm stunned by the way it goes out geographically and professionally, and just the circumstances," he said. "They're physicians and Patriots and Tories and slave owners. And there's African American blood of some sort. There's probably Native American blood of some sort. It's the variety. It's the connectedness to it."

The complexity of Ken's family tree contained in it all the complexity of America itself. The American filmmaker summed up his extensive family tree with one well-known phrase: "*E pluribus unum.*"

Anderson Cooper is one of the most intrepid television journalists of our generation, fearlessly delivering firsthand accounts of the devastation of war, famine, and natural disasters around the world. The fact that Anderson chose the grueling life of a correspondent on the front lines is even more remarkable given the rarefied world in which he was raised. Born on June 3, 1967, in New York City, Anderson Hays Cooper is the son of the writer Wyatt Cooper and the heiress and designer Gloria Vanderbilt. "People always ask me about my mom's side of the family," he said, "but when I think to myself that I come from people, I think that I come from the Cooper side."

Although his father's Mississippi childhood was a humble one, Wyatt and Gloria together hosted some of the most influential writers, artists, and entertainers of the time at their New York City home. Yet Anderson's parents also made their family home a haven for him and his brother. Soon, though, their bubble of comfort and glamour would be punctured by tragedy and loss. Anderson's father died of a heart attack when Anderson was only ten years old, and ten years later, his brother, Carter, committed suicide.

Anderson's own experiences with the press after his brother's suicide informed his way of telling personal stories of suffering. "It was a very public event. He killed himself in front of my mom, and there were reporters camped outside our house for that week," he said. "I remember going to his wake, and there were camera crews waiting outside for us. I remember hating them in that moment and thinking, these people are vultures. I always think about that when I'm on an assignment, particularly in a place where people are grieving or people have lost somebody, because I know what it's like to be on the other side of that camera."

His approach is intimate, always on the individual. "Loss drove me to go overseas and become a reporter, to go to places where people were suffering, because early on I wanted to understand loss and survival. I think experiencing loss has made me much more empathetic and much more understanding, and also being OK with discussing that. We live in this society that doesn't talk about grief, doesn't talk about loss, or doesn't do it in a way that's very comfortable." In his reporting, he seeks to break the silence and anonymity that surround suffering. "I believe in bearing witness to the lives that people led. To have somebody die in silence just compounds the horror of it, and I believe in trying to learn the names and learn the stories of those who are suffering."

Anderson was driven to make sure that people's stories weren't buried in the past and lost. Some were bound to be painful. He was born to a mother whose own story had been splashed across front pages. But what about all those stories, on both sides of his family tree, that had remained untold?

■ Gloria Laura Morgan Vanderbilt was born on February 20, 1924, into one of America's most illustrious families. Her name, Anderson believed, could have been her worst enemy. "There are a lot of people in her situation who could have been ladies who lunch—not that there's anything wrong with that, and I know ladies who lunch, and they're very nice— but she wanted to accomplish something and do something." Not content to rely solely on her family fortune, Gloria started her Gloria Vanderbilt clothing company in the 1970s, establishing her own identity artistically and financially.

In spite of his mother's independence, Anderson was grateful to have the Cooper surname. The Vanderbilt name was too "imposing," he said, carried with it too much baggage. "It wasn't until maybe ten years ago that I would even talk publicly about my mom," he recalled. "I wanted to make a name for myself before people associated me with that background. I needed to focus on work and accomplish things on my own, and paying attention to that name would only lead to bad things."

"That name," as Anderson called it, had been in America for centuries, and the story of its rise to fame was an American rags-to-riches story. We began our journey through Anderson's Vanderbilt past with his grandparents, Gloria's parents, Reginald Claypoole Vanderbilt and Mercedes Morgan, also called Gloria. Reginald was born on December 19, 1880, in Staten Island, New York, and Gloria was born on August 23, 1904, in Lucerne, Switzerland. "I didn't hear much about my mom's parents at all," he said. "I knew that her father had died when she was still an infant, and I knew that he drank a lot. I think maybe he had cirrhosis of the liver. He was described as a sportsman. I'm not sure what that profession is exactly, but to me that means you're rich; you don't really have a profession, and you have horses or something." He would eventually learn about his mother's mother through unflattering media portrayals, but the rest was just fragments. "She never really saw her mother much. She describes her as this great beauty who was always coming in and going out down long corridors." It was an evocative image of a woman who was on the periphery of her own daughter's life.

Young Gloria's life was marked by instability and loss. Her parents weren't together for very long, and her father died in September 1925, when he was thirty-five years old. Like her sons, Gloria lost her own father at a very young age. "I don't think she realized how it affected her. If you grow up in a cave, you don't realize the cave is any different from where anybody else lives." Anderson had lived in that cave himself. He recalled as a child seeing the huge statue of his third great-grandfather Cornelius Vanderbilt that stands in front of Grand Central Station. "This is going to sound absurd, but I thought that all grandparents turned into statues when they died, that everybody had streets in New York named after their families."

Anderson learned soon enough that there were comparatively few families like the Vanderbilts. "I started to realize the fame aspect and the well-known aspect of the Vanderbilt name when my mom got involved in designing clothes, in particular jeans," he said. "Suddenly, when I was eleven years old, people started showing up on the street with my mom's name on their backside. My brother and I had this game of how many people we could see in a day who had my mom's name on their bottoms."

That was fame and recognition his mother courted and cultivated. As a young girl, however, she found herself thrust into the spotlight, at the center of a heated and public custody battle that Anderson said tore their family apart and left his mother estranged from her Vanderbilt relatives. "My mom was taken away by the courts from her own mother when she was ten years old at the height of the Depression and given to an aunt who she didn't know. I always knew growing up that it was an extraordinarily painful thing for my mom and something we never really talked about." Cameras followed his mother everywhere, and the case was called the "Trial of the Century." "There was an incredible newsreel of my mom going to the trial. My mom gets out of this car, and I guess it was, I don't know, 1931, the height of the Depression, and there are these detectives in fedoras who are flanking her, and she's this little ten-year-old girl. I remember the newsreel said something like, 'Money isn't everything.'"

But for the Vanderbilts, it seemed money was the ultimate goal. Anderson had spent most of his life either being protected from or ignoring sad stories about his mother's childhood. As a result, he was cut off from gaining a deep knowledge of both sides of his mother's family, the Vanderbilts and the Morgans. Although the Vanderbilts' history was already well

Ken Burns • Anderson Cooper • Anna Deavere Smith **105**

known, we wanted to go further, to fill in the details Anderson had missed and to take him back to a time when the Vanderbilts were just another immigrant family getting their start in a new land.

We went all the way back to the seventeenth century, to Anderson's eighth great-grandfather Jan Aertsen Vanderbilt. We do not know precisely what year Jan arrived, but he was Anderson's first Vanderbilt ancestor in the United States. A marriage record for Jan and Anneken Hendricks, from the Dutch Reformed Church in New Amsterdam, told us that he arrived long before it was actually the United States—1650. Anderson's eighth great-grandfather was born in the Netherlands in 1627 and died in 1705 in New Jersey, seventy years before the outbreak of the American Revolution. He was born at the height of the Golden Age of Holland, a period during which the Dutch were dominant in the slave trade and building colonies and trading posts all over the New World. Because the Dutch weren't legally required to take surnames until the 1790s, it's likely that he took the name Vanderbilt, meaning "from the town of Bilt," when he arrived in the American colony of New Amsterdam.

In light of the family history, the circumstances under which Jan Aertsen Vanderbilt arrived in America were shocking. The original immigrant ancestor of the family that went on to build this nation—the family whose scion, the railroad tycoon Billy Vanderbilt, would be called the richest man in America—came here as the indentured servant of a Dutch landowner. He arrived penniless in New Amsterdam, working for three years as a laborer to pay off his indenture. In about five generations, the Vanderbilts would go from having nothing to having everything. How did the descendants of an indentured laborer achieve such tremendous success?

Born in Staten Island, New York, in 1794, Anderson's third great-grandfather Cornelius Vanderbilt transformed his small ferryboat operation into one of the largest shipping and railroad companies in the world. When he died in 1877, the Commodore, as he was known, had more money than the U.S. Treasury, more than $100 billion in today's currency, easily making him one of the richest men in the history of the United States and cementing the Vanderbilt family legacy. His son, Anderson's second great-grandfather William Henry Vanderbilt, the aforementioned railroad tycoon known to the world as Billy, only built upon his father's fortune.

Although Anderson felt little bond to these giants of American industry, he had recently begun to collect Vanderbilt memorabilia, one of the items a bowl with Jan Aertsen Vanderbilt's name on it. "It's like collecting stamps or something," he said, "It doesn't feel like me, but I find it interesting, and I know rationally that I'm connected to this family."

The Morgans, Gloria's mother's mother's line, were a very prominent family in their own right. Anderson's cosmopolitan Morgan ancestors had disparate roots, from Switzerland to New Orleans to Chile. Anderson had heard her story: she was married to the Civil War Union general Hugh Judson Kilpatrick, known as "Killer Kilpatrick," according to Anderson, because he notoriously killed many of his own men. On his Morgan side he descended from kings—Edward I of England and Charlemagne, King of the Franks and Emperor of the West. "The Morgan line has more kingly ancestors than the Vanderbilts," he laughed. Then he remembered: the Vanderbilts came from nothing. "This guy was an indentured servant." Both sides of Anderson's mother's family tree were filled with storied and noteworthy characters. His father's family tree, we would learn, was no less colorful.

■ Anderson once wrote of his mother: "My mom comes from a time and place that no longer exists. The world she was born into, the world she managed to escape from, seems so distant to us now." The same can be said of Anderson's father. Wyatt Emory Cooper was born in Quitman, Mississippi, on September 1, 1927. It was the height of the Jim Crow era in the Deep South, when the color line, in law and custom, defined race relations in repressive, often violent, ways. "I know from early on my dad had a very strong sense of social justice," Anderson said. "His brother Harry tells me that when the preacher wasn't available, sometimes my father would be called in to preach the sermon, and he would often preach against segregation, which in the thirties in Mississippi was not something you did in a Southern Baptist church."

The tiny cotton-farming town of Quitman had been the birthplace of Cooper ancestors for generations. Anderson's father loved Mississippi, yet, unlike the majority of his relatives, he ultimately left it. "He loved the stories that he grew up with and all the people he grew up with. He wanted it very much to be part of my life and my brother's life," Anderson said. In 1975 Wyatt published a memoir called *Families: A Memoir and a Celebration*. "That's why he wrote the book. I think he knew that we would learn about the Vanderbilt side, but he wanted to make sure that we knew about the Cooper side and that it was just as interesting."

As a young man, Anderson's father left his home and family to pursue a career in acting. In 1953 he had his premiere on Broadway, playing a Spanish army soldier in a play called *The Strong Are Lonely*. Wyatt's career on the stage was short-lived, and he found work as a screenwriter in California. Anderson called his father "a born storyteller." In a sense Anderson was following in the path his father had set for him.

As far as Anderson knew, before Wyatt left, the Cooper family had never strayed far from Mississippi. His paternal grandparents were both born there, and they both died there. Emmett Debro Cooper was born in 1888, and Rixie Annie Jane Anderson, known as Jennie, was born in 1896. While Wyatt's attachment to his home state was powerful, we learned that Anderson's Cooper ancestors were not originally from Mississippi at all, but were instead part of a wave of settlers who migrated to the Deep South seeking their fortunes cultivating cotton.

The invention of the cotton gin in 1794 created the biggest economic boom in American history to date. In the early 1800s, Anderson's paternal ancestors were still clustered in the Upper South—North Carolina, Virginia, northern Georgia—and they had lived there from colonial times. The soil of the Upper South had been depleted by the staple crops, particularly tobacco, that had been growing there for generations, while the soil of the South was the richest soil for growing cotton on the continent, quite possibly in the world. It also was home to the Five Civilized Tribes: the Creek, Choctaw, Chickasaw, Cherokee, and Seminole. In 1830, Andrew Jackson signed the Indian Removal Act to move the Indians off the precious land and make it available for white farmers. By 1838, the Native Americans had been relocated to Oklahoma following the calamitous journey known as the Trail of Tears. The Deep South was now wide open, and Anderson's ancestors were among those who swooped down on it, part of a mass migration of white settlers accompanied by a million slaves. Cotton completely reshaped both the economy and the demographics of the United States.

Enormous fortunes were made on cotton during this time, and we were curious to know how Anderson's ancestors fared. Using census records from 1850 and 1860, we were able to assess the value of the land they owned and stitch together a picture of what life was like for the Cooper branch after their arrival in Mississippi. "William Anderson, farmer, owning a hundred dollars' worth of land. Edward Bole, farmer, owning five hundred dollars' worth of land. William JG Barry, planter, owning two hundred fifty dollars' worth of land." This wasn't exactly Tara. "There were no Cooper plantation houses as far as I know," Anderson said.

Anderson was correct. His father's ancestors were small farmers and laborers. They followed cotton into the Deep South, but they owned little property and never got rich. Their lives were more typical of white southern families of that period than the big planters who loom so large in American mythology. For every major landowner, there were thousands of small farmers, struggling just to make a living. Of the million men who fought for the Confederacy, the majority of them were defending a way of life that had never been theirs.

Anderson's great-great-grandfather Robert Fletcher Campbell was one of that majority. Born in 1822, he never owned any slaves, but, according to his service record, he volunteered for the Twenty-Seventh Mississippi Infantry, which saw fighting in Pensacola, Florida; Mobile, Alabama; and Tennessee and Kentucky. R. F. Campbell, as his name appeared on his record, was one of many Cooper ancestors who fought for the Confederacy. Anderson's third great-grandfather Burwell Cooper was a private in the Fortieth Alabama Infantry Regiment for the entire course of the war, and he served alongside his father-in-law, Edward Bull. Anderson's great-great-grandmother Annie Boykin had five brothers alive when the war began, and each of them served. Also fighting for the South were many other great-great-uncles and cousins, not one of whom owned slaves. What made them sign up? "It's sort of aspirational, isn't it? People fight for what they hope one day to be able to achieve or the opportunity that they think it may bring them." Anderson pointed out a sad fact that was unfortunately true. "I think in all societies people want to have somebody beneath them," he said. "'I may only have one hundred dollars' worth of land, but at least I'm not like the people down the road.'"

One ancestor of Anderson's, however, could measure his success in terms of the people who he owned: his fourth great-grandfather Burwell Boykin. Born in Georgia in 1787, the year of the Constitutional Convention, he died in Mississippi in 1860, the year before the Civil War broke out. He migrated from the Upper to the Lower South in the first part of the nineteenth century. A muster roll from the year 1814 showed us that Burwell Boykin was a private in Carson's Regiment, a volunteer militia in Mississippi that fought the Creek Indians during the War of 1812. What's fascinating about Carson's Regiment is that it aligned itself with the Choctaw Indians in the region, so Anderson's ancestor was fighting with the Choctaw against the Creek. Anderson laughed. "I remember some family story that we were part Choctaw." This was a common refrain from many of our participants, a rumor of a Native American ancestor. The rumor almost always proved to be just that. Anderson's fourth great-grandfather survived the fierce fighting in the wilderness and became a prosperous man.

According to the 1850 census for Choctaw County, Alabama, Burwell Boykin owned 620 total acres of land, with a farm valued at six thousand dollars, and the Slave Schedule attached to it showed that he had a good deal of his wealth invested in slaves. The only names that appeared in the Slave Schedules belonged to the owners; slaves were enumerated anonymously, identified by age, gender, and color. Referred to as Earl Boykin in the Slave Schedule, Anderson's ancestor owned twelve slaves. Anderson was deeply disappointed, if not entirely shocked. "I never heard anything about it," he said. "Having ancestors from the Deep South I'm not surprised that there's at least one slave holder, but I also thought my relatives were so poor that they wouldn't have had slaves." But Burwell Boykin wasn't poor, and he owned human beings ranging in age from one to sixty. Anderson pored over the nameless list. "It's crazy just to see this ledger. Sixty years old, 50 years old, 45, 45, 22, 16-year-old person, 15-year-old person, 13-year-old child, a 12-year-old child, 11-year-old, a 3-year-old, and a 1-year-old child. The fact that there are no names I find so disturbing, that they weren't even viewed as people to mark down their names. Who is this thirteen-year-old? Who was this fifteen-year-old boy? What happened to them? Where are their ancestors today?"

We had no way of knowing. In 1860, there were 3.9 million slaves in the United States. Slavery persisted in this country with few organized rebellions against it. The only successful slave rebellion in all of the history of slavery occurred in Haiti, then Saint-Domingue, in 1804. Uprisings occasionally happened on a smaller scale in America, but they never succeeded in toppling the system. In some instances, though, individual slaves, acting on their own and often with their bare hands, lashed out against their masters. Anderson read from the 1860 census a most shocking fact: "Burwell Boykin, profession, planter. Cause of death, killed by Negro." Burwell Boykin was murdered by a rebellious slave who beat him to death with a farm hoe.

Anderson's immediate reaction was unpolished, complicated, and extremely heartfelt. "I don't want to offend the other relatives of mine," he said, "but I've got to say that part of me thinks it's awesome." So Anderson thought his ancestor deserved it? "I have no doubt."

His concern was more with the man who committed the murder than with his own blood ancestor. "I wish I knew the name of the person who killed him. I wish I had a picture of him. It would be interesting to know his story." His story ended the same way as would that of any slave who dared commit such a crime against his master: he was hanged. No court records of the hanging exist, but incredibly, we found a personal account of the gruesome event in the Choctaw County library, in a diary written by a neighbor of Burwell Boykin. According to the neighbor, Burwell had locked his slave, whose name was Sham, in a cotton house overnight because he kept running away. When Burwell, hoe in hand, went to let him out the next morning, Sham grabbed the hoe from his master and beat him to death with it.

Both master and slave paid the ultimate price. Anderson bore anger only for his ancestor. "He had twelve slaves. I don't feel bad for him," he stated unequivocally. "I feel bad for the man who killed him, and I feel bad for eleven other unnamed people who God only knows what happened to them. No, I don't feel bad for Burwell Boykin." However horrified he was to find out that his ancestor was a slave owner, he wasn't sorry to learn it. "I feel a sense of shame over it," he said. "At the same time, it's the history of our country. And it makes me feel closer to my dad. It makes me feel fuller in a way, just knowing some of the blank spots. It's good to know."

■ Using the remembrances in Anderson's father's memoir as a jumping-off point allowed us to go back even further on the Cooper family tree. The memoir alludes to a family story that traces its ancestry back to one of the first English families in Virginia, the Wyatts, part of the original aristocracy of America. One of the Wyatts, Sir Francis Wyatt, was the first English royal governor of the Jamestown colony, the first English settlement in North America, founded in 1607. According to Anderson's father's memoir, his own branch were essentially the poor relations. With no paper trail linking Anderson's family to the Wyatts, we turned to DNA to see if we could establish a connection. By comparing Anderson's autosomal DNA, which is inherited from both of an individual's parents and all of his or her ancestors, to that of descendants of the Wyatts, we found a large number of matches. They led not to Sir Francis himself, but to his brother, the Reverend Haute Wyatt, who was born sometime before 1594. Some of Haute's descendants had settled in North Carolina, where many of Anderson's father's other ancestors had also put down roots. We were confident that Wyatt Cooper's oral history of descent from the Haute Wyatt clan was correct. Unfortunately, though, we were never able to document this connection through the paper trail.

As it turned out, we didn't have to stray too far from Jamestown to find Anderson's oldest documented paternal ancestor. A court record from Norfolk, Virginia, dated 1640, gave us not only the name of this ancestor, but also the date of his arrival in the New World. "Thomas Ivey hath appeared to this court," Anderson read, "that he hath transported into said colony two persons, himself and his wife, in *The Rebecca* in 1637." This was just seventeen years after the *Mayflower* brought the Pilgrims to these shores in 1620. Thomas Ivey was Anderson's tenth great-grandfather on his father's side, Anderson's original paternal ancestor on this side of the Atlantic. He was born around 1604 in England, and he died in 1653 in the Virginia colony. "It's amazing to think that both my mom's side and my dad's side came to this country relatively at the same time," he said. "To think that these two strands, these two disparate groups of people, came to the colonies around the same time, didn't know each other, and yet centuries later would be joined by my parents."

Other records indicate that Thomas Ivey was likely a tobacco planter, which would have placed him at the top of early Virginia society. "It never would have occurred to me that my father's ancestors came from any kind of privilege at all, because I've seen the picture of the house my dad grew up in. It's a shack, and there were a lot of kids running around. It was a pretty hardscrabble existence," he said. "It's interesting to see the fortunes of a family rise and fall over generations."

■ Anderson's long paper trail on his father's family brought him back to the early days of colonial America; on his mother's side he descended from kings. His oldest named ancestor on his paternal side was his tenth great-grandfather Thomas Ivey, who was born around 1604 in Wiltshire, England. On his mother's side, through the Morgans, his oldest ancestor was none other than Charlemagne, King of the Franks and Emperor of the West, who was born in 742 and died in 814. Our exploration of Anderson's roots had given him a new perspective on the relative establishment of the two sides of his mother's family. Before learning that the first Vanderbilt to arrive in America came as an indentured servant, Anderson said, "I always assumed, well, it's the Vanderbilt side that goes back forever."

What else could DNA tell us about Anderson Cooper? When we asked him to guess at the results of his admixture text, which measures an individual's percentages of European, sub-Saharan African, and East Asian / Native American ancestry since around the time of Columbus, he was relatively certain: "I'm albino, so I would have to say I'm 100 percent European." Looks can be deceiving, and he had more diversity in his DNA than he expected: 97.8 percent European, 0.7 percent sub-Saharan African, and 1.3 percent Native American. He summed up the percentages as "fascinating."

Anderson's Native American result piqued our interest. It was high enough to be meaningful, but only family lore had indicated a Native American ancestor, not the paper trail. There was circumstantial evidence based on the genealogy that the Native American ancestry came from Anderson's father's line. Anderson's great-great-grandfather Edward Latham Bull was a farmer who lived in Choctaw County, Alabama, in the mid-1800s. Choctaw County gets its name, of course, from the Native American tribe that lived there, and Bull is a common Choctaw surname even today. However, after testing Gloria Vanderbilt's DNA in an effort to rule out her side as the source of this Native American DNA, we were surprised to learn that she and Anderson have Native American DNA on exactly the same chromosomes, meaning that the Native DNA actually came from her family. By consulting Anderson's list of autosomal, or genetic, cousins, we found a very strong match with a person who has four grandparents from Chile. Anderson's great-great-grandmother Luisa Fernandez was Chilean, and she is almost certainly the source of Anderson's Native American DNA.

His comparatively small amount of sub-Saharan African DNA was intriguing, too, and it was identified as being southeastern Bantu in origin, an origin consistent with an African who was enslaved in America. The genealogy would indicate that the African DNA came most likely from his father's side, and Anderson fingered his slaveholding fourth great-grandfather Burwell Boykin, but we couldn't know. The actual ancestors who had contributed his African DNA would remain a mystery, but the surprising diversity of his DNA was a scientific fact.

■ As fascinating as his DNA test results were, Anderson found the paper trail more compelling. "For me the paper trail tells more of a story, because it has people's names associated with it, and there are documents. I'm not much of a science person; I'm more of a storyteller. I respond more to that. But," he continued, "then to see the scientific proof of it and there's not just a story, together it's incredible." Anderson believed stories like these illuminated not only our personal history, but also the history of America. "It's too bad every kid in school can't have this, because it would make them feel so much more connected and interested in the history of this country."

What did Anderson believe made a person American? Was there a defining characteristic? Based on his own family's stories, he believed so. "I think what makes a person American is a drive and a will. I don't think it has anything to do with where you're from, where you were born or who your parents were or who your great-great-great-grandfather was." He was referring to his own third great-grandfather, the history maker Cornelius Vanderbilt. "What makes you an American is a desire for improvement, and I think it's what brought Jan Aertsen Vanderbilt over, and it's probably what brought Thomas Ivey over, and it's what's bringing people over today. Not to sound cliché, but I do think that's the strength of this country, that we're not all related by our DNA and our chromosomes, we're not all related by our experiences, but we all continue to come here to achieve something, to accomplish something. You can call it the American dream. It's the belief in the possibility that this country still has and still holds."

It was impossible to go back in time, but if Anderson could, if a time machine existed, which of his ancestors would he choose to meet? "It definitely would not be the slaveholder," Anderson said. Instead, he stayed much closer to the present. "This may sound silly, but if I could meet anybody, I'd meet my dad." In his fantasy, Anderson, ever the journalist, cast himself as the interviewer and his father as the subject. Anderson recently had had the experience of, in a sense, going back in time. "I recently heard his voice for the first time since I was ten." Wyatt had done a radio interview when his book came out, and it was restored in 2013 for radio broadcast. "I heard his voice talking about me and talking about his book and talking about his family in Mississippi. So if I could sit down and interview anybody, I'd sit down and interview him and find out what he thinks of me and what he thinks of all that's gone on."

Anderson had clearly absorbed so much from both of his parents: his father's need to remain connected to his past, and his mother's drive to keep pushing into the future. So what did Anderson think made us who we are? He believed the circumstances of our birth—both our DNA and our experience—very much shape who we are and who we become. "The accident of our birth unfairly determines an awful lot in this country and all around the world," he said. "We can't help where we were born; we can only help how we live."

The actor and playwright Anna Deavere Smith has had roles on popular TV series like *The West Wing* and *Nurse Jackie,* but she is best known for writing and performing her groundbreaking one-woman shows on subjects ranging from the Los Angeles riots to the American presidency. In her work, she combines journalism with performance, constructing stage plays out of interviews and transforming herself into those real-life characters, bringing to life a menagerie of personalities by perfectly mimicking their voices and mannerisms. She gets this uncanny ability from her lifelong preoccupation with observing everyone and everything around her. "I was always told not to stare as a child," she said. "I did stare for so much of my youth, and I did listen for so much of my youth to stories."

Anna Deavere Smith was born in Baltimore, Maryland, on September 18, 1950, the first of five children of Deaver Young Smith Jr., a shop owner, and Anna Rosalind Young, a schoolteacher. Born just four years before *Brown v. Board of Education* mandated the integration of schools nationwide, she came of age in Baltimore just as racial integration was trying to take hold. When her parents bought a home on Baltimore's Bentalou Street, they were the first and only black family there for quite some time, but Anna's memories of the street bear no trace of this period. "By the time I can remember anything, the whole street, on both sides, was black," she said. "I think the white people ran very fast."

In most parts of the country, integration was neither quick nor easy. Whether in defiance of the law or merely out of habit, the complexion of many schools didn't change much at all, and Anna started her education in an all-black elementary school. By junior high, though, in the early 1960s, she enrolled in a predominantly white school and experienced isolation and unhappiness like never before. "Nobody called me a nigger. They didn't need to." Anna's outsider status afforded her an opportunity to evaluate her surroundings. "I was very curious about those other people, and I didn't appreciate the fact that very, very rarely did you find people walking around who were friends, black and white."

By the late 1960s, when she was a student at Beaver College in Pennsylvania, the country was in turmoil. Anna's response was to embrace her racial identity in a way she hadn't previously. "Many of us have this story: all-white place, seven other young ladies who were Negroes, colored. Nobody was black yet," she said. "We were very nervous about each other. We didn't hang out, didn't want to be seen as the Negro girls. Then when King was killed, we became the Beaver College blacks."

Neither film nor theater had fully embraced black actors when Anna got her start in the early 1970s. She was invited to join a prestigious repertory company only after the one other black actress in the company left. Relegated primarily to the maid roles that were the domain of black actresses of the period, she tried to look beyond the parts. "I didn't really care about the roles," she said. "What I cared about was that I got a union card, and I got a salary, and my classmates didn't." For casting directors, her race was a stumbling block. She was once told, "You don't look like anything," meaning that she was neither easily categorized nor easily cast. "That did plague me for the beginning of my career," she agreed. "I went to get an agent, and she was British, and she said, 'I couldn't possibly send you out because you'll antagonize my clients.' I said, 'What do you mean, antagonize?' She said, 'What will you go as? You don't look black. You're not black or white.'"

For Anna, with her light skin and "good hair," issues of identity have always been at the forefront of her consciousness. Much of her work centers on the differences between how we see ourselves and how others see us. "I've spent my career searching for 'the other' rather than for myself," she said. "It makes me want to know more as a matter of history about my people and how they lived. I think about identity as an amazing jewelry box that most of us don't open. I come today with some trepidation, because I don't know what's there." Anna's jewelry box was filled with greater treasure than she could know.

■ Born on March 16, 1924, in Baltimore, Anna's mother, Anna Rosalind Young, had an unusual upbringing. The fifth of eight children, she spent weekends with her large family but the bulk of the week at the home of a minister and his wife. "Reverend Green and his wife, Mrs. Green, hadn't been able to have any children, and they wanted my mother," Anna explained. The Reverend Green was the pastor at the Grace Memorial Baptist Church in Baltimore, where Anna's parents would marry on June 26, 1949. "I'm told it was quite elegant," Anna said. "She was in a family of eight on the one hand, but really treated like an only child on the other. She had more things than they did because of that." Anna's mother was a brilliant student, the valedictorian of her graduating class at Coppin State Teachers College in 1954. "My mother was innately very smart, and she learned quickly," Anna said. "Even if she'd lived in my grandmother's house,

I think she would have always excelled in school. But that was probably an advantage of being with Reverend and Mrs. Green, who were literate and very well read. My grandmother, I believe, had a sixth-grade education, and I'm not sure what my paternal grandfather had. To be around learned people and to be around the preaching word, that was probably really, really powerful."

Anna's grandmother, Pearl Beatrice Banks, was born on May 30, 1895, also in Baltimore. She died in February 1974. "I have not to date met anyone as kind as my grandma," Anna said. "She went all across the city on buses to take care of all of her grandchildren. She took me from door to door when it was time to collect money for the Harriet Tubman Club that she was a part of. Whenever anybody came to her house, our friends, the first thing she used to say was, 'You're in Grandma's house now, and let me show you your shelf.' We all had a shelf in her house of goodies and things that we liked in her kitchen." Anna's memories extended beyond the walls of the kitchen into the most unlikely of places: the white hair salon. "She would take me where she had her hair done, at Hutzler's department store." Anna laughed. "Oh, it was a big deal, and they would whisper about it."

Anna's relatives described her grandmother Pearl as a real matriarch — strong but quiet, very religious, fiercely dedicated to her children and their education. But there was a mystery about her background that permeated every memory: nobody in Anna's family agreed on Pearl's origins. Anna gave us the version of Pearl's story that she'd grown up hearing. "What I know about her is that she was raised by somebody called Sister Annie, who was a Mason or a part of the Eastern Star, and I know that she lived with her brother George," Anna recalled. "I don't know much except that she had to work very hard for George, her brother George, who had a grocery store, and that Sister Annie was tall, dark, and strict. I know nothing about who her parents were. They must have died."

There were some common elements in what we'd heard from other relatives. According to the family, a couple named George and Annie Banks raised young Pearl alongside their own children after her mother died. From that point on, no two stories were alike. George was Pearl's brother, went one theory. Annie and George were actually Pearl's parents, went another. Another relative speculated that Pearl was born out of wedlock. With no agreement in the oral history, we had to look elsewhere. Fortunately Pearl herself had left a clue, in her family Bible, writing four names, not two, under her own name and her husband's: "Annie S. Banks, George

Banks," followed by "Mary E. Banks, John W. Banks." It appeared that Pearl had listed all four people as her parents. We turned to census records, as we so often did, to try to unravel the mystery.

The 1910 U.S. federal census from Baltimore clarified the confused relationships. George W. Banks was listed as the head of household; Anna, the woman we knew as Sister Annie, was his wife. Pearl B., Anna's grandmother, was described as George's sister, John W. as his father. All four lived together in the same house. Pearl and George were brother and sister, and John was their father, making him Anna's great-grandfather. Anna had never even heard the name before. "Why wouldn't my grandmother talk about John Banks? Why wouldn't she say, 'I lived in this house with that man, John W. Banks'?"

Now that we knew that Sister Annie wasn't Pearl's mother, we continued our search. Key to tracing the ancestry of African American families is the 1870 federal census, the first in which black people appeared by name. Going back a quarter century before Anna's grandmother's birth, we found a listing for Anna's great-grandfather John Banks and his family that allowed us to fill in some pieces of the puzzle: "John Banks, age 25, male, black, oyster shucker; Mary E., age 23, female, black, at home; Benjamin, age 2, male, black; George Jones, age 4, male, black." Anna's great-uncle George Banks, we learned from the census, began life as George Jones. He wasn't John Banks's son; he was Mary's first child, born before she married John. George Welton Jones, whom we now knew to be Pearl's half-brother, was born in about 1866 in Maryland, just one year after the Civil War ended. His father's identity was unknown to us, but he eventually adopted the name of the man who raised him, becoming George Banks.

Was Anna's great-grandfather John Banks born into slavery or freedom? Twenty-five years old in 1870, he was born well before slavery ended in the United States. But Maryland had a tradition of emancipation that other slave states didn't. By 1860, one year before the start of the Civil War, 40 percent of the black population in Maryland was free, as compared to between 10 and 11 percent in the nation. Combing the 1860 U.S. census, though, turned up nothing. If Anna's great-grandfather had been free, his name would have appeared in it. Instead, we turned to the 1860 Slave Schedule, looking for a teenager of his description. The only names that appeared on the Slave Schedules belonged to the slave owners; their human property was recorded by age, gender, and color. Based on John Banks's age in 1870, we knew that Anna's great-grandfather was born in either 1844 or 1845, so we looked for both the name Banks and a boy of about sixteen years old in the Slave Schedule for the Fourth District, Howard County, Maryland. We found both: a listing for a male slave, age sixteen, whose color was described as black, and his owner, Matilda Banks, a sixty-year-old farmer in Howard County, Maryland, who owned fourteen slaves, including, it appeared, Anna's great-grandfather. Digging deeper in the archives, we located the Last Will and Testament of Samuel Banks, Matilda's late husband, dated 1854. "I give and bequeath to my said wife the following slaves," the will read, "namely Dennis, Bill, John, Beale, Jane, Rachel, Louisa, Ellen, and Kitty, and all the increase they may have hereafter."

It was rare to find in documents the name of a slave ancestor, rarer still to find the name of the white man who owned him. The language of the will was chilling. Samuel Banks died long before the Civil War even began, and he, like many of his time, assumed slavery would last forever. When this will was written, Anna's great-grandfather John was only ten years old, yet the will bound him and any children he might go on to father to his master's wife in perpetuity. Anna was stunned by both word and concept. "When I see the word 'increase,' that also means that there's the expectation not only that slavery will last, but this notion of it getting bigger, that there being more people who you could own is extraordinary. That word, 'increase,' is incredible."

Slavery *did* get bigger. The numbers are mind-boggling. Between 1501 and 1866, 12.5 million Africans were shipped across the Atlantic to the New World. Fifteen percent died in the Middle Passage, meaning that 11 million made it to the shores of North America, the Caribbean, and South America. Of that vast number, 388,000 Africans were kept here in the United States. The 42 million African Americans alive today are the result of the increase of fewer than four hundred thousand slaves. "What seems miraculous to me is that they got out of this situation," Anna commented. "That seems astonishing, and that by the time I was with my grandmother, walking on the streets with her to collect money for the Harriet Tubman Club, this wasn't a part of her narrative." This silence is common in African American families, the scars of slavery painful enough to carry, let alone share.

There was no further documentation of Anna's great-grandfather John Banks, but what could we learn about the white man who owned him, Samuel Banks? Parts of the Banks property, Waterford Farm in Howard County, Maryland, including portions of the original house, still stand today. By the time Anna's great-grandfather was born around 1844 or 1845, tobacco had already largely depleted the soil in the region, and most farmers had turned to wheat farming. Compared to those of his neighbors, Samuel Banks's farm was relatively large, and according to the Slave Schedule of 1850, he owned twenty-nine slaves, including the six-year-old boy who was most likely Anna's great-grandfather. The plantation where her ancestor was held in bondage was not far from Anna's childhood home in Baltimore. "I think I've always known that it was likely Maryland or Virginia that they came from," Anna said. "People didn't go far away; nobody traveled down South. And I also think of my people as real Baltimore people."

■ Were there other "real Baltimore people" on Anna's family tree about whom we could learn? We looked for them on her mother's father's side. Anna's grandfather Samuel Maurice Young was born in 1894, also in Baltimore. Anna's grandparents had separated when she was a girl, and her grandfather lived with his common-law wife, Mary. "I knew very little about him growing up, in part because the family alienated themselves from him," she explained. "He had a rough time. He was a very sad man. He usually cried when we went to see him."

Anna's grandfather's parents, her great-grandparents, were Henry T. Young, born in 1850 in Charles County, Maryland, and Ruth Harris, who was born around 1850 or 1860 in Baltimore. Based on the approximate date of her birth, Ruth was almost as likely to have been born into freedom as slavery, as nearly half of Maryland's African American population around 1860 were free. The 1860 census for the Third Ward of Baltimore revealed definitively that Ruth Harris, Anna's great-grandmother, was one of them. The census recorded the "free inhabitants" of her great-grandmother's childhood home: "Thomas Harris, age 34; Mary Harris, age 33; William Harris, age 14; and Ruth Harris, age 1."

Thomas and Mary Harris were Anna's great-great-grandparents, free black people living in a state that still permitted slavery. Abraham Lincoln allowed slavery to continue in the border state of Maryland in exchange for its remaining part of the Union during the Civil War, and slavery was not abolished there until 1864. As the United States headed toward civil war, Baltimore had the largest free black population of any city in the United States, at nearly twenty-six thousand people. It became a magnet for recently freed slaves because it offered relative safety in numbers. Baltimore's free people of color lived within narrow constraints, crowded together in certain neighborhoods and limited to working in certain occupations.

Anna's free ancestors left behind a paper trail that allowed us to trace her mother's father's family further back into freedom. According to the 1830 census, Anna's third great-grandfather Daniel Harris was a free man of color living in Baltimore's Second Ward, working as a brick mason, a trade he passed down to his sons. Daniel was born free in Maryland around 1795, just twelve years after the end of the American Revolution. This was an extraordinarily long line of free people of color. "Then there's no excuse," she laughed. "I should have made something of myself."

Daniel Harris, we would learn, certainly made something of himself. According to Baltimore city directories, Daniel Harris's home was in the Fell's Point area of Baltimore, a crowded neighborhood close to the ship- yard where many free black men and some slaves worked. Prior to 1850, only heads of households were listed by name; their lodgers were recorded simply by age, gender, and status. Although no written evidence existed to prove that Daniel owned his home, in the 1830 census he was listed as the head of household, and under his roof lived nineteen people, including eight free black males between the ages of twenty-four and fifty-five. The free black population in Baltimore quintupled between 1800 and 1830, going from under three thousand to almost fifteen thousand in three de- cades, and many people of color found lodging in informal boardinghouses run by other free black people.

Anna's third great-grandfather left his mark on Baltimore. In 1841 the *Baltimore Sun* reported that Daniel Harris was elected the assistant sec- retary for the Fell's Point Colored Beneficial Society. Although little in- formation about this particular organization survives today, societies like it provided essential support and services to free black communities. By building their own institutions, African Americans showed their determi- nation to help themselves. This community spirit would sustain them in the difficult years leading up to the Civil War. "If there's anything that came down to me from it—which I wouldn't have expected from my maternal grandfather because I didn't know him well enough—it's my own sense of civic responsibility. I'm always asking myself, why are you doing all this? Why am I interested in other artists and bringing them together? Really, as an artist, I should shut the door and write stuff." She paused. "I think it's coming from here."

Daniel Harris continued to make headlines. Once again, on July 16, 1851, the *Baltimore Sun* reported on her ancestor: "The large and commodious steamboat *Relief* has been chartered for a grand moonlight excursion, and splendid displays of fireworks for the colored ladies and gentlemen." The tickets were for sale at 242 Bon Street—Daniel's address in 1851. "What I love about this in particular," Anna said, "is the joy that is evident here." Art and literature, she explained, haven't dwelled enough on this part of the black experience, so it's largely unknown. "We don't have many works of art that show us the diversity of how people lived. We stop short about what is the black experience."

■ Anna's family tree on her mother's side illustrated the diversity of the black experience in antebellum Maryland. Now we turned to Anna's father's side of the family. Her father, Deaver Young Smith Jr., was born on December 2, 1919, in Baltimore. Anna said she inherited an extreme sense of caution from her father, "just this fear that something could happen to somebody I'm responsible for."

Anna's father was a shop owner, working at the Smith Punch Base Coffee and Tea Co., established by his father, Anna's grandfather Deaver Sr., in 1906. Deaver Young Smith Sr. was born on August 20, 1890, also in Baltimore. Located on Pennsylvania Avenue, the hub of Baltimore's black community, culture, and commerce, the company served black businesses in Baltimore and Washington, D.C. "This is when people were drinking Maxwell House, and Grandpop was importing beans from around the world, teas. His shop would be really hot right now. It would be really hip," Anna said.

Anna enjoyed a close relationship with Deaver Sr. "I was crazy about my grandfather. I liked to hear stories from him, so I would like to sit and talk to Grandpop a lot," Anna recalled. "I really liked looking at him. He always wore a tie, a shirt, a sweater vest, and a jacket. He wasn't dapper really because he was too much of a Christian to be dapper. And he smelled like his spices, too." She paused. "You know how you just like some people?"

Deaver Sr.'s shop was only the third black-owned business in this part of West Baltimore. Over the course of decades, until as late as the 1960s, most of the merchants catering to the area's black clientele were Jewish. In March 1914, according to the *Baltimore Afro-American*, at just twenty-four years old, with no more than an eighth-grade education, Deaver Smith Sr. was elected to the executive committee of the Colored Men's Business Association. He was a pioneer in Baltimore's African American business community, and his obituary referred to him as "a Baltimore institution."

"I guess what I got from him is the extent to which I have an entrepreneurial spirit and the extent to which I believe in making things happen myself," Anna said. "I don't have business acumen, but there's something about taking care of yourself maybe." He was a self-made man, and he passed on the traits of self-reliance and ambition to subsequent generations. "There was something really incredible, especially if you met his children, the ones with the fancy cars and the jewelry and the scotch, and I thought, wow, Grandpop made that happen."

Deaver Sr.'s wife, Anna's grandmother Virginia Sally Biggs, was born on July 12, 1893, in York County, Pennsylvania, although her family's roots lay in Carroll County, Maryland. We went back two generations on Anna's father's mother's line and discovered, once again, that Anna was descended from free Negroes on her father's side of the family as well as on her mother's. "Doesn't surprise me about them," Anna commented. Her aunts on this side of her family "were so high yellow. They were very, very light." According to the 1850 census, Anna's great-great-grandparents Basil Biggs and Mary Jackson were free people of color, married sometime around 1843 and in possession of three hundred dollars' worth of real estate in Maryland. Both were born in Maryland, Basil Biggs in 1820 in New Windsor, Carroll County, and Mary Jackson sometime between 1825 and 1827. Basil was a family name; Anna had an uncle Basil, but she had never heard of Basil Biggs. His was an incredible story that should never have been lost.

In 1858, Basil, a free man of color and a veterinarian, moved his wife and four children from the slave state of Maryland to the free state of Pennsylvania. The 1860 census showed the family settled in its new home in Gettysburg, Pennsylvania. "Basil Biggs, male, personal estate value, $1,000; Mary J. Biggs, age 33, female," Anna read. "Here's my aunt Hannah. Hannah E. Biggs, age 13, female; Eliza Biggs—never knew her—age 11, female; Calvin Biggs, age 9, male; William Biggs, age 6; Mary E. Biggs, eight-twelfths of a year old, female; and Edward Byers, age 35, black, male, farmhand." She looked up from the transcript. "He better not have owned him!" He did not; the farmhand was a paid worker. Despite his obvious success, Basil was illiterate. We guessed that his family's move from Maryland to Pennsylvania may have been precipitated by a desire for his children to be educated. The census told us that all of Basil and Mary's school-age children, Hannah, Eliza, and Calvin, attended school. At that time, in Maryland, all black people, including free people of color, were prohibited from attending public school; black children were relegated to segregated, private schools. In Pennsylvania, however, African Americans were allowed to attend public schools, even with white children.

Basil Biggs couldn't have chosen a more dangerous place to move. In the summer of 1863, just five years after relocating his family to Pennsylvania, Anna's great-great-grandfather found himself at the epicenter of one of the most devastating battles in the history of war: the Battle of Gettysburg. For three days, from July 1 to July 3 of that year, the battle raged, claiming more lives than any other battle of the Civil War. An obituary from 1936 for Celia Biggs Penn, Basil and Mary's daughter, described by the headline as the "last of kin who fled [the] '63 battle," gave us a sense of what Anna's ancestors did in the fateful days leading up to the battle. "The only colored persons in this section, the Biggs family, was warned to leave this section with the approach of the Confederate troops." They had no choice. The Biggs family fled, and the Confederates converted Basil's farm into a field hospital. "My God, that's a story right there. That's a play," Anna commented. "What I can't believe is that Aunt Julia and Aunt Hannah never talked to us about this. I mean, we saw them once or twice every single year."

As the battle dragged on, desperate soldiers from both sides ransacked the countryside for food and shelter. When Anna's ancestors finally returned home after the battle was over, the farm lay in ruins. Anna's great-great-grandfather had lost everything: his livestock, his crops, his furniture. A Pennsylvania Civil War Border Claim he filed after the war enumerated the losses in detail: "Wheat, oats, corn, hay, cattle, hogs, a carpet, barrels of vinegar, chains, apple butter, jellies, flour." He valued the loss of his livelihood at $1,506.60, but the state never compensated him for a penny of it. He had to rebuild his life, and the nightmare of Gettysburg provided him with a grisly opportunity to do so.

The human cost of the Civil War was devastating, and thousands of rotting corpses littered the Gettysburg landscape. The rapidly decomposing bodies of Union and Confederate soldiers were both a morbid reminder of the toll taken by the war's bloodiest battle and an impending health hazard. The United States government contracted with a white Gettysburg resident who hired Anna's great-great-grandfather to do the gruesome work of exhuming Union soldiers from their shallow graves. It took nearly eight months, but Basil Biggs, with a crew of eight to ten African American men in his employ, buried nearly 3,500 corpses in neatly ordered rows of graves in what would become the Gettysburg National Cemetery. Anna's great-

great-grandfather played a fundamental role in preparing Gettysburg for the commemoration that followed the battle, and made it possible for Abraham Lincoln to deliver his Gettysburg Address that November. Through the brave work of her ancestor, Anna had a purchase on American history at one of its foundational moments.

This story struck a chord with Anna, one both professional and intensely personal. "I had a play about American history that didn't work very well, called *House Arrest*," she explained. "The most upsetting thing to me about the way people criticized *House Arrest* is that they said that I should go back to doing what I'd been doing, the stuff that's about me, which is about race riots, as if I don't have any claim on American history. I would always say, 'I don't appreciate that,' not knowing anything about this, but knowing that we had to be here before 1865. But to now know some things about my people, it's really upsetting to be relegated to this one place. This is very, very, very powerful. I could have lived my life without having read this paragraph."

After the Civil War ended, Basil reestablished himself in the city he and his family had fled, using the money he made disinterring and reburying the Union war dead to buy a new farm where his family would live and thrive. An article in the 1892 *Cleveland Gazette* described Anna's great-great-grandfather as "reputed to be the wealthiest Afro-American in Gettysburg," the family home as "a magnificent one." The house still stood; Anna's great-aunt had lived in it, and Anna herself had been there many times. "I visited as a child," she said. "My great-aunt was so established here in this very beautiful house. It makes me trust my intuition that there were definitely deep roots there." Yet it had only been intuition; she had never before heard Basil's name. "But they didn't talk about this. Why didn't they?"

Our final story about Anna's great-great-grandfather was the most remarkable one yet, a story showing there was even more to the improbable life of this free man of color. The headline over his obituary in the *Gettysburg Compiler* trumpeted his most impressive, most important achievement: "Leading colored citizen was an active agent in the Underground Railroad." Anna cried. "This man was amazing." The Underground Railroad involved a vast network of people who, like Basil Biggs, provided safe haven for slaves escaping bondage in the South. Runaway slaves who made it across the Ohio River or the Mason-Dixon Line found refuge in the network of the web's secret locations. Basil Biggs was in a unique position to help precisely because he was a veterinarian, which gave him reason to travel without arousing suspicion. The routes around Gettysburg, only ten miles from the Mason-Dixon Line, were treacherous, rife with slave catchers and informants. Although Anna's great-great-grandfather's part in history had been silenced by his family, many historians wrote of the illiterate farmer and veterinarian who took part in the complex and dangerous operation called the Underground Railroad.

Basil Biggs's role in the Underground Railroad was an act of terrific courage. After 1850, when Congress passed the Fugitive Slave Act, it became a federal offense to do what Anna's great-great-grandfather did. "But great thinkers, Martin Luther King among them, in 'A Letter from the Birmingham Jail,' make a clear line between a just law and an unjust law," Anna said, "and what side are you going to stand on?" Basil Biggs, who risked his own freedom to help other African Americans escape from slavery, chose to stand on the side of right.

■ So where did this heroic man come from himself? According to his death certificate, Basil was born in 1819. His father's name was listed as William Biggs, his mother's as Elizabeth Bayne (sometimes as Boyne). These were Anna's third great-grandparents. Examining records of the time, the only William Biggs we could find was a white man, and he was married to a white woman and had white children. He left no will upon his death in 1822, and none of his estate documents made mention of any slaves, a woman named Elizabeth Bayne, or a son named Basil. Was Basil the son of this white man?

At the time of his own death, William, it turned out, was waiting on an inheritance from his father, the late Benjamin Biggs, who died three years before his son did, in 1819. Looking into Benjamin's affairs proved more fruitful than looking into his son's. William had been charged with managing his father's affairs after his death, and a ledger he left behind contained an intriguing entry. On July 19, 1822, he wrote, "Fee paid for going after Negro Basil, $3.50." Our research led us to conclude that the young boy had been living elsewhere, and the three dollars and change were travel costs incurred to return him to the Biggs home. There was no further evidence in the paper trail to tie these people together. Anna's own skin tone was proof of mixing, and a photograph of Basil Biggs had shown him to be light-complected. Then there were her aunts. "They were very light-skinned, those people. Aunt Hannah, I always thought she was a white woman, and so was Aunt Julia, her sister." DNA could solve the mystery that the paper trail couldn't.

■ Anna was descended from free people of color on both sides of her family, and the records they left behind allowed us to trace her ancestors back further than was typical of an African American of Anna's generation. Her oldest identified ancestors on her paternal side were her third great-grandparents William Biggs and Elizabeth Bayne, both of whom were born in Maryland around the turn of the eighteenth century. On her mother's side, the oldest ancestor we identified was her third great-grandfather Daniel Harris Sr., born around 1795 in Maryland. To go back even further, we administered two tests to Anna—an admixture test, which measures an individual's percentages of European, sub-Saharan African, and East Asian / Native American ancestry from the past five hundred years or so, and a mitochondrial DNA test, which would take us back thousands of years on her matrilineal line—and one to her brother, a Y-DNA test, to take us back through her patrilineal line. While mitochondrial DNA is passed from mother to child, regardless of the child's gender, Y-DNA is passed only from father to son. Anna's results showed that she had slightly more European ancestry than African: 50.7 percent European vs. 48.9 percent African. "I have a brother born with blond hair, a sister who looked like a Russian doll. Brother has blue eyes, aunts have blue eyes and green eyes and gray eyes." She laughed. "Something's going on."

Anna's mitochondrial DNA, an identical genetic fingerprint passed from mother to child, one generation after the next, brought us directly back to Africa. Her maternal haplogroup, a genetic population group that shares a common ancestor, is the most common one among African Americans, and it is found only in West Africa. In other words, for Anna, the ancestral source of her mitochondrial DNA was an African woman.

To test Anna's father's line, we analyzed Anna's brother Deaver's Y-DNA and determined that her paternal haplogroup also originates in West Africa. Thanks to a test taken by Anna's maternal uncle William, we also learned that this is the same paternal haplogroup carried by Anna's maternal grandfather, Samuel Young. This tells us that the European ancestry did not come from any of these ancestral lines.

Broken down by region, Anna's matrilineal European DNA came primarily from Great Britain, registering at 41 percent of the total. Otherwise it was quite geographically diverse, with smaller amounts from Scandinavia, Finland, Russia, Italy, and Greece. But it was her African ancestry she was most curious about. While most African Americans descend from ancestors taken during the transatlantic slave trade, few can identify the ethnic group or the region from which they came in Africa. To find out, we compared Anna's DNA results with those of modern-day Africans, allowing us to look back hundreds of years and pinpoint her ethnic roots in Africa, before the Middle Passage. Her largest percentage of African DNA came from the Ivory Coast and Ghana, with smaller amounts from Angola, Cameroon, Congo, and Senegal. The smallest portion of Anna's African DNA traced back to Nigeria.

Even though Anna's admixture revealed an almost even split between African and European DNA, her direct maternal and paternal lines (as well as her direct maternal paternal line) brought us back to Africa. This means that some of the inner branches of her family tree likely carried the substantial amount of European DNA that we saw in her admixture results and that was evident in her own skin.

Finally, we returned to the mystery of her great-great-grandfather Basil Biggs's father and whether he was a white man. The only man of that name that we had been able to locate in the area of Basil's birth was a white man named William Biggs, the son of Benjamin Biggs. Aside from a piece of circumstantial evidence, there was nothing to connect Basil definitively to either of these men. By comparing Anna's autosomal DNA, which is inherited not only from an individual's parents but from all of his or her ancestral lines, to descendants of the white Biggs family, we found many, many matches between Anna's DNA and theirs, particularly to descendants of Benjamin Biggs's parents and grandparents. This was conclusive proof that Anna's black Biggs ancestors were related to the white Biggs family through DNA. She had living white Biggs ancestors who were part of her family tree. "This is fabulous," Anna said. "I hope they're proud of what their descendant Basil Biggs did."

■ Now it was Anna's turn to tell us a story, of a journey she had taken to Uganda. "I went to visit a place where they did traditional healing. They were running in fire and eating coal and getting possessed. At one point, the doctor who was in charge of this spoke English, and he said that one of the witch doctors wanted to know if I would like to be blessed by my ancestors. I said, 'Well, of course I want to be blessed by my ancestors.' You know what the blessing was? I got spat on three times with mouthfuls of banana peels." She laughed. "This acquaintance with my ancestors was a lot more sane than that. I'm glad I didn't get spat on."

There was no question, though, that Anna had been blessed. The stories we told her connected her to a past that her parents and grandparents had never shared with her. When she was a young teacher, she said, she had taken her students to Gettysburg. "We just hung out in the battlefield, just trying to feel it, sense it." At the time she didn't know that her ancestor, her great-great-grandfather, a free black man, had stood on that hallowed ground, prepared it to be the final resting place of the thousands of soldiers who had given their lives there in the name of the Union and in the name of freedom. If she could go back in time, she would go back to that place, to meet him. "Maybe it's too predictable that I would choose Basil Biggs, but it's because of American history," she said. "The story of Basil Biggs makes so much sense to me because of the time in my youth that I spent in Gettysburg. I really love it that he had resistance and courage. That he broke the law, not a moral law but he broke a law that was an unjust law, means a lot to me."

Anna had begun this journey viewing her ancestors more through a historical lens than through "the fact that I'm from them, because I don't really feel that. I don't feel the impact." But after spending more time in their lives, learning of their contributions and experiences, Anna felt differently. She did feel the impact. She believed that our experiences shape our identity more than our DNA does, but, she said, it was the DNA she had inherited that tied her to her past and inspired her to connect that past to her future. "The time we spent today is going to affect my identity. It's going to affect my choices in a huge way," she said, already laying out a plan for herself. "I'm going to go back to Baltimore and go back to Gettysburg and create something out of it. It gives me a lot of courage and a great desire, to live out both the good and the bad in my legacy and to do as much as I can with the time I have left to do something that deserves to be a part of this story."

Ken Burns, Anderson Cooper, and Anna Deavere Smith are consummate storytellers, accustomed to the close and artful examination of individuals both grand and obscure, and they all recognize a good story when they hear one. On their journeys into their family trees, they had each heard several, every one populated with a compelling cast of characters—some of them heroes, some of them villains, some of them ordinary people just trying to get by. The ancestors of Ken, Anderson, and Anna ranged from the famous to the forgotten, and finally, each one had been brought into equal focus, even those long hidden in the branches of their family trees. The details of each story captivated them and gave them a strong sense of their ancestors' place in the history of this country and, by extension, their own.

CHAPTER FOUR

Roots of Freedom

For the actor and director Ben Affleck, the former NAACP president Ben Jealous, and the dancer and actor Khandi Alexander, the past carries both blessings and burdens. Their knowledge of their ancestry ran the gamut: Ben Jealous came to us steeped in the stories of his ancestors, while Khandi Alexander had been cut off from even the nearest branches on her family tree; Ben Affleck stood somewhere in the middle. As we uncovered their fascinating family stories, they would learn that their roots intersected in complicated ways in the defining wars of our nation's history. For all three, the Revolutionary War and the Civil War, and the aftermath of each, were events that existed not only in history books, but in the pages of their life stories.

Ben Affleck (b. 1972)

In 1997, with only a handful of acting and screenwriting credits to his name, Ben Affleck was launched into Hollywood's stratosphere with the success of the film *Good Will Hunting*. Just twenty-five years old at the time, he and his friend Matt Damon won the Best Screenwriting Oscar for the low-budget drama set in Boston. "That was B.C. and A.D. for sure," Ben said. Since then, he has achieved tremendous success behind the camera as well; in 2013, his film *Argo* won the Oscar for Best Picture. He is as committed to liberal political causes as he is to his craft, an active supporter of gay marriage and the antihunger campaign Feeding America, and the founder of the Eastern Congo Initiative advocacy group.

Ben has built an enviable career, but he never perceived success as a given. His triumphs and failures, he believed, have been equally important to his development as an actor and a director, and as an individual. "I really believe the character of a person is defined by adversity rather than by when you know everything is going well," he said. "I've had both in my life, and I've been really, really lucky, and I've grown from the difficult stuff I've had to deal with." He was careful to keep his experiences in perspective. "I don't mean to put my difficulties in a league with folks who are serving overseas and so on, but in terms of character and in terms of this business, there's an up-and-down aspect that's inherent to it, and part of the skill that you need to bring to it is resolve."

Benjamin Geza Affleck-Boldt was born on August 15, 1972, in Berkeley, California, the elder of two sons of Timothy Byers Affleck and Christopher Anne Boldt. Ben's brother is the actor and director Casey Affleck, born Caleb Casey McGuire Affleck-Boldt. When Ben was about three years old, the family moved to Cambridge, Massachusetts. He described the neighborhood as "very heterogeneous, a kind of working-class, middle-class neighborhood. The other kids' parents were police officers and firemen, but it also had the influence of both Harvard and MIT educators and academics, artists, so it was a nice combination. We were part of the first wave of gentrification."

Ben grew up with only the vaguest notion of where his ancestors came from. "It's always been a blank canvas to me," he said. "I'm told that Affleck was a Scottish name, and that there was some Irish." "Some Irish" wasn't enough in the neighborhood in which Ben was raised. He has played Boston Irish American characters onscreen, but offscreen, he makes no serious claims to the heritage. "I consider myself part Irish American, but not to the extent that the kids I grew up around did. They were heavy-duty Irish, really identified as Irish Catholic kids. I didn't have an Irish last name, so if you didn't meet those criteria, you weren't Irish."

What would we learn about Ben's roots, Irish and otherwise? Ben's parents separated when he was young, but together and independently, they set the models of commitment and resolve that have guided Ben throughout his life and career. In our exploration of Ben's ancestry, we would also uncover long-lost stories of ancestors whose actions stood in stark relief to the principles that had been instilled in him since childhood.

■ Ben's father, Timothy Byers Affleck, was born on August 7, 1943, in Detroit, Michigan, the son of Myron Hopkins Strong Affleck Jr. and Nancy Louise Byers. As a child, Tim enjoyed what Ben called "a fledgling child acting career of some sort," and as an adult periodically pursued work in theater as a writer and director. Ben knew little about his father's side of the family. "There was a sense of not wanting to talk about stuff," Ben recalled. "You're a little kid; you don't know enough to try to pry stuff out of your parents, so I never knew too much." Ben's father himself described his family as "difficult and tight-lipped people." We would do our best to open the doors that had been kept shut, and we began our search into Ben's paternal ancestry with his grandmother, the stunningly beautiful Nancy Louise Byers, born on October 16, 1924, a "weather girl" at WJAR Rhode Island in television's early days. Ben's father told us that his mother—talented, intelligent, ambitious—led a troubled life, and she struggled with alcoholism and relationships, committing suicide three years before Ben was born. Tim was twenty-five the year his mother died, the same age as Ben when he skyrocketed to fame with his first Academy Award. "I'm winning the Oscar, and my dad is dealing with his mom's suicide. This is more reason why I have tremendous respect for battling through, pushing through, dealing with adversity. It's remarkable."

Ben's grandmother was a compelling figure, and we wanted to learn more about her beginnings. Nancy's mother, Ben's great-grandmother Dorothy Elizabeth McGuire, was born on February 23, 1903, in Trenton, New Jersey, her surname at birth a strong indication of her Irish heritage. We were curious as to how far back her Irish roots went. But first, we would discover that Ben had deep roots in New Jersey's capital city.

Ben's third great-grandfather George Woolverton McGuire Sr., also born in Trenton, on October 3, 1849, was described in the *New Jersey Biographical Encyclopedia* from 1913 as "one of the most popular and best known men of Trenton, not alone because of the services he has rendered, but because of his manly, upright character and many sterling qualities." After owning several drugstores in New Jersey and Pennsylvania, Ben's ancestor became New Jersey's chief inspector of food and drugs. George Woolverton McGuire's father was similarly admired. Ben's fourth great-grandfather James McGuire, a former blacksmith born on May 1, 1825, also in Trenton, served as a police marshal and as Trenton's health inspector. "What is it with inspecting?" Ben laughed. "My family wanted to be regulators. No wonder I'm a Democrat. We believe in regulation." An article from the *Trenton Evening Times*, dated May 20, 1888, sang James McGuire's praises. "The city owes Mr. McGuire a debt of gratitude for his work during the smallpox epidemic. By utter fearlessness and going where the deadly disease had broken out for the purpose of checking its ravages, he has been the means of stamping out insipient epidemics. When he was marshal, he made notable arrests, and as assistant dairy commissioner, he has rendered valuable services in his suppression of sale of impure milk, bogus butter, and adulterated foods." This was in the days before federal food regulations, and Ben's fourth great-grandfather probably saved countless lives through his work.

With Ben's fifth great-grandfather, we made our way back to Ireland. According to the 1850 federal census for Mercer County, New Jersey, of which Trenton is the county seat, John McGuire was born in Enniskillen, Ireland, in 1789, just six years after the end of the American Revolution. Although we could not track down the precise date of his arrival, we know that he immigrated to the United States sometime before 1825, because his son James was born in that year in this country. John McGuire was Ben's original immigrant ancestor on this line of his paternal family tree.

Irish immigration to the United States reached its peak after the catastrophic potato famine of the late 1840s and early 1850s, when a million Irish died and another million sought a new life outside their homeland. John McGuire was part of an earlier wave. At the end of the 1700s, Ireland's Roman Catholics, suffering mightily under harsh English rule, fled their native land in large numbers. During the period in which Ben's fifth great-grandfather arrived here, the Irish made up a third of all immigrants to America. For many of these immigrants, desperately poor and uneducated, economic opportunity continued to elude them in their adopted home, and the majority took work in the lowest-paid, most menial jobs. Success for future generations was often seen as sufficient reward for hard work in this one. But in the case of Ben's fifth great-grandfather, success didn't wait a generation. We don't know how he did it, but John McGuire became the owner of the National Hotel, located on Broad Street in Trenton. He would own it until his death in 1856. This was not a typical immigrant story. From the time of their arrival in America, the McGuire family established themselves as a fundamental part of the fabric of Trenton.

◼ The paper trail on Ben's McGuire ancestors ended here, so we turned to his grandmother Nancy Byers's father's line. Nancy's grandparents, Ben's second great-grandparents, were both born in Ohio, Allen C. Byers in 1864 and Lulu Lee French in 1869. Lulu Lee's father, Almon Bruce French, was Ben's third great-grandfather, and he had a story as arresting as his name. "I wish I knew it before I had a son," Ben said, "because that would have been his name."

Almon Bruce French was born on September 3, 1838, in West Farmington, Ohio. He became a lawyer but soon abandoned the occupation, influenced by an unusual childhood experience that ultimately determined the course of his entire life. We unearthed the story in a book on the occult called *Gleanings from the Rostrum* written by Almon Bruce French himself, originally published in 1892. Ben's ancestor, we discovered, was one of the leaders of the Spiritualist movement that gripped the nation in the mournful aftermath of the Civil War. The introduction, written by his fellow Spiritualist Hudson Tuttle, tells the story of the night that Almon returned home to find his mother and sister in an altered state. "He sought the house, and on entering, found his mother and sister both entranced," Tuttle wrote. "To him, it was a strange manifestation, which filled his mind with dread and awe at its mystery. He attempted to leave them, but the invisible beings controlling them commanded him to stay, for they had a work for him too great to be revealed at that time." Ben laughed. "This is some sort of possession that he witnessed?"

In the 1870s the idea of Spiritualism gained traction in America, particularly among society's upper classes. The concept wasn't entirely new. Even during the war, Mary Todd Lincoln was known to host séances in the White House. But in the postwar years, millions of people believed that the spirits of the dead wanted to communicate with the living. Two percent of all the people in the United States had been killed during the war—750,000 Americans, the equivalent of roughly 7 million Americans dying today in a war over a four-year period—leaving hundreds of thousands of widows and orphans searching for a way to deal with their losses. Many scholars believe that Spiritualism arose in direct response to the tremendous death rate suffered during the Civil War.

Almon Bruce French was a notable figure in the movement, traveling the country, conducting séances, and delivering talks in which he claimed that he could summon the dead to the very room in which he stood. Newspapers reported on Ben's third great-grandfather's appearances regularly. "Mr. French began to speak. He was mostly unconscious and often would sit before his audience with closed eyes. His condition slowly changed until it became blended with the normal state." His obituary, dated August 30, 1923, called him "an inspirational orator of great force and effectiveness, one of the noted speakers of the time." Ben took pride in his unusual ancestor. "Somebody might call him a nut; somebody might call him an intensely religious and spiritual guy," Ben said. "It's interesting to see interesting people who are using their mind in interesting ways, who are atypical. It's a neat thing to have a guy like that in our lineage."

■ The impact of the Civil War on Ben's third great-grandfather Almon Bruce French was tremendous. Three generations earlier on Ben's family tree was an ancestor touched very personally by the first defining war in our nation's history. Ben's sixth great-grandfather Jesse Stanley was born on December 23, 1757, in Goshen, Connecticut, a town partly founded by his family. (One of those town settlers was Jesse's grandfather Nathaniel Stanley. Though the details of Nathaniel's life fell outside the scope of our research on Jesse, according to plausible genealogical findings reported in the *Daily Mail*, Nathaniel bought a slave named Tobe in 1728 before relocating to Goshen in the 1740s. Our genealogists confirmed Nathaniel as Jesse's grandfather but did not independently verify his ownership of a slave. Nathaniel Stanley died in 1770, when Jesse was twelve.) Jesse was a teenager working as a farmhand when tensions between the colonists and the British began to escalate in the 1770s. His pension application—one among the eighty thousand in the archives of the Continental army—told us that young Jesse had taken up arms in the fight for independence. "The deponent in the month of January, about the middle of the month, 1776, being then a resident in the town of Goshen, in the county of Litchfield, state of Connecticut, enlisted as a soldier in the company commanded by Captain Bezaleel Beebe." Unbeknownst to him, Ben was descended from a Patriot. "I'm developing a movie about the Revolutionary War," he noted. "Now I see why I was drawn to it."

According to this pension application, Ben's sixth great-grandfather was one of two thousand soldiers who served under George Washington during some of the darkest days of the war. In the summer of 1776, Washington's troops had lost a series of humiliating battles, and now they found themselves badly outnumbered, being chased by five thousand well-armed British forces through northern Manhattan. The British expected the Patriots to continue their retreat, but in the Harlem hills, Washington designed an ambush that caught the British by surprise. The Battle of Harlem Heights was Washington's first victory of the war. It wasn't decisive, but it was crucial in building the Patriots' confidence. It proved that they could stand their ground against the larger and better-equipped British force. Some historians say that the Continental army had been on the verge of collapse before the unexpected victory, of which Ben's ancestor was a part.

Ben's sixth great-grandfather Jesse Stanley was just one of three Patriot ancestors on Ben's father's family tree. His fifth great-grandfather Timothy Vinton, born in Dudley, Massachusetts, in 1748, and another sixth great-grandfather, Abel Hinckley, born in Stonington, Connecticut, in 1753, also served in the war and survived it. Their service made Ben eligible for membership in the Sons of the American Revolution. Although the information had been lost over the centuries, Ben had very deep roots in America, going back to colonial times. "We never saw our family like that, so this is a big surprise, and I'm really proud of it," Ben said. "It makes me feel a little more connected to the history of the country. It makes it feel less academic and more personal."

■ With the paper trail at an end for Ben's father's ancestors, we now turned to Ben's mother's side of the family. Christopher Anne Boldt was born on December 1, 1942, in New York City. Ben described his mother as brilliant, humble, curious, and very empathetic, and he traced the roots of his social consciousness back to her. "I hope I'm a little bit like her," he said. "She definitely imbued us with a very strong sense of social justice and social equality that I've carried with me." Chris was a student at Radcliffe College during some of the most turbulent years in the fight for civil rights. By 1964, like many other college students, she had been inspired by the March on Washington and Martin Luther King's vision for racial equality.

In what came to be known as Freedom Summer, thousands of activists from all over the country headed down to Mississippi to protest civil rights abuses, register black voters, and challenge the racial status quo. White supremacists responded by waging a war of intimidation. For some, the war would turn deadly. The Ku Klux Klan patrolled black neighborhoods, where they harassed and beat the so-called outside agitators. The most shocking and horrific atrocity occurred on the night of June 21, 1964. A lynch mob made up of members of the Klan and the local sheriff's department pulled over three civil rights activists: an African American man named James Chaney and his two white colleagues, Andrew Goodman and Michael Schwerner. They tortured Chaney and then shot all three to death at close range.

In Mississippi, the threat of violence was anything but abstract, yet activists were still drawn there because they were convinced that it was in Mississippi that they could effect the greatest change. In short, there was work to be done there—on and beyond the front lines.

Black students had long struggled in neglected, segregated schools, casualties of the falsehood perpetrated by the doctrine of "separate but equal." An important aspect of the broader Freedom Summer campaign was its educational component, organized brilliantly by Bob Moses, who himself was not only codirector of the Council of Federated Organizations but a gifted teacher of math. It was in this sphere that Ben's mother manifested her commitment to social change in Mississippi during Freedom Summer of 1964.

Not yet twenty-two years old, Chris Boldt made her first journey south during that tumultuous time. She was recruited along with a group of other white Harvard and Radcliffe students to teach incoming freshmen at the historically black Tougaloo College, outside Jackson, by a fellow Harvard student named Abbott Gleason. In his memoir, *A Liberal Education* (2010), Gleason explained that he was acting on an idea proposed by Moses, who had earned his master's in philosophy from Harvard in 1957, to organize a group of "wealthy and well-connected Harvard students and faculty [to] give the Tougaloo faculty the summer off to rest and recuperate, and take over summer school teaching—plus participate in local civil rights activities." Of the twenty-five Harvard students Gleason assembled, Ben's mother was one of only four undergraduates. Her course load included, she recounted to us in an interview, "vocabulary, standard curriculum, [and] tutoring incoming freshmen in how to write a paper."

Tougaloo was a logical destination. Founded as an integrated institution in 1869 with the purpose of providing African American students with educational and industrial training, it was long known as an activist campus. In 1963 Tougaloo students and faculty had organized sit-ins at local businesses and "pray-ins" at local churches. The violence with which their peaceful acts were met was still visible when the Harvard group arrived the following year. Gleason noted in his memoir: "Memphis Norman, one of the leaders, still had his arm in a cast, I believe, from having been beaten months earlier." The atmosphere in which the northern white students found themselves was charged with energy and enmity. "Since the late 1940s," Gleason explained, "Tougaloo chaplains, faculty and students had episodically participated in civil rights projects. . . . In the increasingly tense racial climate of the early sixties, Tougaloo had come to be regarded by whites as a hotbed of race-mixing and communism. . . . Whites from Jackson were in the habit of driving their cars around the outskirts of campus, and shooting in the general direction of the administration buildings, particularly after they got off work on Friday afternoon."

The threat of violence was always palpable, but never more so than after the murders of Chaney, Goodman, and Schwerner, which occurred shortly after the Harvard group's arrival at Tougaloo. Chris Boldt did not know them, and Gleason Abbott recalled, "We had no connection with them, . . . but all of us were now afraid."

Despite the combustible environment she had found herself in in 1964, Ben's mother returned to Mississippi for a second time, in the summer of 1965, when she instructed the state's youngest African American students in a Head Start program in the town of Hattiesburg, serving as a bridge to those who needed help at a turning point in American history. It was here, Ben's mother told us, that she "was exposed to much more danger." Tougaloo had seen its share of violence, and Abbott Gleason wrote that the Harvard and Radcliffe group experienced harassment when they ventured into the restaurants of Jackson—"jeered [at] or called names, or spat on, occasionally even punched"—but the campus environment, according to Chris, had provided relative security. In Hattiesburg, however, where the KKK prowled the streets and the black population was distrusting of whites, Chris risked being recognized as "one of those northern troublemakers."

Ben marveled at his mother's commitment, so obviously secondary to her fear. "She had principles," Ben said. "There she was, a college girl, and she goes all the way down to Mississippi to participate in making things a little bit better or more just. That example of a commitment to social justice that my mother set for us has stayed with me." Politically engaged and passionately involved, Ben's mother never cast herself as a hero in the story. "She was not one to tell her own stories or to brag or focus on her own history, probably to her detriment," he said, "certainly to ours."

Ben believed that his mother was greatly influenced by her own father. "I think she did get an example of activism from him," he explained. "They're both quite smart, and he was very political, and I'm sure my mom was encouraged by that." Ben's maternal grandfather, William O'Brien Boldt, was born to Joseph Raymond Boldt and Ann Rita Lenihan on September 18, 1917, in Ridgewood, New Jersey. O'Brien, as he was called, attended Dartmouth College in the years leading up to America's entry into World War II. "He was a very jovial guy. I think he was a good man, a very friendly, kind man. He was very into his progressive politics."

Just as his daughter would do a quarter century later, O'Brien Boldt found a platform for those progressive politics during his college years. Harboring a keen awareness of the wrongs being perpetrated by Hitler and the Nazis in Germany, Ben's grandfather channeled his outrage into irreverence. On December 13, 1938, the *Los Angeles Times* ran an article about a student group called the Adolf Hitler Christmas Stocking Commission. "Its student leader, O'Brien Boldt," Ben read, "said the aim is to send the German Führer four test tube samples of 'Aryan,' Semitic, Negro, and Mongolian blood, with the promise of a five-dollar bonus in pennies if he can tell which is which. The biggest problem, Boldt said, is to find a good sample of Grade A Aryan blood." Ben laughed. "Good for him. He was on the right side."

Ben knew little about his great-grandparents, O'Brien Boldt's parents. Exploring his great-grandmother Ann Rita Lenihan's story took us back across the Atlantic. According to her birth certificate, Ann was born on September 26, 1879, in Rathfriland, County Down, Ireland (today Northern Ireland). Also recorded were her parents' names, Ben's great-great-grandparents, Edward Lenihan and Ann Smyth. Ben's great-great-grandfather was a head constable for the Irish police force, the Royal Irish Constabulary, better known as the RIC. Not only had we found deep Irish roots on both sides of Ben's family tree, but also deep police roots. "A civil disobedience motif and a police motif," Ben said. "At odds with ourselves!"

Already a head constable with a solid income and guaranteed pension at the time of his marriage in 1875, Edward and his new wife, Ann, likely would have been able to live a comfortable life. But everything was about to change dramatically for the Lenihans. Just nine years after he and Ann were married, Edward died after a weeklong battle with pneumonia on March 17, 1884, St. Patrick's Day. Ben's great-great-grandmother became a widow at the age of thirty-three, the mother of five young children. At the time, Ireland was in the midst of a deep depression, and just one year after her husband's death, in 1885, Ann brought the Lenihan branch of the family to the United States.

According to Ben's mother, Ann's early years in her adopted country were very, very difficult. She had likely spent every penny she had to book her family's passage to America, and once here, Ben's great-great-grandmother couldn't provide for those five young children. Her three daughters went to live with nuns, and her two sons were placed in foster homes while she cared for other people's children. By the time the 1900 census was taken, fortunately the family had been reunited. "It was a time when people were so much closer to the end of the rope. People died so young from hunger and disease, and these were the kinds of things that could push people into dramatic immigration choices, like leaving everything you know behind." Once again, Ben had been let into the lives of people battling tremendous adversity. "It gives me a sense of pride to see somebody working against that kind of resistance, struggling to the extent that she did and to make it work in the way she did."

■ If Ben's mother inherited her father's sense of social justice, she inherited her grit and determination from her mother. Ben's grandmother, Elizabeth Roberts, was born on January 16, 1921, in New York City, a Smith College graduate and public relations director for New York's Museum of Modern Art. "She was the brassy woman in a time when there was an active pushback on women who wanted to do too much. She pushed against that herself, and I always admired that."

Ben's grandmother was born at a difficult time in her parents' lives. She was the only daughter of Ben's great-grandfather Lawrence Lester Roberts, born on February 8, 1894, in Washington, D.C., and his great-grandmother Margaret McClain, born in July 1895 in Mississippi. A detailed insurance claim filed by Ben's great-grandfather piqued our interest. "On September 6, 1920," Ben read, "Lawrence L. Roberts was working for his employer. When he arrived at about 37 Wall Street, New York, New York, a serious explosion occurred in the street in the vicinity of Broad and Wall Streets, and as a result, his right leg was seriously fractured. He was disabled from September 16, 1920, to September 7, 1921." Ben's great-grandfather was a victim of the Wall Street bombing of 1920, in which thirty-one people were killed and two hundred injured. The long-forgotten tragedy, the worst terrorist bombing in the history of the United States until the Oklahoma

City bombing in 1995, was suspected to be the work of the Italian anarchist Mario Buda, an associate of Sacco and Vanzetti. Ben's grandmother was born in the midst of her father's long convalescence. He had been "among those reported dead. He came to consciousness after the big blast." It was a dramatic story, yet Ben's mother had never mentioned it. "I wonder why nobody knew this," he said. "I wonder if they did know it and didn't talk about it. My mother should have known this."

■ Painful and traumatic stories are often buried in the past, and eventually silence erases them from a family's memory. We suspected this was the case in the story we next shared with Ben. We went back two more generations on Ben's mother's father's line, to Ben's third great-grandfather, a man named Benjamin Cole. The Benjamin Cole story would illuminate the intricacies of the slave economy of the antebellum South and underscore the nuances of a system in which ownership was not the only means to entanglement.

Ben's third great-grandfather Benjamin L. Cole was born on June 14, 1814, in Savannah, in Chatham County, Georgia. Sometime before 1837 he married a woman named Catherine Norton, with whom he had three sons. The Nortons were not Ben's direct ancestors. Following Catherine's death around 1854, Benjamin Cole married Georgia Speissegger, Ben's third great-grandmother. Benjamin and Georgia Cole would go on to have four children, including Ben's great-great-grandmother Margaret Cole.

During his first marriage, based on the 1840 census, Benjamin and Catherine Cole lived either as neighbors of or under the same roof as Catherine's widowed mother, Ann S. Norton. The record listed mother-in-law and son-in-law side by side as heads of household, but the members of their households were listed separately: Ann S. Norton's included four slaves; Benjamin Cole's, none. Just ten years later, in the next census, however, we found Benjamin L. Cole listed as the sole head of household, and according to the 1850 Slave Schedule, a new addendum to the census that listed every slave owner in the nation by name and the slaves they owned anonymously, by age, gender, and color, Ben's third great-grandfather now owned twenty-five slaves, with his name, not his mother-in-law's, written in the owner's column.

Examining the schedule in isolation, there was nothing to indicate that Ben's third great-grandfather *didn't* own these twenty-five men, women, and children. But a closer look at the surrounding documents either filed by

Benjamin Cole or in which he was named raised questions about whether he was actually the owner. To clarify, the Municipal Records of Savannah, Georgia, included multiple tax and probate records that did not support the fact that he was a slave owner, but rather a trustee or an executor overseeing the estates of close relatives who themselves owned slaves. Specifically, after her daughter's death roughly two years earlier, in 1856 Ann S. Norton named her son-in-law Benjamin Cole in her will as the trustee for her property—which included eighteen slaves listed by name—to be held for the benefit of her three grandsons until they reached twenty-one, as well as for a fourth heir, Ann C. Jones, possibly her daughter.

Ann S. Norton's reliance on Benjamin Cole had started many years prior. In fact, as early as 1837 he had begun filing tax returns for his mother-in-law, which he would do annually for the next twenty years, until her death in 1857. While the number of slaves he reported fluctuated between five and thirteen (far fewer than the twenty-five reported on the 1850 Slave Schedule), one fact remained consistent: over the years, on tax records Benjamin Cole filed for himself through the end of the Civil War, there is no evidence he ever paid taxes on a single slave himself.

As far as pinning down the actual number of slaves owned by his mother-in-law, the most reliable record in our corpus of documents was an inventory and appraisal of Ann's estate, filed in 1859 by three independent assessors who swore to the veracity of their reckoning in court. They counted twenty-three slaves, valued at a total of $15,700. None of the records we unearthed explained the discrepancy between the eighteen slaves named in the will and the twenty-three in the inventory.

By 1860, when the next Slave Schedule appeared, Benjamin Cole had remarried, and he was now identified as the trustee not only for his first mother-in-law's twenty-three slaves, but also for an additional eight slaves who belonged to Samuel Ladson Speissegger, the father of his second wife, Georgia. Also of note, in 1863, Benjamin Cole filed his wife Georgia's tax return, which revealed that she herself owned a slave. That slave was not common property legally, so Georgia—not Benjamin, as her husband—owed taxes on that slave.

This was Ben Affleck's third great-grandfather's personal network, his family and the family of both of his wives. What about his professional alliances? Benjamin Cole was elected sheriff of Chatham County, Georgia, twice before slavery ended. His first term began in 1856 and ended after just a year. His second term, beginning in 1859, spanned nine pivotal years, and in that time he witnessed the secession of Georgia in 1861; the start and end of the Civil War, including the fall of Savannah to Sherman's Union troops in 1864; and the beginning of Reconstruction. It was a convulsive period.

During his tenure as sheriff he was sworn to enforce the laws of property in the state of Georgia, which encompassed the laws of slavery. According to his obituary, he helped organize the Phoenix Riflemen, a local militia, early in the war, reaching the rank of captain, but no official documentation of his service during the Civil War was found. Given Savannah's importance, there was a heavy Confederate army presence there, and a substantial paper trail of receipts and invoices confirmed Benjamin Cole's business dealings with various Confederate officers and agencies. An invoice from 1863 from the Confederate States Engineering Department, for instance, acknowledged payment for slave labor, which indicated that he maintained authority over slaves, and reaped financial benefit as a result of that authority, without being their owner. Tasked with enforcing the laws of the Confederacy as sheriff and with the administration of property as executor and trustee, Benjamin Cole was deeply enmeshed in the slave economy and in the institution of slavery.

Ben's third great-grandfather remained sheriff of Chatham County after the war's end. Once the trustee of estates containing slaves, the postwar sheriff Benjamin Cole was now expected to uphold the laws of the state of Georgia, and by 1868, his last year in office, those laws were becoming more and more inclusive of freed African Americans. In April 1868, on the heels of a Constitutional Convention dominated by moderate and radical Republicans, Georgia voters approved a new constitution that made suffrage for black men possible. An article in the *Daily News and Herald Review*, printed on April 25 of that year, under the headline "Wounding of the Sheriff," placed Sheriff Cole in the eye of the storm. In his role as sheriff, Ben's third great-grandfather was presumably enlisted to keep the peace, but in the chaos surrounding the ratification vote, he was stabbed "in the region of the left hip, which went to the bone." His run as sheriff ended later in the year, just as the progressive phase of Reconstruction in Georgia was beginning. After years of failing health, Benjamin L. Cole died in 1871. His obituary in the *Savannah Daily Advertiser* remembered him as "an honest, upright man, both in his public and private life," with "the reputation of always being willing and ready to do an act of kindness to all." His Phoenix Riflemen were invited to attend the funeral to pay "the last tribute of respect to their former brother soldier." Six years later, Reconstruction collapsed in the South, setting the stage for nearly a century of Jim Crow rule that Benjamin Cole's great-great-granddaughter Chris, Ben's mother, would help to dismantle in the civil rights movement of the 1960s.

For most of his adult life, Benjamin Cole stood in close proximity to the daily business of slavery. In fact, for many of Ben's maternal ancestors, the southern way of life could not have existed without slavery. In the scope of our research, we identified three direct maternal blood ancestors who were slave owners: Ben's fifth great-grandfather John Daniel Speissegger, his fourth great-grandfather Samuel Ladson Speissegger, and his third great-grandmother Georgia Speissegger Cole (the second wife of Benjamin Cole). Additionally, we identified through documentation seven other close relatives of Benjamin Cole's who were slave owners: John D. Cole, whose relationship to Ben's third great-grandfather we were unable to determine but for whom Benjamin Cole administered his estate in 1840; Benjamin Cole's first in-laws, Ann S. Norton and William Norton; Wilhelmina Heinrichs, the stepmother of Ben's fourth great-grandfather Samuel Ladson Speissegger; and Benjamin Cole's three sons from his first marriage, Benjamin T., Robert H., and William H. Cole, who were named as heirs in his first mother-in-law Ann S. Norton's will and were the stepbrothers of Benjamin and Georgia Cole's daughter, Ben Affleck's second great-grandmother Margaret Cole. There may have been others on this and other branches of Ben's family tree who fell outside the scope of our research or whom we were unable to verify based on the paper trail we tracked down. Family trees go on exponentially.

The thought that his ancestors had played a part in the institution of slavery had crossed Ben's mind when he learned of his familial ties to the antebellum South, but the reality of seeing his ancestor Benjamin L. Cole's name written in the Slave Schedule was crushing. "The same way that I feel proud to be associated with Patriots in the Revolutionary War, it gives me a sagging feeling to see a biological relationship with people who are even supervising slaves. It's such a stain and a horrible thing, but there it is, part of our history."

Ben was not the first of the participants in our series to learn that at least one ancestor owned slaves, nor was he the first to be embarrassed by it. "I didn't personally contribute to it, but nonetheless . . . " He trailed off. "That's the tricky thing about ancestry. We don't control it, and yet in some small way it controls us, because it contributes to us and our history in ways that are immutable. I find it tragic in a way, but also an interesting statement on the good and evil in the world." In his own ancestry, Ben said, were "the two polar extremes. What's interesting about it is the progression down through the generations," how "people have changed and evolved, and forged new identities in this country. It's important to recognize, in looking at these histories, how much work has been done by people in this country, of all kinds, to make it a better place, people like my mother and many others who have made a much better America than the one they were handed."

■ Each family story that we had shared with Ben was revelatory. We uncovered deep roots in places he had never felt strongly connected to: Ireland, Trenton, the South. He had also learned of ancestors intimately involved with the two defining wars of our nation, the Revolutionary War and the Civil War. His ancestry dated far back to Europe in the seventeenth and eighteenth centuries. On his father's side, the oldest ancestor we were able to identify was Ben's tenth great-grandfather Richard Platt, who was born in Ware, England, in 1604. On his mother's side, his oldest named ancestor was his sixth great-grandfather Johann Daniel Speissegger, who was born in 1739 in Schaffhausen, Switzerland. There was one last surprise buried deep in the paper trail: Ben and his lifelong friend and screenwriting partner Matt Damon are tenth cousins once removed, connected by a common ancestor named William Knowlton Jr., born in 1614 or 1615 in Knowlton Manor Hall, England. "He's my cousin?" Ben laughed. "That is insane."

Now we turned to Ben's DNA to tell us even more about the origins of his ancestors. In testing Ben's DNA, we analyzed his Y-DNA, which is passed from father to son, unchanged, from one generation to the next, and his admixture, which measures his percentages of European, sub-Saharan African, and East Asian / Native American ancestry from the past five hundred years or so. Ben guessed that he was "just European," and he was almost right. Ben's European result was 99.7 percent European. "Straight white bread," Ben joked. Not quite. His results contained, as we had come to expect throughout Ben's journey, an element of surprise. The remaining 0.3 percent broke down to 0.2 percent Middle Eastern and North African, and 0.1 percent sub-Saharan African. "That's pretty cool," Ben said. "I'll take some tiny slice of flavor with Middle Eastern, North African, and sub-Saharan African." He also had a small amount of Ashkenazi Jewish DNA within the European portion. The largest percentage of the European result was British and Irish, totaling 46 percent. We were also able to determine that one of Ben's parents had passed on to their son a chromosome entirely eastern European in origin. In other words, Ben had a close Jewish ancestor from eastern Europe. When or on which line this ancestor had entered Ben's DNA was impossible to determine in this analysis.

Ben's Y-DNA allowed us to determine his paternal haplogroup, a genetic population group sharing a common patrilineal ancestor. Ben's Y-chromosome did not lead directly back to Europe as we might have guessed. Instead, it pointed us back to a rare subclade, or subgroup, of the haplogroup J2, known as J2a1d or J-M319. The names geneticists give to haplogroups are something of a mouthful, but this alphabet soup has real-life meaning. J-M319 originated in the Middle East and is found today in low frequencies among Cretan Greeks, Iraqi Jews, and Moroccan Jews. In a recent study, it was discovered in the Y-DNA of several Flemish men, indicating that a migration of the J-M319 clan from along the Mediterranean and North Africa to Belgium must have occurred at some point. In the genealogy, we had learned that Ben's direct male ancestor William Affleck was born in Scotland in 1825, but how did his ancestors arrive there in the first place?

We discovered an Affleck Family Surname DNA Project that addressed the same questions we had. According to the project literature, "Although the ancient Scottish name of Affleck is believed to be a derivative of the Flemish surname of Afflighen, the Affleck surname is generally held to be of two origins in Scotland. The first is from the barony of Auchinleck in Ayrshire, Scotland, the second from Affleck in Angus, Scotland." It continued: "Every Affleck male carries that unique code of our family anthropology in his DNA. Let's work together to help unlock this Affleck Code and move toward understanding the mystery of that unique man known as Affleck." Here the literature corroborates what we learned from our analysis of Ben's Y-DNA. It appears that the Afflecks originally may have been Flemish before coming to Scotland, which fits the locations in which the M319 marker has been found.

■ Ben's DNA had revealed some family mysteries that had been absent from the paper trail. Somewhere not too far back, amid all the northern European ancestors, was a Jewish person from eastern Europe. The Scottish surname that Ben bore had Flemish roots, but in his blood was a unique code that revealed the migration of a North African or Mediterranean population to Belgium. Seeing his family tree spread out in front of him, he realized that he came by honestly the identity he had hesitantly claimed on the streets of Boston. He could now truly identify himself as Irish. "For the first time, I could say that I've got immigrants on both sides of the family who are Irish. I wouldn't feel like I was just trying to get by in Boston. That's a line of demarcation from yesterday to today."

He had also met quite a cast of characters along the way. Ben rattled off the ancestors whose stories we'd seen unfold: "I've got a priest. I've got a sheriff. I've got a medium," he said. "I've also got some pretty tough immigrants. I've got a brawler. I've got a meat inspector. I've got three Patriots." If time machines weren't the stuff of movies, where would he go, and who would he meet? "I'm tempted to say I'd like to go as far back as possible, because what a strange and crazy world it would be to us. I think modern people would find the conveniences wanting." A more recent period called to him, too. "Seeing my mom there in college, so lovely and so idealistic, that would be a neat thing to see."

On Ben's family tree we had seen people who struggled and people who succeeded. Ben himself had done both. Do our ancestors' successes and failures inform the choices we make, the things we accomplish? Or is it our DNA that makes us who we are? "Seeing my kids already have fixed personalities at the age of two has impressed upon me the degree to which biological determinants are really powerful." But for Ben, another element came into play when considering the factors that make us who we are: choice. "We tend to want to identify with the people in our genealogy who have done great things and put aside the guys who we don't like—'No, I'm not like that'—which tells us something about ourselves," he said. "We've got dual natures, and we've got competing influences, and I think perhaps this affects us more than we give it credit for. It's important to know the things your ancestors did that were brave and to learn from that, as well as the things that were bad and to learn from those as well."

More than anything, Ben's introduction to his ancestors gave him a sense of his place in the world. "I find this stuff very powerful, because you see history as not only living but as living in you. You leave behind something through your children, and they in turn leave behind something through theirs. It reminds you that life is finite, and you have a brief story to tell," Ben said. "All those start-by/end-by dates, eventually there will be two of those affixed to your name, and that will be what you will have left behind. It encourages one to do one's best."

In 2008, at age thirty-five, Ben Jealous became the youngest person ever appointed president of the NAACP. His career as an advocate for change began when he was in college. When he was a junior at Columbia University, the administration announced plans to tear down the Audubon Ballroom, the building where Malcolm X had been assassinated. Ben led a campaign of civil disobedience to save the African American landmark, and Columbia responded by suspending him for an entire semester. "If you're going to tear down the place where Malcolm was assassinated, where Marcus Garvey organized, where the Puerto Rico independence movement met, where radical Jewish trade unions met, and you're going to replace it with a for-profit biogenetic research center that the EPA says should not be within fifty miles of a densely populated area, it just didn't make any sense to us." He took the consequences and earned a deserved reputation as a passionate, fearless social activist.

Ben's models of social activism came from both his father and his mother, and from her family. "My father was one of the few white guys, certainly in Baltimore, to go to jail for desegregation protests. He went to jail for the Congress of Racial Equality. My mom desegregated her high school in 1955. My grandmother told stories about her battles as a young teacher in the segregated school. My grandfather was a pioneer in law enforcement in Baltimore." Ben embraced the rich legacy that had been handed down to him for generations.

When his parents married in 1966, their union was itself an act of defiance. "They had to get married in Washington, D.C., because it was against the law in Maryland," Ben said. (The following year, the Supreme Court decision *Loving v. Virginia* would overturn the so-called antimiscegenation laws prohibiting interracial marriage.) Although they were of different backgrounds, Ben's parents were of like mind. They met overseas. "When Dr. King gave his 'I Have a Dream' speech," he explained, "they were living among very poor people in parts of the world where their help as teachers was needed, and they had decided that being part of the human family was the most important thing to them, that materialism was of very low importance to them."

Born Benjamin Todd Jealous on January 18, 1973, in Carmel, California, Ben grew up in northern California, in a town called Pacific Grove. His parents chose the area for the relative freedom it offered a mixed-race couple, yet Ben recalled being subject to scrutiny because of his race. At the local five-and-dime, he said, "the manager always followed us, and we would watch our white friends run in and out. The curl of our hair and the color of our skin stood out in that town. I would remember at a very young age feeling like something about the way I looked made other people suspicious." For Ben and his family, race has always mattered. "My whole life, it's always described the same way: 'Dad's white, Mom's black.' That was a big deal then. My father was disowned by his grandfather and his uncle. My mom lost several friends. It was against the law. They moved to California seeking a refuge. For us," Ben said, "the race line, and the fact that we straddled both sides of it as a family, was definitive."

Ben's light skin is evidence of racial mixing even before his own parents' marriage. "My great-grandmother is lighter than my grandmother. My grandmother is lighter than me. So in my family, being light-skinned wasn't different, and it certainly didn't have anything to do with your not being black." Ben's self-identity was never in question. "I remember a story from my mom," he said. "She was young; she was in a foreign country. She wrote a letter to her grandmother about how complex the racial hierarchy was in that country, and our people are African and Native American and European. If we were in this country, maybe we would be considered this or that." Ben said she listed "about thirty-two categories" in her letter. "My mom said her grandmother wrote her the shortest letter she ever received. She just said, 'Baby, you're 100 percent black. Never forget it. Love, Grandma.'"

Ben never forgot it, either. The ties to his African American ancestry had always been celebrated, the ties to his white family severed. Circumstances aside, Ben was a product of two distinct cultures, and he was eager to revisit and restore the legacies of both.

■ Ben once said that it was his family who taught him "to push the cause of progress and justice and human rights in this country forward." As a civil rights activist, his engagement and inspiration has often come through the African American community and through his African American family. His father's family, it turned out, had also taken a very strong hand for freedom, but Ben had been cut off from that side of his ancestry because of a bitter family feud.

Ben's father, Fred Jealous, was born on May 12, 1941, in Maine. In the 1960s, Fred's blueblood New England family tolerated his devotion to civil rights activism at home and around the world, but that tolerance evaporated when he fell in love with Ben's mother, Ann Todd. "His father was dead. His mom stuck by him," Ben explained. "But my father's grandfather and his one surviving uncle gave my father a very clear command: 'A man can fall in love with many women, and if you want to stay in this family, you need to fall out of love with her and in love with somebody else.' It was clear, and it was definitive." Ben's father resisted family pressure to abandon the woman he loved. It cost him and his children a connection to the Jealous side of the family, as well as a large inheritance. "He didn't really talk about the money or the stock. Of all the holdings, all he wanted was one lamp," Ben said. "For my father, his belief was that living your life based on passion and love was the only way to really be free, and that was worth any price."

In dollars, that price was tremendous. In 1865, the year the Civil War ended, Ben's third great-grandfather Edward Sargent, along with his brothers, Joseph and George Sargent, founded the Sargent Hardware Company. Ben had never heard of it. By the early twentieth century, Sargent Hardware was one of the largest hardware manufacturers in the United States, and in 1996, the Swedish firm Assa Abloy, the world's largest manufacturer of locks, purchased the family business. Fred Jealous never saw a penny of the fortune that could have been his. "My father knew, as the eldest grandson, he was losing a whole lot of property and a whole lot of money. He really didn't care. He was in love, and he certainly wasn't going to have his family dictate who he could love. I think for him there was a birthright that was more than money. There was a birthright of heritage, of history, a sense of ownership of this country."

That birthright was Ben's birthright, too, and we wanted to help him claim it. To do so, we traced Ben's father's line back to Ben's sixth great-grandfather Jonathan Harrington, who was born in Lexington, Massachusetts, in 1758. He died in March 1854. His life spanned nearly a century: he was born seventeen years before the American Revolution and died at around the time Abraham Lincoln was running for office in Illinois. An amazing find in the archives of the Continental army told us exactly where Ben's sixth great-grandfather was when "the shot heard round the world" was fired in his hometown. Ben, it turned out, was a direct descendant of someone who actually heard that shot. "In the war of the Revolution," Ben read, "Harrington, Jonathan, fifer, in a detachment from Lexington Militia Company, commanded by John Bridge." Jonathan Harrington served at the Battles of Lexington and Concord, a foot soldier who played the fife during combat. He was sixteen years old at the time, and he outlived every other soldier who fought there, the last survivor of the battle and the only known witness to the Battles of Lexington and Concord who was actually photographed. "He looks a little like Scrooge's brother," Ben laughed, seeing the historic picture for the first time. His sixth great-grandfather's powder horn, which contained the gunpowder he carried into battle, was passed down through the Harrington family for generations and today sits in the Lexington Historical Society.

Ben's Revolutionary ancestry had been hinted at but never before confirmed. "I got glimpses as a child of a sense of ownership of the experiment of this country that was different than other people, that was very particular to the place, to people who lived in Massachusetts for a long time, lived in New England for a long time, and in their marrow understood that none of this would have happened without their family." It was ownership not only of the principles on which the country was founded, but of the republic itself. "The republic, at the end of the day, is just an idea that a bunch of people subscribed to and risked their lives for, and actually seeing a photograph of somebody who did that makes it much more real, much more tangible."

We cross-referenced Ben's family tree and found pension records for eight of Ben's Patriot ancestors. He read the list of family names: "Trask, Choate, Fay, Watson, Baldwin, Craig, Harrington, Harrington again, junior and senior." In total, Ben's family was represented by six captains, a colonel, and a fifer. The experience of seeing the names of eight ancestors who played a significant role in the founding of this nation was, in his words, "pretty humbling." "It speaks to a depth of commitment and sacrifice," he said. "To see I descend from eight men who chose to lead and to take great risk, it closes a loop. It's a missing link in a chain." Ben's direct descent from Patriots qualified him to be inducted into the Sons of the American Revolution. "There's always been a yearning to understand more about the war itself and our family's role in it," he said, "and any association that focuses on how people understand that, I think I'd want to be part of."

Ben's ancestors had been in America long before the Revolution. His eighth great-grandfather William Sargent Sr., who was born in England in 1606, was Ben's original American ancestor, the first of the Sargents to immigrate to the New World. In 1639, William Sr. signed a document called an "Oath of Freedom, Massachusetts Bay Colony," an indication that he was recognized by the colonial authorities as subscribing to and practicing Puritan teachings. The document allowed the signer to become a member of the church, to vote, and to own land. Ben questioned the Puritans' legacy. "The Puritans are kind of a mixed bag when we look back," he said candidly. "They clearly made some big mistakes along the way, but it started out with profound acts of courage, coming across this ocean that everybody was convinced was filled with all sorts of monsters, because of the conviction of your faith."

William Sargent Sr., a landowner in Amesbury, which is roughly thirty miles north of Salem, would be tangentially involved in the Salem Witch Trials years later. In 1669 Ben's eighth great-grandfather and his son, William Sargent Jr., were sued for slander by a man named George Martin (or Martyn), who accused the Sargents of branding his wife, Susannah, a witch. The court considered it a nuisance case, dropping the charges against the father and fining the son a pittance—the equivalent of an eighth of a penny, or a white wampum-peague, an ornamental bead used in trade with Native Americans. Similar accusations dogged Susannah throughout her life, however, and in 1692, in the midst of the fifteen-month panic that gripped Salem and its surrounding towns, the court found her guilty of witchcraft, and she was "hanged by the neck until [she] be dead." Although the Sargents' twenty-three-year-old accusations did not send Susannah Martin to the gallows, they were raised as evidence and corroborated by many witnesses. Ben's eighth great-grandfather's name was a footnote in the history of these tragic events, the outcome of unchecked Puritanical religious fervor and hysteria, an example of the complicated legacy of Ben's ancestors.

Hearing the stories of the family he had been estranged from for his entire life made him feel closer to New England, essentially the Jealous family's ancestral home. "It affirms this strong sense of connection that my father feels to New England. We moved to Pacific Grove because, with its rocky, pine coastline, it looked more like Maine than any other place he could find out on the West Coast." Although his father never expressed regret over leaving his family for his wife, he must have missed New England. "For him and for my grandmother and my uncles who still live in the woods of New Hampshire, it's a very visceral connection to New England. We've been there for a long time, and it's very humbling and a bit overwhelming to be able to look right at the connections, at these court papers and photographs or powder horn."

■ Ben's mother's family was intensely proud of their heritage. On their family tree were individuals who defied the odds, who rose to positions of power at a time when most African Americans were powerless, who gave a voice to the voiceless. Ann Fredericka Todd was born on September 1, 1940, in Petersburg, Virginia. "My mom is a pioneer, a woman of real courage and conviction," Ben said proudly, "a very principled woman who's willing to be an agitator when she has to be." In 1955, she had to be. With ten other African American girls, Ben's mother desegregated Western High School in Baltimore, one year after the *Brown v. Board of Education* Supreme Court decision. She would continue to put herself on the front lines ever after. "I said, 'Well, what did you do in the summer?,' and she said, 'Well, we went down to Petersburg to help desegregate churches.' I said, 'That's what you do when you're on vacation, go to desegregation battles?'" She was part of SNCC (the Student Nonviolent Coordinating Committee) during college and a Peace Corps volunteer afterward. For both mother and son, a lifetime of commitment to the fight for civil rights culminated in dual honors on May 17, 2008. "It was a great convergence, like on that day you feel the universe is winking at you," Ben said. "It's *Brown v. Board of Education* Day 2008. Two thousand eight was the fiftieth anniversary of my mom's high school graduation. It was the first high school graduation she'd ever been invited to. They made a point of locating all the black girls in that desegregated school and making sure they were at the fiftieth." Ben became president of the NAACP on that same day. "To be appointed the youngest president of the NAACP and to have it happen on *Brown v. Board of Education* Day, to have my mom in town for desegregating her high school, was very, very moving."

Ben has called his grandmother, Ann's mother Mamie Bland, his greatest childhood influence. Mamie Bland was born in November 1916, during World War I, in Petersburg, Virginia. "My grandmother told the same stories over and over. She told history as instruction, because she had faith that we would have challenges and that we would rise to those challenges, just like her daughter did, just like she had, and it was those stories more than anything that fixed my DNA." According to Ben, the most important lesson his grandmother taught him was "to appreciate that there's a difference between race and heritage or history, and to appreciate just who you are. You have to understand all of those things and appreciate how they intertwine but also how they separate." Her shorthand for that: "She would just say race is stupid, but we're black." Ben laughed. "In many ways, she was my hero."

Mamie herself was often mistaken for white. "She would tell stories about messing with the cops, walking down Charles Street in Baltimore, the great dividing line of segregated Baltimore, with my grandfather, who was darker than my grandmother, how the police walked up to her and said, 'Ma'am, is this boy bothering you?' She'd say, 'Yes, he is, but he's my husband.'"

Defiance and fearlessness ran in the family. We began our journey into Ben's mother's roots with Ben's great-great-grandfather, Edward David Bland, who was born in 1849 in Dinwiddie County, Virginia. His grandmother "would always talk about him," Ben said of his ancestor. "She would always say he was born a slave, he died a state senator." Edward Bland was a family legend. "He was the one from whom all things flowed for our family," Ben said. "He was the one who amassed the farm and who was credited with creating the opportunity for his children and grandchildren to be educated. Basically anything good that we had, in one way or the other, from character to education, pointed back toward him." After the Civil War, when black people were rendered permanently free and extended citizenship and, to men, the right to vote stripped of explicit racial bans (the result of the ratification of the Thirteenth, Fourteenth, and Fifteenth Amendments), Bland became a prominent politician, elected three times between 1879 and 1883 to the Virginia House of Delegates.

Edward Bland was a source of pride for Ben's family, known not only to them but also to history books. What could we learn about his life before politics? We assumed that he was born in slavery. Ben's ancestor would have been just a year old at the time the federal government introduced the Slave Schedule, a special section of the U.S. census in which slave owners across the nation were required to list their slaves by age, gender, and color only. The owners appeared by name, of course, but their slaves did not. According to the 1850 Slave Schedule for Dinwiddie County, Virginia, a slave owner named Richard Yates Bland Jr. owned twenty slaves, two of whom were a year old, one male and one female. We were fairly certain that we had found Ben's ancestor's slave owner. Ben had little doubt. "I've met some of the white Blands, and both sides wonder. There's a resemblance specifically between my grandmother and some of the people of that generation. There's every reason to believe that they were family, but we've never gone so far as to try to prove that."

We found no documents that definitively connected Edward to Richard Yates Bland Jr., but once we learned the name of Edward Bland's father, Ben's third great-grandfather Frederick Bland, born in Virginia around 1820, we expanded our search, and this time it proved fruitful. Ben read aloud from the Last Will and Testament of Richard Yates Bland Jr., the slave owner. "It is my will and desire that my body servant, Frederick, be kept in the family where my sons may live, to wait on them and attend to home business, gardening, and so for him to make his board, if no more. He is never to work out as a field hand nor under an overseer." Ben was floored. "It ain't quite freedom, but it's a measure of protection."

Slaves were routinely bequeathed to heirs in the wills of their owners, but caveats like these were unusual. Ben suspected that "he was connected to him." "There are patterns in history," Ben continued, "that suggest that oftentimes, people look out for young men who are their sons, if of a different color." It was a logical assumption, and one we shared until we did the math. Richard Yates Bland Jr. was only seven years older than Frederick, which led us to speculate: were Richard Yates Bland Jr. and Frederick half-brothers, both sons of Frederick's owner's father? If this were true, DNA would prove it. But first, we would meet another ancestor on Ben's family tree whose own actions made Edward David Bland's political career possible.

■ Ben's desire to fight for change was inspired by another legendary figure on his mother's family tree, his third great-grandfather Peter G. Morgan, who was born a slave and went on to help rewrite the Virginia State Constitution after the Civil War. "Peter G. is like our personal Frederick Douglass," Ben said. He forged a connection with Peter G., as he called him, at a time when he was questioning his own path in life. "I found an article in a post–Civil War–era newspaper heavily criticizing a speech by Peter G. Morgan, a white newspaper run basically by former Confederates in Virginia, who were very upset about what this pro–human rights, pro–civil rights bad brother was saying on the steps of the state capitol, in the heart of the Confederacy. I was like, 'Well, all right.'" Ben laughed. "It was just nice to know that there was a tradition of resistance that went back generations." In Ben's opinion, his ancestor had passed along more than his intensity and passion. "You look at his eyes in particular," Ben said, pointing to a photograph of Peter G. Morgan. "They look like my grandfather's eyes, my grandfather's mother's eyes. They look like my eyes. And you just wonder where those eyes came from."

After the Civil War, the former Confederate states had to come up with new state constitutions that conformed to the changed constitutional order of the federal government they were rejoining after four years of bloodshed. Above all, that meant having to accept the reality of the Thirteenth Amendment abolishing slavery. This, among other things, was the price of readmission into the Union.

With Reconstruction on the rise, Ben's ancestor was a delegate to the Virginia Constitutional Convention, which met in the former capital of the Confederacy, Richmond, in 1867, and he contributed to the creation of the state's new constitution, which extended the right to vote to black males. Jim Crow would overturn all these measures beginning in the 1890s, but the importance of the Reconstruction constitution, then and in the next century, cannot be understated. By signing this document, Ben's third great-grandfather set a precedent for civil rights for the larger black population and made it possible for Ben's second great-grandfather Edward David Bland, to whom Peter G. Morgan was not related, to hold office. "I was raised to believe that there was no higher calling than service, and this is service, right?"

Ben acknowledged that he had at times literally chosen to follow in his ancestor's footsteps. On the steps of the Virginia state capitol, he felt his third great-grandfather's presence. "I was working to undo a piece of the Jim Crow convention that was still in place, placing a lifetime ban on anybody convicted of a felony from voting in Virginia," he explained. "It was something to walk up the steps and know that my ancestor, Peter G. Morgan, had made arguments to the public for civil rights from those steps. It was a bit of an out-of-body experience. I yearned to hear the echo, and I had to settle for the knowledge that I was there in the same tradition, trying to effect the same thing in fact, trying to undo what they had done to undo this."

Though he is a formidable presence in family lore, many details of his ancestor's life remained a mystery to Ben. "I know that Peter G. Morgan escaped slavery, but I don't know a whole lot about his life before that." Ben's third great-grandfather was born in slavery in Virginia in the year 1816, but by 1859, the year of John Brown's raid on Harpers Ferry, his name was listed in the Registry of Free Negroes for Petersburg, Virginia. We uncovered an incredibly rare document for Ben: his ancestor's manumission paper. "Peter G. Morgan, a free man of color, about 45 years of age, bright mulatto complexion, 5′10½″ high, has a scar in the eyebrow over the right eye, one in the forehead, and is by trade a shoemaker and was manumitted by deed from Thomas H. Faulks on July 7, 1857, and has permission to remain in this state."

"'Bright mulatto complexion' sounds familiar," Ben laughed. "I never imagined I would ever see somebody's handwriting describing the moment that any of my ancestors were freed. It actually makes history feel shorter. I mean, 1960 wasn't that long ago, and 1860 wasn't that long before that. I bet that judge or that clerk had no idea what an impact he would have on that state, that he would push through civil rights legislation, push it into the constitution of the state, and make it possible for an entire peaceful revolution to follow the Civil War in Virginia."

How did Peter G. Morgan come by his freedom? To answer this question, we looked more closely at some critical details of his life. According to his manumission paper, Peter G. Morgan was a shoemaker. Only the most fortunate slaves were taught a trade, and in some cases artisans were allowed to sell their goods to earn enough money to purchase their own freedom from their master. That is exactly what Peter G. Morgan did. "He must have felt tremendously vindicated, to actually save for your own freedom," Ben said. "If you save X, then you'll be free. I'm sure that he had a plan. I've got to make a thousand shoes or two thousand shoes or three thousand shoes, and each shoe has, I don't know, twenty nails? Every nail you pound puts you closer to your freedom. He literally knew that he was sitting there just pounding his way to freedom. At some point, he was going to put in the last nail on the pair of shoes he had to sell before he could get on with the rest of his life."

As a free Negro, Peter G. Morgan was part of a very small minority. In 1860, the year after Ben's ancestor was manumitted, a little over 10 percent of the entire U.S. black population was free, and Virginia was home to more free Negroes—about sixty thousand men and women—than any state in the nation. But their status was always vulnerable, their "freedom" always at risk. Freedmen had limited legal rights, and at any time they could be kidnapped and sold back into slavery. In 1860, for the first time in his life, Peter G. Morgan appeared by name in the federal census for Nottaway County, Virginia. He had amassed a substantial amount of property—five thousand dollars' worth—in his short time as a free man. He also appeared by name in the 1860 Slave Schedule for Nottaway County, Virginia. Slaves, we knew, were merely enumerated in the Slave Schedules of 1850 and 1860, described by age, gender, and color. The only names that appeared in this section of the census belonged to slave owners.

In other words, Peter G. Morgan was a slave owner, and that property valued at five thousand dollars was human property. According to the schedule, Peter owned four slaves: "one female, age 42; three girls, ages 2, 5, and 8." Those four female slaves were Peter's wife and three of their daughters. Ben wept. "In eight months my son will be two, and my daughter will be eight, and my wife will be forty-two." He had difficulty speaking. "I named my daughter Morgan out of a profound sense of gratitude for what this man had done for our family, but it's something to see the paper, to see the ages of his wife and daughters, the sum he had to pay to get them to make them free." He paused. "How many shoes did he have to make to get five thousand dollars?" Ben asked.

For Peter, buying his family didn't mean that he could free them. A Virginia law passed in 1805 mandated that any slave who was freed must move out of the state within the year or face reenslavement. As we saw on his manumission paper, Peter had received special permission to stay in Virginia, but there was no guarantee that his wife and daughters would get the same dispensation. To ensure that his family would be able to remain together, he had to hold them in bondage. Slave ownership among free African Americans was more common than we think. In the year 1830, for example, 42 percent of the free black people who owned slaves owned just one slave, usually a family member.

In 1864, one year before the end of the Civil War, Peter G. Morgan changed course, and he freed his wife and children. "I, Peter G. Morgan, a free man of color, for and in consideration of the natural love and affection which I bear for my wife Julia Anne Morgan and our children, I do hereby manumit, emancipate, and forever set them free from bondage to me or anyone else, my said slaves, and I do furthermore endow them with all the privileges and amenities of free persons of color so far as it is in my power." The war was not over yet, and no one knew it would finally end the following year. Peter G. Morgan had pieced his family together by exploiting the very system that had torn them apart in the first place. Now their emancipation brought with it an inherent risk to their family and to the newly freed slaves' freedom. What did Ben think drove his ancestor to take such a gamble? "He wanted to make sure that his family was free," Ben guessed. "I suspect he wanted his intention to be recorded. There's every reason to believe," Ben continued, "from what little I know about Peter G. Morgan, that if he wanted to do something, he was going to do it. This is a man who seemed to be born with a fire to be free. It was not going to be denied to him."

We learned from the 1870 census, the first census recorded after the Civil War, and the first in which the names of all African Americans appeared, that not only had the family Peter G. Morgan held in slavery and then freed survived intact after the Civil War, but Peter and his wife were also reunited with four older children, now adults ranging in age from twenty to thirty. They had all been owned by other masters, and based on their ages, they had all lived many years in slavery. As a free man in a time of slavery he had not been able to bring his family together, but in freedom they were found. "How proud he must have felt," Ben said, "to have them all under one roof."

■ Peter G. Morgan left behind no documents to explain his motivations for freeing his wife and children when he did. We could speculate, but it was a mystery that would go unsolved. Another mystery lingered on Ben's mother's family tree that we could solve, through DNA science. Exactly what was the connection between Ben's black Bland ancestors and the white Bland family who owned them? In his Last Will and Testament, Richard Yates Bland Sr., the owner of Ben's third great-grandfather Frederick Bland, had left special instructions for what was to be done with Frederick after his passing. His "body servant" was to be "kept in the family where my sons may live," "never to work out as a field hand nor under an overseer." The stipulations hinted at a familial connection that we could not confirm in the paper trail.

To determine whether Ben's third great-grandfather's owner was his ancestor we tested his autosomal DNA, which an individual inherits from both parents as well as all of his or her ancestral lines, and compared it to that of descendants of the slave-owning Blands who had samples in the massive DNA database, which contains the DNA of a million individuals and counting. The comparison turned up multiple close matches that confirmed a genetic relation between the white Bland family and Ben's. Ben's reaction to the news was complicated. It contained a tragic element from which he couldn't look away. "It makes me sick to think about men raping women in any context. And a slave has no rights, so there's no other way to describe it." Yet, he continued, "with that said, I always suspected that the reason that my family owned as much land as they did so quickly after slavery and was able to rise in politics as far as they were and be educated to the extent that they were had something to do with some connection to a wealthy family."

Through the white Blands, Ben had a very famous cousin: none other than Thomas Jefferson. Richard Yates Bland Jr. and the third president were second cousins once removed, meaning that Thomas Jefferson's great-grandparents and Richard Yates Bland Sr.'s third great-grandparents were one and the same. Ben had once described his family as being "black in the Jeffersonian tradition." Now his family was tangentially a part of that Jeffersonian tradition. Ben embraced his new cousin Thomas Jefferson, with all of his complications and contradictions. "The Jefferson Memorial is my favorite monument on the Mall. He is somebody who obviously I have a lot of criticisms of, but ultimately I have a lot of admiration for his contributions to the positive aspects of our history."

We couldn't precisely define Ben's relationship to Thomas Jefferson, just as we couldn't say exactly where the Blands entered his family tree. Through the Blands, Ben's family was connected to many of the oldest and most prominent families in the commonwealth of Virginia. Politics, it seemed, was in their blood. When Ben's great-great-grandfather Edward D. Bland stood for election to the Virginia House of Delegates in November 1879, he beat his opponent, Robert E. Bland, 636–315. Robert Epps Bland, it turned out, was the second cousin once removed of Edward and his father Frederick's owner. By blood they were cousins, but Edward had been born in slavery on one of Robert's cousins' plantations. Ben's great-great-grandfather, born in slavery in 1849, won election to statewide office in Virginia by defeating his blood relation, a member of the family that once owned him. "How different would Virginia be if we could just look across the table of brotherhood and see each other for what we were? We're just a bunch of cousins who descend from different parts of the family."

■ After many twists and turns, the paper trail ended for both sides of Ben's family. Through the genealogy, we were able to trace his paternal side all the way back to his ninth great-grandfather, a man named Thomas Locke, who was born in England in about the year 1600. On his mother's side, the oldest ancestor we identified was Ben's fourth great-grandmother Susan Yates, Edward David Bland's grandmother, born in 1805 in Virginia. With DNA, as we had already seen, we could discover a past never documented on paper.

We began our examination of Ben's DNA with his admixture test, which revealed his percentages of European, sub-Saharan African, Middle Eastern / North African, and East Asian / Native American ancestry from about the time of Columbus. Ben registered as 80 percent European, 18.2 percent sub-Saharan African, 0.5 percent Middle Eastern and North African, and 0.2 percent East Asian / Native American. That three-quarters of his European ancestry coded as northern European was in keeping with the genealogy. We had taken several of Ben's paternal lines back to England, and the white Blands newly added to his mother's family tree went back to England as well.

We were also able to break down Ben's African ancestry. As we have seen with all of the other African American participants in our series, the countries of origin of the African ancestors correspond to those countries that were ravaged by the transatlantic slave trade. According to one company, Ben's largest percentage of African DNA was southeastern Bantu, which encompasses the nations of Mozambique and Angola; 24 percent of slave ancestors came from Angola. The remaining portion of his African DNA included traces from Benin and Togo, Ivory Coast, and Ghana, and very small readings from Cameroon, Congo, and Senegal.

The tiny amount of Native American DNA, 0.2 percent, fell within the range of what is often referred to as "noise." Ben's grandmother "would look at physical characteristics" and had intimated that the family had Native American ancestry. Even Ben said, "When you look at my grandmother, there's a strong Native American kind of look." Oral history notwithstanding, he had no recent Native American ancestors. "It just makes you wonder about the stories," he said.

In addition to the admixture test, we examined Ben's mitochondrial DNA, an identical genetic fingerprint passed on from mother to child. Mitochondrial DNA is just a tiny sliver of a person's ancestry, but it is a sliver we can trace back through tens of thousands of years. His maternal haplogroup, a genetic population group that shares a common ancestor, was rare for an African American. The populations with the highest concentrations of this haplogroup were not where Ben expected to find them. "It's almost the entire world, except for Africa," Ben laughed. "It's South America, North America, East Asia, Central Asia, West Asia, basically everywhere except Africa and Europe—in other words, everywhere except for where most of my people come from."

In the more detailed analysis, our DNA experts discovered that Ben has a unique grouping of mutations in his maternal DNA found among Polynesians, with two additional markers found exclusively in people from Madagascar. Ben's results led us to believe that more than a thousand years ago, his direct maternal ancestors most likely traveled from their native Indonesia to the west coast of Madagascar, pioneers known as the "ancient people of the canoe," or Vahoaka Ntaolo in the Malagasy oral tradition, after the enormous outrigger canoes in which they made their journey. Ben, once a member of the crew team at Columbia, laughed. "I can row a canoe, too."

How did this ancestor from Madagascar end up in his genome? The slave trade in Madagascar, with its remote location off the coast of southern Africa, was never very extensive. But between 1678 and 1721, at least seventeen ships made the journey around the Cape of Good Hope and crossed the Mozambique Channel to carry slaves from Madagascar to the United States. Most of the four or five thousand enslaved people who came from Madagascar landed in New York and Virginia. This explains how Ben's direct maternal ancestors, who have been living in Virginia for the last 150 years or so, have Malagasy mitochondrial DNA. "It's fascinating to narrow it down," Ben said.

■ Ben's introduction to his ancestors, both ancient and recent, didn't change his perception of himself. Without hesitation, he said, "I'm black." He had done the math. "The law in Virginia at the time that I was born was one-thirty-second. One-thirty-second would be 3 percent. I'm a lot more than one-thirty-second. Ultimately it's what my great-grandmother said to my mother: 'You're 100 percent black, baby, and never forget it.'"

Ancestors on both sides of his family had instilled in him a fighting spirit, yet his connection to his black maternal ancestors remained strongest, and if he could go back in time to meet one of them, it would be the man who had loomed so large for so long: Peter G. Morgan. Ben had been planning this trip for a long time. "This is a man who escaped slavery not by deception, but literally by planning and hard work and execution. He knew in his own heart that there was no way that he would have gotten there without his own hard work and persistence." After his journey through his roots, he recognized that a side trip might be in order, too, to the other side of his family. "I would want to meet all of those captains and colonels. I would like to talk to the fifer who was at the Battles of Lexington and Concord. I would like to talk to all of them."

Ben and his ancestors, it seemed, looked at the world through similar eyes. He, too, had witnessed defining moments in history, tremendous changes in society, some steps forward and some steps back. In light of everything he had learned today, what did he believe makes us who we are? Is it our experiences or those of our ancestors? Or is it the DNA we carry within us? "For me, it always comes back to my conversations with my grandmother," Ben said. "There is race, and race is a creation. The definition of 'black' has always been very inclusive. If you had one drop, you were black. White, very exclusive. And there's heritage, and heritage is everybody you descend from, you're related to, everybody you claim, everybody who claims you—even sometimes the ones who don't claim you."

All those parts, Ben felt, made up a whole, and the whole was the individual person he had become as a result of each of these factors. "Who I am is somebody who has spent their entire life fighting for human and civil rights for other people. I look at my family tree, and it's clear that on both sides, that's been a big part of what people in my family have chosen to do for a long time." Long after the history books said freedom had been won, Ben's family was still fighting this fight. "I knew the stories about my parents and the stories about the black side of the family being active in the civil rights movement. I knew somebody was involved in the Revolution. But to look at the names of eight men who all risked their lives and who led other men into battle in what was at the time the greatest crusade for civil rights that the world had known is humbling and grounding, and it affirms what my grandmother's point always was. At the end of the day, we are a very small human family, and it's important to be on the right side of history, but it's also important to understand that you're connected to everybody on every side of history." His journey into his family's roots had grounded him. "I feel like the other foot is planted."

Khandi Alexander (b. 1957)

The dancer, choreographer, and actress Khandi Alexander has never been comfortable identifying herself as African American. "Where I grew up and in the time I grew up, I identify more with black. My father used to tell me when he was growing up, calling someone black was the worst thing you could say to them. So I truly identified and have always identified as a black woman. I loved it," she said. "When African American became the new terminology, I didn't warm to it. I'd like to be able to say I'm African American, but I've never felt African American. I felt black."

Born Harriet Rene Alexander on September 4, 1957, in Jacksonville, Florida, Khandi moved with her parents and sister to Queens, New York, when she was still in elementary school. Her family was part of the mass population shift called the Great Migration, the period between 1910 and 1970 when more than 6 million African Americans from the South relocated to the urban North, Midwest, and West. Khandi didn't know what in particular motivated her parents' move. "We always heard that it was you leave the South to go north," Khandi said. "My mother was very dark-skinned, and my father was extremely light. I'm sure they had a rough time." Her northern home, Queens, was the proverbial melting pot. "It was so much fun, because we were all together," Khandi reminisced. "There was no divide. We had Polish, Jewish, Puerto Rican, black, Caribbean, Asian. Everyone was together, all of us."

From the time Khandi was about three years old, her mother wanted her to be a dancer. It wasn't until Khandi saw Alvin Ailey perform at the Brooklyn Academy of Music that she herself became convinced of her direction in life. Her father was less so. "I saw Mr. Ailey dance, and the top of my head flew off. I got swept away with it. My father was furious. My father was not having it. He said, 'Nope. If you're going to do this, you have to learn how to type.'" Her father's practical streak ran deep through her. She developed an interest in acting early, displaying a flair for both comedy and drama, but she felt that Broadway was a more secure option for her than either screen, big or small. "I saw the landscape, and I've always been very realistic because of my dad. I didn't see a consistent through-line of employment for black women. I thought, I don't want to do one or two movies and then fall away and never be seen again. I need to pay my bills. I stuck with theater and Broadway because it looked like I would be able to work and pay my bills."

Khandi had a long career in theater, both on stage and behind the scenes, traveling the world and working as a dancer and choreographer for, among others, Whitney Houston. Once she began to work on television, in the 1990s on *News Radio* and *ER*, and more recently on *CSI*, *The Wire*, and *Treme*, Khandi the actress eclipsed Khandi the dancer. While *ER* and *CSI* could boast diverse casts in a largely white landscape, network television was a difficult fit for Khandi initially. Parts for black actresses weren't yet fleshed out. "I put in the sassy-black-girl sort of thing," she recalled. She has witnessed a tremendous change in the roles available to black women in recent years. When Khandi started on Broadway, she joked, as long as there was a maid's role, a black actress could always find work. Change was slow, but she had seen opportunities expand and perceptions shift. What role had race and color played in the lives of her ancestors as they navigated worlds that still hewed closely to the color line?

■ Like many African Americans, Khandi knew almost nothing of her ancestors. There were no names, no dates, no photographs. Rather than dwell on a painful past, her parents' focus was on the future. "They were very much, 'Let's move forward. That's over.'" She inherited this trait. "I always wanted to move forward. We grew up in Queens, and Manhattan was one bus and one train ride away. Those are my fondest memories—running away and being in the city and just running wild."

The allure of New York was strong, and Khandi's mother felt it, too. Alverina Yavonna Masters was born on October 7, 1932, in Jacksonville, Florida. Members of Khandi's family told us that Alverina was a real "people person," that she could light up a room with her sense of humor and her warmth. Khandi was twenty-two when her mother died. Many of her memories revolved around her mother's physical presence. "I remember her beautiful smile. She had this beautiful, dark skin and this bright white smile. She was so pretty," Khandi said. "I remember that. I remember looking at her figure when she would get dressed up. She loved great music, and I loved that about her."

In Florida Alverina sang in church, but once the family moved to New York, she took to the nightclub stage. Khandi told us that her mother was a classically trained singer who loved Mahalia Jackson and Marian Anderson. "We always had a piano in my house, and my mother would sing arias on Sunday mornings. She had fancy friends from Manhattan who would visit. This was her nightclub clique that she had in Manhattan." Khandi said that her mother strived in her own life to excel much in the way she pushed her daughter to. "My mother was very educated. She was very artistically inclined on a higher level. She didn't go for all the coonish stuff. She said, 'You have to reach higher. We're going to see the elite, and this is exactly what I want to influence your life.' Back in those days," Khandi explained, "it was important for black people to really be a part of the elite."

Like many African Americans of her generation, Alverina felt she had to represent the race in the best possible light.

On Khandi's mother's side, we found a story that shows the price her ancestors paid for trying to get ahead in the segregated South of the 1930s. Khandi's grandfather Joshua Pinckney Masters Jr. was born in Savannah, Georgia, around 1910, at the height of Jim Crow segregation. She had heard "not a word" about him. Khandi stared at his picture, his face instantly familiar. "He's got that very dark chocolate skin that my mom had, that I love. And I'm sure it's a sign of the times, but he has this sadness in his eyes." When he was about nineteen years old, Joshua Masters joined the flood of rural blacks migrating to southern cities in the 1920s and 1930s, looking for work in factories. Khandi's grandfather settled in Jacksonville, Florida, where he found a job at a rosin plant. In a strange coincidence, rosin had been part of Khandi's life literally for as long as she could remember. "As a dancer, you put rosin on your hands before you touch the ballet bar," she said. "I grew up with rosin on my hands."

Rosin is a chemical derived from the sap of pine trees, and in the 1930s, it was a key ingredient in glue and soap. The process of extracting rosin from pine sap was extremely dangerous, the steam it produced toxic. Prolonged exposure could lead to lung disease, and the rosin itself was extremely flammable. Khandi's grandfather was one of the very few black men allowed to work his way up to a skilled position in the company. He was a distiller in the plant, charged with running the stills and guarding against fires. It was an enormously responsible job generally reserved for white men. He seemed to be moving up in the world.

On December 2, 1935, an explosion rocked the rosin factory, and according to a report in the *Florida Times-Union* the next day, there was just one injury. "Negro Workman Is Seriously Burned in Plant Accident," the headline read. "Joshua Masters, Negro distiller, was critically burned shortly after 1 o'clock this morning in an explosion at the Godwin Medlin Naval Stores Company. The east side of the distilling plant was blown out when one of the vats exploded. The explosion blew hot turpentine for more than 50 feet."

The outcome was devastating. Two days after the explosion, the *Times-Union* ran a follow-up article. "Negro Burned in Explosion Died," Khandi read. "Joshua Masters, Negro, who was burned early Tuesday morning in an explosion, died yesterday in Brewster Hospital." The death certificate revealed the grisly, painful truth: "Principal cause of death: Burned over the entire body." Neither Khandi's mother nor her grandmother had ever breathed a word to her about her grandfather or his horrific death. "Maybe it was just too painful," she said sadly.

A veteran of the rosin industry told us that an explosion like this one was extraordinarily rare, and two of Khandi's distant cousins who had lived in Jacksonville said that Joshua's death was no accident: white workers resented having a black boss, so they intentionally rigged the explosion that killed Khandi's grandfather. Under the circumstances, this tragedy amounted to a workplace lynching. "You don't need historians to tell you that," Khandi said. Her cynicism quickly turned to sadness. "My goodness. At twenty-five. Imagine what he could have done."

Khandi's family coped with the tragedy as many do, by attempting to blot out its memory. But in doing so, they cut themselves off from an entire branch of their family tree. Fortunately, with diligent research, we managed to travel more deeply into Khandi's grandfather's family. Her great-grandparents on her mother's line were both born in South Carolina, Joshua Masters Sr. around 1883, probably in Beaufort, and Charity Murry around 1887, probably in Kingsville County. By 1910 they were living in Savannah, Georgia, where their son, Khandi's grandfather, was born, and according to a 1924 Savannah city directory, her great-grandfather was the pastor of Mt. Hermon Baptist Church. She looked at pictures of her great-grandparents; their names were completely unknown to Khandi, but she had seen the faces somewhere before. "He looks like my cousin Benny, and she looks like Benny's mom, Benny's mom and Benny's sisters. Yes, Charity definitely looks like my aunts on my mom's side, my mother's aunts."

Next we followed Khandi's great-grandfather back more than two decades to Beaufort, South Carolina, where we suspected he was born. According to the 1900 census for Beaufort County, seventeen-year-old Joshua Masters Sr., a farm laborer, lived with his parents, Khandi's great-great-grandparents Joshua and Alice Masters. (Although her great-great-grandfather's name was recorded in the census as Joseph, we found other documents that led us to believe that his name was Joshua.) Both of Khandi's great-great-grandparents were born in South Carolina, and both were born deep in slavery, Joshua in February 1843 and Alice in May 1845, in Barnwell County.

Khandi had often contemplated the fact that slavery was part of her history, but she had never described her ancestors as "slaves." "I always said my ancestors were people who were enslaved," she explained. "I've thought about that a lot, especially as I was going through very hard times in my life. The blood that runs through my body is of the survivors. So no matter what they do to me, I've got to get up and keep going, because if they did it, I can do it, too. It's more than a responsibility. They survived; that's why you're here. How dare you let this overwhelm you. Have your cry, go to bed, get back out there, five, six, seven, eight."

We continued to search the archives for vital records and found Khandi's great-great-grandmother Alice Masters's death certificate, and in doing so, the names of her parents. Alice Masters was about seventy when she died in Jasper County, South Carolina, on April 14, 1915. Her parents' names were D. Savage and Alice Savage. Unbelievably, we had just introduced Khandi to her third great-grandparents, both of whom were born in Barnwell County, South Carolina, most likely in the 1820s. Nothing else is known about their life or death. What we had found for Khandi was exceedingly rare: nearly two hundred years of African American roots, with names attached to them. Khandi was tearful. "I don't know any part of this. I don't know any part of my life from my history, and now I have this. I feel full. I feel grateful."

■ The paper trail for Khandi's mother's line ended with her third great-grandparents. We had gone back far into slavery, into the early nineteenth century, against all odds. How far back could we go on her father's side of the family? Harry Roland Alexander was born on August 25, 1930, in Jacksonville. "I just thought he hung the moon," Khandi said. Family members recalled Harry Alexander as lovable and easygoing, if a bit old-fashioned. He wasn't supportive of his wife's singing career, we were told, and wanted her at home. "It was a reflection on a man's manhood," Khandi said. "If your wife could stay home with the children, that meant something. He wanted that 1950s housewife. He wanted his dinner on the table. He wanted his kids clean. He wanted that." Khandi's mother wanted something different. "She wanted to be Josephine Baker. She wanted to be in Paris."

Khandi's knowledge of her father's family was as sparse as that of her mother's had been. "He was very thin about it," she said. Our exploration of her paternal ancestors began with her great-great-grandparents, Nicholas Harrison and Lenora Love. "My goodness, Lenora Love," Khandi laughed, studying their photograph. "Strong-looking woman. And that's a stage name for you." To see her great-great-grandparents' faces, Khandi said, was "a miracle." Like her maternal great-great-grandparents, Nicholas and Lenora were slaves, both born in Fairfield County, South Carolina, Nicholas in December 1849, twelve years before the Civil War started, and Lenora in June 1850. Once again, we discovered that Khandi had deep roots in South Carolina on her father's side as well as her mother's.

To go back as far as we could with Khandi's great-great-grandfather, we turned to some of the most reliable documents for genealogical research that exist: censuses and death certificates. Her great-great-grandfather Nicholas Harrison was described as "MU" on the 1880 census for Fairfield County, shorthand for "mulatto." "Halfrican," Khandi joked. In his photograph, Nicholas's skin tone indicated some white ancestry, but a picture could never tell us how far back that white ancestry went. If we could trace his family back into slavery, we might get our answer. We consulted Nicholas Harrison's death certificate for his parents' names. Khandi's great-great-grandfather died of pneumonia in Duval County, Florida, of which Khandi's birthplace of Jacksonville is the county seat, on November 26, 1918. His father's name was recorded, but the space for his mother's was left blank. Khandi's third great-grandfather was a man named John Harrison, and when we began our search for him, we landed upon something startling: the name John Harrison in the 1860 census for Fairfield County.

Slaves' names did not appear in the census. It included only the names of free people, and in 1860, less than 3 percent of South Carolina's black population was free. The census also included the race of those free people, and beside John Harrison's name was not a "B" or an "M" or "MU" for "mulatto," but a "W." If we had the right John Harrison, then Khandi's third great-grandfather was a white man. Only DNA could tell us conclusively.

■ Nicholas Harrison, Khandi's great-great-grandfather, had been described in the 1880 census as a mulatto. Now the name of his father on his death certificate, John Harrison, corresponded in the records not to a black slave but to a white man. If Khandi were indeed the third great-granddaughter of this man, then she would share DNA with some of his ancestors' descendants. To test this theory, we compared Khandi's autosomal DNA, which an individual inherits from both parents and all ancestral lines, to that of documented descendants of John Harrison's ancestors. The analysis revealed match after match after match between Khandi and John Harrison's extended family. Notably, these matches descend from not just one or two, but on several of his ancestral lines tracing back to

South Carolina, England, and Scotland. Based on these findings, we had no doubt that John Harrison was Khandi's third great-grandfather. There is no record of her third great-grandmother's name, but she was almost certainly the property of John Harrison, the man who impregnated her. That would make John Harrison, the white man, both the master and the father of Khandi's great-great-grandfather Nicholas Harrison.

Although it was unlikely that we could ever recover the name of Nicholas Harrison's mother, we wanted to confirm the master-slave relationship between father and son. We started with the 1860 Slave Schedule for Fairfield County, South Carolina. The 1860 census had first given us the name and race, and therefore legal status, of John Harrison, but in the Slave Schedule, the only names that appeared belonged to the slave owners. Slaves themselves were enumerated by age, gender, and color only. From the Slave Schedule we learned that Khandi's third great-grandfather was one of the largest slave owners in the entire state of South Carolina, counting 156 black people among his property. For the sake of comparison, in 1860, the year this census was conducted, only 1 percent of all slave owners owned one hundred slaves. John Harrison's vast cotton plantation stretched for acres and acres. In fact, his total property, which was assessed that same year, was valued at more than two hundred thousand dollars. In today's currency, that's roughly $5.5 million.

In terms of the people he owned, his son Nicholas, though anonymous, was accounted for: he was one of three young slaves described as "10MM," or ten years old, male, and mulatto. Beyond his parentage, we know nothing of Nicholas's life in slavery. Not knowing his mother's age, there was no way to find her among the many anonymous female slaves in John Harrison's possession.

Now on both sides of her family Khandi could identify two generations of slave ancestors by name, but, unlike 99 percent of African Americans, she could also name one of her white ancestors. In our series, we had never tested a black guest whose DNA didn't reveal a significant amount of white, or European, ancestry. "It's strange," Khandi said. "You feel half and half, because I'm sure she was raped. It wasn't like she willingly had sex with him and had these children." Although she had always identified herself as black, she didn't dismiss the white side of her family tree, nor did she feel anger toward her white third great-grandfather, even if the son he fathered, Khandi's great-great-grandfather, was the product of rape. "I never had a family tree to start shaking until maybe an hour ago," she laughed, "and I couldn't any more change the color of my skin tone than I could deny that he got shaken out of that tree. What can you do?" she asked. "I don't hate anyone. I understand history as it was. It was something that wasn't real to me before, and now suddenly it's very real to me. It was what it was, and I'm grateful that I'm here right now with all of this inside me."

■ John Harrison's family tree was now Khandi's family tree, and it was vast. Her third great-grandfather was born in 1790, when George Washington was president. In this country, her ancestry stretched back to the end of the seventeenth century, to colonial times, long before the American Revolution. Her sixth great-grandfather James Harrison was born in Westmoreland County, Virginia, in 1690. His grandson, Khandi's fourth great-grandfather Reuben Henry Harrison and the father of John Harrison, was her first direct paternal ancestor born in South Carolina, in Craven County, in 1760; he was fifteen years old when the Revolutionary War broke out. South Carolina was one of the wealthiest of the Thirteen Colonies thanks to slavery, since 45 percent of all the slaves that came into the United States entered through the Port of Charleston. It was also one of the most strongly opposed to paying taxes to the king, and in the years leading up to the war, political tension in South Carolina was mounting.

The British had suffered a humiliating surprise defeat at the hands of the Continental army in Charleston during the early part of the war, in 1776. But in the spring of 1780, they returned and lay waste to the city in the Siege of Charleston, handing the Patriots their worst defeat of the Revolution. By the end of that summer, the British had seized control of the entire colony. Khandi's fourth great-grandfather, now twenty years old, was living in occupied territory, and in 1781 he took up arms to protect his home. "Reuben Harrison," his military record read. "Served in General Henderson's Brigade on an expedition at Four Holes and Edisto River in Captain Stark's Company." On April 7, 1781, Reuben Harrison took part in a surprise attack on Four Holes Bridge, a valuable post in the British army's lines of communication. In South Carolina, the Patriots had adopted the strategy of guerrilla warfare, harassing the British with small-scale attacks, ambushes, and raids. Harrison's company's successful raid, in which the British commander was fatally wounded and more than twenty British soldiers were captured, ultimately helped break the back of the British forces in South Carolina.

Khandi's fourth great-grandfather was a Revolutionary War hero, yet the more we looked at his life after wartime, the more complicated his story became. This man who fought bravely for the cause of freedom, according to the 1810 census for Fairfield County, South Carolina, owned eighty-five slaves. The story of Khandi's fourth great-grandfather Reuben Harrison speaks to a painful truth about the American Revolution. It was a noble fight for freedom, but not freedom for all. The majority of the men who signed the Declaration of Independence were slave owners themselves, a fact that prompted the English writer Samuel Johnson to ask, "How is it that we hear the loudest yelps for liberty among the drivers of Negroes?"

Many Patriots viewed slavery as a necessary evil, so crucial to the economy that a majority of the Founding Fathers feared the fledgling nation would collapse without it. Perhaps this is how Khandi's fourth great-grandfather reconciled the contradiction that she called "the divide." "I don't think he saw them as equals, as human beings," she said bluntly. "You're property, and I know you breathe and eat and work, but you're like an animal. You're a step above an animal because I can talk to you, and if you don't understand I can make you understand. I can beat you to a level of understanding." Khandi paused. "Or maybe he wasn't this cruel person. It doesn't matter. You use people like that, you don't see them as human." Khandi recognized a conflict within herself as well. "I'm very proud to be American. As a woman, to be American, there's no place else I think on this earth I would be as free." Yet, she continued, "I've always been amazed by this country's blind spots, its choice to ignore others or the other, which is sometimes how I feel that they referred to myself, my history."

Khandi's descent from a Patriot qualified her for membership in the Daughters of the American Revolution (DAR), the same group that had prevented her mother's idol, Marian Anderson, from performing at Constitution Hall in 1939 in our still-segregated nation's capital. A disgusted Eleanor Roosevelt resigned from the DAR in the wake of the decision and invited Anderson to perform instead at the Lincoln Memorial on Easter Sunday. In enforcing a whites-only policy, the DAR succeeded not in preventing a great artist from performing before an adoring crowd, but in inadvertently making racism a part of the national conversation. "I would be proud to be a member," Khandi said. "It's symbolic, and it's important, and I would do that for Marian."

■ The paper trail for Khandi's family, both black and white, was longer than she ever could have imagined. On her mother's side we traced her ancestors back to her third great-grandfather D. Savage, who was born a slave in Barnwell County, South Carolina, sometime during the 1820s. On her father's side, we traced her ancestors all the way back to her seventh great-grandfather George Harrison, a white man born in 1665 in England. She had deep roots in this country, in England, and in Scotland, as we had already seen. "I didn't know where anything happened," she said. "My knowledge stops at Jacksonville. But now I know where my family picked cotton. I know where they were enslaved." DNA would reveal more about her origins in these countries, and also in Africa.

We performed two DNA tests on Khandi, one focusing on her mitochondrial DNA, an identical genetic fingerprint passed from mother to child, virtually unchanged from generation to generation, and one to reveal her admixture, which measures an individual's percentage of European, sub-Saharan African, and East Asian / Native American ancestry from the past five hundred years or so. (There were no males from her direct paternal line available to test.) First we looked at Khandi's admixture. Her percentages revealed numbers in keeping with her genealogy—73.9 sub-Saharan African, 24.1 percent European—but also a surprise found nowhere in the paper trail: 1.3 percent East Asian / Native American, a result higher than typical for African Americans. Her DNA tests confirmed a diverse ancestral record. "So I am African American, aren't I?" she mused.

We broke down her European DNA, and it corroborated the family history our research had uncovered, with nearly a quarter coding for Europe West and Ireland, an expected result for a person with ancestry going back to England and Scotland. Her African component dovetailed with the historical record of the transatlantic slave trade. Khandi's largest percentage of African DNA came from Nigeria, specifically eastern Nigeria where the Igbo people live, at 25 percent. Of the 388,000 Africans brought to the United States from Africa, about 18.6 percent of them, or seventy-two thousand Africans, were taken from eastern Nigeria.

The second test we administered to Khandi was on her mitochondrial DNA, which follows a direct line of matrilineal inheritance over thousands of years. Khandi was our first guest whose test ever revealed this unusual maternal haplogroup. Khandi's haplogroup, a genetic population group that shares a common ancestor, originated in the Near East tens of thousands of years ago. At that time, the population began to migrate out of East Africa; whether it was Tanzania, South Africa, or Ethiopia has been the subject of much debate. Khandi's ancestors, instead of continuing to make a path out of Africa, returned to North Africa in what is called the Back Migration. North African Berber women carried one branch of Khandi's DNA signature from the northwest Atlantic coast of Africa to the Canary Islands, and another branch traveled to Ethiopia. The mutations in Khandi's mitochondrial DNA are exclusively found in the Ethiopian branch. "White people always ask if I have Ethiopian blood," she said. As far as her slave ancestors went, descent from Ethiopians was impossible; there were no slaves from Ethiopia. But Khandi's Ethiopian ancestors went back much, much further, through her direct maternal line. They came from Ethiopia by way of North Africa in the reverse migration. Fifty thousand years ago people walked out of Africa; Khandi's went back. There's no way to know what caused the reverse migration: hunger, cold, fear. The movements were slow; people were on foot. This is the history of humanity, and it is encoded in Khandi's genome.

■ Khandi's ancestry was a painful reminder of the contradictions and cruelty that have defined the United States since its founding. She met two generations of slaves by name and two generations of slave owners, too. If a time machine could take her back to meet one of the many ancestors we'd introduced to her, who would it be? Khandi's answer came as a surprise. "I wouldn't want to meet any of them," she said matter-of-factly. "I think the gypsy in me would have to take over, and I would choose to go forward." She had always suspected that her parents didn't share their past with her because it was simply too painful, and now she understood. "I think about my grandfather on my mother's side, her father"—Joshua Masters Jr., who was burned to death in a workplace fire—"and I think, my God. I don't think I could get out of bed from crying after meeting him, yet at the same time I'm proud of him." Then there was the matter of her white ancestors. "It's a little complicated over there. For me the knowledge of their existence is enough."

Khandi seemed content to keep her distance from her ancestors, but did she feel that they had any impact on the person she is today? Which was more important in shaping her, the DNA she inherited from those who came before her or her family and life experiences? Khandi believed that her work ethic came very strongly from her own father, but stories of work—her grandfather in the rosin plant, her pastor grandfather, even her white ancestors who made their money from the unpaid labor of her own ancestors—permeated her family history. "I think part of it is a bit DNA as well as being reared watching my dad get up and go to work, watching my mother put on all that makeup and gussy herself up in the latest styles, and listening to her play the piano, run her scales, train her voice, waking up in the morning to this opera singing. It had to be a combination," she answered. "But I also don't want to discount the spiritual. I cannot discount a higher power, because even going back to my grandfather, there was something about that rosin that hit me, that I was three years old with it on my hands at the ballet bar." The chemical that she rubbed on her skin as part of her ballet warm-ups was an integral part of the story of her grandfather's apparent murder in the early 1930s. Coincidence, yes, but it was a meaningful detail in the story of her life. "I don't ever want to think it's by my own power."

We had taken Khandi on an amazing journey, one on which she had never intended to embark. "I'm a gypsy. I've been a gypsy all my life, certainly all my career," she said. "I never had a curiosity about my history because I was always forced to keep it moving. That's what my parents' idea was: You keep moving; you don't look back." But her exploration of her roots had a comforting effect that took her by surprise. "I feel a little bit at peace. Something I never was interested in, never focused on or even thought about is flooding me, and I feel warm, and I feel like I belong to something bigger than me." Learning about her DNA and her genome changed the way she saw her family and herself. "I never thought about how much of what I have inside me."

For Ben Affleck, Ben Jealous, and Khandi Alexander, joy and sorrow mingled in the stories that had been hidden on their family trees. Ben Affleck, the son of a civil rights activist, was also a direct descendant of a southern sheriff for whom the institution of slavery was part and parcel of his day-to-day world. Ben Jealous's third great-grandfather bought his own way to freedom but was forced to enslave his wife and daughters as his only means of keeping his family together. Khandi's grandfather had achieved a modicum of success in a world where black people were expected to know their place, and he lost his life because of it. All three accepted and embraced the incongruities in their family trees that our exploration of their roots had revealed, and recognized that in those very incongruities lay the impulse that had compelled each of them to make their own mark, and propelled them to always move forward.

CHAPTER FIVE

The Melting Pot

Tom Colicchio, Ming Tsai, and Aarón Sánchez are three world-renowned chefs who have won fame by cooking the dishes of their ancestors, and those dishes—Italian, Chinese, and Mexican—form the holy trinity of American cuisine. American cuisine, after all, is ethnic cuisine, a mixture of ingredients from all over the world that blend together to form a distinctly American flavor. Theirs is a story of how America's food has been shaped by its immigrants, with recipes passed down from one kitchen to the next, bridging cultures and generations. Maybe that's why America is called the melting pot.

Tom Colicchio (b. 1962)

Tom Colicchio is a culinary superstar. Though he owns more than a dozen award-winning restaurants across the country, he's still as comfortable at his local farmer's market as he is on the set of his hit show, *Top Chef.* He is a man who adores food and has for his entire life. In the eyes of his large Italian family, he said, "food was important. So much revolved around food." But there was another aspect to it. "I think what it really did is brought people to the table."

Thomas Patrick Colicchio Jr. was born on August 15, 1962, in Elizabeth, New Jersey, in the embrace of a close extended family, the middle son of

Thomas Patrick Colicchio Sr. and Beverly Corvelli. He grew up identifying more as Italian American than as Italian. "We didn't speak Italian at home. My father barely spoke Italian, since he was the youngest of his siblings and he wasn't forced to speak it. When my grandfather passed away in 1966, that was the end of it. I didn't hear much Italian after that." He heard no stories about his immigrant grandparents' lives in Italy, so he felt little connection to their homeland. "We identified with Italian American, especially around food. Christmas came, and there may have been ham, but there was lasagna first, and Easter came, and there may have been lamb, but there was manicotti first, or manigot, as they would say in Elizabeth."

Tom described Elizabeth as a typical "blue-collar town," with many ethnic enclaves. "You had an Italian American section; you had a Polish section; you had a Jewish section. There was an African American section; there was a Spanish section. They were all just slightly separate." He felt that food played a role in his family that was typical of Italian Americans, but not necessarily of others. "I don't remember my friends rushing home because they were going to eat," he said. "I had one good friend whose parents were divorced, and he would have dinner by himself in front of the TV. We thought it was pretty cool." Today, though, Tom saw it as lonely and disconnected. "Food was always something that we cared about. It could have been something very simple, but it was important that my mother have something on the table. That was her way of taking care of her family." Tom traced his love of cooking to this basic instinct. "Food is one of those things where you cook for someone, there's immediate gratification. It's an immediate connection to them."

Growing up in Elizabeth, surrounded by grandparents, aunts and uncles, and cousins, meals weren't formal, but they were something of a ritual. "We had to be home every night at the table. Dinner was seven days a week, usually around 5:30 or 6:00," he recalled. "Sunday was when we had macaroni. It wasn't 'pasta.' It was macaroni and gravy, but the gravy was tomato sauce, and that was around three o'clock in the afternoon." These Sunday dinners bear little resemblance to the dishes Tom has become famous for. "If you talk to most chefs, no matter how fancy their food is, it's not what they want to eat. We want to eat peasant food. That's what we like, and I think it's because we all realize that's where it all started."

Food was a link to Tom's past, to his family and their traditions. "My wife just recently said, 'You've got to start making gravy. Our kids have to grow up this way.' It's one of those things I'm promising myself, trying to take the time to do stuff like this. You feel the pull." Tom's relatives may not have passed down written recipes to him, but they had passed down their rich heritage. It was time now to gather his ancestors around the table and meet them.

■ We began our journey back to the "old country" with Tom's father's family. Thomas Patrick Colicchio Sr. was born on March 17, 1936, and given the middle name Patrick in honor of his St. Patrick's Day birth. His middle name was the only thing Irish about him. Father and son shared a name, but there were significant differences between them. Tom believed his decision to follow his heart and pursue a career as a chef was influenced by the fact that his father, a barber-turned–corrections officer, never "found that thing he loved, and I think it always frustrated him," Tom said. "He encouraged all his sons to follow their dreams because he couldn't. We all learned that lesson, although it wasn't one of those things where he ever sat us down and said, 'I want you to do this,' because we didn't talk much." Tom's father was only fifty-two years old when he died of lung cancer. "We had just gotten to the point where we were starting to have adult conversations, and we probably missed more than anything else having those conversations." We would now tell Tom family stories that Thomas Sr. had never shared, whether out of reticence or a lack of knowledge himself we didn't know.

Tom's paternal grandparents, Felice Michael Colicchio, who went by the name Felix, and Olga Marino, were immigrants from Italy. They settled in Elizabeth, New Jersey, where Felix worked at the Singer Sewing Machine Factory and Olga was a homemaker. Olga was quite a character, and she always had plenty of food prepared whenever family visited. "We would see my grandmother on Sundays only, and we'd get there in the late morning, and there was always prosciutto and some kind of summer sausage and salami on the table," he reminisced. "There was always a bottle of anisette on the table. Sunday morning was always anisette and coffee. We weren't allowed to drink it, but every now and then, my dad would sneak us a little sip to let us know what we were missing."

Tom didn't remember his grandfather Felix at all. He was only four years old when he died in 1966. But he had heard the stories, and once again, food was a theme. "They had this garden that they would tend that would have been the envy of all these Brooklynites that are gardening on the roof. It was a kind of arbor with grape vines, and my uncle Felice would make wine. It was always this brown-tinted wine that I'm sure had a kick. We weren't allowed to go near it." Tom's grandfather would even buy whole pigs and lambs and butcher them in the basement. Tom's aunt Theresa told us that Felix and Olga used their basement for special events, and every Sunday, they put out a big spread for the entire family. "I wish I were a little older sometimes," Tom said, "because I missed this." Even though his memories of Sunday afternoons came courtesy of others, his face lit up when he talked about them. "This is how they grew up. You got the pig, you butchered the pig, you made sausage, you hung a leg for prosciutto, you made your soppressata, and you did everything yourself. They were from Italy; they were doing things the old way."

They had brought Italy with them to Elizabeth. We had a clear picture from Tom about their life in Elizabeth; now we wanted to paint a picture for him of their life in Italy, and how his family got to America. We began with his paternal grandmother's line, the Marinos. Everything we told him, he said, would be new. "I have not heard a single story about how they grew up," he stated matter-of-factly. According to her birth certificate, Olga Marino was born to Gaetano Marino and Raffaela Donata Schiavina, Tom's great-grandparents, on April 15, 1911, in Vallata, Italy, a farming village of two thousand people about seventy-five miles west of Naples that is today a haven for hunters of black truffles. Tom's great-grandparents were also born in Vallata, around 1881. Olga immigrated to the United States with a younger sister in 1928, aboard the SS *Saturnia*. Olga was seventeen years old, her sister Annina fourteen. Had the girls left their parents behind in Italy?

Yes and no. Olga's father, Tom's great-grandfather Gaetano, had arrived at Ellis Island seven years earlier, on May 26, 1921, aboard the SS *Caserta*. According to the ship manifest, Gaetano Marino, described as a thirty-eight-year-old tailor, was accompanied not by his wife but by another daughter, Concetta, then age sixteen. Immigration experts told us that it was very common for the breadwinner of the family, who in this case would have been Tom's great-grandfather, to move to the United States and save up enough money before bringing the rest of the family over. In the case of Gaetano Marino, however, we would learn that his family's staggered immigration was not purely a financial consideration.

A headline from a *New York Times* article dated April 27, 1924, held a clue: "America of the melting pot comes to end." In 1924, the U.S. Congress passed an immigration act limiting new immigrants to 2 percent of the people already in the country. The effect on Italian immigration was profound. Prior to the act, twenty thousand to thirty thousand Italian immigrants had been arriving on these shores annually; in the wake of the act's passage, that number was sharply reduced, to between one thousand and three thousand.

After World War I, people from battle-ravaged eastern and southern Europe flooded the United States. They were a new kind of immigrant—Jewish, Italian, Polish—and they were seen as diluting the national character. Because the 1924 quota system was based on the percentage of people already established in America, it greatly favored the immigrants who had come much earlier: the English, the Irish, the Germans. As a result of the new law, Tom's great-grandfather's family was forced to immigrate piecemeal over the next eight years. It would be 1929, when Tom's great-grandmother Raffaela and two sons finally arrived at Ellis Island, before the Marinos and their five children were finally together for the first time in America. Anti-Italian discrimination wasn't a topic that Tom's relatives discussed often. "Growing up, occasionally you would hear something, but I grew up in an era of race riots between African Americans and whites," he said. "I guess we knew that one generation removed, it was Italians that were being discriminated against."

The family made huge sacrifices to immigrate. What did Gaetano and Raffaela Marino want to leave behind? In the early twentieth century, their tiny mountain town of Vallata was a hard place in which to live, and in 1910, the year before Tom's grandmother's birth, an earthquake demolished most of it. Hundreds were killed. The village square was turned into a camp where much of the town was forced to live, outdoors, for several months. This wasn't an isolated event, either. Earthquakes were common in southern Italy. At the same time, with the population swelling and farmland eroding, poverty was widespread. "I knew they had a difficult life even when they got here, but I never heard about a hard life back in Italy. They never spoke about it." Tom guessed that his ancestors dealt with the trauma they experienced in the way that many people do. "Maybe because it was so difficult, they decided that they didn't want to repeat that history. They wanted to leave it behind."

Tom's roots in Vallata took us back to the beginning of the nineteenth century. Incredibly, we located the marriage record for Tom's third great-grandparents, dated January 24, 1835. Giuseppe Marino and Maria Gallo were also born in Vallata, Giuseppe around 1807 and Maria around 1810, and they lived through a defining period in Italian history. For centuries, from the fall of the Roman Empire until the mid-1800s, Italy was a loosely structured series of fractured city-states and small kingdoms, often dominated by foreign powers. In the 1840s, a man named Giuseppe Garibaldi launched a revolution to expel foreign influence and bring all the disparate kingdoms together into a single nation. His consolidation of the kingdom was known as Il Risorgimento, literally "The Resurgence," and it created modern Italy. He proclaimed the new kingdom on March 17—Tom's father's birthday—of 1861, just a month before the outbreak of the Civil War in the United States.

For some, unification was a huge leap forward, but the people of Vallata saw few improvements. The newly formed nation, based in Turin in the north, levied high taxes that many in the south were simply too poor to pay, and in Vallata, the rule of law broke down. While beautiful to behold, the town was buffeted by poverty and violence, as it had been for centuries. Groups of bandits roamed the countryside, preying upon the rich. They even robbed city hall. The problem became so severe that on August 1, 1861, a local newspaper in Vallata published a plea to its citizens: "Sons of Abel," it began, "charged with defending your territory, the best defense is yourselves. Take up arms, and if you don't find yourself with any, buy some. Lend yourselves to this event. At the first sight of the brigands, ring your bells like crazy."

Vigilantism worked, and several months later, the townspeople captured seven bandits, their names listed in a document detailing the criminal proceedings. One name stood out from all the others: "It says Vito Marino," Tom noted. "He was twenty-seven years old, from Vallata." Vito Marino was Tom's third great-granduncle, the son of Tom's third great-grandparents Giuseppe Marino and Maria Gallo. Tom assumed poverty had driven his family member to take his chosen path. We have no record of Vito's motivations. While some bandits were simply thieves, many of them were lashing out against the newly unified kingdom of Italy by stealing from the wealthy and the government itself and giving to the poor. "So," Tom remarked, "he was Robin Hood."

These primitive rebellions were so widespread that by the late 1860s, almost 5 percent of the entire Italian population was in jail. For many of those imprisoned, punishment was harsh and final. Proceedings from the ensuing trial of the seven brigands revealed Tom's third great-granduncle's fate. "The bandits were condemned to death and killed by a firing squad outside of the Church of St. Vito," Tom read. "That tells me he wasn't a thief. You don't put a common thief to death." If Vito was indeed Vallata's version of Robin Hood, Tom considered his actions heroic, even if criminal. "If he was doing it because he thought that he was being oppressed, I'm fine with that." On that dramatic note, we reached the end of the paper trail on Tom's father's mother's line.

■ We now turned to Tom's father's father, Felice "Felix" Colicchio, also born in Vallata, on September 23, 1903, to Maria Muscaritolo and Francescantonio Colicchio. Tom's great-grandfather Francescantonio was the first member of the Colicchio family to come to America, but it would turn out that his immigration story unfolded over the course of many, many years, and many, many journeys.

Francescantonio's immigration record from 1901 showed us that he had made his journey from Italy to New York alone. According to the ship manifest for the SS *Tartar Prince*, the twenty-year-old laborer arrived from Naples on June 11, 1901, with twenty-seven dollars in his pocket. It was not as little as it seemed; immigrants were known to arrive in this country with no more than two dollars to their name. But this record raised a question: Francescantonio arrived in New York in 1901, but his son Felice, Tom's grandfather Felix, was born in Vallata in 1903. If Francescantonio was Felix's father, then the numbers simply didn't add up. Was Felix illegitimate? Tom had never heard about any such scandal, but would something so shameful have been discussed in front of the children?

There was no need for discussion. We found our answer in a second immigration document, this one dated 1906: "Colicchio, Francesco, 28 years old. Last residence, Vallata, Italy. Final destination, Elizabeth, New Jersey." We already knew that Francescantonio had come to the United States in 1901. Now he was coming back. At some point after 1901 he had returned to Italy, where he fathered Tom's grandfather Felix, and then returned to the United States for a second time in 1906. Felix was about three years old, but he remained in Italy with his mother. Unbelievably, we found yet another immigration document for Francescantonio—his third—this one from 1913, and once again he was traveling back from Italy to America alone. Tom's great-grandfather seemed to spend his first decade in America returning to his homeland.

Leading experts on Italian American immigration said that Francescantonio's back-and-forth crossings actually fit an established pattern. In the early twentieth century, more than half the Italians who came to America made repeat trips across the Atlantic, earning money in the United States to bring home to Italy. Some made dozens of crossings, living apart from their families for years at a time. Francescantonio was what historians called a bird of passage. It's a sweet term for what must have been a hard and lonely life. The trip took two weeks and cost around twenty-five dollars, which is about five hundred dollars in today's money. The tough passage was made even tougher by the fact that Francescantonio and most of his fellow birds of passage traveled in steerage, with up to four hundred passengers crammed into tiny berths.

Italians were near the bottom of American society on both land and sea in the early twentieth century. Once they arrived in the United States, they were mostly confined to crowded cities, where they did menial labor. They were despised for their Catholicism, their social customs, and their dark skin. Yet it seemed that Francescantonio never gave up on America. But, we wondered, was it his ultimate goal to return to America or to return to Italy? Tom posed an interesting question: "I'm wondering why he didn't bring his family back with him at some point, save enough money instead of making two trips and leaving money there. At what point do you bring your family with you?"

To this day Vallata remains a fairly small village, so we sent a researcher there to go house to house, asking if anyone had ever heard of Francescantonio Colicchio. The house at 69 Strada San Giorgio was of particular interest. Above the door the initials "CF" had been carved. The current owner said they belonged to the man who built the house, one Francescantonio Colicchio. "So he was going back and forth not to bring money home but to build this house." The current owner, Pasquale Quaglia, is Tom's second cousin; Pasquale's great-grandparents are also Francescantonio Colicchio and Maria Domenica Muscaritolo. In the house hung portraits of Tom and Pasquale's great-grandparents, which had been taken in Italy, before Tom's great-grandfather ever left for America. "You keep the ancestors around," Tom said. "That's great."

A transcription record from World War I proved how strong Francescantonio's ties to Italy remained, even though his time on Italian soil was divided. "It says Francescantonio Colicchio, serving from June 9, 1917, until December 9, 1918, in the 64th Regiment." In July 1914, Europe was engulfed by the First World War. When he was about thirty-six years old, Tom's great-grandfather was pressed into service in the Italian army, and he soon found himself in one of the war's great stalemates. For three years, the Italians struggled to take a tiny stretch of Macedonia from Germany and its allies. Although the Italians ultimately triumphed, 15 percent of Francescantonio's fellow soldiers were killed or wounded, and many more were taken prisoner. Francescantonio survived, returning to an Italy that was economically ravaged, that would soon descend into fascism and the chaos of World War II. As we'd done so many times before, we turned to immigration records to track Tom's great-grandfather's whereabouts. The fourth and final document we found for him was dated September 24, 1947. Completed two years after the end of World War II, this voyage was Francescantonio's last across the Atlantic. But this time he had company. The manifest listed two names. "It says Colicchio, Francescantonio, 69 years old, and Maria Domenica, 69." The SS *Saturnia*—the same ship that had carried their daughter-in-law to America nearly two decades earlier—now carried his great-grandparents home, together at long last.

Francescantonio spent the rest of his life in Elizabeth, New Jersey, where he and Maria joined Tom's grandfather Felix and Olga's family. The house that Tom's great-grandfather worked so hard to build and traveled so many miles to perfect remains in the family to this day. Vallata is truly Tom's ancestral home. His people have lived there for many generations, and though records are scant, we were able to add another rung to his family tree, with two fifth great-grandfathers from two different Colicchio lines born in Vallata before the American Revolution: Felice Colicchio, who was born in 1730, and Salvatore Colicchio, who was born in 1744. From the middle of the eighteenth century on, everyone on Tom's family tree that we could trace was born in either Vallata or Elizabeth. This was a family that was incredibly rooted. Tom had always been surrounded by family; he didn't know another way. "They didn't go far," Tom laughed. "They put down roots and stayed there."

■ Would we find a similar trend of rootedness on Tom's mother's side? Beverly Corvelli, born on February 28, 1936, during the Depression, was also a child of Elizabeth, New Jersey. "Everybody loves their mother," Tom said, "but we really believe that our mother's special." Beverly stayed at home with her sons when they were young, but then went to work as a manager at the Elizabeth High School cafeteria. Unbeknownst to Tom, his mother had a side business of her own that made the two more similar than he realized. While Tom was a student there, Beverly earned extra money selling Italian food to the other teachers. "I've never heard that!"

Tom laughed. "She would do these little parties and stuff, but I had no idea she was actually selling." There was always food on the table at home, too, and she was the primary cook. "She had her fifteen dishes that she kind of worked through," he said. "She was a good cook, and my father liked to cook, but he was more adventurous. They both cooked, and they both just love food." In the Colicchio house, food was love. The sense of security his mother gave him as a child was still evident in the way he spoke of her today. "My mother was one of those mothers where she made sure everything was served and everything was set before she sat down. She was the one who took care of us. She made sure that everything that we needed was there," he said. "Growing up, you don't think much of it until you have kids of your own. She was our rock."

As we had done with the Colicchios, we shared wonderful old family photos of the Corvellis with Tom. He looked at a picture of his grandparents in their younger years. "As you can see, my grandmother was a good cook, because my grandfather clearly put on a lot of weight," Tom laughed. Tom's mother's parents were both born in 1910 in New Jersey, Michael Corvelli on May 7, and Conjeta Migliore, who went by the name of Esther, on November 11. "I can go on and on with memories of my grandparents," Tom said fondly. "I love fishing. I love being on the water so much, and I get that from my grandfather. Fishing to me is, it's still dark out, and I smell pepper and eggs. I smell peppers and onions frying, and there's an omelet, or what I would call a frittata now, but that smell is something that the rest of my life, I'll associate with fishing"—and with his grandfather. Tom grew up across the street from Michael and Esther. "It wasn't like I had to go take a trip to see my grandparents. I saw them every day. I didn't know kids grew up without this. To me, this was the way families were. Your aunts and uncles lived upstairs. Your grandparents were right there. My grandparents were almost like parents to me, we spent that much time with them."

Both of Tom's grandparents were born in the United States, and they never talked about the old country of their parents. "There's a pattern here," he said, recalling the silence that also surrounded his family history on his father's side. "Every now and then you hear, 'Oh, the old country,' but they weren't born there. I don't think they ever set foot in Italy." That's exactly where we were headed, back to Italy to see what we could learn about this branch of Tom's family. On Tom's mother's mother's line, we could get back to the second half of the nineteenth century, but no further. Tom's great-great-grandparents were Vincenzo Migliore, who went by the name of James and was born around 1869, and Rosa Patrizia, who was born around 1883. James was a shoemaker, Rosa a homemaker. Both were born in Italy, but details were scant, and we hit a dead end in the paper trail after this point.

We had greater luck tracing Tom's mother's father's line. Tom's great-great-grandparents were born in Alberona, Foggia province, less than one hundred miles from Vallata, Avellino province. Both are about two hundred miles south of Rome. His great-great-grandfather Francesco Conte was born on March 19, 1853, and his great-great-grandmother Concetta Maria Franchino was born in 1857. Their marriage record, "posted on the doors of city hall" on January 4, 1877, brought us back one more generation on Tom's mother's family tree. Concetta was an orphan, so her parents' names did not appear on the license, but through Tom's great-great-grandfather Francesco Comte's parents we went back one more generation still. Tom's third great-grandparents were both born in Alberona, like their son: Biase Conte in 1829 and Giuseppa Nicolina Frazzano on December 21, 1827.

The paper trail for this branch of Tom's maternal ancestors ended with Biase the farmer. Tom broke out in laughter. "On both sides of the family, farmer keeps coming up. My wife will get a kick out of this, because I want a farm for some reason, and she keeps laughing: 'What are you, crazy?' Now I know why: it's in my blood."

◾ To find out what was truly in Tom's blood, we would turn to DNA. The first test we administered to him was an admixture test, which reveals an individual's percentage of European, sub-Saharan African ancestry, and East Asian / Native American ancestry ancestry since about the time of Columbus. Tom's percentages corroborated the history we had shared with him: 95.6 percent European, 4.3 percent Middle Eastern and North African, and 0.1 percent unmatched. The Middle Eastern and North African finding was less surprising than it might seem initially. Because there was a substantial amount of migration from the Middle East into southern Italy, it's not unusual for people of southern Italian ancestry, like Tom, to have small amounts of Middle Eastern DNA. Tom's Middle Eastern result was fairly significant, though, indicating that he might have a second or third great-grandparent from that region, most likely North Africa. A geographic breakdown of Tom's European DNA was proof of how complex our ancestry can be. A tiny portion of his DNA was Finnish. "I don't understand that at all," he said. But with an Italian reading of 82 percent, the science confirmed what Tom had always known: he was deeply, deeply Italian. "There's nothing to suggest otherwise," he said.

Tom's admixture test connected him to the countries from which his ancestors came, but DNA could also connect us to specific ancestors and individuals on lost branches of our family tree. In researching Tom's maternal grandmother's parents, Vincenzo "James" Migliore and Rosa Patrizia, we had hit a dead end in the paper trail. Once an individual takes a DNA test, his or her information is stored in a massive database, allowing DNA companies to automatically connect individuals who share identical DNA with each other, and thus to turn complete strangers into autosomal, or genetic, cousins. Tom Colicchio, we discovered, had a new cousin. She had never made it to one of his family gatherings, but her name is Elena Biondi, and she and Tom share a huge amount of DNA. A familiar name and place caught our eye on her family tree: the Petrizzos in New Jersey. As we know, many immigrants, especially Italians, underwent name changes in America. They were often illiterate, and their names were often rendered phonetically on their vital records. Here the names were too similar to ignore. Elena Biondi gave us the name of the Petrizzo family's church in Newark, Our Lady of Mount Carmel in Newark, and that church gave us exactly what we were looking for: an opening into Tom's Petrizzo past. On a marriage record stored in the old Latin books at the church, the connections were spelled out. "The name of the groom is Vincenzo Migliore, son of Gerolomo Migliore and Maria Manafra," Tom read. "Name of bride is Rosa Petrizzo, daughter of Giovanni Petrizzo and Nicolina Santarsiere." Tom's new cousin Elena had led us to the marriage certificate of Tom's great-grandparents, which revealed the names of the couple's parents. It turned out that Rosa's parents were Elena's great-great-grandparents, making Tom and Elena third cousins. That marriage certificate took us back another generation in Tom's tree to two sets of his great-great-grandparents, enabling us to trace those lines back to Italy. Tom smiled. "My mother's going to love this."

■ Tom was justifiably overwhelmed by all he had learned today. When we unfurled his family tree for him, he laughed. "Look at all these Italians!" He was amazed at how far back his ancestors went, and how little he had known of most of them before. On his father's side, we were able to go back to Tom's fifth great-grandfather Felice Colicchio, born in Vallata in 1730. On his mother's side, through the miracle of DNA science, we went back to his sixth great-grandfather Giovanni Petrizzo, who was born in Sessano, Italy, around 1750. Both sides of the family went back to a period in Italy before the United States was founded. "It's humbling to know that all these people came before, and they all had their lives and their families. This is just a kernel of it. It just continues." Of particular interest to Tom were the names—every single one familiar, not through family history, but through the streets of Elizabeth. "All of these names, Muscaritolo, Melchionna, Marino, Nigro, these were all names that are very familiar names to grow-ing up in Elizabeth," he said, poring over his family tree. "I've heard these names all my life. Half the village moved," he laughed, "and the village is so related. If I looked at my parents' yearbook, these are all the names you'd see." If Tom went to Vallata, he would probably find all those names still there, too. "I have to book a flight to Vallata very soon. Because I cook, I need to honor dishes and food from this region and understand it more, because maybe it will unlock a key as to what I do and why I do it."

Tom looked at his family story in a context that went far beyond Eliza-beth, even beyond Vallata. "This is an immigration story, and this dovetails perfectly into what is happening today. When you think about what people will do to cross a border, to go through the desert, to leave their families behind, leave their children to try to make a better life, when you see this, you realize that someone going through this struggle, they're doing it for a reason, and they're doing it probably to feed their family. They're doing it because they want a different experience and a richer experience. It's the same struggle. It doesn't change." As the grandchild and great-grandchild of immigrants, he put the nature of the American experience for them beautifully. But why the amnesia? We found ancestors of Tom's who were born before the American Revolution, yet in family lore, he couldn't tell us anything beyond a generation or two. "It's an old adage," he said, "that once you get in, you want to pull in the ladder behind you. I don't under-stand that. I think when you get here, maybe it is amnesia. You just forget. You forget the struggle. But you know what? This country was made great because of people who were willing to work hard and sacrifice a lot, and I don't understand why we forget."

What was never forgotten in Tom's family was the food. While specific recipes weren't passed down from generation to generation—no one wrote anything down, he said—food was always a central part of his family's life, and it connected him to his long-lost roots and the land on which his ancestors lived. "You are what you eat. Your ancestors were doing certain things, and they were typically doing them because that was what was available, so the way you made one particular dish from that pig may have been slightly different than someone the next country over, the next region over. When you say recipes or dishes, I'm looking at it as more the significance of the culture, because that will inform you what people were farming, how people were farming, how people were surviving."

Tom came from a huge family, with so many cousins he had lost count. But today he had met many, many more. If he could cook a meal for any one of the ancestors we'd introduced him to today, who would it be, and what would he cook? It came as no surprise that he picked his great-grandfather, whom he considered "the key to my family," Francescantonio Colicchio. "He made the trip back and forth," Tom said. "I want to cook for him, and I want to cook for him what they were getting in first class on that boat, not what he was getting in steerage. Whatever was going on on the upper decks, that's what he deserves." Vito Marino, the Robin Hood of Tom's family tree, was a close second. "I'd like to cook his last meal," Tom said, referring to his ancestor's execution. "They give you that last request. He deserves a first-class meal."

In light of everything we had discussed, what did Tom think makes us who we are? Was it our lived experiences from the time we're born? The families we're born into? The DNA we inherited from all these people? Tom couldn't separate nature from nurture. "If you look at the nurturing that happens from your parents or from your family, and some of your extended family, you can't help but go back to the nature part of that to actually find out why certain people show nurturing. Why was my mother so nurturing? The answer's probably in here somewhere." He pointed to the family tree. "The key is all here. And when you see it in front of you like this, it all becomes very clear."

Ming Tsai (b. 1964)

There are over forty thousand Chinese restaurants in the United States, more than all the McDonalds, Burger Kings, and Pizza Huts combined. Two of them belong to Ming Tsai. For thirteen seasons, Ming has been celebrating Chinese food on his signature show, *Simply Ming*. Whether he's dazzling diners with his East-West innovations on air, at his restaurants Blue Ginger and Blue Dragon, or on television, his recipe for success is simple: "With a smile and good food, you can build friendships forever," he said. "I love making other people happy. There are very few things, besides maybe music, that can do that, that can change your mood for you, but food goes inside of you, literally, physically." In Ming's family, the love of food is intergenerational. There was never a time in Ming's memory that food didn't play a central role. "My whole life, really, has been based around food, period."

Ming Hao Tsai was born on March 29, 1964, in Newport Beach, California. He grew up in Dayton, Ohio, part of a tiny Chinese American community. "Our family joke was, when we had the two or three Chinese families over to our house, we were Chinatown," he recalled. "We were always surrounded by food. All we did was cook and eat." Dumplings and spring rolls were often on the menu, but his first foray into the kitchen with his mother didn't involve Chinese cuisine. "At six years old, I went into the kitchen, and I wanted to learn how to make a Duncan Hines cake, the vanilla," he said. "I was just fascinated, and she helped me—eggs, boom, mix, cake. I just thought this was amazing. You just mix stuff like this." As a world-renowned chef, Ming has built his reputation on "mixing stuff," rejecting the word "fusion" commonly used to describe his style. "Fusion is what you learn in engineering for nuclear energy, and you're forcing atoms together. That's not food. America is famous for putting labels on things, and they didn't have a name for this. 'East-West' was too long, so they said, 'Fusion, perfect.' They were fusing two things; you are bringing East and West together. I just think cooking is more gentle, more of a blending."

A first-generation American, Ming himself is a blend, describing himself, proudly, as Chinese American. "By being American, I've enjoyed all the benefits of fantastic schooling, the security, the safety, everything America has to offer," he said. America has always been his home, but it was China, the home of his ancestors, the birthplace of his parents and grandparents, that formed his foundation. "I read enough Chinese to order Chinese food, but that's it. The most important thing for me, to be honest, is being able to go into Chinese restaurants and order food and cook for people Chinese food, the whole banquet. Cooking family-style is the best way to eat." Through food he connected with the culture of his ancestors. "My mindset, the way I was brought up, was very Chinese, meaning respecting the elders, family first. Food is very important. Education is very important." Ming played sports and excelled in school, becoming the third generation of his family to attend Yale. He is possibly the only chef to have earned a degree in mechanical engineering. Cooking was never far from his mind, though. "I always gravitated toward the kitchen."

Ming's parents were both born in Beijing, but they met and fell in love in America. It's no surprise that they first bonded over food. It's the Tsai way. Ming's mother was a teenager living at home, his father a student at Yale; their fathers knew each other from Yale as well. "When my dad first got to New Haven, his father says, 'Go see Pao Chen Lee'—my mom's father—'and they'll give you a good meal.'" Ming laughed. "Again, based around food. I doubt he was going because he fell in love with a fourteen-year-old, but he would go frequently to the house because there was Chinese food. That's how they fell in love." Cooking was a family affair, and Ming said both of his parents have always been great cooks. "Mom is more exact. She'll follow the salt-and-pepper shrimp recipe to a T. Dad is more that Iron Chef—open the fridge, see what there is, and there's fried rice or fried noodles on the table in five minutes." When Ming was sixteen, his parents opened a restaurant in Dayton called Mandarin Kitchen. Whether at home or during their frequent travels, food was the primary attraction. "It would always fall back to food," he said. "'When we go to the Great Wall one day, we'll show you where we can go fish,' and then they'll make the fish."

Food and family are intertwined for Ming. What his grandparents and parents were forced to leave behind in China on their difficult journey to America, they made up for by instilling in Ming a deeply ingrained, deeply nourishing feeling for his people's ancient culture.

■ We began our journey into Ming's roots on his mother's family tree. Puhong Lee, who goes by the name of Iris, was born on February 18, 1935, in Beijing. From his mother, Ming inherited what can only be called his zest for life. "The glass is definitely half full," he said. On the road to success, the destination is only part of it. "I learned very early that if you're not enjoying the ride getting there, you're missing out on half of it. Success is success, but if you don't enjoy the way to success, you blew it." His mother wore many hats in the Tsai house and in the Dayton community. She was a homemaker, a cooking teacher, and ultimately a restaurant owner. He caught "the restaurant bug" when his parents opened Mandarin Kitchen, but it was long before that that he learned what it takes to make people happy. "She instilled this whole hospitality inherent in being a Chinese family," Ming explained. "The first question in Chinese culture you ask is

'Have you eaten?,' not 'How are you doing?' My mom instilled that in me: you can at a minimum feed people, and everything else will be fine."

Iris came to the United States in 1946, a year after World War II ended. She was eleven years old, and her memories of her girlhood in China were limited. She resettled in this country with her late brother, Ming's uncle Jim, and her parents. Iris's father, Pao Chen Lee, was born in China's Hebei province on July 18, 1907, and her mother, Tsui Lee, who went by the name Gwendolyn, was born on April 27, 1911, also in China. Gwendolyn, whom Ming called Lala (Chinese for "grandmother"), was a nutritionist at a hospital in Iowa City before moving in with her daughter during the latter part of her life, when she worked as the manager of Mandarin Kitchen. "Lala became one of my best friends, having lived with us for probably twelve, thirteen years," Ming said of his beloved grandmother. "But she was the antithesis of me. I love bold, spicy flavors. She would actually take her stir-fry dishes and rinse them with water in a strainer to get all the oil, fat, and salt off of it, all the flavor, which still kills me." He may have disagreed with her tastes, but Ming loved to sit with his grandmother while she ate. "After Mandarin Kitchen, she would come back, eating her food, and she would chew super-slowly for digestion reasons, but we got to hang out a lot." In her younger years, though, she was ahead of her time. "We would visit as kids. We would buy frozen pizzas, which we loved. She would take chicken in hoisin sauce and put it on the pizza and bake it, and we'd say, 'What are you doing? We want pepperoni. We want normal!' Fast-forward fifteen years, there's Wolfgang Puck putting Thai chicken and all these flavors on top of pizza."

Ming was thirteen when his maternal grandfather died. They had spent little time together, but he remembered a grandfatherly man who was willing to keep secrets with his grandsons and buy them ice cream. In his homeland, however, he was a hero known as the father of modern choral composition in China. "I saw pictures of the funeral, and it was a national funeral. It was the prime minister, the president—everyone was there," he said. "Subsequently I went to Taiwan for the summer to master Chinese, and I was always introduced as Lee Pao Chen's grandson. Everyone wanted to shake my hand because I was his grandson."

In 1931, after decades of tension and conflict between China and Japan, the Japanese launched an invasion of Manchuria in northeastern China. Infuriated by what he saw as unchecked Japanese imperialism, Ming's grandfather, Pao Chen Lee, the director of the National Conservatory of Music in China, responded in the only way a conductor could. "After the Mukden Incident," his grandfather's biography, available only in Taiwan, read, "he composed several songs: 'Triumph Return,' 'Fighting for Our Country,' and 'The Great China I Love.'" Ming's grandfather's music is still being sung and recorded today. "This is amazing that back in '31, he just knew the best way to fight back is through music." Ming believed that only music came close to having the same effect on a person as food.

In addition to being a Chinese patriot, Pao Chen Lee was also a very religious Christian. His own grandfather, Ming's great-great-grandfather, was a man named Qing Feng, born around 1845 in the Hebei province. "Pao Chen's grandfather, Qing Feng," Ming read from the biography, "in the end of the Qing dynasty, converted to Christianity and helped the Christians to translate the Bible." The Qing dynasty was a long-running dynasty, obtaining between 1644 and 1911. While the mass publication of Bibles in the Chinese language began in 1813, the vast majority of nineteenth-century Bibles remain unpublished translations done by hand, one of them penned by Ming's great-great-grandfather.

Ming had no idea that his ancestor had been responsible for such an enormous undertaking. Qing Feng's task was not only difficult; it was also extremely risky. Almost everyone in China followed Confucianism, and many feared that the spread of Christianity would undermine core social values and potentially have political ramifications for the emperor. Starting in the early nineteenth century, Chinese promoters of Christianity, like Ming's great-great-grandfather, were often ostracized or, even worse, targets of violence. Ming speculated as to why his ancestor was willing to take such a risk. "I think it was just inherent in himself that he wanted to spread something that changed him, and he wanted to hopefully better the people around him. He was for the people. He was trying to help the common folk."

Whatever his motivations, the outcome of his religious fervor was devastating. The biography put it bluntly: "Qing Feng was expelled from his clan." This was a severe punishment. The formation of clans and the recording of one's family lineage were cornerstones of Chinese society before Mao Zedong's Cultural Revolution of the 1960s, when he ordered all genealogies destroyed. Clan genealogy dates back to the Shang dynasty, which ran between 1523 and 1028 B.C., at a time when family histories were written on turtle shells, cow bones, and bronze. Expulsion from one's clan was extraordinarily rare, and it carried with it an enormous sense of shame and loss. The name of the expelled member was expunged from all genealogical records. If not for this biography, Ming's ancestor's name would have been entirely erased from memory.

Our research into Qing Feng brought us to the Boxer Rebellion, a famous uprising in northeastern China that lasted from 1898 to 1900, led by a group of martial artists known as the Yihequan, the Righteous and Harmonious Fists. One of their slogans was "Beat the foreign devils and burn their books"; another, "Support the Qing, exterminate the barbarians." In this case, Qing referred to the dynasty, not to Ming's ancestor; he, in fact, was one of the barbarians. The Yihequan, named the Boxers by the English, were landless peasants who wanted to purge China of all foreign influence. They were particularly angered by Christian missionaries and their supporters, and beginning in 1898, the Boxers burned churches and killed both foreign missionaries and Chinese converts to Christianity, dumping their bodies in mass graves. More than thirty thousand people died.

Ming's great-great-grandfather would have been a prime target for the Boxers. A map of their path through China revealed that some of the worst massacres of the Boxer Rebellion took place in Hebei province. We could find no evidence of Qing Feng's outcome, but a photograph of the ruins of a church in his home province, with the caption "It was here that a great number of missionaries and native Christians were condemned to death," painted a grim picture of Qing Feng's likely fate.

Qing Feng's family, with or without Qing Feng himself, survived. After the Boxer Rebellion, Qing Feng's son, Ming's great-grandfather, Lee Ben Gen, also known as Zong Zhi, rebuilt the Bao Ding Presbyterian temple at Hebei. Despite the violence and turmoil, Qing Feng's family continued to practice Christianity. "I didn't realize how strong the faith was," Ming said. "Both grandparents were religious, and they went to church. That is how my other grandfather got to Yale, through the Yale in China program, and thank God—no pun intended—that's what got him to this country. But that's about as far as I thought Christianity went in our family." It went so far, in fact, that it might have cost one of his ancestors his life. "Obviously it's much more deeply rooted than I ever imagined. I don't think, potentially, I'd be here if it wasn't."

■ The paper trail for Ming's mother's family ended there, in the middle of the nineteenth century, with Qing Feng. Ming's father's family tree would take us much further back than that, further than we'd ever gone into any of our subjects' ancestries before.

Ming's father, Wei-Lun Tsai, who goes by the name Stephen, was born on July 6, 1929, in Beijing. A true rocket scientist and, according to Ming, "the only genius I've ever known really well," Stephen also taught his son to treasure food and family. His work involved a great deal of travel, but he always brought his children with him, and he always fed them as well as he could. "One thing about my father that I love is he would be in charge of setting up these engineering symposiums, and he could pick any time to set it up. He would first call the three-star Michelin restaurants to make sure he got a reservation. Then he says, 'OK, we'll do this symposium this week.' Again, his priority was food." Like father, like son. Ming followed his father to Yale, and almost into engineering, but he stopped short of making it his career. In every other way, Ming said, he always tries to emulate his father. "My dad was an engineer. He was always home at 5:30. I'm not home as much, but I try my darnedest to get home for dinner, make them dinner, so we just have that hour together. That's how I was brought up. The gathering at the dining room table around great Chinese food, that was our epicenter." His father also modeled for him "to treat people well all the time, regardless if they happen to be a janitor, a driver, a dishwasher, your boss, your boss's boss. Doesn't matter. Treat them well; you will be treated well."

Ming's father came to America to study at Yale University, as had his father before him. We showed Ming his father's arrival record from September 8, 1948, aboard the SS *President Wilson*: "Stephen Tsai, arriving to United States, 19 years old. Final destination: Yale University, New Haven." He had gotten out of China just in time. Just four months after he left, in January 1949, the Communists captured Beijing, and Mao Zedong declared the People's Republic of China later in October 1949.

Ming's grandfather, we would learn, was directly affected by Mao's Cultural Revolution. He had to flee his homeland to save himself. Yi-E Tsai, who like his son went by the name Stephen, was born on September 4, 1898, in the Hunan province of China, and he died on April 1, 1991, in Santa Clara, California. Ming's grandmother, Yunqing Li, who went by the name Lily, was born in 1899 in Zhejiang, China. She died in 1994, also in Santa Clara. They were married for more than seventy-five years. "They were the most loving couple ever," Ming said. Toward the end of their lives they lived near Ming's family in Dayton, and every Friday night they ate dinner together. "Yeye, my grandfather, grew everything. He'd say, 'Look at this cucumber. Look at these chili peppers.' They would do their own noodles, their own wonton wrappers. I would try to out-eat him in chili paste. We'd always have that."

Yi-E Tsai was a student of economics at Yale, graduating with the class of 1923. Yale and China developed a relationship in 1901, when the Yale Foreign Missionary Society chose China as the focus of their work, in part to honor an 1892 Yale graduate and missionary slain in the Boxer Rebellion. Upon graduation from Yale, he returned to China and became the comptroller of Yenching University, founded in 1919, which *Time* magazine called "the single biggest expression of U.S. educational philanthropy abroad." Incidentally, Ming's maternal grandfather, Pao Chen Lee, graduated from Yenching University in 1930. It was there that the future in-laws met.

In 1937, when Ming's grandfather was thirty-eight years old, the Japanese again invaded China, part of a conflict that would soon expand into World War II. Within months, Japanese forces entered Beijing. By that time Ming's grandfather had been employed by Yenching University for more than ten years, serving in several different capacities, designing sidewalks for the school and installing the first underground sewer system at a Chinese university. As the Japanese drew near, most of the university's employees fled, but a handful remained behind, including Ming's grandfather. "Yenching was his home. I think that defined him," Ming said. "He was the comptroller, but he already did so much to the university, and the last thing he wanted to see is everything he did destroyed. He was so strong in the mind that he probably realistically thought he could take care of the Japanese himself somehow."

This confidence was noble but misplaced. The situation in Beijing only worsened. On December 7, 1941, Japan bombed Pearl Harbor, and the tensions at Yenching escalated. The Japanese began to arrest professors and staff of the university whom they viewed as American loyalists. An article published in the *Zong Heng Journal* mentioned Ming's grandfather by name: "After Pearl Harbor, the Japanese army seized Yenching University and arrested many professors and students, including Tsai Yi-e." He was one of sixteen professors and administrators arrested by the Japanese army and taken to a military police base. He was thrown into a prison camp and repeatedly tortured, and soon contracted typhus. Ming's grandfather spent six months in these horrid conditions, and he would have died, according to news accounts and family lore, if not for "the kindness of a Japanese nurse who gave him penicillin."

When the war ended in 1945, he remained in Beijing and returned to his beloved university. But now he faced a new threat. Almost as soon as the Japanese were defeated, China erupted into a civil war between the Communists and the Nationalists. The Nationalists were supported by the United States, their ranks filled with China's emerging middle class. The Communists, backed by the Soviet Union, promised to liberate China's huge population of impoverished peasants. The conflict between the two groups had been fomenting since the early twentieth century. Now war consumed the entire country, a war that was ultimately won by the Communists. In the wake of their victory, China's new leader, Mao Zedong, moved to consolidate his power, authorizing the execution of anyone with ties to the Nationalists. Landowners, businessmen, and intellectuals were killed in droves. This kind of violence would mark Communist rule in China for the rest of Mao's life. It would culminate in the notorious Cultural Revolution, which claimed tens of millions of victims and placed Ming's grandfather, a prominent intellectual, in grave danger. Fortunately he saw it coming. "They knew early on," Ming said, "when these rumors started coming, that they would be targeted. And my grandfather fled immediately." Not all of Yi-E's circle had the same foresight. "A lot of his friends who stayed were killed, just because they were 'threats to the government.' People don't realize the simple fact, more people were killed during the Cultural Revolution than the Holocaust. Both are horrific. The reasons are equally stupid, one because you're Jewish, one because you're a thinker."

Yi-E finally left China in 1948. The following year, the Communists took control of Beijing and shut down Yenching University for good. Ming's grandfather spent three years running from the Communists, fleeing from Beijing to Shanghai, to Guango, to Macau. Thankfully, he reached Nationalist-controlled Taiwan in 1951. Many so-called American sympathizers escaped Beijing only to be arrested while they were on the run. But Yi-E made it out with the help of a man named John Leighton Stuart, the son of Presbyterian missionaries and Yenching University's first president. It was he who had hired Ming's grandfather at Yenching in the first place. Stuart always retained ties to China, and in 1946, he was named the U.S. ambassador to China. According to Ming's father, Stuart used his diplomatic influence to help move Yi-E out of Beijing before the Communists could capture him. He probably saved Ming's grandfather's life.

Yi-E could bring little with him on the journey that would take him and his wife away from the land of their birth. He took just one object with him: a precious book tracing the family's genealogy back to the year 891 A.D. As the youngest of the male descendants of his generation, Ming had been in possession of the book for some time. "This really comes full circle to roots," he said. "It just speaks volumes that the most important thing in his life was family and where he came from. You can always, in theory, get another Bible or another cross, but family history, if that was lost, you can't get that back."

At the height of the Cultural Revolution, Mao had ordered the abolition of the Four Olds: old thinking, old culture, old customs, and old habits. In an effort to break down family structures and make the Chinese people rootless, he ordered all clan genealogies destroyed. Ming called it "archaic brainwashing." "Let's get rid of all history, and if there is no history, then the only person you can listen to is Mao, the new father, your new god," Ming said. "If you have no ties to Christianity and no ties to old ways of thinking, you can no longer be a threat." For centuries, only the names of male descendants were recorded in the clan genealogies; women were identified merely as "female" or "woman." For thirty-four generations there had always been a son in the Tsai line; any daughters were lost to time. "My father, who is forward-thinking, decided, 'Look, this is the twenty-first century. We live in America. We married women. They have to be in the book.' Maybe one of the great-great-grandfathers turned over in their graves, but you have to be progressive."

The clan genealogy recorded oral history, as set down by Ming's ancestors. Our goal was to confirm its veracity with sources outside the book. It was a long shot. Before communism, the Chinese landscape was dotted with hundreds of thousands of steles, the stone tablets that record family genealogies. Unfortunately, 85 percent of all genealogical records in Hunan province, including the majority of the steles, were destroyed in the Cultural Revolution. In the village of Yi Yang, Ming's family's traditional hometown, one stele remained. Intact and alone, it stood in an area called Quin Jao Her, which means "the meeting of two rivers." Unbelievably, on the stele was carved the name Tsai Ying—Ming's thirty-sixth great-grandfather. The only stele to survive the Cultural Revolution in Hunan province belonged to Ming's family. "I just got goose bumps," Ming gasped. "I have to take my father there."

Tsai Ying was born in the year 891 and died in 924 in Hunan province, the birthplace of Ming's grandfather a thousand years later. The clan genealogy contained a biography of Tsai Ying, the ancestor who was responsible for initiating this genealogical record. Tsai Ying brought Ming's family to Hunan province more than a millennium ago from the city of Chang'an, the capital city of the later Tang dynasty, with a population topping 2 million—more than all the people inhabiting the British Isles at that time. Hunan province was at the very edge of the empire's holdings. What could have drawn Ying to this remote place? According to the genealogy, the later Tang dynasty emperor Zhuang, who ruled for just three years, from 923 to 926 A.D., had personally selected Ying to resettle in Hunan after it had been ravaged during the wars of the early tenth century. "Tanzhou had been damaged during the war," Ming read. "People were out of work. Ying dealt with famine and reshaped the army. Tanzhou," it concluded, "revived very soon." Tsai Ying was Ming's original Hunan ancestor, a region he had been drawn to through its food. "My grandfather was from Hunan, hence the affinity for spicy foods was a natural." A picture of his ancestor's gravesite transported him to his family's ancestral home. "When my grandfather passed, I never cried so much in my life with all my uncles. It felt like hours we were bowing," he said, referring to the Chinese tradition of bowing to the deceased at funerals. "I've already visualized me there with my family, bowing."

That lone remaining stele in the village of Yi Yang had pointed us to the Shanghai Public Library, which allowed us to construct a Tsai family tree that stretched back an unprecedented ninety generations. It was the largest family tree we had ever done. The list of ancestors seemed endless. Ming's forty-fourth great-granduncle Tsai Lun was born in 50 A.D. in Guiyang, China, and in the year 105 invented paper. Like Ming's great-great-grandfather Qing Feng, who translated the Christian Bible into Chinese in the middle of the nineteenth century, Tsai Lun literally changed the course of history.

The originator of the Tsai name was Ming's eighty-second great-grandfather Shu Du. Born in the year 1046 B.C., he received the fief of Tsai in central China from his elder brother, King Wen of Zhou. It remained in the family until it was conquered by the Qin dynasty in the third century B.C. At this point in Chinese history, surnames had been reserved for the aristocracy, but following the Qin conquest, they spread to all classes, and many people from the former state of Tsai took it as their own. The Tsai surname has been continuous in Ming's family for an incredible eighty-four generations, going in a straight line from Shu Du down to Ming and his sons.

The stele took us back even further in time, all the way back to a legendary figure in Chinese history named Huang Di, one of China's first Five Emperors, who is often cited in folklore as the father of the Chinese language and the centralized Chinese state. Huang Di, the Yellow Emperor, lived around the twenty-seventh century B.C. The record skips several generations, so precise genealogy is impossible, but we estimate that the Yellow Emperor was Ming's 116th great-grandfather, and he reputedly lived from 2698 to 2598 B.C. "To go back to Huang Di, one of the original Five Emperors, is just mind-blowing," Ming said. "But it's already set in motion in my head: what did he eat? What did they all eat? How did they eat? That's an immediate new quest, because there was definitely food tied into every one of those Tsais." We laid out a menu for Ming. By 5500 B.C. the Chinese were eating domesticated chicken. By 3000 B.C. they had domesticated pigs. Early imperial delicacies included jellyfish with cinnamon, puffer fish, and pickled mutton. Ming had cooked for many, many people in his life, but this was certainly the largest family gathering he had ever attended.

■ We had been able to take Ming Tsai's magnificent history all the way back to the twenty-seventh century B.C. If imaginable, DNA could take us back further still. We administered three DNA tests to Ming: an admixture test, which would reveal his percentage of East Asian / Native American, sub-Saharan African, and European ancestry, going back to the time of Columbus, or, more appropriately to Ming's family, the Qing dynasty. Ming was 99.8 percent East Asian, of which 89.3 percent was Chinese. Although each of Ming's ancestors was Chinese in the paper records, some of his DNA most closely matched that of people living in Korea and Mongolia today, both of which are very close to the Hebei province in northern China, home to Ming's maternal ancestors.

We also traced Ming's Y-DNA, which a man gets from his father, and his mitochondrial DNA, which all children get from their mother. Both Y-DNA and mitochondrial DNA are an identical genetic fingerprint or signature. Ming's paternal haplogroup—a genetic population group that shares a common ancestor—is found in about 15 percent of all Han Chinese males. This corroborates the paper trail. Interestingly, it's also been found in up to 85 percent of Tamang males. Believed to be the oldest tribe in Nepal, the Tamangs trace their ancestry back to Tibet and, anciently, to Mongolia. Ming's mitochondrial DNA revealed that his maternal haplogroup is particularly common among Koreans, where it reaches nearly 22 percent. It is also found in about 18 percent of Siberians and is present at about 20 percent in Manchuria, which is just north of the Korean Peninsula. This means that it's possible that the Korean component we saw in Ming's admixture comes from his direct maternal line.

■ In tracing Ming's genealogy, there seemed to be miracles at work. Displaced by revolutions and wars, erased from genealogies, Ming Tsai's ancestors could have been entirely lost to time. Through strange twists of fate, we were able to explore thousands of years in a day, those years populated by ancestors with names and stories. "Every star had to align for this to even come to fruition," Ming said. "I thought thirty-four generations was a long time, but you tripled it. Most extraordinary is the three coincidences or accidents or happenings. Yeye, my grandfather, had to grab the book when he fled China. The researcher goes to a village with no chance in hell of finding anything; the steles are all destroyed except one, and it's down where the rivers meet, and that's my family's. Then the stele points to the book that adds another sixty generations. Obviously it's meant to be," Ming said matter-of-factly. "I actually don't believe in coincidence. I think this was fate, and it further solidifies how blessed I am."

Ming had spent his whole life cooking for people, filling the bellies and satisfying the souls of family, friends, even strangers. He had met many ancestors today, some beloved, some unknown till now. If he could cook for any one of them, who would it be, and what would he cook? Ming went way back. "It would have to be Huang Di, because Huang Di was the first, and he was an emperor. What would I cook?" He paused to consider the meal. "I would cook my heart out with all my Chinese-influenced dishes, from Beijing, from Mongolia, and I would give them the tasting of all of China my way—not traditional, because they've all had traditional, but my reinterpretation of those classics."

It was obvious that Ming wanted to give back to his ancestors as they had given to him. And what exactly did Ming feel he had taken from them? Did the emperor make Ming the person he is today? Did the paper inventor or the Bible translator? Was it our family tree, or was it our DNA, or was it our experiences? Ming was certain in his answer: it was family. "You're molded by your family. You have to know going in that without your two parents, you would never be here physically, but you also would never act this way and have these values and these wishes and these wants. I still have my two parents on this planet; I'm still learning from them and will continue to." His dedication to his family and his gratitude to his ancestors was ingrained in him. "Just like all my Jewish friends, Mexican friends, Chinese friends, all the immigrants are family first. Family is the most important element of all of our cultures. That hopefully will never die, because you have to have it." For Ming, family sustains him and nourishes him more than anything else.

Aarón Sánchez (b. 1976)

Aarón Sánchez—Food Network luminary, host of *Heat Seekers*, and judge on *Chopped*—is a third-generation chef. Simply put, he said, "Everybody in my family can cook." It's in his blood. His daring, expertly prepared dishes all owe something to his training and to his heritage. In 2002 his restaurant Paladar in New York was named Best Latin American Restaurant by *Time Out*, and in 2005 he won the James Beard Award for Rising Star Chef of the Year. For all his success, though, Aarón holds himself to a higher standard still. "I want to cook 50 percent as good as my mom, and 50 percent as good as my grandmother. Then I'm doing something right." When Aarón was a young boy, his mother, the caterer and social worker Zarela Martínez, made a bold decision: in financial ruin following her divorce from Aarón's father, she packed Aarón and his siblings into their van and moved from Texas to New York to open a restaurant. Zarela took New York by storm, and she has been called the queen of New York's Mexican culinary scene. When Aarón's grandmother Aída Gabilondo was in her seventies, she published the cookbook *Mexican Family Cooking*. For Aarón's family, those cookbooks are akin to history books. "We've actually put down a tangible piece of our lives that people can have," he said.

Aarón only recently began to describe himself as Mexican American. "For a long time I identified myself as Mexican, but in reality, I'm Mexican American. I'm born here in the States, but the duality of being able to see Mexico every day when I go back home really resonated with me," he said. That duality plays a significant role in his cooking, too. "I say I do contemporary Latin food," he explained. "Every dish that I conceive of has to come from a cultural lens. I don't put a Chinese dish with a Latin dish and call it my food. It has to stem from somewhere original. It has to have a cultural significance."

New York has been the backdrop for much of his success, but he doesn't call it home. "No matter how far you travel, home for me is in your heart, and El Paso is that for me. It's a place where I go and eat all the favorite food. It's where I see all my crazy aunts. It's the place where I get the particular cowboy boots I like, and all those things that you can't find here in New York." His brother still lives in the house that belonged to their father before he died. "When I come back home to visit, it's not something that feels sad or somber. It's really a celebration of my upbringing and my father's life. The pace slows down, the stories come out, the tequila comes out, people start singing—all the things that are essential in people's lives."

Aarón and his fraternal twin brother, Rodrigo, were born on February 12, 1976, in El Paso, Texas. Their parents, Adolfo Sánchez and Zarela Martínez, married on Valentine's Day in 1975 and divorced when Aarón was just seven years old. Aarón went back and forth between his parents' homes before moving to New York, and he felt firmly grounded in both sides of his family. He had always relished listening to "the matriarchs and the patriarchs" of the family spin the tales of his ancestors, and he came to us with considerably more knowledge of his ancestry than many of our participants. Yet he still hungered to know more.

■ Aarón's mother, Zarela Martínez, is a force to be reckoned with, both in and out of the kitchen. She was born on October 17, 1947, in Agua Prieta, Mexico. Zarela has always been proudly Mexican, and she famously pours her heritage into each dish she prepares. Interestingly, it was an experience that she had as a chef that made her feel, for the first time, American. In 1983, Zarela was one of a group of chefs invited to cook for President Reagan at the G7 Summit in Williamsburg, Virginia. "She was so enamored by the whole thing. She was there in this very patriotic environment," Aarón said, "and that was one of the first times she ever really identified as being American. She just said, 'Wow, this is it. This is the glory of being an American.'"

Throughout Aarón's childhood, his mother eagerly shared memories of her own childhood and of her family's Mexican roots. She grew up on a three-thousand-acre ranch in San Pedro de Ojitos, in a valley just south of the Sierra Madre Mountains in Sonora, Mexico. "My mom told us very romantic stories of growing up on a ranch. It was really the place that forged the strong woman that is my mom, and she speaks so highly of it, from all the cowboys to the food to the riding of the horses to the killing of the rattlesnake with a bullwhip to my grandmother making fresh cheeses," Aarón said. "A dream of mine was always to come back and somehow buy this ranch." The ranch symbolized the sense of permanence and posterity that were so important to Aarón and his family. Aarón had heard the ranch was an old Apache fort, but he knew nothing about how it came to be a part of his family's history.

We started with the owners of the ranch, Aarón's maternal grandparents, José Martínez, born on November 9, 1914, in El Paso, Texas, and Aída Gabilondo, born on March 7, 1918, in Douglas, Arizona. Grandpa Pepe died before Aarón was born, but Aída, whom he called Mima, was an integral part of his life. "For me, she was the sweetest, most elegant person I've ever met. She was the best cook I've ever seen," he said. Aída was a towering figure in his memory. He immortalized her with a tattoo on his arm of her name and, underneath it, *"Escuela vieja"*—"Old school." She graduated as valedictorian of her class at the Loretto Academy and went on to prepare meals with world-renowned chefs and publish a cookbook long after most people have retired. She had passed her drive and determination to her daughter and to her grandson, but who had passed those traits to her?

We went back another generation on Aarón's mother's family tree, to Aída's parents, Aarón's great-grandparents Hilario Gabilondo and Ana Acuna. Hilario was born on January 17, 1895, in Nogales, which is in Sonora, Mexico, and Ana was born in 1897 in Banamichi, also in Sonora. There had been talk of political ties and the Mexican Revolution, but Aarón only knew bits and pieces about the lives of his great-grandparents. "When I was younger," Aarón said, "that generation seemed like the movies. People lived back then? People had horses? It was one of those things that was very far-fetched." That generation he had seen as unreal was about to become very real.

Hilario and Ana's marriage certificate told us that they were married in Santa Monica, California, on July 7, 1916. World War I was already under way. The certificate, which described Hilario's occupation as "ranchman," brought us back yet another generation, to Hilario's parents, Aarón's great-great-grandparents, Rafael Gabilondo and Josefa Corella. Rafael was born in Sonora, Mexico, in 1867, and Josefa Corella was born in 1866. According to Aarón's mother, the man the family called "Papi Rafael" was quite a character: a bootlegger, a cattle rancher, a kingmaker, and even a patron of the arts. He was also Aarón's first maternal ancestor to move across the border. On May 14, 1912, Papi Rafael crossed from Mexico into the United States for the first time, his final destination Douglas, Arizona, where his granddaughter Aída would be born just six years later. "A lot of my family still has ties in Douglas. I was always interested to see how they found Douglas and why my mom's extended family decided to stay there," Aarón said. "I guess it really derived from Papi Rafael making the move over there."

At the time of his immigration, Aarón's great-great-grandfather Rafael owned a large cattle ranch in Colonia Oaxaca in Sonora, but he left it behind. Born into a prominent family, he was one of the wealthiest cattle owners in northern Mexico by the time he was a young man. But his fortunes began to unravel in a flash. In 1910, just two years before he and Josefa came to the United States, Mexico exploded into a revolution, a bloody, all-out war that would ultimately claim nearly a million lives. Aarón had a strong grasp on Mexican history and was familiar with the Mexican Revolution, but he never knew that his ancestors were affected by it so deeply. For more than thirty years, Mexico had been ruled by the dictator Porfirio Díaz, whose government worked to concentrate power and wealth into the hands of a few. Laws made it impossible for peasants to own their own farms. In November 1910, a group of rebels led by Pancho Villa and Emiliano Zapata rose up, calling for the overthrow of the government and widespread social change, starting with land reform. Aarón's great-great-grandfather, as a member of the land-owning elite, feared for his life, so he abandoned the ranch, all his cattle, and virtually everything he owned to make a run for the U.S. border. That's how Aarón's ancestors first arrived in this country, with almost nothing, as part of a massive wave of refugees. More than 890,000 Mexicans fled north to the United States, fugitives from their own people. "I did not know that," Aarón said. "I didn't know that our land was threatened, but I can imagine why. They were probably frowned upon. 'Look at you guys; you're living pretty high on the hog, and we're over here fighting for this country.'" Rafael's wealth made him the enemy.

The ranch didn't fare well. An article from the *Tucson Daily Citizen*, dated March 17, 1915, detailed its fate. "Before the Mexican wars began, the Gabilondos were rated among the richest families in Sonora," Aarón read, "but the various armies have tramped back and forth over their holdings, and large numbers of their cattles and horses have been run off by the bandits." Aarón could only imagine his great-great-grandfather's despair. "Imagine how that must have made you feel as a Mexican national to have your countrymen trampling over your land and disrespecting what you have. That must have been hard for a person to have dealt with that, like your country let you down." But Aarón suspected that his ancestor didn't take the news lying down, and a newspaper article from the *El Paso Herald*, dated April 12, 1913, confirmed that. "Rafael Gabilondo has received permission from the Secretary of Treasury to cross 2,000 head of cattle from the ranches of the Gabilondo Brothers at Monument 66 east of here." After four years of near-constant effort, at the height of the Mexican Revolution, Aarón's great-great-grandfather somehow persuaded the U.S. government to allow him to bring two thousand head of cattle from his ranch to Arizona. How he did it, we don't know. "From my understanding, the Gabilondos were very connected politically, so I'm sure he had ties back in that part, and somebody talked to somebody," Aarón speculated. "He probably had what you call nowadays 'game.'" He certainly had a fortune at risk. Two thousand head of cattle in 1913 cost $34,000; that's the equivalent of close to $800,000 today. Rafael saved his cattle but not his land. In 1920, the rebels finally defeated the Mexican government, and as promised, they redistributed the land, including Rafael's ranch.

A land deed from 1931 proved that Rafael had never given up on returning to his homeland. "I have noted the transition of property between Mr. Augusto Brabazon Urmston and Rafael Gabilondo and Mr. Hilario Gabilondo on the first day of March 1931," Aarón read. The area of the ranch was 39,332 hectares, or 97,000 acres; its price, $45,000 in 1931 dollars. Nineteen years after fleeing his homeland, Rafael and his son Hilario had saved up enough money to buy a new ranch in Mexico, the very ranch where his descendants would live for generations to come and that Aarón dreamed of buying back himself one day. What did Aarón think had drawn his great-great-grandfather back to the land he'd fled? "It was his birthright," he said. "He probably felt, 'That's my land. It was taken from me temporarily, and I'm coming to get it back.'" To Aarón, it was significant that Papi Rafael purchased the land with his son Hilario, Aarón's great-grandfather. "He must have felt like there was a story untold. He probably bought it purposely with his son to show him that 'You're going to carry this legacy. Let me make sure my legacy is preserved.'"

The connection Aarón had always felt to the ranch and to the land where his mother grew up was now even stronger. "I've always been drawn to that part of Mexico, the north. It's very rough out there, and it's dry, and it's arid. It really challenges you as a person to survive in an environment like that. It makes you look at the important things in life, like the people around you and singing songs and listening to one another and eating and all the things that we sometimes forget, living very busy lives. Hopefully down the road somewhere, I'll go back, just like Papi Rafael did."

◼ Rafael's father, Aarón's third great-grandfather Hilario Gabilondo, was a legendary figure in Aarón's family and in Mexican history. "My mom always says that one of your grandparents was celebrated in Mexican history books, and this is the one," Aarón commented. Hilario lived through a very contentious time in Mexican history. He enlisted in the National Guard when he was eighteen, around 1840. After Mexico won its independence from Spain in 1821, its vast northern territory included present-day Texas, Arizona, New Mexico, and California—and expansionist politicians in the United States set their sights on it. Groups of Americans known as filibusters were routinely crossing the border to claim Mexican land as their own. Sonora, where Aarón's third great-grandfather was stationed, was a hotbed of such raids. In January 1857, when one hundred filibusters entered Sonora, the local governor, Ignacio Pesqueira, issued this proclamation: "The people who want to be free must be free. Viva Mexico. Death to the filibusters."

By this time, Aarón's third great-grandfather had risen to the rank of major. The leader of the filibusters was the former U.S. senator Henry Crabb. He ignored the governor's warning and with his men marched ninety miles through the desert to the town of Caborca. It all clicked for Aarón here. "My grandfather was known as the hero of Caborca," he said. On April 1, 1857, the Mexican army ambushed Henry Crabb and his men, but the Americans gained the upper hand and drove the Mexican soldiers into the local church. The Mexicans called for reinforcements, and Aarón's third great-grandfather answered the call. The governor of Sonora received a letter on April 3, 1857, the third day of the battle of Caborca. "Don't be at all surprised when my force arrives, and with the help of the angels, the filibusters will receive an exemplary punishment. The victory will be ours because my heart tells me so." The signature at the bottom belonged to the commander of Mexico's National Guard in Sonora, Aarón's third great-grandfather. After six days of fighting, Hilario Gabilondo and his men, in the little church in Caborca, forced the Americans to surrender. Aarón was blown away. "I guess everybody wants some badasses in their family," he said. Aarón considered his own qualities of leadership. "I'm sure he was the first guy charging. Maybe that's the place where I get it from."

On May 14, 1857, an American newspaper detailed the "horrible atrocities" that occurred in the aftermath of the standoff. "The expedition into Sonora under the command of H. A. Crabb," the article cried, "had the most disastrous end." Following the victory, Aarón's third great-grandfather and his men ruthlessly executed all of the American prisoners, sparing only the youngest filibuster, a sixteen-year-old boy—a mercy carried out, according to an official military account of the massacre, of Hilario's own accord. The leader of the Americans, Henry Crabb, was found dead, his body riddled with more than one hundred bullets. His head was completely severed and preserved in mescal. The bodies of the other Americans were left in the desert to be eaten by birds. As gruesome as the scene was, Aarón wasn't ready to condemn his ancestor and his men for their brutality. "Mexicans must have been really resentful toward Americans and what they were probably telling people Mexico was like, that it was overrun with people who had no scruples and no morals. They were probably thinking to themselves, we were fine down here before you guys tried to take our land. So I can't tell you I feel sorry for these gentlemen, these filibusters. When you try to take something by force, this is what happens. The rubber met the road, as they say."

There was more to the story of the executions than we first suspected. Our researchers found a letter Hilario submitted to the *Weekly Arizonan* on April 7, 1859, two years after the battle of Caborca. "It comes to my hearing that the American populace charge me with the execution of the unfortunate men who perished at Caborca on the 7th of April 1857 at the time of Crabb's invasion, but I did not give such an order," Aarón's third great-grandfather wrote. "The duty of every officer is to obey without having a right to investigate the case. The boy who was saved by me visited the school and lived with my family until he preferred to return to California." Hilario had been called a butcher, but he said he was just following orders. Aarón was skeptical. "Can you say honestly, 'Hey, man, I put to rest one hundred people'? I'm sure there had to be some chain of command, some sort of accountability, but I'm pretty sure he acted with strong conviction."

In Mexico, Aarón's ancestor is still celebrated as a hero, the man who saved the Sonora region from American imperialism. But in researching Hilario's life, we came across his baptismal record, and made a surprising discovery: Aarón's third great-grandfather, the hero of Caborca, the cele-brated Mexican soldier, wasn't born in Mexico at all. He was born in Bilbao, Spain, in the Basque region, in 1822, one year after Mexico gained its independence from Spain. He migrated to Mexico when he was eighteen years old, in 1840, and enlisted in the Mexican military shortly after his arrival. Was Aarón's third great-grandfather seeking a land of opportunity, a promised land, or was there something more behind his decision to leave his native land of Spain?

Hilario, it turned out, was fleeing a country in turmoil. In 1833, when Hilario was just eleven years old, the Spanish king, Ferdinand VII, died, and the country broke out into a bloody civil war over the succession to the throne. The fighting was especially fierce in the Basque region, and Hilario's birthplace of Bilbao was the site of a major battle in 1836. More than a thousand people died in that battle alone, a tenth of the population of the small town. To escape the war in Spain, Hilario fled to Mexico, thus launching Aarón's Mexican family. But he left deep roots behind. We were able to trace Aarón's maternal ancestors all the way back to his sixth great-grandfather Martín Andrés Gabilondo, born on March 31, 1713, in Guipuzcoa, also in the Basque country.

In Aarón's mind, his family history had started in Mexico, but his roots in Spain were actually far deeper. It was a part of his heritage he had never embraced. "I do love the way Spaniards live their lives. It's very free-flowing, and they concentrate on the important things of life, like eating and having holiday with their family," he said. But he had always felt detached from his Spanish roots. "I've researched a little bit of the Spanish atrocities in Mexico, and it's not a really nice history, everything from the eradication of indigenous Mexicans to slavery to all those things that are not pretty, so maybe subconsciously I don't want to be associated with that." But in looking at his own ancestors, he looked beyond the history books. "If you look at my family's history, it had nothing to do with conquering people and subjugating them to pain and hardship. I guess I need to be a little bit more open-minded. I need to shake a little bit of that chip off my shoulder and understand that the family tree has very deep roots in Spain."

Aarón noted the bravery and determination that ran through all of his mother's ancestors. "One of the things I'm seeing out of all these different generations is the fact that they're all very courageous. They wanted some semblance in their life of stability. That's why they wanted to have a place where they could have ample land and provide for the generations to come." For Aarón, that stability was still found in Mexico, but we had opened a new window onto his past, and he felt that it would change the way he described himself. "I consider myself having more Mexican roots, but now I'm saying we're from Mexico by way of Basque country." He remembered a project he did years ago, when he was in junior high school, and he had to make a family tree. "I did a family cactus instead of a family tree. Maybe my son will do a family cactus."

■ The paper trail for Aarón's mother's family had taken us across the ocean, back to eighteenth-century Spain. Now we turned to his father's family tree. Adolfo Sánchez was born on August 7, 1939, in Valentine, Texas. His father kept stories about his family close to the vest. "There's an old saying—you don't talk about things that hurt you sometimes—and my dad was one of those guys." Valentine was a very small town, and Aarón's paternal grandparents led a hard life. According to the 1940 census for Jefferson County, Texas, the highest level of school Aarón's grandfather completed was first grade, his grandmother second. "They were just these real simple people," Aarón said of his Sánchez grandparents. "His mom, my grandmother, was illiterate, and my grandfather, he worked laying track for sixty years in Texas, and when he died, he wanted to be buried in a burlap sack by the railroad. My dad must have been very affected by that, because he probably thought he couldn't go farther than just down the road." But he did go much farther, through sheer force of will and determination. "At that time, he was one of the few Mexican Americans to go to college, and he got a master's in criminology at a time when Mexicans Americans didn't even finish high school."

Adolfo Sánchez died from complications of bypass surgery when Aarón was only thirteen years old. His memories of his father were vivid, and the pictures he painted of him made it seem as if Adolfo were standing in front of us. "My dad used to pick us up from the airport at the gate, and he used to wear his cowboy boots, and there was this gentleman who always shined his boots, so every time we'd leave the airport, he'd always get his boots shined." He was what Aarón called "a man's kind of man." "He had a soft spot for the ladies. He was always impeccably dressed, always looked sharp, always smelled great, very well groomed." When we first met Aarón, he had described himself as nurturing. This trait came from his father as much as it did his mother. "I'm like my dad because I have this real need, like he did, to take care of people and be Big Papa. I do that a lot in my life. I want to be the strong one." His father's loss was still very profound for Aarón. "I miss him dearly," he said. "Anytime you lose your old man, it hurts you in many different ways, because he's your first hero. Now as a father to a son, I'm very conscious of that."

Who was this complicated man? We started with a look at his parents, Aarón's paternal grandparents, Francisco Sánchez and Ramona Rodriguez. Aarón's grandfather Francisco was born on March 9, 1912, in Ojinaga, Mexico, and his grandmother Ramona was born on New Year's Day, January 1, 1913, in Brackettville, Texas. His grandfather, he said, "was a very tough guy, very big man. He had this old washed-out tattoo on his arm, and he didn't talk much, to me at least. He was sweet when he had to be, but we didn't have that connection." It was entirely different with his grandmother. "She lived not far from us in El Paso, and she was the grandmother who gave the wet kiss. But I never used to mind it," he said. "She had this high-pitched voice. She was so sweet. She was very textbook grandmother."

Francisco Sánchez, Aarón's grandfather, was his first immigrant ancestor. He had emigrated from Mexico to Texas to work for the railroad, and he and his wife settled in the town of Valentine. Aarón had visited Valentine; in a word, he said it was "bleak." "It was cryptic. You walk in, and it's like one light doing that thing. No one's there. Everything's dilapidated, like a movie set." It was sobering for Aarón to see where his grandparents lived and where his father was born. "I can imagine growing up in that, and seeing his parents live like that, he's like, I'm not going to do that."

We wanted to see how far back we could trace Aarón's paternal ancestors in Mexico. A birth certificate for Aarón's third great-grandmother Trinidad Oros, who was born in Mexico on June 28, 1828, led us to an interesting, never-told family story. Her parents, according to the birth certificate, were José Ignacio Ronquillo and María Antonia Oros, Aarón's fourth great-grandparents. José was born in Chihuahua around 1781, two years before the end of the American Revolution, and María was born around 1800. Mexican birth records and marriage records were a key part of our search for Aarón's ancestors, revealing as they often did not just one but two generations of forebears. But the marriage record for José Ignacio Ronquillo and María Antonia Oros was nowhere to be found. There was a simple reason for that: it didn't exist. Aarón's fourth great-grandfather was already married to someone else, a woman named Rafaela Gabilondo. According to their marriage license, they were married on January 9, 1803, in Jiménez, Chihuahua. In 1894, several years after her father's death, Aarón's third great-grandmother Trinidad Oros gave a deposition in a Texas courtroom that confirmed this. Her father and her mother had had an affair, she explained, and her parents and her father's "legitimate wife," along with José and Rafaela's three daughters, Trinidad's half-sisters, all lived within the walls of the Presidio del Norte.

A presidio is a fortress, and we wondered what brought Aarón's ancestors there. The Casa Ronquillo in Ojinaga, Mexico, which still stands today, was built by Aarón's fourth great-grandfather in the early 1830s on the border of Mexico and southwestern Texas. The land here was undesirable. There was no gold, no silver, and few laborers. It was farm country, but the land wasn't particularly fertile, and Apache Indians constantly raided the communities of non-Indians that tried to take root there. The military forced convicts to work the desert as farmers, to serve as a buffer against the Apaches. The Mexican government tried to attract settlers through land giveaways, but very few people came to the uninviting spot. "If you ever go to Valentine, Texas, and see where my dad's side of the family is, it's very bleak as well," he said, referring back to his father's birthplace. "So there's something in their bloodline that they can see something out of nothing."

José Ignacio Ronquillo, it turned out, had a perfectly good reason for setting up his families inside the walls of the presidio. We found a military service record for soldiers in the Nueva Vizcaya province, a region on the border of Mexico that later became Chihuahua and Durango. Aarón's fourth great-grandfather was the don of several of the frontier presidios, and he played a crucial role in helping the Mexicans defend their territory. In 1832 he negotiated a peace treaty with the Apaches, who agreed to suspend their raids in exchange for food and rations. Unfortunately, the peace didn't hold. An obituary published in the Mexican newspaper *El Fanal* on February 20, 1835, revealed the sad outcome of the failed treaty. "Lieutenant Colonel José Ignacio Ronquillo left with 155 men. The party returned to the Presidio without their leader, the aforementioned, Lieutenant Colonel Ronquillo, whose life ended in Ojo Caliente." Aarón was intensely proud of his ancestor. "Zapata had this great saying that I had tattooed on my back that says, 'I'd rather die on my feet than live my life on my knees.'" Aarón's ancestors, on both sides of his family tree, had been engaged in every major contretemps in the history of Mexico. They fought the Spanish; they fought the Apaches; they fought the Americans. "This is good to see, not just that they were soldiers, but they were also people that wanted peace. They were doing what they had to do."

What became of José Ignacio Ronquillo's families? After he was killed, Rafaela, his wife, took their three daughters and left the presidio, but his mistress, Aarón's fourth great-grandmother, was left behind with her young daughter Trinidad. A woman alone on the frontier must have been quite vulnerable, but she made a life for herself. She raised Aarón's third great-grandmother in Ojinaga, where, remarkably, Aarón's family stayed for four more generations. His grandfather was born there almost 150 years later, and Casa Ronquillo remains. Aarón had deep, deep roots in Ojinaga, and deep ties not only to the Mexican landscape but to Mexican history.

■ Aarón's astonishing paper trail ended here. We had traced his ancestors on his father's side as far back as José Ignacio Ronquillo's father, Aarón's fifth great-grandfather José Ramón Ronquillo, who was born in Sonora, Mexico, in 1751. On his mother's side, we were able to go back to his sixth great-grandfather Martín Gabilondo, born in Guipuzcoa, in the Basque region of Spain, on March 31, 1713. Looking at his unfurled family tree, he was awestruck. "You're looking at a legacy that's so strong, that really affects everything that I do currently." Not least of all, it would affect his cooking. "I feel that it's my duty to research the food of the Basque country now. I have to pay homage to them," he said. "On the flip side, I also want to learn a little bit more about northern Chihuahuan cuisine, especially from that area where my dad's side of the family is from."

Now we would look even more deeply into Aarón's ancestral past by analyzing his DNA. As many of our participants do, Aarón suspected he had Native American blood. "It calls to me a lot," he told us. "I feel that when I travel in Mexico, any Latin American country, I'm drawn to the story and the family circle of indigenous people." For most of them, long-circulated rumors among family members proved to be just that: rumors. Would his DNA tell us something that his genealogy hadn't? We gave him three different DNA tests. The first measured his admixture, his percentages of European, sub-Saharan African, and East Asian / Native American ancestry from about the last five hundred years. Aarón's breakdown was 66.4 percent European, 3.7 percent sub-Saharan African, and a very substantial 24.5 Native American. At nearly a quarter of his genome, Aarón's percentage translated to the equivalent of having one grandparent who was fully Native American. In Aarón's case, some version of the prevailing myth of the Native great-grandmother that so many Americans insisted they had was true. Furthermore, the 3.7 percent sub-Saharan African reading was significant enough that one of Aarón's third great-grandparents, or possibly even a second great-grandparent, could have been fully black. "This is very interesting for me," Aarón said, "because you think about the travels of your family ancestors, and you think about what it means in hard numbers. It's pretty cool."

By breaking down the components of Aarón's European ancestry, we uncovered a secret heritage that was nowhere to be found in his paper trail. While more than half of his European DNA was Iberian, or Spanish, he also had small percentages of Ashkenazi Jewish, North African, and Middle Eastern DNA, all of which suggested a history of hidden Sephardic Jewish ancestry. The genealogy didn't reflect Jewish ancestry, but historically it made sense. In 1492, the same year that Columbus discovered America, Queen Isabella and King Ferdinand expelled all the Jews from Spain, forcing them to convert or be killed if they stayed. Those who converted were called Conversos or Reversos. We believe that some of Aarón's ancestors may have migrated to the New World in search of refuge. These so-called Crypto-Jews concealed the practice of their Jewish faith in public, adopting the ways of Catholics, but at home they remained practicing Jews. According to DNA analysis, Aarón likely had up to 20 percent Sephardic Jewish ancestry—approximately the equivalent of one grandparent—a mixture so substantial that it appears his Jewish ancestors may have continued to marry within the Jewish community in Mexico for generations, Crypto-Jews marrying Crypto-Jews. Interestingly, Aarón said that his mother always had an affinity for Judaism. "That's why my name is Aarón. My mom loved Judaism because it was really about community and about family and tight-knittedness." Maybe that pull was encoded in Zarela's DNA.

In addition to his admixture, we also tested Aarón's mitochondrial DNA, which he inherited from his mother, and his Y-DNA, which came from his father. His maternal haplogroup, a genetic population group of people who share a common ancestor, was a distinctly Native American signature. Although we were unable to determine to which tribe Aarón's ancestor belonged, we could say with certainty that he was descended from a Native American woman. His Y-DNA told us a less surprising story. His paternal haplogroup took us directly back to Europe, where it is found in low frequencies in many populations across the continent, including Iberia. Aarón's DNA results were the reverse of what he'd expected. "The way I always perceived my dad is they lived in more of a rough part of the country, and where they came up with the Apaches and all that, I just would have thought he would have had more of the Native blood, and my mom more of the European." Mexico was a place where Spanish colonists, Native Americans, and African American slaves had mixed in a violent history that ultimately produced a profoundly diverse people. Aarón was the heir to that legacy.

■ For all that Aarón knew coming into this journey, he had never realized how deeply entwined his family's personal history was with that of Mexico. "The most insightful thing or surprising thing was the fact that we come from a family of warriors on both sides," he said, "and that people made enormous sacrifice to be able to provide a better life for my ancestors. It makes me feel proud. We've made our mark."

Both of Aarón's family trees were populated by people who exhibited tremendous determination and bravery. Did their experiences inform the person Aarón was today, or was it his own experiences, or possibly DNA, that had the greatest impact? Aarón felt that hardships he had faced defined him. "Who knows that I would have been the man I am today if my father were still alive? I felt like I had to be the man of the family, and I think that's really a big part of it, losing my father." But his heritage, and the Spanish language itself, also shaped his identity. "I've traveled a lot in Mexico to understand that side of myself, kept up with my Spanish, which is a big part of it. A lot of people claim, 'I'm Mexican,' 'I'm Latino,' 'I'm Hispanic,' and they don't speak their language. There's a big saying in Spanish: 'When you lose your tongue, you lose your country.'"

If Aarón could cook for just one of the many ancestors he'd met today, who would it be, and what would he serve them? "Every time someone asks me that, I always say my grandmother," Aarón responded. "But now, considering this lineage, I think I would have loved to have cooked for my great-great-great-grandfather, Hilario, the hero." Hilario's significance not just to Aarón's family but to all of Mexico had left a tremendous impression on his third great-grandson. "I would have loved to have been able to make the meal after he won that victory. I would have served him maybe a bunch of whole roasted pigs. I would have had some women making tortillas. We would have had chickens. We would have had to slaughter some animals to hammer home how special it was. Maybe mole, something that takes a long time. When the battle was over, I would cook the fiesta for them."

Aarón clearly believed in food's ability to connect with our roots. "Food tells a story. It's a language we all speak," he said. "I think we chose food to be the one thing that reminds us of our past and our roots, and in this case, it's so evident that, just as the DNA in my background has been exposed today, the recipes are that constant factor that's always there, that's getting passed down. I'm still cooking my grandmother's food that she grew up eating from Anita, her mom. I'm still cooking those recipes to this day at my restaurant." For Aarón, food was the link. "It's a way of paying respect to your legacy and where you're from."

With every dish they prepare, Tom Colicchio, Ming Tsai, and Aarón Sánchez honor their ancestors and enrich their legacy. Just like their ancestors, new immigrants come to America every day, bringing their own recipes and their own ideas, broadening our sense of who we are as people, adding new flavors to our country's history as they celebrate their own.

CHAPTER SIX

We Come from People

African American families were too often casualties of the Civil War and the long years leading up to it, children sold away from their parents and marriages between enslaved men and women not recognized or respected. The utter disregard for the sanctity of slave families did not prevent them from forming and even from flourishing, as we would see in the case of the ancestors of the hip-hop artist Nasir Jones, the actor Angela Bassett, and the presidential advisor Valerie Jarrett. The relationships we found on the family trees of Nas, Angela, and Valerie, the connections we uncovered, were astounding in both their complexity and their endurance, often straddling the line between slavery and freedom.

Nasir Jones (b. 1973)

Nasir bin Olu Dara Jones, the musical pioneer better known as Nas, released his first album, *Illmatic*, in 1994, and he has been an unstoppable force in hip-hop ever since. Born in Brooklyn, New York, on September 14, 1973, he has always felt a strong connection to his community, both past and present. "I've always rapped about African kings and queens," he said, "and I've always read about African history and Timbuktu and all these great places that taught the world everything they know." He borrowed equal inspiration from his immediate surroundings. Nas grew up in New

York City's Queensbridge Apartments, the largest public housing project in the United States. "Queens to me felt like the Emerald City. It felt like Manhattan, Brooklyn, Bronx, Staten Island. It felt like all the cities combined in one. It was exciting, a great place to meet people from all walks." As a child, he was in awe of his surroundings, and the people around him were his kings and queens. "I thought everybody was strong. I thought everyone was powerful, because I was so small. Everyone else, they looked like they were monsters, mountains. There was a community to it, definitely."

That community began to fracture as crack insinuated its way into the city in the 1980s, taking its toll on people he knew. "It got out of control when you started to see people who you had respect for become nothing. Beautiful queens, beautiful women who you looked up to, like, 'That's going to be my wife when I grow up,' become the total opposite," he said. "When friends of mine, their moms would succumb to it, that was hard."

Nas didn't always want to be a musician. "I was looking at being a writer," he explained. "I had a typewriter, so I would set up our room like an office." School didn't engage the restless teenager, and he never graduated from high school. He admitted that he could have worked harder, but that was only part of the equation. "I felt like school should have done more to reach me and not allow me and people like me to get lost," he said. He became enamored of the philosophy of the Black Panthers. They were long gone by that time, but they were his models for political engagement in the black community. "I was still enraged by the injustice around the world at that point and the injustice even in the schools, with the fact that I wasn't learning this stuff in school, and that all people weren't learning enough about their roots in school. No matter if they were Italian, whether they were Chinese or whatever, we weren't collectively learning about each other. I thought that was a big problem."

In the 1980s, Queensbridge was a mecca for the burgeoning hip-hop scene, a place where talented young artists were expressing their frustrations about a system that seemed stacked against them, but it was also becoming an increasingly violent place. When Nas was eighteen, he went through what he calls "one of the darkest moments of my life." His younger brother, Jabari, and his close friend William Graham were shot during an argument in the projects. Jabari survived, but Will didn't. "It affected me in the most deep way. At that moment it didn't change me. It brought me down. I felt like I was in a war. I felt like Vietnam soldiers must have felt. I thought I was next. I didn't see any light down the tunnel." Will's death had a lasting impact on Nas's music. "I shout him out a lot—Ill Will." At that point, though, Nas hadn't yet found his voice. "I didn't have music at that point. I didn't have anything. You know, we was just there."

Before long he embraced hip-hop as his art. "Hip-hop was the raw expression of American youth, and the rhythm of it was like a combination of all musics combined into one," Nas said of its pull. "It was so raw and so honest that you couldn't mistake hip-hop for shucking and jiving or trying to just be mainstream, trying to fit in. It was the music of my soul." Hip-hop is the voice of Nas's generation, but it also keeps the tradition of the past alive through sampling, through citation, through echoing, through quotation. Just as Nas's musical ancestors play a part in his art, he believes that his African ancestors play a part in his life. "I'm cut from that cloth. I'm a part of them, and I feel like they're helping guide me today. They're around me."

■ Nas's music may be synonymous with life in New York's tough inner city, but his family's roots are deeply southern, beginning with his mother. Fannie Ann Little, known to her friends as Ann, was born in Steeles Township, Richmond County, North Carolina, on September 19, 1941. Nas's mother died in 2002 after a long battle with cancer. Despite her many years of living in the city, her rural North Carolina upbringing came through to her sons. "She was New Yorker–fied, but the country, the southernness, it was there in her cooking and how she grew up. She'd tell us about where she grew up. It was there, yeah."

Ann was determined that Nas and his brother forge ties with her ancestral home in North Carolina, and each summer she made a ritual of sending the boys down South to spend time with their grandparents, Mack and Nannie Little, and her extended family. For Nas, it was "culture shock in its highest form." "Now it's not such a long trip from New York to North Carolina, but then it felt like we were on another planet. Two weeks at Grandma's house, and it felt like a year." Despite his mother's best intentions, North Carolina never felt like home. "At first it felt like we were in a time machine and had wound up back on the plantation," he said. "They weren't into TV, and actually where my grandma stayed, out there they had outhouses, bathrooms outside, and then sometimes even a bucket." He learned to appreciate it on a certain level, but New York was never far from his mind. "Walking around with no shoes on, just bare feet on hot rocks and dirt and grass, that was cool. But I wasn't really an outdoorsy kind of dude. What I noticed is that we could see the skies better. There were no skyscrapers and probably less smog. And I noticed the Big Dipper for the first time in my life out there." He laughed. "I appreciated skyscrapers more."

Nas didn't know that this small township in North Carolina was home to an entire branch of his family tree. To get started with our journey into his roots, we consulted the 1940 federal census, where we found Nas's grandparents, Mack Little Jr., born on February 6, 1918, and Nannie Little (maiden name also Little) born on February 29, 1920. Both were born in Steeles Township, just like their daughter. Nas was very close with them. "My grandfather Mack, everyone called him Snoot. Snoot walked with one leg that was stiff because he had been shot in the knee. He didn't properly take care of it. He would slide that leg because it was stiff, and you'd hear him coming from the back of the house to the porch. He had these cool trousers on, these old-school trousers on, his shoes and his button shirt. Very stern figure, stern individual, and he was the man of the house." Nas's grandparents seemed to come to life as he spoke of them. "And Nan was the cutest thing. She was more down-to-earth, not strict at all, more let the kids do what they want to do. Very southern. They both talked with real southern accents. I have her name tattooed on my back."

As we went further back on Nas's family tree, we discovered a distinct naming pattern in his family. We had already seen that his grandmother's maiden and married name were the same: Little. A staggering five generations of male and female Littles had married spouses also named Little, and almost every one of them came from the same town. We methodically collected the names of all of the Little ancestors of every branch of Nas's mother's family tree, tracing each of these lines as far back as we could through the 1870 census, the first in which African Americans were recorded by name. We recovered the names of three sets of Nas's third great-grandparents, all born deep in slavery, and every single one with the surname Little: Wade Little, born around 1837, and Frankey Little, born around 1830 (Nas's great-great-grandfather Mack Sr.'s parents); Andrew Little, born around 1814, and Fannie Little, born around 1825 (his great-great-grandmother's Celie's parents); and Calvin Little, born around 1824, and Pocahontas Little, born around 1844 (his great-great-grandfather Patrick's parents).

How had all these people come by the same last name? The 1910 census for Richmond County contained an intriguing detail. Living next door to Nas's great-grandmother Fannie, then twenty-two, and her parents, Nas's great-great-grandparents Mack Sr. and Celie, was a seventy-eight-year-old woman also named Fannie Little. But this Fannie Little was white, and, we learned, she was more than just a neighbor. She was the daughter-in-law of a man named Thomas Little, whose name we discovered in the 1850 Slave Schedule, a part of the federal census on which the only names recorded belonged to slave owners; slaves were listed anonymously, identified only by age, gender, and color. Thomas Little owned ninety-nine slaves. Because of the tremendous number of slave descriptions recorded, it was impossible for us to identify Nas's ancestors among them. To know for sure that his ancestors were the property of the Little family, we needed names, and the only document that could be reliably counted upon to contain slaves' names was a will.

The will Thomas Little left in 1857 confirmed what we had suspected to be the truth. On his death, Thomas Little left stocks and bonds, livestock, more than two thousand acres of property, and sixty-seven slaves to his widow, Elizabeth. He divided the remainder of the slaves in lots among his three children. Nas's third great-grandfather Calvin, part of a group "consisting of Jim, Rosetta and child, Mariah, Haywood, Rodney, Tillman, Calvin," was willed to Thomas Little's youngest son, Benjamin Franklin Little, a lawyer who would six years hence lose an arm in the last day of fighting at Gettysburg on July 3, 1863. When Benjamin Franklin Little inherited his slaves in 1857, there was no indication that slavery would ever end. Nas contemplated the lives and minds of his slave ancestors. "I wonder how they felt about themselves," Nas said. "I wonder about the love of selves. I wonder what they thought about life, and what kind of people they were. I try to picture how they looked, how they got through the day, what were the happy times like." Nas guessed that joy and sorrow mingled. While nothing had been left behind to offer insight into their emotional lives, the meticulous record keeping of Calvin's owner, Benjamin Franklin Little, afforded us a rare glimpse into the daily lives of his slaves.

In 1854 Nas's third great-grandfather Calvin was about thirty years old, and his master's "Ledger of cotton picked per slave, October 1854," details the pounds of cotton Calvin picked every day. Nas read the daily reckoning: "One hundred fifty. It looks like 200. Next to that, 78, 49. He must have been tired that day. The next day he's picking up 54. The next day is a blank. He probably told them to go screw themselves." The list continued: "96, 120, 123. On the 13th, 134; the 14th, 173." In front of Nas was a slave owner's take on the measure of a man, Nas's third great-grandfather. "It was his money; it was his business," Nas commented. On another ledger,

Benjamin Franklin Little recorded Nas's ancestors' value in dollars. According to his owner, Calvin was worth $900—$25,000 in today's currency. "This is painful now. To see that, that hurts." Nas was disgusted. "You can't put a price on a human being," he said. "Just to think that they were OK with doing this, OK with this system. I mean, money will drive man into madness, the need of it."

Slaves were extremely valuable commodities, and for the first time in Benjamin Franklin Little's exhaustive records we came across a mention of Calvin's wife, Nas's third great-grandmother Pocahontas. What we found was the rarest document an African American can find when researching the roots of their slave ancestors: a bill of sale. Written on a preprinted receipt, the transaction was dated March 27, 1859, the year of John Brown's raid on Harpers Ferry and two years before the Civil War broke out. "Received of Benjamin Franklin Little $830 being in full for the purchase of a Negro slave named Pocahontas." Pocahontas was about fourteen or fifteen years old when Benjamin Franklin Little bought her. "This is a receipt for a human being," Nas said. "What was in the mind of Pocahontas, knowing she was stock, like she was like cattle? This is real people," he said. The next year, according to yet another document compiled by Benjamin Franklin Little, this one labeled "Birth of Negros," Pocahontas gave birth to "her first child, a daughter, born June 14, 1860, and died age three days." Nas's own daughter's birthday was just one day later, June 15. "Letty, another girl, was born June 10, 1861. Her third child named—left blank, born March 12, 1864." That third child was a son, one of Nas's great-great grandfathers, Patrick Little.

In the winter of 1861, the year the Civil War began, Nas's third great-grandparents' owner detailed all of the winter clothing he distributed to his slaves. Calvin received a winter coat, and Pocahontas received a winter dress. "I'm wearing gold. They had to wear chains," Nas said. "I'm wearing a gold chain. This chain means so much more to me now than just style or flash or status. It means we changed those chains of pain into chains of freedom." Nas connected with his ancestors on virtually every level. And while he felt "anger, amazement, sadness" on seeing a dollar sign next to the names of his great-great-great-grandparents, he also felt something else: gratitude. "I'm grateful to the record keepers, to have this here. These are the records of these people's existence, whereas without going into this, maybe no one would ever mention their names again, ever. Something is becoming alive in me."

■ The end of the Civil War would profoundly change the lives of African Americans at the most intimate levels. As we learned from the plantation records of Benjamin Franklin Little, Nas's third great-grandmother gave birth to three children while enslaved on his plantation. Marriage between slaves was not recognized, but it was clear from a court document filed with Richmond County's justice of the peace on August 11, 1866, that Nas's third great-grandparents Calvin and Pocahontas had begun to build their family together in slavery, with no guarantee that their family would be allowed to remain intact. "The following named persons, Freemen, have given me their names and wish to be recognized as man and wife, and state that they have been living together as such before they were freed." Calvin and Pocahontas's names were among the seven couples listed, most of whom shared the surname Little. A second set of Nas's third great-grandparents, Fannie and Andrew "Andy" Little, the parents of his second great-grandmother Celie, who was the neighbor of the white Fannie Little, stated that they had been living together as husband and wife within the institution of slavery for a stunning thirty years.

Almost to a person, the Little slaves and their descendants stayed in Richmond County, North Carolina, for generations, keeping their master's surname and marrying each other. Their families had not been divided during slavery; children weren't sold away from their mothers. The ties they formed—with each other, with the land, even with their masters' family—endured in freedom. They didn't change their name, because that name linked them to each other and to their past. "It's like changing the word 'Africa,'" Nas speculated. "It wasn't made up. Africa comes from a guy's name. But the name has a great ring to it. So they're in this place where they were born; they worked hard; they survived. They fought to survive. This is home. This is every bit of their home as it was for Benjamin Franklin Little. They built this place. They were used to it, down-home country people." A book called *From These Ruins*, written by a descendant of Benjamin Franklin Little named A. W. McAlister, hinted at the connection. "Family lore holds that the Emancipation Proclamation was read to the slaves at the end of the war and that they were told that they were free to go," Nas read. "Supposedly, only one chose to do so and subsequently is said to have returned."

Fifty-five years after the end of slavery, in fact, we found Nas's ancestors still living next door to the woman whose family had owned them. Furthermore, as free people, they continued to work for her, although a document called "Plantation Rules and Regulations" revealed that, on the land of Fannie Little, there was little difference between slavery and freedom. "During working hours no general conversation is to be allowed," Nas read. "And all stopping of work for the purpose of talking except what may be necessary to the carrying on of work is strictly forbidden." Nas paused. "I thought slavery was over." Nas's ancestors were sharecroppers, and sharecropping was a system that supported the former masters' attempts to hold on to slavery in everything but name. More than a half century after emancipation, freedom was not yet synonymous with equality.

Nas now understood why his mother, Ann, sent him and his brother down South every summer. "I'm born in New York, and for me the whole world starts there. But what this means right now is that it doesn't start with me, of course. It starts with my mom and my pop, but this goes before even them, and I'm learning more about my purpose and why I'm here. I'm starting to feel like I'm here for a reason, and these people didn't live in vain. These people didn't die in vain. This is because of them. They made this happen."

■ On both sides of his family, the born-and-bred New Yorker Nas had deep roots in the South. His father, Olu Dara, given the name Charles Jones III at birth, was born on January 12, 1941, in Natchez, Mississippi, the oldest of seven children. A well-known and respected musician himself, Nas's father chose the Yoruba name, meaning "God is good," for himself and then passed it on to his son. "That was the age of consciousness, maybe the '60s. People were becoming more aware, more free, and he wanted to connect back to his roots," Nas said. "As a kid I didn't like that name. I wanted a name like Michael or Tony, but I grew into it, and I love it now."

Nas's parents separated when he was still in elementary school. His father traveled extensively as a musician, and Nas became entranced by his vagabond lifestyle. As a young man he decided to follow in his father's footsteps. "I was really fascinated by all the countries he had been to," Nas recalled. "The music he played at the time with the trumpet, it was cool, but I didn't understand it. It was really old school. And then even with the African rhythm he's playing, from the moment when I heard it, it was like, 'I get what you're doing, but it's not what I would listen to if you weren't around.'" They collaborated on Nas's album *Street Disciple*, his father playing the trumpet on a song called "Bridging the Gap."

Nas's father had been playing music for his entire life. By the time he was seven years old, little Charles Jones was playing drums and trumpet in Natchez's College Heights Community Center's traveling children's band, the Rabbit Foot Minstrels, their tour bus emblazoned on the side with the words "The Greatest Colored Show on Earth" and a large "Sambo" face. The Rabbit Foot Minstrels were a legendary performance troupe. Founded in 1900, they traveled throughout the South on the famed Chitlin Circuit, singing, dancing, and performing comedy skits for segregated black audiences. They launched the careers of Ma Rainey and Rufus Thomas. In the 1960s, Nas's father played in the Navy Band, one of the oldest professional musical organizations in the United States, where many notable jazz musicians, including John Coltrane, Clark Terry, and Cannonball Adderley, got their start.

Who were the individuals who had raised this independent, talented man? Nas's father's parents were both born in Mississippi, Charles Rufus Jones II in Natchez on August 16, 1914, and Ella Mae Jones in Canton on March 17, 1911. Coincidentally, Ella Mae's maiden name was Jones, but this was an extremely common surname, very different from the story on the Little side of the family. As he had done with his maternal grandmother, Nannie Little, Nas had Ella Mae's name tattooed on his neck, literally displaying a deep passion for his roots. "Those are like the queen empresses," he said. "My mom was a hell of a woman, but even before her there were more serious women, and those women were amazing women."

Nas's paternal grandparents were both teachers, having met as students at Campbell College in Jackson, Mississippi, which is now part of the historically black university Jackson State University. His grandfather was also a musician. In the 1930s he performed with a group called the Melotones, which traveled to churches and college campuses singing gospel and Negro spirituals. For musical inspiration, though, Nas turned not to his father or grandfather, but to his great-grandmother Rosa Johnson, whom everyone called Rosie. She was born in Natchez, Mississippi, in 1878. According to Nas's father, Rosie sang spirituals constantly around the house, and when the children asked her a question, she answered in verse. It was Rosie, in fact, who sent Nas's father for his first formal music lessons, at the College Heights Community Center, and connected him with the Rabbit Foot Minstrels. The musical talent in this family hadn't skipped a single generation. If musical aptitude was genetic, scientists hadn't yet been able to prove it, but Nas was willing to believe such a gene existed. "There's got to be something," he said. "This is not by accident."

The 1920 census for Madison County, Mississippi, allowed us to go back to Nas's great-grandparents on Nas's father's mother's line. Nas's great-grandparents were both born in Mississippi, his great-grandfather Charley Jones Jr. in Madison County on December 16, 1881, and his great-grandmother Letitia Jackson around 1883. Like so many of Nas's ancestors, his great-grandparents lived under the horrific conditions of Jim Crow Mississippi. Black people who didn't own property barely entered the public record. Without land deeds, wills, or property records in their names, it was hard to learn much about their lives. The common names Jones and Jackson posed a problem as well. Fortunately it was not insurmountable, and we successfully located two sets of Nas's paternal great-great-grandparents in the 1870 and 1880 censuses: great-grandfather Charley Jones's parents, Charles and Pleasant Jones, who were both listed as farm laborers, and great-grandmother Letitia Jackson's parents, Thornton and Ella Jackson. Ultimately we managed to identify nine of Nas's paternal ancestors who were born in slavery in Mississippi. Even without the detailed records that we'd been so fortunate to find on his mother's line, we took Nas back almost two hundred years on his father's side, too. Jones was simply too common a name for us to find the name of the white man who owned them.

■ DNA couldn't give us names, but it would take us further back in Nas's ancestry than any paper trail could. We had traced his genealogy back, on both sides of his family, to the first half of the nineteenth century. On his mother's side, the oldest ancestors we identified were both born in North Carolina, Pierson Jones, born around 1815, and Liney Green, born around 1820. On his father's side, his oldest ancestors were his great-great-grandparents George Saunders, born around 1831, and a woman named Isabella, born around 1835, both in Mississippi.

Every one of Nas's ancestors we had documented was born in either North Carolina or Mississippi. His DNA would take us far from the American South. We administered three DNA tests to Nas: one using his mitochondrial DNA, which would allow us to trace his mother's direct maternal line; one using his Y-DNA, which would allow us to trace his father's direct paternal line; and one called an admixture test, which measures an individual's percentages of European, sub-Saharan African, and East Asian / Native American ancestry since around the time of Columbus. We started with his admixture results, which were 82 percent sub-Saharan African, 15 percent European, and 1.5 percent Native American. His Native American result was approximately double that of the average African American and translated roughly to descent from a fourth or fifth great-grandparent of full Native American ancestry. A breakdown of Nas's European ancestry showed that it was primarily from northern Europe, most likely Great Britain.

We turned our focus to Nas's African DNA. The largest percentage of his DNA, 36 percent, had its roots in Nigeria, with the second largest amount, 15 percent, from the countries of Benin and Togo, home to the Yoruba people, from whom Nas's father had taken his name. "He must have felt it. Something in him felt it, and he named himself Olu Dara. Thank God it was the right choice," Nas said. "It turns out he knew what he was doing." Other countries represented in Nas's DNA were Mali, the Ivory Coast, and Ghana, each measuring at 10 percent; Cameroon and Congo, at 7 percent; and Senegal, at 3 percent. Nas's African DNA came to him through people brought over from the countries represented in the transatlantic slave trade. His genome presented us with something unusual: 3 percent traced back to the hunter-gatherers of South Central Africa. Out of the 388,000 slaves brought to the United States, only about 1,200 came from South Africa. This was an extremely rare finding in an African American, one he shared with the actor Angela Bassett.

An analysis of Nas's mitochondrial DNA, an identical genetic signature passed from mother to child, from generation to generation, gave us Nas's maternal haplogroup, a genetic population group that shares a common ancestor. Although it is of African origin, this haplogroup is extremely rare among African Americans. It arose in eastern Africa thousands of years ago but is commonly found today among the Yoruba and Fulbe populations in western Africa. Through his mother's line we had another affirmation of his Yoruba identity from Nigeria.

Nas's Y-DNA, which a man gets from his father, who gets it from his father before him, virtually unchanged across the generations, revealed that Nas was among the 35 percent of all African American men descended in his recent ancestral history not from a black man at all, but from a white man who impregnated a black woman, almost certainly during slavery. The majority of this 35 percent descended from white men with their roots in Ireland, England, or Scotland. Nas's Y-DNA, however, brought him much farther north. His paternal haplogroup is also known as the "Viking subclade," a signature he shares with the British musician Sting. Nas laughed. "That was a wild bunch," he said, "Just imagine a huge ship coming out of the mist and these big dudes with swords." He would have "never, ever,

ever" expected to find Vikings in his ancestry. Nas, who had said he "wanted to be full-on African," felt his mixed heritage made him part of something bigger. 'It's like we're a beautiful mixture, American blood through and through. You can't get more American than Native American, European, and African mixed. That's what the original country is about."

■ As a teenager Nas felt that the school curriculum didn't speak to him, didn't engage him or represent him. But after his journey into his roots, he felt himself a part of American history in a way he never had before. "In school you read about slaves. You read it like it's some story about these unfortunate people. No. They are our ancestors, our predecessors, forefathers. They are the whole purpose we're in the classroom reading in an integrated setting. They are the reason," he said. "It makes me want to know more and more about the history of America as a whole, because I'm so linked to every part of American history in some way, not just because of today, not just because of anything that's happening in my lifetime. There's a direct connection with you and the history here. It's not about some other people. The fiber of my being," he concluded, "exists in American history, and to be an American, the first thing you should learn is your history."

If he could travel back in time through American history and meet just one ancestor, who would it be? He answered quickly: "It's Calvin." Calvin was Nas's third great-grandfather who so vividly came to life in the diligent record keeping of his owner, Benjamin Franklin Little. We knew how much cotton he picked in slavery each day, and we knew what dollar value that owner put on his head. We also knew from the public record that as a free man, Calvin stood before a justice of the peace and legitimized a union formed in and sustained throughout slavery. "He had a family and he had a relationship with Pocahontas that lasted for decades, and he was a great man. I couldn't imagine. I would love to meet him."

Nas carried Calvin's DNA in him as he did that of all his other ancestors. In part, Nas's history was Calvin's history, and that was the history of slavery. But Nas's history was also the Queensbridge Apartments, summers in North Carolina, and a great-grandmother who rapped to her children in lieu of speaking. Considering all that, did he think it was DNA that most determined our identity? Our experiences since birth or those of our ancestors? The families we are born into? "It all starts with DNA. That fills in the blanks, because there will be blanks from any other way you look at it. Is your grandmother telling you a story, or if there's a photograph that's been passed on—those things are really, really good things to know. But," he said, "my history didn't start from my enslaved ancestors, and the DNA proves that, and takes you directly to where it began."

Angela Bassett (b. 1958)

The actor Angela Bassett has won fame and adulation for her moving portrayals of some of the most iconic women in African American history: Tina Turner, Coretta Scott King, Rosa Parks. Within her own family was a line of strong, independent women, some who were forced to forge their own path and some who did so by choice. Born Angela Evelyn Bassett on August 16, 1958, in Harlem, New York, she had a transient childhood. When she was only ten months old, her parents sent her to live with her aunt Golden, her father's sister, in North Carolina. Most of her childhood, though, was spent in St. Petersburg, Florida, living with her mother and sister, with grandparents and great-grandparents always close by. Her first exposure to theater came in eleventh grade, on an Upward Bound trip to Washington, D.C. She sat in the audience and watched James Earl Jones perform in *Of Mice and Men*, and her path was set. "I remember the theater just emptying out, and I'm the only one in the theater left crying, and I remember saying, 'If I could make people feel as bad as I feel right now, how wonderful that would be.'"

She tried her hand at local theater in St. Petersburg, but the program was small, and the few roles available hadn't been designed with a black actress in mind. She joked about her early experiences there. "'Oh, we have a St. Pete Little Theatre. Let me go over there.' And they're like, 'Well, hello, little brown girl. Yes, let's put her in here somewhere.'" "Somewhere" was more often than not in the role of the maid. She was undaunted, though, and soon found herself at Yale, a double major in Afro-American studies and theater studies. She remembered the precise moment that she decided to pursue acting as a career. "It was the first snow of my junior year in New Haven, Connecticut. Snow was very different for me coming from St. Petersburg, Florida. Snow to me was just glorious and magnificent and from heaven," she said. "So it was a beautiful day, and I was going back and forth. Should I be practical, or should I follow my dream?" Angela's mother had insisted that her daughter go to college, but her expectations ended there. "She told us from the time we were kids, 'You are going to college.'

You knew there was no other choice." But Aunt Golden, who raised her as a toddler, had remained very influential in her life, and she was the standard to which Angela aspired. "Our only family vacation my mother took me and my sister on was to Carbondale, Illinois, to see her walk and get her PhD," Angela recalled. It was Aunt Golden's voice that Angela heard in her head as she wrestled with her own future. "I remember her saying, 'Oh, Angela, don't waste your education on theater.' She wanted me to be able to keep the lights on and feed myself and clothe myself. I tried to be practical."

Instead, Angela followed her dream. She enrolled at the Yale School of Drama, where she would meet her future husband, Courtney Vance, and make it to Broadway in a renowned 1988 production of the August Wilson play *Joe Turner's Come and Gone. Joe Turner* is about slavery, religion, and migration. "I saw how families were separated so easily and how precarious life could be, finding yourself on the road and you get snatched up." Wilson's play forced her to examine herself as a descendant of slaves, something she wasn't ready to do at that time. "It was almost overwhelming to imagine what they could have gone through. I try to place myself in that situation: If I were born of that day as opposed to this day, how would I have survived? Would I have been bold like those in history that I admire? Who might I have been?" Angela was ready to face her history now, no matter how difficult. Her first step would be getting to know who her ancestors were, how they survived and who they had been.

■ Angela didn't spend much time with her father growing up. Her formative years were spent with his sister, Golden. Her paternal grandparents were always nearby, but she didn't recall hearing stories about her family's past. "You just assume it was something traumatic or something you're not proud of. And of course many of our generation, if it was that painful or shameful, we didn't go around telling it—as we say, letting our slips show. You kept your business to yourself or to the family."

We started our journey into Angela's family tree with her father. Daniel Benjamin Bassett Jr. was born on December 16, 1924, in Winston-Salem, North Carolina. Unwittingly, we had already given Angela her first piece of new information. "Born in 1924?" she asked. "I didn't know that, because my mother says he told her that he was ten years younger than he actually was when they got together." She established more frequent contact with her father when she was in college in New Haven and he was living in New York, but the proximity didn't amount to closeness. "I never held it against him, because everyone doesn't know how to be what they've never been before. Some men know how to be fathers but not daddies." She was grateful for him in spite of the distance, "and grateful for the family that I come from."

Angela's memories of her father's mother, her grandmother Brownie Younger Bassett, who was born on January 8, 1890, in Caswell County, North Carolina, were as sweet as her name. "Oh, I remember that big, high, soft bed of hers, and I remember that we drank coffee in the morning. Of course mine was a bowl of milk with one spoon of her coffee in it, and we watched the soap operas together, and she would let me fill in those books with those Green Stamps. She let me go on up the street and get my Mountain Dew and my peanuts that I put in the soda." Angela lit up talking about her. "She lived right across the street from Winston-Salem University, which is where my aunt Golden taught at the time, so she was my caretaker/babysitter/grandmama."

Brownie was widowed at age forty-five. Her husband, Angela's grandfather and her father's namesake, Daniel Benjamin Bassett Sr., died suddenly of a heart attack in 1935, when he was forty-two years old. According to the 1930 census for Forsyth County, North Carolina, taken five years before he died, the Bassetts owned their own home, valued at $1,500. Angela's family was in a privileged minority: only about 28 percent of African Americans in North Carolina were homeowners in 1930. Angela had always believed that her grandfather was an itinerant preacher, but in the census his occupation was recorded as "pastor at Disciple Church." Far from being itinerant, Daniel Bassett Sr. ministered regularly to the congregation of the Cleveland Avenue Christian Church, in the Disciples of Church denomination. Brownie worked outside the home as well. She was a tobacco leaf roller for the R. J. Reynolds Tobacco Company. "Well, Winston-Salem, North Carolina, you can smell the tobacco in the air, so that makes sense," Angela said. Brownie's was a difficult job—long hours, harsh conditions, and very low pay. The money for the home, we guessed, had come from Daniel's work in the church.

We guessed wrong. The house had been Brownie's long before she married Angela's grandfather. To Angela's surprise, her grandmother had been married once before, to a fellow tobacco roller named Lemuel Adams. The October 26, 1908, marriage of "Brownie Younger, aged 19, colored, and Lemuel Adams, aged 23, colored" was recorded in a Winston-Salem registry, and according to a property deed from 1910, the house was purchased for $550. Although we never located a death certificate for Lemuel, we knew that he died sometime before 1920, because his name wasn't recorded in the 1920 census. Her first husband's death left Brownie as the owner of the house. For a black woman to own property at the time was extraordinary. Her granddaughter noted the pattern: one strong woman begat another. "When I think of her daughter, Golden, who was the first PhD in our family, who raised me and all that she was able to do, and what she amassed and saved and took care of, it flows. It makes sense."

Sometime after Lemuel's death, the 1920 census found Brownie living in her own home with her mother and grandmother, each one a widow—three generations of widows living under one roof. Brownie's mother, Angela's paternal great-grandmother, was named Snow Younger. Families stories swirled around Snow. Her own daughter, Brownie, had wondered if Snow had Native American ancestry, and there was talk of a connection to the Trail of Tears. Angela herself, with her high cheekbones and almond-shaped eyes, had often been told that she "looked" Native American, and the name Snow piqued our interest. We searched for its origins, and learned that Snow Younger's first name wasn't Snow at all; that was her husband's last name. A North Carolina marriage license dated February 11, 1902, confirmed this: "A license for the marriage of William Snow, aged 32 years, and Harriet Younger, aged 42 years." "It's nice to meet her," Angela said. "I just go back to Grandma Brownie, because I could see her, touch her, hug her. Snow had lived with her for a time, so it's marvelous to be able to go even further back to see where she comes from, where I come from."

As we probed more deeply into the paper trail for Angela's great-grandmother, we encountered mystery upon mystery, all the result of the many names that we found associated with her. Her marriage license to William Snow gave us the names of her parents, Angela's great-great-grandparents, E. Cunnigan and Isa Roberson. Neither was named Younger, Harriet's last name when she married William Snow. It turned out that she had come by the name Younger in an earlier marriage, on October 26, 1881, to a man named Henderson Younger, Angela's biological great-grandfather. From this license we learned that Harriet and Henderson had both been born in slavery, Henderson in 1834 and Harriet in 1860. Once again, there was confusion. On this marriage license Harriet's last name was Jeffreys, and her father's name was no longer listed as Cunnigan, but as Dunham or Dunningham. Errors were frequent in those days, the names spelled— often misspelled—based on the recording clerk's best guess.

We solved the riddle of the Jeffreys name with the discovery of still another marriage license—the third—dated Christmas Day, 1874. "A license for the marriage of Taswell Jeffreys, aged 20," read Angela, "and Harriet Roberson, aged 19." Seven years before she married Angela's great-grandfather Henderson Younger, using her mother's last name of Roberson, Harriet married a man named Taswell Jeffreys. Now we had answered the questions about the origin of Angela's great-grandmother's surnames. The same license described her as the "daughter of James Cunningham."

Though Harriet's father's name was now unmistakable as James Cunningham, his identity was not. Five men who lived near Harriet's mother, Isa Roberson, shared this name. Four were listed in the federal census of 1860; the fifth, a black man, appeared only in the 1870 census, the first census to record African Americans by name. Of the four white James Cunninghams listed in the 1860 census, three—ages twenty-three, forty-nine, and seventy-two—were married; the fourth was sixteen. None could be ruled out. The sole black James Cunningham in the area, we gathered from the 1870 census, was twenty-two years old and married, making him twelve at the time of Harriet's birth in 1860; however, his death certificate recorded his birth year as 1843, which would make him seventeen in 1860, and therefore still a contender for paternity.

We went through census record after census record to get to the bottom of this. In the fifty years' worth of censuses through which we traced Harriet, beginning in 1870, her color was described sometimes as mulatto, other times as black. Racial classifications were subjective, based on the perception of the census takers. Harriet's daughter Brownie had light skin, and Angela shows signs of mixed ancestry, but without documentation, there was no way to resolve this quandary.

Tracing Angela's great-grandfather Henderson Younger, we encountered obstacles all too common in researching African American genealogy. The second husband of the woman Angela knew as Snow Younger was born in 1834 and died in 1899, leaving his wife, Harriet, to raise their five children, one of whom was Angela's grandmother Brownie. The 1881 marriage license for him and Harriet had included his parents' names, so we could give Angela the names of her great-great-grandparents, Jeff Younger and Charlotte Hodge, who were also born in slavery, but their names were all we had. To learn more about Angela's great-great-grandparents, we needed the names of their white owners. There were two slave owners in Halifax County, Virginia, with the surname Younger. But no records listing the names of their slaves existed, and without the ability to identify Henderson's owner conclusively, we hit a dead end. Henderson was described as a mulatto in some census records, so it was possible that one of these two white Youngers or their relatives had fathered him. It was only speculation, though, and speculation didn't allow us to proceed any further.

We ended our search through Angela's father's mother's line with two question marks, both revolving around indeterminate paternity, but Angela was fulfilled by simply seeing the long list of names we had given her. "It's wonderful," she said. "As a woman of faith, the Bible says we have 'so great a cloud of witnesses,' and these are the witnesses—the ancestors, my blood."

■ What could we tell Angela about her direct paternal Bassett line, her father's father's line? We traveled up her family tree from her father to her grandfather, Daniel Benjamin Bassett Sr., who was Brownie's husband, to his father, Angela's great-grandfather, William Henry Bassett. As is so often the case, William Henry Bassett's death certificate, dated October 6, 1918, proved to be a good starting place to learn more about his life. Age seventy-two at the time of his death, he was born in Henry County, Virginia, in 1846. After emancipation, he became a preacher; his son, Angela's grandfather, Daniel Benjamin Bassett Sr., would follow the same path. The woman of faith had two generations of ministers in her family. "We needed it to come through this," she said. "We had to believe in something other than what we saw. We needed faith."

The panoply of names that had appeared on documents related to Angela's great-grandmother Harriet ultimately stymied our research into her line, and now a marriage license in the Henry County archives for Henry Bassett unearthed a similar mystery. On October 29, 1885, Henry Bassett, described as a widower, married a woman named Martha Price. On the certificate, Angela's great-grandfather listed his parents' names as G. and J. Ingram. What were their first names, and why was their last name different from their son's? The 1870 census was crucial to finding the answers to these questions. In 1870, five years after emancipation, Angela's great-great-grandparents the Ingrams had made a home in Franklin County, Virginia. Angela read the record: "Ingram, George—there's your 'G,'" Angela said, "67 years old, male, black, farm laborer, and Jinny, 55 years old, female, black, housekeeping. Sally, 14 years old, female, black, and Fleming, 9 years old, male, black." George and Jinny Ingram, Angela's great-great-grandparents, were living with two of their younger children. There was no mention of William Henry in this record.

Another Ingram lived next door to George and Jinny: "Ingram, Elizabeth, 87 years old, white." This white next-door neighbor would be the key to unlocking Angela's past. Elizabeth, we learned was the daughter-in-law of the man who owned both George and Jinny, and incredibly, we discovered two wills that established the long connection between the black and white families. The first was filed in the year 1816 by a man named James Ingram. "I, James Ingram," Angela read, "think it proper to dispose of what God has given me as follows. I give and bequeath to my son, Alexander Ingram, one Negro named George. I give unto my daughter, Sarah Ingram, one Negro girl named Jin." At the time this will was filed, Angela's great-great-grandfather George would have been about thirteen years old, and her great-great-grandmother and George's future wife, Jinny, would have been about six. "My heart's just beating," Angela said.

Moving forward thirty-three years, James Ingram's son Alexander filed a will of his own, on April 2, 1849. "I, Alexander Ingram Sr., give my beloved wife, Elizabeth Ingram, all my estate, both real and personal, consisting of my land and Negroes, namely George, Bob, Stephen, Sophia, Amanda, Henry, Moses, Matilda, and Rhoda, together with all of my household and kitchen furniture." In this document Jinny's name wasn't listed—she had been bequeathed to Alexander's sister—but it included father and son, Angela's great-great-grandfather George and her great-grandfather William Henry, called Henry here: two generations of Angela's family, itemized alongside furniture and other belongings. Angela had told us that she and her husband spoke to their children about being "quality" people, whose value was measured in good deeds and upright behavior. Alexander Ingram put a different sort of value on Angela's ancestors, according to an inventory he had taken the same year he wrote his will. "One Negro man named George, $200. One Negro woman named Sophia, $200. One Negro woman and child, Matilda and Mara, $400. One Negro boy named Robert, $400. One Negro boy named Stephen, $500. One Negro boy named Henry, $300. One Negro girl named Rhonda [Rhoda in the will], $400. One Negro girl named Amanda, $250. One head of sheep, $6. Thirty-three head of hogs, $40. One gray mare, $40. One bay mare, $30. One bay colt, $14. Two cows and a yearling, $26." Here it was, in black and white, the "worth" of human beings and animals listed side by side. Angela was deeply pained. "Well, property and three-quarters of a human being, all that history you learned growing up, but to have your family name and your people so tangibly associated with it, you can't help but ache for what they came through, what they went through," she said. "They cost more, but they were put on the same level as hogs and sheep and horses, thought of as property, as animals, as less than human, as having the brain, intellectual capacity of animals." She felt tremendous pride in what her ancestors had come through and marveled at their resilience. "Nameless, faceless, but now at least I have the names. I can call them by name."

George and Jinny were connected to the Ingram family for at least fifty years before slavery ended in 1865, growing up together on the Ingram plantation and then making their home next door to the daughter-in-law of the man who had owned them. Intimate bonds sometimes grew between slaves and their masters in ways that may seem inexplicable to us. And under the harshest of conditions, despite the constant threat of being separated from each other at the whim of a master, slaves built and maintained families of their own on the plantation. Even though the law didn't recognize marriage between slaves, we know that George and Jinny had a son together, Angela's great-grandfather William Henry.

At least in William Henry's earliest years, father and son remained together. He was three years old at the time that Alexander Ingram wrote his will. This was the last time William Henry's name appeared in any documents until after the Civil War. It was a painful truth of slavery that children were sold away from their parents routinely, and the fact that William Henry and his parents had different names in adulthood strongly indicated that this was the case, but we could find no bill of sale to prove it. Our research hinged on the name Bassett, and we turned to the 1860 Slave Schedule for Henry County, Virginia, which bordered the Ingram plantation's home of Franklin County to the north. A man named John Henry Bassett owned two slaves, one of whom was a fourteen-year-old male. This teenage boy was most likely Angela's great-grandfather. According to family lore, Angela's great-grandfather worked at a sawmill, eventually becoming a foreman. This slave owner, John Henry Bassett, and his sons owned sawmills and went on to create the Bassett Furniture Company in the early 1900s. We could find no other corroborating documents to prove this, but the circumstantial evidence was compelling and convincing. The discovery of William Henry's separation from his parents, George and Jinny, on the Ingram plantation solved the mystery of their different last names, and also explains why Angela bears the last name Bassett. We showed her a photograph of John Henry Bassett and his wife, who owned her ancestor and whose name she bore. "I'm just looking at their eyes, their expressions," she said. "That's our history in America. That's our history. Or that's my history."

■ In the 1930 census, Angela's paternal great-grandmother Martha Jane Price, by then the widow of William Henry Bassett, was living with her son and daughter-in-law, Angela's grandparents Brownie and Daniel Bassett Jr., in Forsyth County, North Carolina. We had traced her husband back to two different plantations in Virginia and learned that he was born of a relationship that formed in slavery and survived in freedom. What could we learn of Martha's earliest years? We already knew that she and William Henry Bassett had legally married on October 29, 1885, in Henry County, Virginia. Almost twenty years earlier, on February 27, 1866, less than a year after the Civil War ended, Martha's parents, Angela's great-great-grandparents, made their union legal in Henry County as well. Marriage, as we knew, was not recognized between slaves. The ceremony known as "jumping the broom" carried great weight among slave communities, but legally it meant nothing. After emancipation, former slaves were able to have the marriages and family units they formed in slavery recognized as legal by filing a document called a cohabitation record, and we found Angela's great-great-grandparents'. "Cohabitating together as husband and wife," Angela read, "Oscar Price, aged 35, and Charlotte. Last owner, Duke Price. Children, Martha J., aged 7, Daniel, aged 5, Frank, aged 3, and Mary A., 9 months of age." Oscar and Charlotte Price had been "cohabitating" since 1854 and had three children, including Angela's great-grandmother, born in slavery. (Based on her age and the fact that the Civil War ended on April 9, 1865, baby Mary was most likely born free.) They managed to keep their family together under the most uncertain of conditions, and they had their union recognized by the law as soon as they could.

Also on the record: the name of the white man who owned them, Duke Price. According to the 1860 Slave Schedule, Duke Price owned eleven slaves, listed by age, color, and gender. Knowing their ages from the cohabitation record, we could determine that three of Duke Price's slaves were indeed Angela's ancestors: "32 years old, male, black. 22 years old, female, black. Three months old, female, black." Angela looked at the record of her great-grandmother, just an infant, with her parents—no names, just descriptions, but they were her people. "I'm amazed," Angela sighed. "I'm about to fall off my seat."

As we had done with her great-grandfather's Bassett slave owners, we

showed Angela a picture of Duke Price. For the second time, she was looking into the eyes of an American slave owner, one who had owned her
ancestors. "It makes it real in a whole new way and fashion," Angela said.
"Coming up, studying African American history and reading about slavery
and knowing about it and where we come from, but now, to actually see the
faces of the slave owners, that's pretty amazing. I'm in awe." She paused.
"I can't say I'm mad. I'm in awe."

■ We had been able to look into the lives of an astonishing number of
Angela's slave ancestors on her father's side. Now we turned to Angela's
maternal ancestors. Her mother, Betty Jane Gilbert, was born on August 3,
1935, in St. Petersburg, Florida. Her marriage to Angela's father "had its
challenges," as Angela described it, and as a child, Angela experienced
feelings of rejection because of it. "A child yearns to know who they are
and who they belong to, and to have a mother and a father. It's a mother's
love, a father's love, and without that, there's a hole. There's a space that
needs to be filled."

Although her earliest years were spent living in North Carolina with
her father's sister, Golden, Angela grew up with her mother in Florida,
with grandparents and great-grandparents nearby. The memories Angela
shared were undeniably warm and loving, of a family with strong bonds
in spite of struggles. Her maternal grandparents were both born in Georgia, Emma Jane Stokes on March 22, 1917, and Leroy Gilbert on May 23,
1908, and married on January 14, 1935, in the state of Florida. "We never
called her Grandma. We called her Mama Emma, and we called him Daddy
Leroy. That's what my mother called him."

Week in and week out, Sunday afternoons meant Sunday dinner with
Angela's great-grandparents. Her great-grandfather, Slater Samuel Stokes,
was born on April 1, 1893, in Quitman, Georgia. A preacher, he left an in-
delible impression on Angela. "We were very close. When Poppa came, you
knew you were going to get a little something. He always gave my sister
and me a silver dollar." He was a natural storyteller and sparked Angela's
imagination with African American folk tales. "He would sit and tell us
stories about how the buzzard would fly, those sorts of old wives' tales,
like Br'er Rabbit and those sorts of things." Slater Stokes was an associate
minister for thirty years at the AME Zion Church in St. Petersburg, according to Angela "one of the founding pastors of the church," and "a very

kind and generous soul." He also had a flair for the dramatic that wasn't lost on the budding actress. "I remember going to his church once and seeing him preach, and he sang, and he walked down the middle of the aisle, and he had a white handkerchief on his shoulder, and he'd talk about your troubles, and you take it to the Lord, and then he took the white handkerchief off, and in a flourish just threw it on the altar, and he'd say, 'And you leave it there.' It was just so dramatic, so dramatic." She laughed. "He was just arresting." He was also her "standard." "I didn't grow up with my father, but I grew up with my great-grandfather. I looked to Slater Samuel Stokes as my measure of a man, as what I should look for in a man, and they would have to meet or exceed the quality of this one." She named her own son Slater in his honor.

Slater Samuel Stokes died in 1980, the same year Angela graduated from Yale. His funeral program gave us the names of his parents, Angela's great-great-grandparents Judge Stokes and Henrietta Cohens—names she had never before heard. Having his parents' names allowed us to trace Poppa Slater back to the 1910 census for Brooks County, Georgia. He lived in the household not of his father, Judge Stokes, but of his stepfather, Monroe Cohens. Slater and his mother, Henrietta, were both described in the census as mulatto, Monroe Cohens as black.

We had to go back a full forty years to find Slater's biological father in the records, to the federal census of 1870, the first in which all African Americans were recorded by name. Judge Stokes was just ten years old at the time, living with his two siblings and their parents, the forty-five-year-old farmworker Henry Stokes and his wife, forty-two-year-old Emily. This record introduced us to yet another set of Angela's ancestors who were born in slavery, her third great-grandparents Henry and Emily Stokes.

As we had seen with Angela's paternal ancestors, to learn more about the lives of Henry and Emily Stokes, we needed to find the name of their owner. There was only one white Stokes living in the area at that time. "Well, that narrows it down," Angela commented. According to the 1860 Slave Schedule for Baker County, Georgia, J. W. Stokes owned a male and female slave close in age to Angela's third great-grandparents, and we believed with great certainty that a baby described as "one year old, male, black" was her great-great-grandfather Judge. J. W. Stokes owned thirty-five slaves, all crowded into six slave houses on the plantation. Angela shuddered to think of the life within those walls. "I've been able to visit slave cabins in New Orleans, some that still actually exist, and to be able to walk that land and to go into those very tight quarters, to imagine what it sounded like, what it smelled like."

Henry and Emily lived most of their lives on the Georgia plantation of a diehard Confederate, the very first man in his county to volunteer to fight in the Confederate army. On May 13, 1861, J. W. Stokes and his fellow volunteers signed an oath in which they pledged "to tender our services to the governor of the state of Georgia and to the president of the Confederate States, to go at a moment's notice to whatever point we may be ordered to in the capacity of soldiers." Captain J. W. Stokes was captured and killed during the last day of fighting at the Battle of Gettysburg on July 3, 1863.

Angela's third great-grandparents were owned by a man who fought to the death to preserve the southern way of life. He did not live to see that life upended, to see Henry and Emily and all his other slaves freed. On June 25, 1867, just two years after the end of the Civil War, Henry Stokes, a free man, made his mark and registered to vote in the state of Georgia. Angela read his oath: "I, Henry Stokes, colored, do solemnly swear in the presence of Almighty God that I am a citizen of the state of Georgia, that I will faithfully support the Constitution and obey the laws of the United States, and will, to the best of my ability, encourage others to do so." Angela, who had taken part in voter registration drives in South Africa and stumped for then-candidate Barack Obama, felt deeply connected to her ancestor. "That's beautiful," she said. "That feels so good, especially knowing how important the ability to vote is, that it was withheld from you, and years later, for it to be important to me to register to vote as a young person as soon as I became eighteen, that's the line, the lineage." Angela imagined how her ancestor, once nameless and voiceless, felt at the moment he made his mark. "He must have felt so proud that he had come through so much to come to this moment, that everything was moving forward."

■ We were amazed at how far back we had been able to go in the history of Angela's family, considering her descent from slaves on the many lines we explored. On her mother's side, the oldest named ancestor we could identify was a man named Nathan Love, who was born in slavery in Tennessee in about 1810. On her father's side, her oldest named ancestor was George Ingram, born in slavery in Virginia around 1793. "I just had no idea that it was written down, that it was there, just waiting," she said.

The paper trail had ended, but what was written in her genes? We turned to DNA to find out. Angela was most curious to know what parts of Africa her ancestors came from, and also whether we could substantiate the family story about their Native American ancestry. To find these answers, we administered an admixture test to her, which measures an individual's percentages of European, sub-Saharan African, and East Asian / Native American ancestry from roughly the last five centuries. More than three-quarters of her DNA was from Africa—just under 78 percent—and her European ancestry registered at 21 percent. Despite suspicions that her great-grandmother Harriet may have been fathered by one of the several white men named James Cunningham who lived near her when she became pregnant, we had not located any white ancestors by name for her family tree, but as with almost every African American we had ever tested, she carried substantial European ancestry; it was the legacy of slavery. Her Native American result was small but not insignificant—0.6 percent—which translated roughly to the equivalent of DNA one would inherit from a fifth or sixth great-grandparent.

We were able to break down Angela's admixture results by region, and 20 percent of her European DNA originated in Great Britain. We broke down her African result the same way. Her greatest percentage of African ancestry—32 percent—came from Nigeria. She also had substantial amounts tracing back to Benin and Togo, Cameroon and Congo, Mali, southeastern Bantu (Angola), Ivory Coast and Ghana, Senegal, and even the South Central hunter-gatherers at 1 percent, a rare finding she shared with the hip-hop artist Nasir Jones. Angela has a pan-African genome, representing the nations from which her ancestors were taken during the transatlantic slave trade five hundred years ago.

■ Angela had long been a student of African American history, but that history had become much more personal for her. She was particularly taken with the story of her great-grandfather William Henry, and if she could go back in a time machine and meet any one ancestor, she would choose him. "Who just jumped out? That little boy, that little three-year-old, Henry. I would want to know who he was, who his parents were, and how he traveled. He went away or was sent away and took another name, and why? And what was he able to do and to become?" Her great-grandfather's story embodied slavery's ability to tear families apart, but also to persevere, to overcome adversity and move forward. Their struggle, she had said earlier, was not for nothing. "They were on earth. They had a footprint. They had a life, and they meant something. It's astounding to see people who were considered three-fifths of a human being, to find them, and know they were five-fifths, one whole human being, a child of God."

After meeting so many unknown ancestors and being reacquainted with others, did Angela see her ancestors in herself? She shared their DNA, but was that what made Angela who she is today? Was it her experiences, or was it theirs? "All of it," she said. "A combination of all of it. If you look, if you take an assessment, there are some traits and qualities that are similar. And then to go back, without even your knowledge, there are perhaps some more traits." She thought particularly of the strong women who had come before her, to whom she felt a direct connection. "Grandmother Brownie owning land, taking care of business. I said, 'Oh my God, that makes sense, because her daughter did the same thing.' All of that plays a part, is a part of the fabric of who we are, the DNA, the nurture/nature. There's some truth to that."

Her world had expanded before her eyes, and she described the experience of finding her roots as "breathless." "I thought I was from a small family," she said. "I just knew the people I grew up with, and I felt blessed we could go back a couple of generations on my mother's side, but to see it before me is remarkable. It means a great deal." The papers and photographs she had seen gave her family a permanence and a history she hadn't known existed. "I feel proud to know where I'm from, to hear their names, to see some of their faces, to see their names in print, to see they were remembered, to see it inscribed."

Valerie Jarrett (b. 1956)

She's been called the president's First Friend, big sister, and consigliere. As a senior advisor to Barack Obama, Valerie Jarrett is one of the most influential political figures in the country. In her role, she oversees the Office of Intergovernmental Affairs and the Office of Public Engagement, and she chairs the White House Council on Women and Girls. She's a crusader for equality and social justice, a passion born on the South Side of Chicago, where in 1983 she threw herself into the campaign of Harold Washington, earning a front-row seat to the improbable election of Chicago's first African American mayor. "It was just an extraordinary time in Chicago," she recalled. But once the campaign was over, she went back to work as a lawyer. She had a position, it seemed, anyone would envy. "I had this incredible office on the seventy-ninth floor of the Sears Tower in Chicago, with a view of Lake Michigan. You could just imagine all the sailboats in the water," she said. "By anybody's definition, I should have been really happy, and I was miserable. I had recently divorced, and I had my daughter, and I was leaving her every day. I wasn't feeling good about what I was doing. So my friend said, 'Join a movement. Be a part of something bigger than yourself. Give back to the city that you love.'"

Valerie did just that, and she joined Mayor Washington's staff. After his death, Valerie stayed on in city hall, working as deputy to Chicago mayor Richard Daley. It was during this time that a résumé landed on her desk. "At the top it said, 'Outstanding young woman, has no interest in being in a law firm.' Right away that caught my eye, since obviously I had left a law firm." The outstanding young woman was named Michelle Robinson. "What was supposed to be a twenty-minute interview turned into an hour-and-a-half conversation. She was just trying to figure it out, with the same kind of hunger for public service, would there be a fit in the mayor's office." Apparently her fiancé, a Chicago community organizer named Barack Obama, wasn't so sure, and Michelle proposed that Valerie join them for dinner to discuss it. "The rest is history," she said. "Thank goodness for that dinner."

She has always been quick to answer the call to service. "None of the jobs I've had in public service were ones where I was immune from someone coming up to me in the grocery store and complaining about a bus route when I chaired the Chicago Transit Authority. Or now, who knows what they might come up and say?" She laughed. "In a sense, public servant really does mean twenty-four hours a day, but that's also the best part of it, that you feel as though your responsibility is to someone other than just yourself." Valerie has worked closely with history makers, people who broke the color barrier of the offices they were elected to, but, she said, "I don't really have a whole lot of time to reflect. The future will be better off if I'm thinking about what I have to do ahead of me as opposed to what our legacy might be."

Valerie knows something about legacies. Born Valerie Bowman on November 14, 1956, in Shiraz, Iran, she came to us knowing a great deal more about her ancestry than most of the participants in our series did. After all, her grandfather and great-grandfather have both been written up in history books, and the knowledge of those who came before her has motivated her throughout her life. "It made me feel there were no excuses," she explained. "I could not possibly come home and fabricate any reason why

I should not be able to work hard and succeed. That's really the perspective it gave me." Little did Valerie know that, despite the rich family history that had already been passed down to her, many generations of stories had been lost over time. Valerie's perspective was about to become even broader.

■ Valerie needed to look no further than her own home to find figures to inspire her. It was the illustrious past of her mother's family that captivated historians, but Valerie's father was himself a "trailblazer," in his daughter's words, and we began our journey into Valerie's roots on his side of the family. Valerie's father, the pathologist and geneticist James Edward Bowman Jr., was the eldest of six siblings, born on February 5, 1923, in Washington, D.C. In 1947 he became the first—and, at the time, the only—African American resident at St. Luke's Hospital in Chicago. Jim Crow laws were still in effect. "My father was not a get-along kind of guy," Valerie said proudly. "St. Luke's had a history of everybody who was black going in the back door, and my father just wouldn't have it. He figured, 'I'm going to be here, and I'm going to be a physician; I'm coming in the front door.' He loved to tell the story about how he walked in that first day, and all of the orderlies and the nurses were going, 'Oh, my gosh, Dr. Bowman walked in the front door.' Then the next day, they were all waiting and walked in the front door, too."

During the "happy days" of the Eisenhower era, an African American physician's prospects in medicine were limited, and Valerie's father sought work overseas. "I don't think either of my parents were even fully sure where Shiraz, Iran, was on the map at the time, but they thought it would be an adventure." Valerie's father helped found Nemazee Hospital in 1955. Valerie was born the following year. "The city of Shiraz had never had a hospital before the Nemazee Hospital," Valerie explained, "and I was the second baby born there." After five years in Iran and one year in London, her father received an offer to join the faculty at the University of Chicago, and the Bowmans returned to Chicago. "In a sense, he had to go all the way around the world to come back home." Back in Chicago, James Bowman became the first African American to receive tenure in the Division of Biological Sciences at the University of Chicago.

James Bowman was the son of a demanding and successful father. Valerie's grandfather James Edward Bowman Sr. was born on May 10, 1904, and he practiced dentistry in Washington, D.C. He put himself through dental school at Howard University working as an elevator operator, and he instilled in his children the same work ethic. Valerie's grandfather "really believed that, even though he was a dentist, that his children should make it on their own and pull themselves up by their bootstraps. He just thought that the young people needed to be tough and resilient and get out there. He was not financially as supportive as my father might have wanted him to be, but his children all did really well."

There was an abiding mystery surrounding Valerie's grandmother's paternal ancestry. Valerie's father's mother, Dorothy Peterson Bowman, was born on May 30, 1907, in Washington, D.C. Tragically, she died in 1946, only thirty-nine years old. "The sad thing is that he was actually on duty on the floor the day she died. That was very painful," she said. "But boy, he loved his mother. He loved her." Valerie didn't know a lot about her grandmother's family, but according to her relatives, Dorothy's father, Valerie's great-grandfather, was Jewish. Valerie recalled the first time she heard this surprising news. "A very dear friend of mine whose family lived outside of Chicago was all alone at Passover, and she said, 'Do you think I could come to your house, and I will cook a seder dinner?' My parents said, 'Absolutely.' And in a very matter-of-fact way, in the course of dinner, my father said to her, 'Well, we're very good at this because my grandfather was Jewish.'"

To see what we could learn about Dorothy's parents, we turned to her death certificate, which identified her parents as George Peterson and Mildred Waddy. George Peterson, Valerie's great-grandfather, was the ancestor rumored to be Jewish. But the 1910 census described him as black. For that time period, it seemed unlikely that an individual would be black and Jewish, so we wondered if George was not Dorothy's biological father and perhaps she was illegitimate.

We looked in the paper trail but found few clues. There was no documented evidence that helped us solve the mystery of Valerie's Jewish great-grandfather; we would have to turn to DNA for that. Tracing any of Valerie's paternal ancestors proved to be difficult. From her grandfather James Bowman Sr., we were able to go back only one generation into slavery. His father, Valerie's great-grandfather Nelson Bowman, was born about 1835 in Virginia. On her grandmother Dorothy Peterson's side, we reached back two generations into slavery, to Valerie's third great-grandfather James Peterson, who was born in 1815, also in Virginia. James was the first of Valerie's Peterson ancestors to migrate north to Washington, D.C. The paper trail ended here for Valerie's father's family, as it did for so many African American families, with few names and in slavery. Valerie's mother's family tree, however, would take us back generations, to places we never expected to go.

▪ Although Valerie was born in Iran, home is and always has been Chicago. "I say I'm from Chicago, because that's the city I remember most," she said. "It's where my mother grew up, so I consider Chicago home." Her strong professional ties to the city are rivaled by her personal ties to it. Her mother, Barbara Taylor, was born there on October 30, 1928, and she has devoted her career as an educator to improving opportunities for the city's youngest students. In 1946, Barbara was among the very few African Americans enrolled at Sarah Lawrence College in New York. She went with the intention of becoming a city planner, but after receiving her bachelor's degree in liberal arts, she switched tracks, going on to get her master's in education at the University of Chicago. In 1966, she cofounded a pioneering graduate school in early childhood education, which became known as the Erikson Institute. She remains active there today. "She discovered early, really before there was a clear profession in early childhood education, that if we invest in these little people while they're still little, you get an enormous return on that investment."

It was in Valerie's genes, it seemed, to educate, to innovate, to look out for the community around her. Perhaps mother and daughter had both gotten that drive from Valerie's grandfather, the housing activist Robert Rochon Taylor. Born in Tuskegee, Alabama, in 1899, he died in his adopted city of Chicago on March 1, 1957. A prominent business leader in insurance and real estate, he fought tooth and nail to improve living conditions for impoverished African American families in Chicago. His legacy, however, was complicated. "He was chairman of the board of the Chicago Housing Authority," Valerie explained, "and interestingly enough, the reason why he resigned was because he was unable to get the Chicago City Council to be willing to integrate public housing throughout the city in a way that allowed it to blend into the urban fabric, as opposed to standing alone in isolation. There was a rather painful irony that the then–Robert Taylor Homes, which was the largest, most notorious housing project in the world, was named after him, because it really symbolized the opposite of what he stood for."

Valerie's mother and aunt told her countless stories about her grandfather. The career was part of it, of course, but there were intimate details, too. "He loved ice cream," Valerie said, "and he used to get up in the middle of the night and eat, and my mother, to this day, eats in the middle of the night. She told these stories my entire childhood about the conversations that they would have, sitting around the kitchen table, eating in the middle of the night. She talked a lot about his discipline and his commitment to hard work, and he, too, had very high standards."

High standards and high expectations were passed down to Valerie's grandfather by his own father, Valerie's great-grandfather, the renowned Robert Robinson Taylor, who was born in Wilmington, North Carolina, on June 8, 1868. In the late 1880s, when Valerie's great-grandfather enrolled at the Massachusetts Institute of Technology, he was the only African American in his class. In 1892, he became not only the very first African American to graduate from the prestigious university, but also the first professionally trained African American architect. "The president of MIT has a photograph of my great-grandfather on the mantelpiece, taken his first year there, together with another photograph of a group of women taken the same year," Valerie said. "He said it just reminds him of the roots of the university."

Shortly after Robert's graduation from MIT, the prominent and powerful African American leader Booker T. Washington enlisted him to help build his Alabama-based Tuskegee Institute, one of the earliest colleges committed to providing vocational education as a means of social and economic uplift for African Americans after the Civil War. Booker T. Washington's philosophy, including a focus on economic uplift within the constraints of America's racially separate spheres, was not universally embraced by other black leaders in the rising generation, however. Particularly outspoken was the Harvard-trained scholar W. E. B. Du Bois, who, along with others active in establishing the NAACP, emphasized political and legal action to dismantle Jim Crow segregation and achieve civil rights. Regardless of which side one comes down on regarding his positions and politics, there is no question that Booker T. Washington was one of the most influential leaders in African American history, and in his Tuskegee Institute he left a permanent, tangible legacy, one which Valerie's great-grandfather helped build.

Robert Robinson Taylor was at Tuskegee for almost forty years. In 1898 he completed his masterpiece, replacing a ramshackle pavilion that had been widely used as an auditorium with a glorious chapel that would be considered the jewel of the campus for decades. It was constructed with student-made bricks, and it was the first building in Macon County, Alabama, to have electricity. Valerie knew all about the student-made bricks. "When I was at MIT giving a lecture, I said, 'You all may have some complaints, but at least you're not out there in the hot sun in Tuskegee making the bricks that then formed the buildings that you will live in."

Robert Robinson Taylor was born just three years after the Civil War ended, and his father, Valerie's great-great-grandfather Henry Taylor, was born in slavery in Cumberland County, North Carolina, in 1823, exactly forty years before Abraham Lincoln issued the Emancipation Proclamation. How did Valerie's great-grandfather, the son of a former slave, manage to accomplish so much in the Jim Crow era, a nadir in American race relations characterized by the punishing segregation, disfranchisement, and violent, often deadly, treatment of black citizens emerging out of centuries of enslavement? A clue lay in a letter dated 1929, found in the Tuskegee archives, in which Robert spoke of his father's ancestry. The letter was addressed to a man named Charles Taylor in Glasgow, Scotland. "My grandfather, Angus Taylor, settled near Fayetteville, North Carolina," he wrote. "I do not know very much about him except as I have heard my father speak of him. As I understand it, he accumulated large property holdings, but at his death, these were dissipated in some way. I am sure that none of his kin inherited any of it."

Only a free man could have property holdings, so we looked in the census records for an Angus Taylor. We found his name in the 1850 Slave Schedule for Bladen County, North Carolina. The only names that appeared in the Slave Schedule were those of slave owners; slaves were listed anonymously, described by age, gender, and color. Angus Taylor was a white man of Scottish descent, and he owned a small farm in North Carolina. Valerie's great-great-grandfather had been born in 1823; the "26-year-old male, black" listed among Angus's seven slaves was certainly Henry Taylor. Based on Robert's letter, we assumed that the master of Henry Taylor must also be his father. Though quite common, such claims are usually impossible to prove, as white slave owners rarely acknowledged their black children in any legal way.

We continued to search for conclusive evidence. In the second volume of *The Story of the Negro*, Booker T. Washington included a tantalizing detail about the unusual status of "the father of Mr. R. R. Taylor," Henry Taylor. "Mr. Taylor's father," Washington wrote, "was nominally a slave, but he was early given liberty to do about as he pleased." This semi-free status that his master allowed him suggested, ostensibly, a degree of affection, yet Angus Taylor never went so far as to free him. One of the cruelest ironies of trying to live as a freed black person in a slave state was the ever-present risk of illegal reenslavement. We can only speculate on the reasons why Angus Taylor may have kept Henry in bondage. Perhaps it was to afford him a measure of protection that he wouldn't have had in freedom. Definitive proof of the identity of Henry Taylor's father still eluded us, though the circumstantial evidence was convincing. Whatever Angus Taylor's motivation for granting Henry this quasi-freedom, there was no question that it gave him a tremendous advantage when slavery finally ended.

In the 1870 census, the first to list all African Americans by name, Henry Taylor was described as a mulatto, an indication of mixed ancestry. And only five years out of slavery, as a house carpenter, he had managed to accumulate substantial real estate holdings valued at five thousand dollars, in today's money the equivalent of ninety thousand dollars. That was an exorbitant sum for a white man to possess in 1870; for a black man it was extraordinary. It appeared he was also compensated well for his work. A receipt for payment received by Valerie's great-great-grandfather showed that he been paid "for building schoolhouse, $1,000. For building fences, $220. Received payment, Henry Taylor, $1,300." He had a respectable income, but what's more, he seemed to have a solid foundation, which was a plausible explanation for how Valerie's family had risen so quickly in the uncertain years after emancipation.

All that we had uncovered led us to believe that Henry Taylor was the son of Angus Taylor, whose own ancestral roots we could trace back to the early eighteenth century, to a place called Skipness in Scotland. Valerie's great-great-grandfather died in 1891, before death certificates were required by law in North Carolina, so that valuable source of parental names wasn't available to us. Because of a massive loss of records in Bladen County, the identity of Henry's mother, a slave, could never be known, and his father's identity was suspected but still not proven. We would have to deploy DNA science to determine the truth of Henry Taylor's parentage once and for all. Even without scientific proof, Valerie accepted that she was most likely descended from her great-great-grandfather's master. "It's about as common as anything," she said. "I didn't get this complexion by accident. It's not like it's something that makes me very angry or anything, because it's always been a part of my life. We always knew our history." She stopped for a moment. "In a way, maybe it's worse, because it's just almost a matter of fact."

▓ It was hard to top the legacy of Valerie's great-grandfather Robert Robinson Taylor. But in the branch of Valerie's family tree that extended from

Robert's wife, Valerie's great-grandmother Beatrice Rochon, we would find another formidable character in her lineage, Beatrice's father, Valerie's great-great-grandfather, a man named Victor Rochon.

Valerie knew very little about her great-grandmother's Rochon family. "I don't have stories about Beatrice, just know her name." Born in Louisiana in 1874, Beatrice Rochon Robinson was a music teacher at Paul Quinn College in Waco, Texas, one in a long line of female educators in Valerie's family, including, of course, Valerie's mother. Beatrice's parents, Valerie's great-great-grandparents, were Kate McKay, born somewhere in Louisiana around 1855, ten years before the end of the Civil War, and Victor Rochon, who was born in 1843, in St. Martinsville, Louisiana. Unbeknownst to Valerie, her great-great-grandfather was a political pioneer, one of the first black men elected to the Louisiana State House of Representatives during Reconstruction, representing St. Martin Parish first in 1872 and then again in 1888, during the period known as Redemption.

After the ratification of the Fifteenth Amendment in 1870, which gave African American men the right to vote, freed blacks were now poised to stand on equal footing with white southerners—in theory. In practice, however, this would not be. Disgruntled southern whites pushed back, and as they sought to reassert their supremacy, the newly elected black legislators confronted a hostile white opposition. On the floor of the Louisiana State House, Victor Rochon argued passionately against the injustice of the Separate Car Act of 1890, the opening salvo in the legal war to establish the doctrine of "separate but equal" as the law of the land. On May 12, 1890, speaking before the legislature, Representative Rochon put forth his argument: "Why, Mr. Speaker, the idea that you and your family would not be offended in traveling hundreds of miles with a dozen or perhaps more Negro servants, but you would be insulted to travel any distance with me and my family on account of our color, the logic of this proposition is beyond my understanding." It would be, he said, "an abrogation of self-respect and an injustice to the colored people of Louisiana to remain silent and not raise my voice against the passage of this bill." In Valerie's family, somehow Victor Rochon's legacy had been lost. "How could I not know this?" she marveled. "It makes sense that I'm doing what I'm doing."

Valerie's great-great-grandfather's argument was ultimately unsuccessful, and the Separate Car Act passed in Louisiana. Six years later, in the case that arose from a challenge to the act, the United States affirmed the legality of "separate but equal" in *Plessy v. Ferguson*. It would take decades to dismantle.

The fiery Victor Rochon piqued our interest. As we had seen with Valerie's Taylor ancestors, most African Americans' names did not appear in the federal census until after the Civil War. They were enumerated in the Slave Schedules of 1850 and 1860, but anonymously. In the federal census for 1850 — not the Slave Schedule — Valerie's great-great-grandfather Victor Rochon appeared, by name, a seven-year-old boy who was among the small minority of black people who were free before the Civil War.

This census record, in fact, contained the names of an astonishing three generations of free people of color, ranging in age from seven to seventy-one, every one described as "mulatto." Victor, of course, was Valerie's great-great-grandfather; Sterille and Elizabeth Rochon, Victor's parents, were her third great-grandparents; and Jean or John Narcisse and Charlotte Rochon, her fourth great-grandparents. The head of household, called Narcisse, was born free in Orleans Parish, Louisiana, in 1778. Valerie's free roots went as far back as America itself.

Born in the middle years of the American Revolution, Valerie's fourth great-grandfather was one of the few men of color who fought in the War of 1812. His service record revealed that from January to March 1815, thirty-five-year-old Narcisse Rochon served as a sergeant in the Fifteenth Louisiana Regiment, a segregated company of fifty men led by a white man named Captain Alexander Lemelle. Narcisse enlisted just ten days before the pivotal Battle of New Orleans. As the large and well-trained British forces prepared to march on New Orleans, poised to take the city easily, American forces under the leadership of General Andrew Jackson mobilized the local population — including, out of desperation, the colored troops — and built a defensive line just outside New Orleans. They turned back the British, and they won decisively. The British suffered two thousand casualties, the Americans fewer than one hundred. This was America's greatest land victory in the entire war, and one of the first documented instances where black troops fought in large, cohesive units under the American flag. In fact, when Frederick Douglass lobbied President Lincoln to allow black men to bear arms in the Civil War, he pointed to the five thousand men of color who served in the American Revolution, and to the few that served in the War of 1812. Valerie's fourth great-grandfather was among them. Her ancestor's service in the War of 1812 qualified her for membership in the Daughters of the American Revolution. "Wouldn't that be something if I showed up there?" Valerie laughed. Her membership would serve as a reminder that African Americans had long fought alongside their white countrymen for this nation's freedom, a nation that for so long kept so many unfree.

■ We discovered generation after generation of free people of color on the Rochon family tree. To find out how Valerie's ancestors became free in the first place, we went back to Valerie's sixth great-grandmother, a woman named Marianne Rochon. When we first found her in the paper trail, she was a free woman of color living with her six children. But Marianne herself had not been born free, nor were her children. Documents revealed that Marianne had been enslaved on the Rochon plantation in colonial Mobile, Alabama, property of the prosperous white plantation owner and Mobile native Pierre Rochon. Pierre was the father of Marianne's six children, and on March 20, 1770, he set their children free. "Pierre Rochon, being moved by a paternal affection for six mulatto children," the rare manumission document stated, "grant such children their freedom, and after my decease, their mother, Marianne, aged about 26 years, to be free to all intents and purposes from slaveitude to any person or persons whatsoever." Valerie's sixth great-grandfather was a white man, acknowledging his children and their mother legally. Marianne would have to wait for her freedom until her lover's death, but the release of the children from bondage was immediate. "I'm very grateful that he did the right thing, because obviously, many chose not to," Valerie said. However, her praise for her sixth great-grandfather was measured. "An unusual man, a good man—a good man at least in doing that. You wonder in the first instance how you have slaves. I can't imagine how anyone could think they should own another human being."

In August 1770, five months after he emancipated his children and acknowledged his intimate relationship with their mother, Pierre Rochon married. His bride was a French Canadian woman also named Marianne, Marianne Benoist. We found no evidence to help us understand Pierre's motivations for either his new marriage or his decision to emancipate his children. Perhaps it was for their protection; in the event of Pierre's death, his legal wife would be entitled to his property, including his slaves. By freeing them prior to the marriage and Marianne Rochon upon his death, he prevented his legal wife, Marianne Benoist, from selling or separating them.

The marriage license couldn't answer our questions about the complexities of human relationships, but it did allow us to go back another generation on Valerie's Rochon family tree, providing the names of Pierre's parents, Valerie's seventh great-grandparents Charles Rochon and Henriette Colon. A map of colonial Mobile revealed that the Rochons were among the first families to settle the area, and Charles Rochon was one of the city's four founders. Valerie's seventh great-grandfather Charles Rochon was a French Canadian fur trapper. At an early age he left his birthplace of Quebec City and traveled south along the Mississippi River, ultimately settling in Mobile in 1701, at about age thirty-one. From his baptismal record we learned the names of his parents, Valerie's eighth great-grandparents Simon Rochon and Mathurie Bisson. Simon Rochon, born Simon Rocheron around 1633, made the journey from Normandy, France, to Quebec in 1657, when he was twenty-four. At some point before his son's birth, Valerie's eighth great-grandfather anglicized, or at least shortened, the family name to Rochon. Simon Rochon was Valerie's first immigrant ancestor.

The baptismal record for Valerie's seventh great-grandmother Henriette Colon, the wife of the French Canadian fur trapper and Mobile founder, had survived as well, and it told a very different story about Valerie's origins. It was recorded in French on November 27, 1698, in the Immaculate Conception of Our Lady of Kaskaskia Church. The baby then called Henrica was baptized at one month, born to Jean-Baptiste La Violette Colon and Catherine Exipakinoa, Valerie's eighth great-grandparents. Henriette's mother was Native American. The Kaskaskia were one of a group of approximately twelve Algonquin-speaking Native American tribes of the Illinois River Basin, a region frequented by French explorers, fur traders, and missionaries making their way south. The Native American village of Kaskaskia, where Henriette was born, became home to a Jesuit mission in 1675, and many French men took Native wives who converted to Christianity. "I'm speechless, and I'm never speechless," Valerie laughed. "I'm good and mixed, aren't I?"

■ Valerie's family tree embodied the paradox of American democracy, with slavery and freedom coexisting on its branches. On both sides of her family, the paper trail brought her further back than she could have imagined. On Valerie's father's side, her oldest named ancestor was her third great-grandfather James Peterson, who was born in slavery in Virginia around 1815, the same year that her maternal ancestor Narcisse Rochon, a free man, served as a soldier in the War of 1812. On her mother's side, her oldest named ancestor was Julien Rocheron, born in Saint-Come-de-Ver, France, in 1610, whose descendants came to the Louisiana Territory from France by way of Canada.

We had already traveled great distances with Valerie's ancestors in the paper trail, and DNA would prolong the journey. We administered an admixture test to Valerie, which measures an individual's percentages of European, sub-Saharan African, and East Asian / Native American ancestry from about the last five hundred years. On Valerie's family tree were many white ancestors, many ancestors described as mulatto, and her admixture results were in keeping with these findings: 49 percent European, 46 percent sub-Saharan African, and 5 percent Native American. She had considerably more Native American ancestry than most African Americans tested. In fact, only 5 percent of the African American population has at least 2 percent Native American ancestry. That she had more European DNA than African DNA didn't rattle her. "I could have gone either way," she said.

We broke down Valerie's African DNA to determine which countries it represented. Valerie had traveled to Africa many times. "I could have been from any one of those countries," she said. "I felt right at home everywhere we went." As for almost all of the African American individuals we tested, Valerie's results reflected the countries most affected by the transatlantic slave trade. Her breakdown was 24 percent Nigeria, 8 percent Congo, 6 percent Ivory Coast and Ghana, 5 percent Senegal, 2 percent southeastern Bantu, and 1 percent Benin and Togo. The majority of her slave ancestors would always remain nameless, but Valerie's DNA was able to tell her something of their origins.

Similarly, we broke down Valerie's European DNA and found a large portion of Irish/Scottish ancestry in it, in addition to 16 percent from Scandinavia, which was not represented in the paper trail, and 3 percent from western Europe, including France, which was, on her mother's mother's line. Angus Taylor, whom circumstantial evidence pointed to as her third great-grandfather on her mother's father's line, was of Scottish descent, so this result lent more support to the argument for paternity; however, it established only location, not identity.

Further analysis of Valerie's DNA could solve definitively the lingering mysteries on both sides of her family tree, that of the paternity of her maternal great-great-grandfather Henry Taylor as well as her paternal Jewish great-grandfather. We started with the Taylors. On her mother's side,

Valerie's great-grandfather Robert Robinson Taylor had written of "my grandfather Angus Taylor," who appeared to be both owner and father of Valerie's great-great-grandfather Henry Taylor. We tested the Y-DNA of one of Valerie's male cousins, Edward Taylor, on her direct maternal line. Because Angus Taylor was from Scotland, we would expect to find Edward's Y-DNA carrying a European Y-chromosome, ideally one that was Scottish. When we ran Edward's Y-DNA, we found two matches in particular that provided the results we needed to help prove paternity. Valerie's cousin's two closest matches were Martyn Taylor from Skipness, Scotland, Angus Taylor's ancestral home, and John Creed Taylor from Bladen County, North Carolina, Angus Taylor's American home. Furthermore, both men had identified Angus Taylor's grandfather Archibald Taylor as a direct paternal ancestor. That was all the proof we needed, but we went further anyway. When we tested Valerie's autosomal DNA, which an individual inherits from both parents and all of his or her ancestral lines, and compared it to that of a woman named Pat Matthews, a descendant of Angus Taylor's sister Catherine, we discovered that they shared a tremendous amount of DNA. There was no question that Angus Taylor was Henry Taylor's father. Valerie's third great-grandfather was her ancestor's father and master.

On Valerie's father's side, there was an often-repeated rumor of a Jewish ancestor. If that rumor were true, we would know from Valerie's DNA. Did some of her European ancestry come from her paternal great-grandfather, her grandmother Dorothy Bowman's father, who was purportedly Jewish? Ashkenazi Jewish DNA was present in Valerie's admixture, but at only 2 percent of her European total, it was too small a figure to indicate a Jewish great-grandparent. One Jewish great-grandparent would have contributed an eighth, or 12.5 percent, of her European DNA. In other words, Valerie's great-grandfather could not have had primarily Jewish ancestry. A reading of 2 percent indicates that Valerie's Jewish ancestor entered her family tree somewhere between five and nine generations ago, or at the level of her third to seventh great-grandparents. Valerie laughed. "Maybe the story started, and they just kept saying 'great-grandfather' generation after generation, and they forgot to add a 'great-great-great-great' after each one," she said. "It looks like folklore."

■ Valerie admitted that she had never given equal weight to the many lines on her family tree. "I always focused on my great-grandfather, not so much on my great-grandmother," she said, referring to her Rochon ancestors. "I gave her short shrift, and I shouldn't have."

Our exploration of Valerie's roots had leveled the field. Her great-grandfather, Robert Robinson Taylor, was a great man, deserving of the place of honor he occupied in Valerie's family as well as in history books. But perhaps because of his prominence, many of the other rich stories we shared with Valerie had been lost over time. Did one strike a chord with Valerie more than others? If a time machine could take her back to one ancestor, traveling across the more than three centuries they had been in this country, which one would it be? Valerie had a lot of questions for her sixth great-grandmother Marianne Rochon, the mistress of her master and the mother of his children. She wanted to know "how she felt the moment he told her she would be free when he died," Valerie said. "What did that mean to her, not just as his lover, but as a mother of six children who she knew would have a very different life as a result of his act?"

Looking into one's genealogy personalized history. On just one branch of Valerie's family tree, one ancestor, a free black man in a segregated regiment, fought to assert America's independence against the British in the War of 1812; another stood in the Louisiana legislature and railed against the Separate Car Act, which threatened to undermine, and ultimately did undermine, the civil rights of African Americans. Had her perspective on American history and our country changed? "It clarifies for me, in a very personal way, the fact that I have as rich and as strong a heritage in this country as anybody, probably more than most people," she said. A particular point of pride for her was her multicultural heritage. "I'm very proud of the diversity in my history. In a sense, that's what this country is all about. We are a nation of immigrants. We come from all over, and as the arc of the universe spins a little bit closer toward justice, we accept each other a little bit more than we have historically."

Valerie's family tree was filled with individuals who overcame tremendous odds to achieve unbelievable success. What did she feel was the most important factor in shaping our identities and our outcomes? Was it the DNA inside us, or was it our experiences in the world around us? She did not deny that her ancestry was "a great motivator." All of her ancestors lived in her through DNA and inspired her through their lives and works. But, she said, "you pave your own way, and you make your own decisions, and you can't be limited by your history. But you also can't rest on your laurels as a result of your history." For Valerie, it came back to her no-excuses outlook on life. "The onus is really on you to do honor to your ancestors by doing the very best that you can do. I feel that extra sense of commitment to get back to work." She laughed. "I've got a lot to live up to."

One of the greatest ironies of black genealogy is that to learn the identities of our slave ancestors, we have to turn to the records left behind by their masters—the very people who denied them their humanity. Through the paper trail, we had traced the lineages of Nasir Jones, Angela Bassett, and Valerie Jarrett back through three hundred years of American history and identified a stunning number of their slave ancestors by name. On multiple branches of their family trees, we saw relationships formed in blood and forged by choice. Through these relationships, Nas, Angela, and Valerie gained a deeper understanding of how their ancestors confronted the brutalities of slavery and affirmed their humanity, which slavery so cruelly sought to erase.

CHAPTER SEVEN

Our People, Our Traditions

Jewish Americans share much in common with other European immigrants who crossed the Atlantic seeking a better life. But there is one crucial difference: the long history of their persecution, and the many attempts to systematically annihilate them, made the Jewish quest for haven in the New World literally a matter of survival. The criminal defense attorney Alan Dershowitz, the singer-songwriter Carole King, and the writer Tony Kushner all descend from Jewish immigrants who fled Russia and eastern Europe to find sanctuary in America and the freedom to practice their faith in the way they chose. While Alan, Carole, and Tony have their own individual relationship to their faith and their culture, their family's stories of perseverance in the face of prejudice and poverty unite them.

Alan Dershowitz (b. 1938)

Alan Dershowitz has been described as one of the nation's "most distinguished defenders of individual rights." In 1967, when he was just twenty-eight years old, he became a full tenured professor at Harvard Law School, the youngest in the history of the institution. Over his long career he has written more than thirty books, some on law, but also novels and the memoir *Chutzpah*, and he has argued more than one hundred cases for high-profile clients ranging from O. J. Simpson to Patty Hearst to Leona Helmsley to Klaus von Bulow, cases that have made his name as famous as those of his defendants. He is less well known, however, for the pro bono work he does on behalf of clients who can't afford an attorney at all. The drive to fight for those who can't fight for themselves comes from the values ingrained in him as a child, in his home and in his synagogue. "It was always just an automatic part of our growing up that it was the job of the Jew to always be out there defending the underdog," he explained. "We were the underdog. I feel like I have to remember that it was only very recently that I was the underdog, and I may become the underdog again."

Born on September 1, 1938, in Brooklyn, New York, Alan describes his notion of being Jewish as "complex." Like many modern Jews, Alan emphasizes the divide in Judaism: that one can identify strongly as Jewish without adhering to strict religious practice. "Judaism is a civilization. It's a religiously based civilization, but it's a civilization and a culture and a history, and for me, I'm part of all of that, though I'm not particularly theologically religious." Alan recognized this division from an early age. "My family was completely observant, and I have no idea whether either my father or my mother believed in God. Nobody ever said to me, 'God's watching you.' Nobody ever said to me, 'You're not going to go to heaven.' It was, 'Did you make the right blessing? Did you wash your hands before the meal? When you woke up, did you thank God for allowing you to wake up?' It was all about observance. There were 613 *mitzvot*, 613 obligations, in the Torah, and they counted. They checked it off. You had to perform every one of them."

Yet being Jewish informs every aspect of Alan's life, as it did his parents', and never once did he consider rejecting their teachings or traditions. "I don't think I ever said a cruel word or even a harsh word to my mother or my father or any of my grandparents," Alan said. As great a hold as his parents had on him, they couldn't keep him in Brooklyn forever. "My parents were terrified that I and my brother would assimilate and leave the fold, and they wanted to hold on to us as long as they could. Going to Yeshiva University High School wasn't so much the education; it was the control. They knew that I would only meet Jewish girls, Orthodox girls. They sent me to Jewish summer camp at the same time. They wanted to constrain the externalities."

Those externalities began to change for Alan at Yale Law School. In his 1992 book *Chutzpah*, he wrote that leaving Brooklyn and Brooklyn College, where he completed his undergraduate degree, to attend Yale Law was almost as traumatic as the journey his ancestors took when they were up-rooted from their homes in the old country to create a new life in America. In a word, Alan said, Yale was "alien." "The first time I spoke up in class, I got laughed at, because I talk with a pretty thick Brooklyn accent," he recalled. Alan's "overt" Jewishness raised obstacles for him upon graduation from Yale Law, too. "Yale Law School, first in my class. I'm editor in chief of the *Yale Law Journal*. I'm like the number-one draft choice in the NBA," he joked, "and no law firm wants me. Thirty-two out of thirty-two Wall Street firms find excuses for not hiring me. It became clear to me that being Jewish was not an advantage in getting a job in a Wall Street firm." Yet Alan, perhaps not surprisingly to those familiar with his public persona, "didn't feel a moment of pain." "I was always taught by my father to fight back and never let it get you. Don't get ulcers; give ulcers." Alan is well known for bringing this fight into the public arena, be it in a courtroom or a television news studio. After all, he comes from people for whom fighting was the only means of survival.

Alan once wrote that there's no legacy comparable to the commitment to Jewish tradition and practice that his ancestors left him. As an adult, he adapted this legacy to fit his life and his own beliefs. "My ancestors, from the time of the Bible until the time my brother and I essentially left the Orthodox fold, had observed for thousands of years. This is a strong legacy, and they did it at enormous cost to themselves—persecution, pogroms, the Inquisition—and it took an enormous amount of chutzpah and maybe even disrespect for me and my brother to decide that we were going to break that chain," Alan said. "But I couldn't live a life that I didn't believe, so I live my own Jewish life, consistent with my own Jewish beliefs. Part of Jewish tradition is to reject parts of Jewish tradition."

And part of that tradition is to keep the faith at all costs, no matter how dire the circumstances or how difficult the challenge. Now it was time to explore Alan's family tree, to meet the people who kept the faith and handed down their age-old traditions in a new world.

■ We started our journey into Alan's roots on his mother's side. Clara Ringel, known as Claire, was born in Manhattan on July 21, 1913, a first-generation American. Alan described his mother as "very, very smart." A high school graduate by the age of fifteen, she was the first person in her family admitted to City College in New York. Like many women of her generation, she wanted to be a schoolteacher, but the Depression hit before she could fulfill her dream. Forced to leave school to help support the family, she was never able to go back. "She always regretted it," Alan said. "She could have been almost anything. She had a real deep intelligence." She also had a deep commitment to Judaism. "Judaism meant everything to my mother," Alan explained. "For her, being part of the Jewish community was crucial, and observance was crucial. Again, theology, not so much."

Alan's maternal grandparents figured prominently in his life. "My grandmother dominated the family," Alan recalled. "Her word was law. My mother listened to everything she said. My mother was a child at age fifty or sixty when her mother was there." Both grandparents, he knew, put a premium on being Jewish, but their approaches were entirely opposite. His grandmother's story exemplified the often difficult process of assimilation for eastern European Jews coming to this country, struggling to balance their Old World values with those of modern, twentieth-century America. "My grandmother had a very negative approach to Judaism. Her favorite word was *matornisht*. 'You're not allowed; this is not permissible.' If I would ever do anything, I was smacked on the fingers. You're not allowed to have a chocolate bar so soon after having a hamburger. *Matornisht, matornisht.* You're not allowed to drink water without making a special blessing. You're not allowed to speak during prayers." As for his grandfather, "I didn't know him very well, except through my mother's memories. My mother loved him, admired him. He was the greatest man in the history of the world. He could do no wrong. He had a very positive approach to Judaism. He loved my mother and encouraged her in every way."

Alan's grandparents were born in an area that was then called Galicia, his grandfather Naftali Ringel around 1878 in the town of Przemysl and his grandmother Blima Newman in 1887 in nearby Cieszanow. Nothing was known of Naftali or Blima's parents, Alan's great-grandparents, beyond their names: Naftali's were Abraham Mordechai Ringel and Ann or Chane Lea Helenwreich, and Blima's were Yitzriol Svi Newman and Dworja. "I know nothing about who they were, what they did," he said. Little evidence survived of his great-grandparents' downtrodden generation. "They were Galicianers, which is the lowest level of eastern European Jew," Alan explained. "We were the peasants, the nonintellectuals."

Now located in Poland, Galicia was an agricultural center in the Austro-Hungarian Empire, extremely poor, but with a tight-knit Jewish community. Naftali's hometown of Przemysl was home to just under eleven thousand Jews. They made up about a third of the entire population. The town had a thriving Jewish culture, and it was a center of the Hasidic movement. "In some ways, it was very idyllic," Alan related. "There was a very good Jewish community. There were synagogues and schools." Yet, he continued, "there had been periods of pogroms. There had been periods of anti-Semitism. Of course you couldn't progress from Przemysl. You couldn't get to university. It was very difficult if you were Jewish."

On January 15, 1898, an influential Catholic journal called *Prawda*, which was distributed widely across Galicia, printed an article called "Defense against the Jews." Alan read the incendiary passage: "Jews are a plague and a punishment for every soil they inhabited, as their enterprise ruins it, and their moral values are poison to the societies that welcomed them. One has to defend oneself from destruction that their actions bring upon the Christians." Galicia was in the grip of a severe economic crisis, the sad result of a decade of crop failures, and Jewish merchants and bankers were used as scapegoats. That summer, rioting erupted throughout Galicia. Naftali was twenty years old, Blima only eleven, when this was going on, and in June, an event so horrible happened in the Galician town of Frysztak, about sixty miles from Przemysl, that it made headlines around the world. Whipped into a frenzy by anti-Semitic rhetoric, Christians looted and destroyed hundreds of Jewish homes and businesses. On June 16, a German newspaper published details of the mayhem. "At eight o'clock in the evening," Alan read, "approximately 1,000 unemployed persons gathered. The police incited the crowd, saying, 'Cut down the Jews. They have bread and cakes.' The excitement among the crowd began to grow tremendously. The residents who are Jews made a great noise, shouting, 'Violence, robbery!' Some street youths began smashing windows. By ten o'clock, many were injured and bleeding heavily." The next day, across the Atlantic, the *New York Tribune* wrote of the event that Galician Jews called "The Plunder." Alan guessed that their proximity to the hateful events affected his grandparents deeply. "I can tell you one thing: it had a profound influence on their love for America," he said. "My grandmother loved America. She would make my brother and me recite the Pledge of Allegiance, go to the Statue of Liberty. Her biggest holiday was July Fourth. She loved America. America," he concluded, "was everything that Poland was not."

Almost exactly a month later, on July 15, 1898, an editorial in a Galician Jewish newspaper called *Der Israelit* posited: "And all this, namely the plundering of Jews in one's own soil, the seed of a moral poison has been sown, that dulls the sense of right and justice and order, making social life wild and impossible, threatening the future of the nation. It has made life as we had known it impossible and puts into question the future." Being Jewish in turn-of-the-century Poland was exceedingly dangerous. Wouldn't it have been easier for those Jews who survived to reject the heritage that caused them such pain? "For my grandparents, there was no option," Alan said. "They couldn't reject their Jewishness. Their Jewishness was who they were. They could reject their Polishness, and they did. They left Poland."

Between 1900 and 1910, nearly 170,000 Jews fled persecution throughout the Austro-Hungarian Empire, the vast majority coming from the Galicia region. According to a passenger record from the SS *America*, which arrived at Ellis Island on August 17, 1907, Naftali Ringel made the journey to New York alone, with ten dollars in his pocket, the first person on Alan's mother's side of the family to come to the United States. It would be two years before Alan's grandmother Blima joined her husband. Blima was actually Naftali's second wife. Her sister had died, leaving Naftali a widower with two children. Alan explained that it "was Jewish tradition" for a man to marry the sister of his deceased wife. Like Naftali, Blima arrived on the SS *America*, on October 31, 1909, with her stepchildren, Berl and Dworye Ringel. It had taken Naftali two years to earn enough money to bring over his family.

Arriving in America without a penny in her possession, Blima Ringel and her stepchildren were detained by Ellis Island officials. Each year thousands of immigrants, without someone to meet them and vouch for them, were sent back to their native countries. Fortunately Naftali arrived later that day and proved to immigration officials that he would take care of her. Alan looked at his grandmother's name. "Detained. I never heard this. She probably thought this is like Poland, where the police would arrest you and detain you, and you'd never be heard from again. She was probably embarrassed about this. This is not part of our family memory."

In 1910, Naftali and Blima were living at 242 Rivington Street with their children, who now went by the Americanized names Benjamin and Dora, in the heart of the Lower East Side, by some estimates home to a half million Jews. It was one of the largest concentrations of Jewish people anywhere in the world. "My grandmother said they thought it was paradise," Alan said, "even though the streets were packed. There were pushcarts, people selling old clothes and fruit. But for my grandparents, it was paradise. This was New York. It was America." Alan's grandfather worked as a peddler of dry goods, one of thousands of merchants crowding the streets of the Lower

East Side. It was noisy and dirty, and the families living there were scraping by. Did Alan's grandparents ever regret their choice to leave Galicia? "It never occurred to them in a million years to regret it," Alan stated matter-of-factly. "They knew their life would be hard. Their goal was to improve the lives of their children and grandchildren." They had no nostalgia for Poland, but plenty for Rivington Street. "'Oh, Rivington Street, oy, what a great place,'" Alan remembered his grandparents saying. "It was filled with synagogues and filled with Jewish cultural centers and with friends from the old country—and safety. It was a safe place. There were no pogroms."

On July 15, 1914, seven years after he immigrated to America on the *America*, Naftali Ringel became an American citizen. "It was ordered by the court," Alan said, looking at a copy his certificate, at his grandfather's signature, "that he be admitted as a citizen of the United States of America. I can imagine how proud he must have been." With Naftali's naturalization, Blima also won American citizenship. To Alan's grandparents, America was the proverbial promised land. "America was the place that the streets were paved with milk and honey and gold. America was, for them, the salvation and the solution of every problem."

As much as he loved his new home, Naftali never forgot his old one. On July 18, 1924, he filed an application for a passport "for use in visiting the countries named for the following purposes: Poland, visit relatives." By 1924 Przemysl had become part of Poland, and three brothers and several nieces and nephews still lived there. Less than two decades later, in 1942, the Jewish population of Naftali's hometown would be decimated by the Nazis. Almost all of Przemysl's nearly twenty thousand Jews were deported to concentration camps and killed, two of Alan's great-uncles and several other relatives among them.

■ The Holocaust, Alan said, "has affected my whole life in every way. For me, 'Never Again' is not a slogan. Family members were killed. I grew up in Borough Park. In 1945, Borough Park was flooded with immigrants, so I grew up with survivors. I grew up with people with their numbers tattooed on their wrists. I grew up with stories, mostly untold because they were embarrassed and ashamed to talk about it. It was really a generational silence. But we knew." As we explored his father's side of Alan's family tree, we would learn the remarkable story of Alan's grandfather Louis Dershowitz and the extraordinary lengths to which he went to save his family from certain death in Nazi-occupied Poland.

Alan's father, Harry Dershowitz, was born on May 8, 1909, in Manhattan. A salesman and co-owner of the Merit Sales Company, Harry was, according to his son, a very hard worker and dedicated Jew, a founder of the Young Israel Synagogue in their Borough Park neighborhood. "Worked six days a week, and on the seventh day went to the synagogue," he said. "He influenced me by teaching my values, values of defending the underdog, the value of fighting back, the value of not taking it." But, Alan said, his father "didn't like arguing with people. He was a very likable man, so he would always be elected to be the vice president or the president of various organizations. He was a consensus builder. In that respect," Alan laughed, "I don't think I take after him."

Alan had strong memories of both of his paternal grandparents, both of whom were born in Galicia, Louis Dershowitz in September 1881 in Pilzno and Ida Maultasch around 1887 in Tarnobrzeg. Today both towns are part of Poland. Alan said that his father was extremely close to his own mother, a figure "more domineering than likable." "My grandmother was like a mother bear. You couldn't say anything critical of any of her children. Nobody was good enough for her children." He described his grandfather as "a lovely man." "My grandfather, although he came over when he was very young, had no memories of eastern Europe. He was an all-American guy, wore a straw hat, liked the Brooklyn Dodgers. Liked America and liked being an American." More than his other grandparents, Louis Dershowitz "was very anxious to meld Americanism and Judaism." In an effort to do so, he cofounded the Yeshiva Torah Vodaath in Brooklyn, a Hebrew school and seminary. Alan's grandfather was extraordinarily proud of the school, which "all of our family" attended. "The very words *Torah Vodaath* mean Bible and knowledge, secular knowledge," Alan explained. "It was a way of trying to bring together America and the old country, Bible and modern knowledge."

Alan knew little of his great-grandparents. "I did know Louis's mother. We used to call her Bubba Meyer. Why I don't know. I have vague memories of her as a little old lady, sitting on the stoop." Based on records we found in the United States, we confirmed that Alan's grandfather's parents were named Zacharia Dershowitz and Lea Bender. We continued our search in Poland, although we weren't hopeful. On his mother's side, we hadn't been able to find any Galician records about his ancestors, a common problem of Jewish genealogy. Our luck changed on Alan's father's side.

Amazingly, we found Alan's great-grandfather's birth certificate, preserved in a Polish archive since a year before the Civil War broke out in America. Zacharia Serschowitz was born on July 6, 1860, to father Chaskel and mother Chane Riwke. "It all goes back to him," Alan said of his great-grandfather. "He's the man who came to America. He's the reason I'm alive today. He's the reason I was not a victim of the Holocaust. I owe a tremendous amount to Zacharia Dershowitz." Although we couldn't find his great-great-grandparents' birth certificates, we assumed that they were most likely born in Galicia also, around 1840. "This really makes me feel like I'm touching the past, like I'm going back in history," Alan said. "It makes me feel like part of a chain, and makes me feel a little guilty about abandoning the chain to the extent I have. I'm no longer Orthodox. They would not regard me as part of their tradition of deeply Orthodox, observant Jews."

Life for the Jews of Galicia, as we had seen with Alan's maternal grandparents, was harrowing. Zacharia immigrated to New York in 1888 and sent for the rest of his family three years later. The passenger list for the *Furst Bismarck*, which arrived in the Port of New York on August 8, 1891, contained the names of Alan's great-grandmother Lea Dershowitz, great-aunts and great-uncles, and of course his grandfather Louis, just nine years old at the time. "In 1988, the family did have an event celebrating the hundredth anniversary of the arrival of the first Dershowitzes in America," Alan recalled. "We've been in America now more than half of America's existence, and it's amazing."

According to the 1900 census, the Dershowitz family was living in an apartment on the Lower East Side, the center of Jewish life in Manhattan. Alan's great-grandfather Zacharia worked as an operator in a suit factory in the Garment District. "My family myth—I don't know whether it's true—is that he worked in the Triangle building that became the place where there was this terrible fire that killed hundreds of Jewish women particularly, who were operating machines," Alan explained. "The family myth is that he was saved because the fire occurred on Saturday, and he was Sabbath-observant, and therefore was not at work that day." We couldn't confirm any connection to the Triangle Shirtwaist Factory, but the conditions in which Zacharia worked were probably equally grueling. In spite of the hardships of immigrant life, Alan said, to Zacharia, America meant two things. "One, it meant he wasn't in Poland anymore, which was a very, very important thing. Second, it meant his children would have better opportunities. For him, it was very, very difficult. I mean, a sweatshop, working long hours, very difficult for him because he was Sabbath-observant, but it was better than what he had."

By 1920, the Dershowitzes had relocated to the Williamsburg section of Brooklyn. Here, the seeds of a bustling Orthodox community were being sown, and the Dershowitz men would eventually establish the neighborhood's first *shtiebel*, a small Orthodox community synagogue in the basement of their South Tenth Street home. "This was a synagogue without a rabbi," Alan explained. "This was a family synagogue, and the cantor was my grandfather. The lay leader was my great-grandfather, but he wasn't a rabbi. There were no employees. Nobody got paid." The *shtiebel* filled a need for the neighborhood's Orthodox Jews, who could often only obtain work if they agreed to work on Saturdays, the Jewish Sabbath. The basement synagogue allowed them to pray at home and to pray communally. The little shul remained an important part of the fabric of Jewish Williamsburg for many years to come.

The Dershowitzes' basement synagogue would be the lifeblood for an entire branch of Alan's extended family. By the 1930s, Jews desperate to escape the growing Nazi menace in Europe were fleeing the continent in great numbers. In response, the United States resorted to immigration quotas and other onerous visa restrictions to stem the flow of Jewish refugees. In 1939 the Roosevelt administration turned away the *St. Louis*, a ship carrying 907 passengers, most of them German Jewish refugees, forcing its return to Europe, where hundreds of those onboard would ultimately die in concentration camps.

Many Dershowitzes had stayed behind in eastern Europe at the turn of the century, at the time that Alan's great-grandparents had fled. Now they were in graver danger than ever before, and Alan's grandfather Louis hatched an ingenious plan to rescue them: suddenly his tiny basement synagogue was in need of a staff. By issuing affidavits guaranteeing they had employment, Louis proved that his relatives had a purpose for coming to America. "My grandfather would have affidavits saying, 'Our synagogue needs a rabbi. It needs a *hazzan* [cantor]. It needs a circumciser. It needs a *shochet* [kosher butcher]. It needs a *shammes* [caretaker].' You'd have these affidavits, so they would have an opportunity to say, 'We have a job,' and they would come over," Alan said. "And that's the way we saved twenty-eight members of our family."

A set of passenger records from 1939, from ships departing ports in Germany and Poland en route to the United States, listed Dershowitz upon Dershowitz, every one of them saved by Louis Dershowitz from almost certain death at the hands of the Nazis. "Chaskel Deresewicz, Aron Deresewicz, Hirsh Deresewicz, Wolf Deresewicz," Alan read. "I knew all these people. My God, it's 1939. Hitler invades Czechoslovakia just in about that period of time, and my grandfather saves all these people." Sadly, not all of Alan's relatives could be rescued, and they met with the tragic fate of so many Jews who perished at concentration camps like Auschwitz and Treblinka. By the time Nazi Germany surrendered, more than 6 million Jews had been exterminated. Well over half of them came from Poland. Alan felt he owed a tremendous debt to his ancestors. "The most important decision in my life was not made by me," he said. "It was made by my grandparents to leave Poland and to come to America. If they had remained in Poland, I would have been four years old at the time of the Final Solution, and I would have been part of that solution."

Alan's grandfather put his own freedom at great risk by forging the documents that saved his relatives from death at the hands of the Nazis. "He loved America, but he committed crimes in America, and he was proudest of the crimes he committed." So was his grandson, one of the leading criminal defense lawyers in the country. "You might ask me why I'm so sympathetic to illegal immigrants in the United States. Because my family were illegal immigrants. Some of the most successful members of my family were brought over on fake affidavits. These folks, who came in as illegal immigrants, on the eve of the Holocaust, became among the most productive American citizens."

In the face of unmitigated evil, Alan's grandfather had saved twenty-eight lives, "using lawlessness to protect the innocent." Alan's journey into his father's roots ended on a triumphant note.

◼ The documents—legal and otherwise—that we uncovered for Alan's ancestors told us an enormous amount about the eastern European Jewish immigrant experience. The paper trail brought us back to the middle of the nineteenth century. On his mother's side the oldest named ancestor we could trace was Alan's great-grandfather Abraham Mordechai Ringel, born in Galicia around 1860. On his father's side we found rare birth certificates that took us back further than was typical of Jewish genealogy:

we identified four sets of great-great-grandparents born during the 1840s. Alan's oldest named ancestor was his great-great-grandfather Chaskel Dershowitz, born around 1840, also in Galicia.

To delve more deeply into Alan's ancestry, we turned to DNA, and we administered three tests, the first of which was an admixture test, which measures a person's percentages of European, sub-Saharan African, and East Asian / Native American ancestry from the past five hundred years or so. Alan's result was, he said, "so pure it's amazing": 99.9 percent European. When we broke down that number to measure his Jewish DNA specifically, it also came back remarkably pure, to use Alan's word: 98.5 percent Ashkenazi Jewish, with trace bits of DNA from other population groups, including southern European and Balkan. His Ashkenazi Jewish roots ran very, very deep.

Next we tested Alan's Y-DNA, which every man gets from his father, in an unbroken line from generation to generation. His paternal haplogroup, a genetic population group sharing a common ancestor, is the most common Y-chromosome among men throughout the Arabian Peninsula. It's found only rarely in Europe except among Jewish men whose male ancestors brought it from the Near East as a consequence of the Diaspora.

A test of Alan's mitochondrial DNA, an identical genetic signature that passes from mother to child, male or female, revealed that his maternal haplogroup is commonly found around the Caucasus region. This haplogroup reaches its highest frequency in Lebanon, where it is carried by up to 20 percent of the population. While it isn't one of the mitochondrial haplogroups associated primarily with Ashkenazi Jews, neither is it unusual to find it among people of Jewish heritage.

An analysis of Alan's autosomal DNA, which an individual inherits from both parents and all of his or her ancestral lines, would tell us which of our other participants Alan was related to genetically. Because of Ashkenazi Jewish communities' tendency to live in isolation from their gentile neighbors, the rate of "cousining" among Jews of eastern European descent is exceptionally high. With this in mind, we would look at Alan's autosomal DNA at the end of the chapter, alongside that of his cousins, Carole King and Tony Kushner.

■ Throughout our time together, Alan noted his gratitude to his ancestors frequently. He believed that their courage in leaving their homeland not only allowed him to live a better life, but, frankly, allowed him to live. The

Holocaust had touched his family very personally, as had the rampant persecution that was part of Jewish life in nineteenth-century eastern Europe. Did going on this journey with them today change anything about the way he sees himself? "Absolutely," Alan answered definitively. "It really makes me think that no man is an island, how much I am connected to my past and also how much I am connected to others in the present. Now I feel much more connected to the human family. It's affirming to me."

Alan knew his grandparents on both sides. He had grown up surrounded by family. But if he could hop into a time machine and meet just one of the ancestors we'd introduced him to, who would it be? He chose his great-grandfather, Zacharia Dershowitz. Alan knew Zacharia had left behind a difficult life in Poland, but the one he found in this country wasn't without its trials. "I'd want to ask him directly why he gave up so much to come to America, and I want to thank him for doing that, and tell him how much I appreciate the sacrifices that he made to work in a sweatshop. Probably in some ways, his life would have been more comfortable staying back in Galicia, but he came here, enduring this boat ride and leaving his family for years so that I could be what I have become. And my brother and my children and everybody else, we're all part of this one connection."

The Jewish people have a unique history, one filled with sorrow and pain. Yet, as they did in Alan's family, they have clung to the religion that has been the source of much of their suffering. Is it the culture or the religion itself that is so deeply ingrained? In other words, could Alan pinpoint what makes a Jewish person Jewish? Is it the lived experiences, our families, our DNA, our history? "It's obviously a combination," Alan responded, "and for different people it's different things. For me, it's clearly my DNA. When I think about the leadership qualities and the boldness that some of my relatives showed over time, clearly there's something I've inherited," he said. "But the experiences of persecution, the historical incidents that surround Jewish life, play a very important role in my own life, and then, finally, the opportunities we've had. The quest for education and the fact that Jewish parents put learning so high on the scale of values, all of that contributed to who we are."

Alan, a high-profile attorney, scholar, and author known for his bravado, was humbled in the face of his own history. "What this has done for me makes me feel less confident in my own self and much more gratified that I'm part of a chain. I owe my success to so many," he said gratefully. "I've stood on the shoulders of giants."

For many of us, Carole King is the voice of a generation. A four-time Grammy Award–winning singer and songwriter, she achieved pop superstardom with her 1971 album *Tapestry*. With more than 25 million copies sold, it remains one of the best-selling albums of all time. The iconic album contains some of her best-known, best-loved songs: "So Far Away," "I Feel the Earth Move," and, of course, "(You Make Me Feel Like a) Natural Woman," which was seared into our collective consciousness by Aretha Franklin. Whether made famous through her own recordings or others', Carole's heart and soul are unmistakable in each of these songs, making them the classics they have become.

Born Carol Joan Klein on February 9, 1942, in New York City, she was a "nice Jewish girl" to whom music came naturally and early. She began to "tinkle notes" on the family piano "when I could first reach it." By age fifteen, she knew her life would be in music, and she changed her name to ease the transition. "I adopted the name King as a songwriter, and I also adopted the "e" around the same time. There were other Carol Kleins in my school, so I decided to give mine a different spelling," she said. She changed the spelling of her first name to be more distinctive, her last name to be less so. "In those days, Jewish performers typically changed their names to anglicize them, and that appealed to me. I think there was something about me that I didn't like just then, so I thought, OK, I'm going to give myself a little bit of a new identity."

To Carole, being Jewish means being part of "a chain" not easily broken. "It's less about the religion for me. It's a way of living, about leaving the world as good or better than you find it. I identify that as a Jewish teaching. Be compassionate to people; treat everybody with kindness and equality." While not observant herself, she finds meaning in the rituals. "My grandsons and granddaughter have been bar and bat mitzvahed. I wasn't, but I don't mind that I wasn't. The point is that just being part of a cultural chain that goes back so far is exciting to me." For her parents it was the same. "It wasn't about the religion. We were the Jewish family that went to synagogue only on the High Holy Days." She laughed. "It was about the cultural connection, what Jewish families did. It was the people that I came from. I wanted to learn about that."

Through music, specifically the emerging accessibility of rhythm and blues during the 1950s, Carole began to embrace other cultures. "I wasn't exposed to world music or African American music until my teens. I listened to Alan Freed when he was playing the R&B versions, like Fats Domino's 'Ain't That a Shame' instead of Pat Boone's 'Ain't That a Shame.' I heard them both, and you know which one I liked better." She laughed. The impact was immediate. "I was like a blotter, and any new music that I heard, that I loved, I absorbed and played it back. It spoke to me, but it spoke to my generation. I was not unique." Rock 'n' roll was a powerful unifying force for the black and Jewish communities. "I remember my neighborhood did not have black people except those who came to clean people's houses," Carole recalled candidly. "So for me to go to a place where the people are pouring in of every color, and we're all going to the same theater, and we were not a segregated audience, it was just dots of people of all colors, and everybody loved all the music, and everybody was dancing, it was a phenomenon." Perhaps there was a level of simpatico between Jewish culture and black culture, a cultural connection that went even beyond the music. Both cultures have survived unparalleled suffering, yet have an uncanny ability to embrace joy as well. "There is that commonality," she agreed. "Here's the thing about Jewish people. I think that black culture helped us come to a greater awareness of our essentiality, because we lived more in the head than in the body." For Carole, it always came back to music. "When you are enjoying the same music as someone from another culture, you are not judging their culture. There was no sense of racial difference."

Carole's career in music spans more than fifty years, but the roots of her success were planted well over a century ago, when her grandmother came to this country with a massive wave of other Jewish immigrants, carrying with her little more than her love of music and her dreams of success.

■ Not surprisingly, Carole's earliest memories revolve around music. Her mother's own record collection was extensive and eclectic. Eugenia Cammer, known as Genie, was born on July 31, 1916, in Brooklyn, New York, the daughter of Jewish immigrants. "My mother came from a household in which culture was very much valued, particularly music," she explained. "The first piece of furniture in my mother and father's home was a piano, paid for, I suppose, by my grandparents. It was always in my home, always in my field of vision, always someplace I went to explore, to have fun, to play."

Carole grew up in the predominantly Jewish neighborhood of Sheepshead Bay in Brooklyn, surrounded by a large extended family. Her maternal grandparents, both immigrants from what was then the Russian Empire, were always part of her life. Her grandfather Israel Benjamin Cammer was born on July 7, 1890, in Wloclawek, which is now in Poland, and her grandmother Sarah Besmogin was born on April 15, 1890, in Orsha, which is today in Belarus. "Grandma was all about food. She was an amazing cook, the typical Jew with the chicken soup, with the brisket. She was always cooking, always feeding us." Israel worked hard to provide for his family. "My grandfather had a wood-turning business," Carole said. "He was a carpenter and made things. He made hat blocks at his little wood-turning factory. It was a little bitty factory, and he did well, and Grandma Sarah liked that."

Sarah Besmogin was driven by a desire to build a better life for her family. "My grandmother was the child of a baker. She would deliver the bread to the rich girls' homes, and she'd press her nose up against the window and see the rich girls playing piano. She would never get to do that in her status as a Jewish woman of her generation." Things would be different, she believed, for her American daughter. "Genie was going to do that. As the child of immigrants, my mother had a lot of expectations placed on her by her mother. My grandmother wanted her to be a concert pianist and play in Carnegie Hall," Carole said. "It didn't come to pass, but isn't it interesting that I played in Carnegie Hall, because Genie had the knowledge to teach me the music? I really think about how life works and how things skip generations."

Carole's grandmother never spoke about her childhood in Russia. "She didn't want to speak Russian. She didn't want to tell any stories," Carole said, "not to me." In Sarah's hometown of Orsha, more than half of its thirteen thousand residents were Jewish, and like most eastern European Jews, they were desperately poor. She spent her childhood among the nearly 5 million Russian Jews confined to an area along the empire's western border known as the Pale of Settlement. At the time it was home to the largest community of Jewish people in the world. Established in 1791 by the Russian empress Catherine the Great, it was the only part of Russia where Jewish people were permitted to live—although they were not permitted to live well. Jews in the Pale were forbidden from buying farmland, and restrictive quotas prevented most from obtaining higher education. Economic opportunities were severely limited, and much of the Jewish community was left to languish in dire poverty. "No wonder she didn't talk about it," she said. "No wonder she aspired to wealth and culture and all the things she wanted my mother to be."

At fifteen Carole had changed her name and taken her first steps into professional songwriting. When her grandmother was fifteen, however, mere survival was a challenge. In 1905, the Russian tsar Nicholas II, responding to social unrest among the peasants, issued the October Manifesto, a proclamation that ostensibly would have put all Jewish people on an equal footing with other Russians. "We grant to the population the essential foundations of civil freedom," it promised, "based on the principles of genuine inviolability of the person, freedom of conscience, speech, assembly, and association." With centuries of anti-Semitism in Russia expected to come to an end, the Jews of Orsha celebrated. "Thousands of people came out into the city streets, notably Jews," a newspaper account from the time read. "The streets filled with an unprecedented liveliness. Many Jewish youth started trickling into the town square. The protesters carried red and black flags with slogans such as 'Hail the social democratic republic.'"

The celebration, unfortunately, was short-lived. On October 21, just four days after the manifesto was read, a local police clerk named Tikhon Sinitsky addressed a mob gathered in the Orsha town square. "My brothers, now the Jews are rebelling," Sinitsky warned. "We must stand up for ourselves. Otherwise we shall be in their hands. We have to continue to annihilate them until there's not one Jew left." Rather than emancipate Russia's Jewish population, the manifesto set off a rash of reactionary pogroms, outbreaks of anti-Semitic violence that spread throughout hundreds of towns in the Pale, including Orsha. In the archives of a Russian newspaper an eyewitness account detailed the brutality that befell Carole's grandmother's hometown. "The assailants used stakes to kill three people. They killed another person after torturing him for a long time. The screams and moans of those beaten did not bother the assailants, and the young lives were extinguished under merciless blows with clubs and axes."

This was only the beginning. A few days after the pogrom, the Russian newspaper *Belorussky-Vestnik* published a report on Orsha's destruction. "The town is completely torn apart. Terrorized for two days, destroyed houses, stores, and looted Jewish property. Masses of killed and wounded. The town was burning in several places." In the end, thirty-two Jewish people died, and hundreds more were severely injured. Two years after the pogrom, in 1907, a provincial court brought charges against more than fifty perpetrators of the violence. Almost half were acquitted; the rest were found guilty of only minor charges, and most were ultimately pardoned by the tsar. Carole had never heard a word about any of this from her grandmother. "My grandmother put a wall up," Carole said, and she understood why. "I put up walls, too. If I had lived through this, I wouldn't be talking to my grandkids about it, especially not my American grandkids, because this was the Promised Land. This was the land where this would not happen, so why would I bring this into my grandchildren's consciousness?"

Anti-Semitic attacks like these throughout Russia prompted tens of thousands of Jewish people to flee to the United States. In the early decades of the twentieth century, waves of impoverished Jewish immigrants made the grueling weeks-long transatlantic journey crowded together in the fetid underbelly of steerage compartments and passenger ships. Searching records for any sign of Carole's grandmother, we discovered a passenger list for the SS *Kursk*. It docked at Ellis Island on December 14, 1911. "Sheina Besmogin," Carole said, examining the ship's manifest. "I don't know who he or she is. Is that my great-grandfather?" Sheina Besmogin was Carole's grandmother; she Americanized her Yiddish name to Sarah only after her arrival.

For several years, Sarah lived in an apartment in Brooklyn with her mother, Riva Leah, her brother, Oscar, and her sisters Mary and Lillian. On October 17, 1915—exactly ten years after Tsar Nicholas II issued his October Manifesto—Sarah Besmogin and Israel Cammer filed for a marriage license. Carole's grandfather Israel had emigrated from Russia in 1910, a year before his new wife. As a creator and purveyor of hat blocks, Israel worked hard to establish himself, and he moved up quickly. In the 1921 *Millinery Trade Review*, his name was listed among the officers of the Gussoff Hat Block Company, Inc. "With Samuel Gussoff as president," the announcement read, "the Gussoff Hat Block Company, Inc., has been organized. The other officers of the company are Israel B. Cammer, vice president; Harry Fluenstan, treasurer; and Morris Gussoff, secretary." In little over a decade, Israel had seen his status improve, his opportunities grow. He had made something of himself, and his religion had not hindered his rise. His was a classic immigrant success story.

By 1930 Carole's grandparents had reached what many immigrants considered the pinnacle of success: they had purchased a home of their own in Brooklyn. "They're immigrants," Carole said. "They came to America and just went up the ladder, which was free for everybody, including Jews.

That's a long way from Orsha." Carole said that her grandmother felt that she was living a dream "and protected it fiercely." "I never saw any evidence of her identifying as an American and saying, 'I'm proud to be an American,'" Carole said. But, she continued, "she loved this country. She loved being in it. She loved the opportunities it gave her and her girls. What she was was very happy to be where she was."

The paper trail for Carole's maternal ancestors ran out only two generations back from Carole, with her great-grandparents Riva Leah and Itzak, or Isaac, Besmogin. The fate of Carole's great-grandfather was, in fact, unknown. His name didn't appear on any ship manifests, nor was it listed among the victims of the pogrom in the documents we consulted. He may have died before the family made the trip across the Atlantic; we couldn't know for sure. The destruction of Jewish records that went hand in hand with the Jews' persecution has erected many obstacles in the search for Jewish ancestry.

■ Carole's father, Sidney Klein, was, like his wife, a first-generation American, born on May 6, 1916, in Manhattan. His parents were Jewish immigrants named David and Mollie Klein, born David Henry Gleiman and Malke Topf. "My dad had the character of see a problem, go fix it," Carole explained, "and the problem he went to solve was putting out fires and saving people." A firefighter, he belonged to the Naer Tormid Society (Yiddish for "Eternal Light"), an organization founded by Jewish New York City firefighters in response to the anti-Semitism they encountered within the department. Carole said that she had never personally felt the sting of anti-Semitism, and if it was there, she ignored it. "My hair wasn't always blonde. I have a nose that's associated with Jewish people, and certainly my accent is not without reference. I tend not to see evil if I don't have to, and I think racism of any kind is evil, so if it was there, it may have been targeted at me, but I never saw it." Her father, however, didn't look away. "He didn't talk about it specific to the fire department. He just talked about it specific to him or to people he knew," Carole said. "Yes, he was aware of anti-Semitism."

The survival of vital records for eastern European Jews of Sidney's parents' generation was extremely rare, but in a book of Russian birth certificates from the late nineteenth century, we were fortunate to locate his father's, Carole's grandfather's. "Herszek Glajman, tailor, 35 years old, presented to us a male child born in the town of Zamosc, on February 4,

1885, of his wife Dworja nee Both, 27 years old. This child at circumcision was given the name David." With this birth certificate, we brought Carole back one more generation, to her great-grandparents Herszek and Dworja Glajman, to a town that was then part of the Russian Empire and is today in Poland. "I always thought they were from Poland, but Poland was part of the empire," Carole said, "so this is amazing to learn."

Most immigrants came to America in search of a better life, for the safety and prosperity they were denied in their homeland. Carole's grandparents had another reason to make the journey: love. Their story was almost operatic. "David was a tailor. Mollie's family had a little more money. They looked down on a tailor," Carole said. "So they fell in love, and to my understanding, they ran away together. They made that crossing over land and sea. They really wanted to get to America, where there would not be those class differences." David and Mollie married in Zamosc. "They could have just gone to another village, but I think they had the dream. They wanted to live the dream, and they did."

That dream was nearly dashed. We found their names on a passenger list for the SS *Giulia*, which arrived at Ellis Island on November 25, 1904: David Gleiman and Malke Gleiman. As Carole's maternal grandmother Sarah had done, Mollie Americanized her Yiddish name, Malke, after her journey. David was nearly twenty years old; Mollie was eighteen. The young lovers arrived in America "in possession of two dollars between them," Carole noted, "and unable to read." Immigration officials doubted that Carole's grandparents could support themselves in the United States, so they didn't let them into the country. After crossing a continent and an ocean to be together, Carole's grandparents, like other detainees, were separated by gender and held in on-site dormitories at Ellis Island, penned into hot, crowded, lice-ridden cells. Some Russian immigrants compared the wretched detention centers to Siberian prison camps. The newlyweds were herded together with those men and women whose physical condition or economic circumstances might prevent them from entering the country. If they couldn't demonstrate that they had a means of support in the United States, Carole's grandparents risked being sent back to Russia.

Thanks to a man identified in the passenger record as "cousin, Mr. Sam Kline," the worst-case scenario never came to fruition. Sam Kline vouched for David and Mollie at Ellis Island and convinced immigration officials of their merit, and after three days in detention, they were admitted to the United States. We searched everywhere, but we could find no other record of anyone named Sam Kline. Whether he was friend or relative, we couldn't say. Sam Kline's identity would forever remain a mystery, but his role in the history of Carole's family was immeasurable. Had this enigmatic so-called cousin not come to meet Carole's grandparents, David and Mollie could have been sent back to Europe, and the rest of Carole's story might never have been written. "My goodness. Cousin Sam Kline, spelled K-L-I-N-E. That may be where they got the name," Carole mused. "I thought an official had changed their name when they came in." This was a common immigration myth, but in actuality it almost never happened. Ship manifests were filled out at the point of departure in Europe, by speakers of the native tongue, and not on arrival at Ellis Island. "Do I have to rewrite my book now?" Carole joked. After going through several legal name changes herself, Carole had recently returned to the name she left behind as a teenager, the same one her grandparents adopted while practically still teenagers themselves. "I am still Klein," she explained. "I've incorporated that. My legal name is now King-Klein. I went through four marriages and changed my name every single time, and then I finally came back to, 'No, I'm Klein!'"

The young couple David and Mollie Klein began their lives in America on Broome Street, in the heart of New York's Lower East Side. Carole's grandparents never told her about those days; they didn't have to. "It's legendary Jewish lore what it was like," Carole said, "crowded, hot, pickle barrels on the street and delis. It was seething with humanity." By 1915, there were 350,000 Jews living on the Lower East Side, all of them packed into two square miles, one of the largest concentrations of Jewish people in the entire world. Conditions in the tenements that housed these families were so unsanitary that each year thousands of people died from tuberculosis, and diseases like cholera and typhoid were rampant. It was in this squalid environment that David and Mollie's family would grow to include six children by the time Carole's father was born in 1916. "They did what they had to do, didn't they?" Carole said.

David eked out a living in a work environment that rivaled the degradation of the tenements. In the teens, New York's garment industry was booming, and it provided employment for thousands upon thousands of Jewish men, women, and children. According to letters written by Carole's father, her grandfather David, a tailor, worked in a factory much like the one made famous by the Triangle Shirtwaist Factory, a touchstone for the labor movement and early-twentieth-century Jewish immigration. Likely for six grueling days a week, from sunrise to well past sunset, Carole's grandfather tolerated the tedious work, back-breaking hours, and deplorable, exploitative conditions of the sweatshop. Carole sensed what kept him going. "He was in America, and believed in the future and believed that it would get better. Again, I come back to they did what they needed to do. This brings it together, because I come from a long line of people who see a problem, do what they need to do to fix it or make something better, or wait it out. We are a practical people, and I've learned that from my family."

Carole's father's family ultimately made their way out of the Lower East Side, by 1930 settling in Brooklyn's Bedford Stuyvesant neighborhood, at the time a diverse melting pot of a community. The overwhelming majority of its residents were European immigrants — Irish, Italian, German, and the list goes on — nearly a fifth of them Jewish; more than a tenth of the population was African American. It was here, in 1936, during the height of the Depression, that David Klein took the momentous step of becoming a U.S. citizen, renouncing "all allegiance and fidelity to any foreign prince, potentate, state, or sovereignty, and particularly to the state of Russia and/ or the republic of Poland, of whom I have heretofore been a subject." Carole admired her grandfather's handwriting, his signature, and his perseverance. "That was the dream," she said. David Klein arrived in this country impoverished and illiterate, yet he sent his sons to college. For a poor Jewish tailor in Russia, that would have been impossible, but for a poor Jewish tailor *from* Russia, now living in America, it became reality. The moral of the story, Carole said, was "Dare to live the dream." David Klein lived the dream, and he passed it on to his granddaughter. "When I was first setting out to write songs and sell my songs to a publisher at age fifteen, why would they pick me above anybody else? But the idea is they've got to pick someone; why not me? And Grandpa must have had the same idea: Let's go to America; let's make it happen."

■ When Carole's grandparents set sail for America, they left behind countless relatives. For most Jewish people, the names of their ancestors who remained in Europe were lost forever. But on Carole's father's side of the family, the obstacles we encountered in tracing her mother's genealogy, and many of our Jewish subjects', did not present themselves. Miraculously, through birth, marriage, and death records, we took Carole's family back, in an unbroken paper trail, to the end of the eighteenth century. The marriage certificate of Carole's great-grandparents Herszek Glajman and Dworja Both, dated 1881, gave us the names of their parents, Carole's great-great-grandparents, Abram Glajman and Gitla Teperman and David Both and Baila Resza, all of whom were born in the 1820s or 1830s. Another marriage certificate, filed in 1851, ten years before the Civil War broke out in America, gave us Abram and Gitla's parents' names, Carole's third great-grandparents Herszek Glejman and Ida Glat, and Lejbus and Laja Janklowicz. Based on his death record, we determined that Carole's third great-grandfather Herszek Glejman was born in Russia in 1795, just over a decade after the American Revolution ended.

From generation to generation, the chain was intact. Carole was, in her words, "blown away." "Going to something spiritual," she said, "even if people don't believe there's a heaven or an afterlife, this is what happens when you die. You leave that. And even if you don't leave descendants, you leave your imprint on the earth." She looked again at her great-great-grandparents' marriage license. "The DNA that's signed on to this paper here is in me and in my children and my grandchildren." All the ancestors we'd met today in some way, through her music or her perseverance, or perhaps a little of both, lived on in Carole.

■ George Washington was president when Carole's third great-grandfather Herszek Glejman was born in Russia in 1795. Herszek was her oldest known ancestor on her father's side—and in fact the oldest of many of our participants' Jewish ancestors. We traced her mother's side back to her great-grandmother Riva Leah Borkin, born around 1870 also in Russia, a finding far more typical of Jewish genealogy because of the widespread destruction of Jewish records. DNA, however, could not be destroyed, and it would take us back further than any paper trail.

We administered two DNA tests to Carole. The first was her admixture, which measures an individual's percentages of European, sub-Saharan African, and East Asian / Native American ancestry over the past five hundred years or so. Supporting all that we had learned today, Carole's admixture was 100 percent European. Of that, her Ashkenazi Jewish ancestry comprised 96 percent. She had a smattering of other European ancestry, from both eastern and southern Europe, but what surprised her most was to see small traces of Middle Eastern and North African DNA, which, when looked at in conjunction with the southern European DNA, is possibly an indication of Sephardic Jewish ancestry. The Sephardic Jews are descended from Spanish Jews who were expelled from Spain under the rule of Ferdinand and Isabella, in the same year Columbus discovered America, 1492, and make up only about 20 percent of the American Jewish population. The remaining 80 percent are Ashkenazi Jews, who trace their roots back to eastern Europe, as Carole does.

The second test we administered to Carole was of her mitochondrial DNA, which is an identical genetic fingerprint passed down from mother to child, from generation to generation. Her maternal haplogroup, a genetic population group with a shared ancestor, is found in low levels all over Europe. While not considered one of the primary Jewish maternal haplogroups, it is not uncommon among people of Jewish descent.

We had come to expect a high level of "cousining," of interconnectedness, among our Jewish participants when examining their autosomal DNA, which an individual inherits from both parents and all of his or her ancestral lines. We would look at Carole's autosomal DNA at the end of the chapter, at the same time we examined that of her cousins, Alan Dershowitz and Tony Kushner.

■ In our exploration of Carole's family tree, we met young people willing to take tremendous risks to follow a dream and make a better life for themselves, and ultimately for their families; we met people who exchanged their given names for chosen ones, perhaps in an effort to make the path a little smoother for themselves and for those following after them. Carole herself had taken such risks, followed her dream, changed her name. Her history was rich, her roots long and deep. She was awestruck not just by the connections she felt to her ancestors, but by the consistency she saw in all their stories. "Everything that has informed me psychologically comes from all of this, knowing this," she said. "My favorite books are journeys." The book of her life that we'd prepared for her was one such journey, but it was not nearly over. "What is not in this book but what is in the next room and onward are my children and my grandchildren, and the future of these people being carried forward, the moxie of these people. I see it going forward."

Looking back, Carole saw a line of pragmatic people whose drive to move forward, both literally and figuratively, brought them to these shores. "It makes me want to fight even harder for America to be the best place it can be," Carole said. "In my family history there is a caring about keeping the world a better place, making it a better place, the best place it can be. That's what these people have fed me. I love this country because it was a place my family came to to get away from where it wasn't such a nice place to be."

If she could meet one of those people who fed her, as she put it, it would be "the one who saw things in a similar way to me, who sees the big picture as well as the little picture."

Carole's greatest surprise, perhaps, had come when she recognized in her family tree "the me-ness of it all." Ambition and integrity and strength manifested themselves in different ways for her and her ancestors, because of the opportunities that were available to them. We went back hundreds of years and saw the same tendencies and characteristics repeat themselves on every branch of her tree. What made Carole who she was? Was it her DNA? Her family culture? Even her religion? "All of it," she said definitively. "All of it combines to make us who we are, and I have been blessed. I have had a really, really good life, and I'm still having one." And she never, ever took it for granted. "When I sign my emails to friends," Carole concluded, "the bottom line says 'Gratitude.'"

Tony Kushner (b. 1956)

Tony Kushner is one of America's most acclaimed writers, best known for his Pulitzer Prize–winning play *Angels in America* and his Academy Award–nominated script for Steven Spielberg's *Lincoln*. Born Anthony Robert Kushner on July 16, 1956, to William Kushner and Sylvia Deutscher, Tony grew up in Lake Charles, Louisiana, far from the lights of Broadway or the hills of Hollywood. In many ways, Tony's description of his childhood sounds typically southern, that of a "country boy." "The house that I grew up in was a house in the woods," he reminisced. "There was a swamp in the backyard, and there were water moccasins in the grass. We had a pet raccoon when we were little. We had pet goats. We played in the woods all the time. We were barefoot all the time." But Tony's family was Jewish, and this made them part of a very small minority.

Like most towns in the Deep South, Lake Charles was overwhelmingly Christian. Jewish people made up less than 1 percent of the city's population. What he called "low-key, low-rent anti-Semitism" surfaced only occasionally in conversation with neighbors, but there was one incident that had affected him deeply. "When my mother was dying in 1990, in the hospital in Lake Charles, my mother's hair had started to fall out, and this very nice woman who was a nurse in the hospital—she was in her forties—said, 'Can I just ask you something? Where are the horns?' She literally thought not that we had devil's horns, but the old myth that Jews have these little bumps, and she thought that under the hair there would be horns." The comment was shocking, but Tony characterized anti-Semitism of this sort as stemming more from confusion than hate. "People were more curious about it, didn't quite understand how we didn't believe that Jesus was the Messiah and so on, but very little in the way of anything virulent."

In spite of its small size, the Jewish community in Lake Charles flourished. "There were about one hundred families in Lake Charles, but the temple was a very impressive building," Tony said. "As far as I could tell, all the way back to the founding of Temple Sinai, the Jews in Lake Charles were absolutely unapologetic about being Jews. There was an enormously powerful and absolutely proud affiliation with Jewish history, Jewish culture, and Jewish affinity. We were all told, 'You don't apologize for it. If anybody has a problem it's their problem.' And we all went through our childhoods feeling proud that we were Jews."

Being gay was another story. Tony said he knew he was gay from the time he was a little boy, but sadly, he intuited that this was not something to be proud of, or even discuss. "I started asking my parents questions about it, and from the answers I got or didn't get, I could start to figure out that I was wrong in some way," he said. "I wanted to play being Mary Poppins and things like that, and I learned very quickly not to share that with anyone." He was twenty-six years old before he came out to his parents. Acceptance came slowly, but it came. Tony has said that being Jewish prepared him for being gay. "I think a lot of gay, Jewish kids had this experience when it came time to understand how to be gay in a homophobic world. I already knew the model to follow because I knew how to be Jewish in an anti-Semitic world, or in a predominantly Christian world," he explained. "I grew up in a minority community that was absolutely unapologetic about its minority status and was not in any way willing to accept any negative definition of itself imposed by the majority. Of course," he continued, "when I was coming out to my parents, I beat them up with that mercilessly. I said, 'You taught me not to apologize for who I am and to be proud of who I am, and this is who I am. I'm Jewish, but I'm also gay, and I'm just doing what you taught me to do.'"

When asked what he considers home, Tony said his first answer will always be Louisiana, but when asked how he identifies himself, his response was far more complex. "I'm a Jew in America, so I feel myself very much the inheritor of Jewish history and of American history, and I'm a southerner, and all of those things have shaped my consciousness, my understanding of the world," Tony said. "If you ask who my people are, my first impulse would be to say Jewish. Then, of course, right after that, I would say I'm gay. I'm on the Left, and I'm from the South, and I'm an American. Most people have fairly complicated identities, and you pick the one that you want to use strategically, depending on the circumstance."

In his work, Tony often draws inspiration from history. He believes that absorbing the lessons of the past is the only way to move effectively into the future. "We turn to the past to provide models and examples for ourselves. You have to be very much in the present moment to really understand how to get into the future, but without any grasp of how we got to where we are, you can't really understand how we're going to move forward," Tony said. "There is this contradiction at the heart of the American project in that we're both something very new and have a freedom that comes from rootlessness, but every single one of us comes from very deep origins and very deep roots, and one way or another, whether we're conscious of it or not, we carry all of that stuff—if we're hillbillies, if we're the descendants of slaves, if we're Jewish peddlers, whatever we are, we bring all of that with us, and it's in us. That working dialectic is part of the dynamic of this country." That dialectic, as Tony called it, was part of his dynamic as well.

■ Tony described his mother as "an enormous, artistic soul." Sylvia Deutscher was born on December 15, 1924, in New York City. Raised in the Bronx, she was a professional musician. "She was a small woman with enormous lung power, a really extraordinary bassoonist," Tony said. "The bassoon was the perfect instrument for her, because she had a tragic soul." Tony credits his mother with setting him on the path toward theater. "I know it had to do with her being an actress," he said of his decision to become a playwright. He described her as "a creature of impulse, somebody who would change a story to make it more dramatic."

The dramatic edge may have come from her own mother, Sarah Bard. "I could go on forever about her," Tony mused about his grandmother. "She would come and stay with us in Louisiana for four or five weeks out of the year, and the day she arrived, she said, 'I want to go back.'" Sarah said she was from a town called Chorostkow that Tony had never been able to identify on a map, and that her nationality was Austrian, a claim Tony questioned. "I used to say to my parents that Chorostkow was Russian for 'Brigadoon' because we didn't think that it existed." Tony's grandmother filled his head with "incredible stories" and "intense fantasies," sharing with her grandson "a kind of fairy-tale version" of her youth. "She told us about this Polish countess who took her for a sleigh ride. There was some guy with blond hair who was a Polish student who would take her piggyback riding. I think she said that her father had an inn." With his grandmother, Tony always had a hard time separating fact from fiction.

While the recollections may have been something out of a young girl's imagination, the rest, we were able to confirm through her birth record, was true. Sarah Judes Bard was born to Mendel Bard, a grain merchant, and Ruchel Gellman, in Chorostkow, Austria, on June 22, 1888. Mendel and Ruchel were Tony's great-grandparents. Chorostkow, with a population of about two thousand Jews, or one-third of the town's population, was a market town in the kingdom of Galicia, then part of the Austro-Hungarian Empire and a center of European Jewish life. Galicia no longer exists; what was once western Galicia is now in Poland, while the eastern part, where Chorostkow was located, is now part of Ukraine. The Jews of Galicia were desperately poor, restricted in their professions and their movement, but Tony knew little of his grandmother's life there. With the exception of "these stories that kind of made sense and kind of didn't," Tony said, "she didn't really elaborate on her memories there. She was not particularly forthcoming about that."

She was similarly evasive about her early life in New York City. We knew from a passenger list for the SS *Moltke*, which arrived in New York on May 1, 1904, that Tony's grandmother was just fifteen years old when she made the two-week voyage across the Atlantic without her family, with four dollars in her pocket, in steerage. It would be six years before we found Sarah Bard in the paper trail again. According to the 1910 census, she lived as a boarder with an Austrian Jewish family, and she worked as a "waist operator." In other words, like so many other Jewish immigrants, Tony's grandmother found work in one of the notorious sweatshops of New York's garment industry. Tony suspected that the "ferociously pro-union politics" she espoused even late in life grew out of the drudgery of the endless days and nights she spent hunched over a sewing machine in the Garment District.

On March 22, 1913, Sarah Bard married Tony's grandfather, Benjamin Deutscher. Benny, as he was called, died before Tony was born, and "a big part of his identity," Tony had been told, was his membership in the glaziers' union. As with his grandmother, Benny's wife Sarah, there were many gaps in Tony's knowledge about his grandfather. Benjamin Deutscher, whose given name was David Ber Deutscher, was born on January 23, 1884, in Nadworna, also in Galicia. In 1904, Benjamin became the first member of his family to immigrate to America, leaving behind his siblings and his parents. Tony's great-grandparents were Pinkhas Deutscher, born in Nadworna on July 8, 1860, and Chany Somer, born on August 1, 1867, possibly in the neighboring Galicia town of Jablonica. Like his son, Pinkhas Deutscher worked as a glazier. Although he knew that eventually three of his grandfather's brothers, including his youngest brother Jack, escaped Poland, Tony was never sure of the fate of his ancestors who stayed behind during the time of the Nazi occupation.

Initially, Tony's great-uncle Jack, born Aaron Jacob Deutscher, chose not to follow his brothers to America and instead remained in Europe, opening a medical practice in Gdansk, Poland, in 1935. By this time, Galicia had dissolved, and Nadworna was part of Poland. As Hitler brought more and more of Europe under his control, the situation for Jews became increasingly dire, and Jack finally fled Poland in 1938. He arrived in the United States on March 14 of that year, just two days after Nazi troops crossed the border into Austria. His brothers had managed to save up enough money to secure his passage.

Their reunion made the local paper. "Dr. Aaron Deutschler finds U.S. a happier place to live," the headline read. Although rife with misinformation and misspellings, including his uncle's last name, the article offered its American readership insight into the desperation that had gripped Jews in eastern Europe. "His parents are still in their little home in Nadworna," the article read, "and last night, the brothers and sisters made a pact to bring them to this country as soon as possible." Tony wasn't sure their efforts ever came to fruition. "I know that there was a money question. Jack arrived with nothing because he had to leave everything behind, and what he found when he got there was an occasionally employed glazier and a waiter at the Waldorf Astoria," Tony said, referring to his grandfather and his great-uncle. "There was definitely not much money. And I've always been told that by the time they had enough to get the sisters passage on a boat, they couldn't contact them anymore. They couldn't make contact."

By 1941, the Nazis were rounding up Jewish people throughout Poland. Nadworna was under German control, and no Jews could leave. We found eyewitness accounts of the bloody events that took place in Tony's ancestral home, Nadworna, on the morning of October 6, 1941. "We could hear the smashing of windows, the breaking down of doors, rifle shots, loud and wild screaming in German and Ukrainian, accompanied by the barking of dogs, lamenting of people dragged from their homes and crying of children." Said another eyewitness, a resident of Nadworna who had managed to elude the roundup of the town's Jews: "By moonlight, one could see what a great tragedy had taken place here by the scattered dresses, children's little clothes, little suits, tiny children's shoes, caps, and more, which the victims before they were killed had been forced to take off."

The massacre took place in what is known as the Bukowinka forest, and roughly two thousand Jews were gunned down on that single day, thrown into a mass grave, their names never recorded. Hauntingly, the Nazi officials who planned this massacre referred to it in their correspondence as a wedding, their victims as guests. A twenty-six-year-old German soldier present on that day recounted the day's horrific events. "Three or four trucks brought the Jews to a ditch about ten kilometers from Nadworna, to a forest," Tony read. "With one of the first trucks, I arrived at the shooting site. The executions were already in progress. Many of the Jews lay naked in the ditch and were already dead. More and more trucks of Jews arrived, and they only had to partially undress. The shooting continued as long as we saw that there were any living Jews laying in the ditches. The only time we stopped was to wait for the next truck to arrive."

The Nazis typically executed anyone who wouldn't be of use in labor camps, and Tony's great-grandparents Pinkhas and Chany would have been eighty-one and seventy-four years old, respectively, at the time. But without documented proof, Tony couldn't be certain if his ancestors were among the victims of the massacre. More than seventy years later, we turned to oral histories from survivors and their descendants to find the answer. Their testimony appears in what are known as *Yizkor Books*. *Yizkor* is the traditional Jewish mourning service, and the word literally means "remember." There we found a reference to Tony's family members in testimony submitted by his great-uncle Jack: "Pinkhas Deutscher and Chany Deutscher, my sister Malka Kerner, Vludwig, their kids Marta and Manek, my sister Leica Hecht, my brother-in-law Metist Hecht, and the kids Lanek and Manek, all killed by the German murderers."

Yizkor: Remember. "Memory is essential," Tony said. "There's a difference in not just quantity but quality in the Holocaust from most other horrors that human beings have been subjected to. I feel the same way about slavery. I think it's enormously important that people are scrupulous about understanding that genocide is a specific thing; slavery is a specific thing.

It's a kind of soul murder that is unlike other forms of oppression and produces a whole set of difficulties that have to be overcome and worked through. You can't understand contemporary Jewish reality anywhere in the world if you don't understand two millennia of really horrendous oppression and suffering, culminating in the Holocaust. And you really can't speak about it if you aren't willing to come to terms with it." Tony understood the impulse toward silence. Painful memories were more easily buried than discussed.

"It's unspeakable." He referred to the horrors of the events themselves and the fact that they were literally "never spoken about." He recalled a time in Lake Charles, during the late 1960s, when the older members of the Jewish community opposed a screening of Alain Rensais's documentary *Night and Fog*, which incorporates Nazi footage of the concentration camps. "They really didn't want the movie shown," he said. "They didn't want to talk about it. The Holocaust was known; it was an established fact of history. But there was still a kind of World War II–era reaction to this, like, 'It's the old country where these horrible things happened, and we don't need to think about this.'"

The impulse toward silence, Tony believed, had to be overcome. Studying our family histories, telling our stories, was a way of doing that.

■ Like Tony's mother, his father, William Kushner, was a musician. Born on March 14, 1924, in Lake Charles, Louisiana, he was a Julliard-trained clarinetist and conductor. "I never met anybody who loved a particular art more passionately," Tony said. His father's influence on him was profound, but their relationship was not always easy. "I owe him an incalculable amount. He taught me a great love of language. My father had an absolutely remarkable ear for language that was really shaped by his ear for music. He couldn't read anything that was badly written. He paid us a dollar for every poem that we learned and would recite back when we were kids." Tony spoke candidly of his father's difficulty accepting the fact that his son was gay. "All the way up until my early twenties, we were at loggerheads," he said. "But we became very close. He told me a couple of years before he died how proud he was of me, not just as a writer but as a person, and that meant a lot. He loved my husband, and that was a great thing."

Tony described his father as "a serious, analytical mind, a very scrupulous man." He was also one of Tony's earliest teachers. "He was the first person to explain to me the difference between World War I and World

War II, the first person to tell me about the Holocaust," Tony said, "so some of my sense of history I get from him." Now we wanted to delve into Tony's father's personal history and climb up the Kushner family tree.

Tony's paternal grandfather, Sam Kushner, was born on July 6, 1898, in Shreveport, Louisiana. At the time, Shreveport was developing rapidly, and it had an established Jewish community. Jews made up only 4 percent of the total population, but they were among the city's civic leaders. In fact, in 1900, Shreveport elected its second Jewish mayor. When Sam was about twelve years old, he moved with his family 185 miles south to Lake Charles. Sam Kushner was, literally, a large presence in Tony's memory. "He was an astonishing person," Tony said. "He was 6'2", 6'3", huge. He was very dark-skinned. He told us that he had gotten a suntan when he was a child and that it had never gone away. He was very olive-skinned. He had a very dark complexion, and a massive head, and a huge body." He loved to write poetry—"rhymed verse, not very good, but witty and funny"—and had an amazing penchant for reciting facts from memory. His memories of his grandfather were rich, but most important to Tony was the fact that he was a principled man. Tony told us that Sam's older brothers had gone into real estate and bought land outside Lake Charles, forming what was called a covenanted community. "Everybody who bought had to agree that you wouldn't sell to black people," Tony explained. "They offered my grandfather a chance to buy in with them, and he refused to do it. He said he thought it was wrong. I admired him enormously." According to Tony, his grandfather was well loved in both the black and white communities of Lake Charles. "Black people and white people still, when I go to Lake Charles, people say, 'Oh, your grandfather'—everybody, black and white, called him Mr. Sam—'he was such a good man. He was such a great man.' I think he really was a profoundly good and decent man." While Tony had described anti-Semitism as relatively "low-key" in Lake Charles, "the racism there was institutional," and blacks lived in separate communities from whites. So how did Sam Kushner exist in both communities, and how did his family get to the South in the first place? To find out, we would go back one more generation, to Tony's great-grandparents.

Tony's great-grandfather Ezrael Kushner was born on July 1, 1873, in Kovno, Russia. His great-grandmother Hannah Packman was born on August 1, 1867, in Vilnius. Both of these cities today are part of Lithuania. Ezrael and Hannah emigrated to the United States around 1890, a period of intense immigration for Russian Jews. When he left his homeland, Ezrael was almost eighteen years old, the age of conscription at a time when the Russian military was a very dangerous place for Jewish men to serve. "This may be complete fiction," Tony began. "Legend was that he had worked as a tailor for the Russian navy and that he fled when he became afraid that he was going to get enlisted in the draft, which for Jewish men frequently meant the end, because they were killed by their own comrades as often as anything else. The story I was told was that he took a spool of gold thread, stuck it in a jar of chicken fat, and smuggled it, somehow used the gold thread to pay for his passage." Tony laughed. "It's very romantic. I don't know that any of this is true, but that's what I was told."

We couldn't confirm the story, but Tony shared another piece of family lore that might have explained why Ezrael chose to put down roots in the southern United States. "This is a story I was told: that among the permissible trades in Lithuania and in the area of the world in Kovno for Jews was lumber milling, and that the pine forests were business opportunities for Jews," Tony said. The story had merit. Jewish immigrants had begun to make their way south in significant numbers following the Civil War. The end of slavery created new economic opportunities: supplying goods and services to recently freed slaves and their descendants, now suddenly thrust into the marketplace as consumers. When Ezrael Kushner moved his family to Lake Charles, he found both opportunity and community.

Lake Charles had a smaller Jewish community than Shreveport. Out of a population of more than eleven thousand residents, only about 125 were Jewish. In spite of the low numbers, a synagogue, Temple Sinai, had been established there in 1907. Starting in the late nineteenth century, the local abundance of pine and cypress made for a bustling business in timber. Between 1900 and 1910, in fact, the population almost doubled. It was an up-and-coming town, and the Kushners were part of its growth. In the Lake Charles directory from 1927, we found a listing for "Kushner Lumber and Building Company, Ezrael Kushner, president; Sam Kushner, secretary/treasurer; 1417 Broad." Kushner Lumber was a family operation, with aunts and uncles filling every position. Tony called it "a fairly small-potatoes thing." "I don't think anybody in my family was great at business," he said, "and I think they saw an opportunity in the African American community, because there were just very few businesses that catered to them." Ezrael hired an African American man named Rufus Berard as the foreman, and

Rufus's son Carlbert many years later became part owner of the business, which was renamed the Kushner-Berard Lumber Company. The family dissolved the company in 2013, nearly ninety years after its founding.

The Kushner family made its mark in the Lake Charles community. In laying a foundation here in America, Tony's great-grandfather Ezrael established a business that provided for generations of Kushners to come, taking advantage of present opportunities to build for the future. Now we were curious to learn more about Ezrael's past. We couldn't locate his birth certificate, and his death certificate didn't contain his parents' names. The document that ultimately allowed us to go back in time was one that focused on the future: his will. There we found his mother's name. "It is my desire," it read, "that there be paid out of my estate to my mother, Mrs. Cecelia Kushner, a resident of Brooklyn, New York, the sum of $25 per month during her lifetime." Cecelia was Tony's great-great-grandmother, and according to the 1930 census, she lived in Brooklyn with her daughter and grandchildren in Crown Heights.

Records show that Cecilia was born in Russia in 1838, when Tsar Nicholas I still reigned. At the time there were roughly 2 million Jews living in Russia, out of a total population of 60 million. She immigrated in 1898, making her sixty years old when she started her new life in this country. There was no evidence that her husband, Louis Kushner, had ever made the voyage. She died in 1931, just a year after the census was taken. Her death certificate opened a window onto her past: it listed the names of her parents, Isidore Abrams and Fruma Levine, both from Russia. Remarkably, although we couldn't find their birth dates or precise birthplaces, we now knew the names of Tony's third great-grandparents.

On all the branches of Tony's rich family tree were Jewish immigrants who came to this country around the turn of the twentieth century to pursue greater freedom and opportunity. His tremendous artistic success was possible because each of them dared to make the Great Voyage. "To be a Jewish American and to have this," he said, looking at his family tree. "I was thinking of the people who survived in the forest outside Nadworna, standing on that hillock, and that's the wall that most of us hit. It's meaningful that I can at least trace it all the way back to the beginning of the nineteenth century, the beginning of modernity. It expands my sense of the world a little bit."

DNA would expand Tony's sense of the world exponentially.

■ Destruction of records and dislocation and displacement of populations makes genealogical research for eastern European Jews extremely difficult. Yet Tony's paper trail had taken us all the way back to the beginning of the nineteenth century. On his paternal side, we traced his ancestors back to Isidore Abrams and Julius Donn, who were both born in Russia in the early part of the 1800s. On his maternal side, the oldest named ancestor we found was Aron Jacob Deutschler, born around the same time, probably in Galicia.

Tony's DNA would take us back much further. We administered three DNA tests to Tony: one to determine his admixture, which measures an individual's percentages of European, sub-Saharan African, and East Asian / Native American ancestry from about the time of Columbus; his Y-DNA, which a man gets from his father; and his mitochondrial DNA, which a child inherits from his mother. Tony's admixture dovetailed precisely with his genealogy, which showed that all his ancestors came from eastern Europe. His European ancestry registered at 99.9 percent. Broken down further, we determined that 97.5 percent of his European result was Ashkenazi Jewish DNA—again not surprising in light of the ancestry we had been able to trace. But there was a very small amount of DNA from an area Tony never expected. "I'm intrigued by the Finn that got in there somewhere, and somebody from Scandinavia," he laughed.

Our test of Tony's Y-DNA, an identical signature that fathers pass to their sons across the generations, did contain a surprise. His paternal haplogroup, a genetic population group that shares a common ancestor, is one that is usually associated with Asians and Native Americans. Further investigation revealed that while his subclade, or subgroup of the haplogroup, is found in about 6 percent of Jewish men, it's almost entirely nonexistent in all other Europeans. Our best guess is that this finding could reflect the Jewish population's migration out of the Levant thousands of years ago.

Likewise, Tony's mitochondrial DNA, also an identical signature passed from mother to child, unchanged generation after generation, took us to a part of the world we hadn't expected. His maternal haplogroup is a Eurasian haplogroup not specifically associated with Jewish populations. According to an expert on this haplogroup, his subclade arose long ago and in itself doesn't imply Jewish origins, but there are some Jewish families who fall within this subgroup of this signature.

Interestingly, both his Y-DNA line and his mitochondrial DNA line yielded results that are, on the surface, surprising in light of the percentage of Ashkenazi Jewish ancestry that Tony possesses. In their diversity they tell the story of the Jewish people. On his father's side, it's a biblical story, tracing back to ancient Israel; on his mother's side, it's the story of the Diaspora, of a people settling in eastern Europe and mixing, only occasionally, with the outside population there.

In examining Tony's autosomal DNA, which an individual inherits from his or her parents and from all of his or her ancestral lines, we experienced something that is unique to people with Jewish ancestry, which illustrates just how occasional that mixing was. For that reason, it's worth looking at the autosomal DNA of Alan Dershowitz, Carole King, and Tony Kushner together. All three of them are related to each other, and all three are also related to virtually every Ashkenazi Jewish participant we've ever had in our series. Alan is related to both Carole and Tony, and to Barbara Walters, Maggie Gyllenhaal, Robert Downey Jr., Angela Buchdahl, Gloria Reuben, Harry Connick Jr., and Jessica Alba. Carole's list varies only slightly; it includes Kyra Sedgwick, but we did not find a relation to Robert Downey Jr., Angela Buchdahl, or Jessica Alba. Tony was related to every single one, with the exception of Jessica Alba. Ashkenazi Jews have one of the highest rates of "cousining" of any population group in the world. For centuries, isolation from the non-Jewish world, both forced and self-imposed, led to a high rate of intermarrying within Jewish communities of eastern Europe, resulting in a smaller overall gene pool. Marriage partners were often extended cousins. That history is evident in the shared genes of Tony and our other Jewish participants. "It's a ghetto thing," Tony joked, "but other than that, that's cool. That's wild."

■ Throughout Tony's career, he has revisited different periods in history and brought to life historical figures, real and imagined. Today we had introduced him to his own history. If given the chance, and a time machine could transport him back in time, which ancestor would he choose to meet? It was difficult for Tony to narrow it down. His ancestors had been witnesses to, and victims of, some of the worst atrocities against humanity in the history of the world. "I'd be afraid to do it, but I would probably want to meet one of the two sisters of my grandfather who probably died in Nadworna," he said. "I don't know what I would ask them, but I guess there's a sort of lingering terribleness of not knowing. I'm very drawn to the idea that we didn't get to talk about it very much." He was also curious to meet his third great-grandparents, born more than one hundred years before the Holocaust, "because that's as close as I'm going to get mitochondrial Eve." The journey up his family tree had opened his eyes to a new line of inquiry. "Once you start to get an appetite for this, you keep wanting to go to where and who were we ultimately connected to."

Our exploration of Tony's roots, he said, had shed light on what he called "a darkness at the center of the family history." That darkness, of course, emanated largely from the village of Nadworna and the forest around it, where Tony's ancestors died for being Jewish, but there was also joy in having met the brothers and sisters, sons and daughters of those left behind, those who had the foresight, luck, or pluck to know that to continue being who they were, they had to leave their home. "I feel very moved, thinking about this sort of slow build of people who came from what sounded like very modest circumstances and modest aspirations, who built and built on that, and finally got us all safely to where my cousins and I, the people of my generation, are in my family," he said.

Tony's journey today affirmed the one his ancestors had begun more than a century ago. "It confirms what I've been saying, which is that I think they made a good choice. I'm glad they got here." In spite of the hardship they faced in leaving their home and establishing a new one, a family tradition told him they were glad they got here, too. Every year at the Passover seder, the festive meal in which the story of the Jews' freedom from slavery in Egypt is recounted, Tony's family sang "America, the Beautiful." "I always loved Passover for some reason. I was moved by it," Tony said. "At the end of the seder, the last thing that you say as part of the official ceremony is 'Next year in Jerusalem,' which is an expression of the immemorial yearning of a people of a Diaspora to return home, to have an end to the suffering of the displacement and rootlessness. There's a certain sense that there's an absolutely critical relationship between home and freedom, that you can't really be free if you don't belong to a place." Whether in a rented room in New York City or a house in the woods in a small southern town, Tony's family had found that place in America.

On each of their family trees, Alan Dershowitz, Carole King, and Tony Kushner had ancestors who struggled against intolerance and whose unshakeable pursuit of religious and personal freedom laid the foundation for the lives their descendants enjoy today. Through their stories, we learned that for Jewish people, the United States of America was more than a mere symbol of freedom and opportunity. It was a haven where the Jewish people could hold on to their culture, practice their religion, and commemorate their traditions, as they embarked on their journey of becoming Americans.

CHAPTER EIGHT

British Empire

The musician Sting, the alternative-medicine guru Deepak Chopra, and the actor Sally Field were born and raised thousands of miles apart, but all are bound to each other by the tiny island nation in the North Atlantic that in its glory once reigned over 400 million people. Each of them descends from ancestors who spent their lives as subjects of the British Empire, serving kings and queens on four continents. Of the three, only Sting was born in England; Deepak is Indian by birth, and Sally is an American icon. Their own origins embody the empire's far reach, proving that what Shakespeare called "this little world" of England is not so little after all.

Sting (b. 1951)

He is known by one name the world over, an iconic performer who is equal parts rock star and humanitarian. He shot to stardom with the Anglo-American trio the Police and went on to have an enviable solo career. Sixteen Grammys later, with 100 million albums sold, Sting ventured onto Broadway in 2014 with the evocative musical *The Last Ship*, which was inspired by memories of his childhood in the fifties and his adolescent yearning to escape the narrow confines of his hometown. "Isn't that ironic," he noted, "that you have to go back to the place that you escaped from to find yourself in many ways?"

Born Gordon Matthew Thomas Sumner on October 2, 1951, in Wallsend, a working-class shipbuilding town in the northeast of England, he was raised during the post–World War II years, when Great Britain's role in the world was changing dramatically. "When I was a kid, we used to look at the map of the world, and most of it was red. There was a tiny little island that invaded most of the countries in the world and conquered them." At its peak in the 1920s, the British Empire was larger than the Roman Empire ever had been and held sway over nearly a quarter of the world's total population. By the time Sting was born, however, the empire had begun its decline. The complicated legacy of the British, of being British, was felt even by Sting and his young classmates. "There was a kind of pride about it but also a sense of shame. We have a checkered history, not a perfect history." But there was the flip side. "There's lots to be proud of, too. We've given many gifts to the world—literature, democracy. I don't think I'm blind to many of our faults, but I am British, and I'm proud to be British."

Prior to World War II, northeast England was the largest shipbuilding center in the world, and ships and the shipbuilding industry dominated Sting's childhood. Yet he wanted no part of it. "Most people either worked in the coal mine at one end of the town, or they worked in the shipyard at the end of my street," Sting recalled. "I was attracted to neither. I would do everything in my power not to end up there. So I studied hard. I found a guitar, which became my best friend and my mentor, my accomplice in my plan to escape."

Wallsend has always occupied his thoughts and shaped his psyche. "It was a surreal industrial landscape to grow in. The ship was a massive symbol in my life, literally a symbol that covered the sky." It loomed large, too, over his relationship with his parents. His mother played the piano, and his father sang well, but they couldn't imagine a world in which music had primacy. Even before he launched his career, school had begun to drive a wedge between Sting and his parents. He attended the prestigious St. Cuthbert's Grammar School in Newcastle between 1962 and 1970, followed by Northern Counties College of Education, where he trained to be a teacher. "I had aspirations to the world of the mind, the world of literature," he said, "but pretty soon after I was at grammar school, a kind of chasm opened between my parents and myself. My mother inspired me to play, to be a musician, but she had no idea where that can lead. My father actually wanted me to go to a technical school so I could learn skills that to him were useful. He was a practical man." They lived to see their son's success, and while his mother celebrated it, his father continued to harbor reservations. "'When you gonna get a real job?' He literally said that to me. My dad actually told me to go to sea."

It was understandable. In his small town, sons followed the well-worn path their fathers had paved for them. But for Sting, there was much to see outside the walls of Wallsend. Even his sense of music, influenced by his mother's, was informed by a desire to explore new worlds. "She liked a bit of classical music, a bit of jazz, a bit of pop, rock 'n' roll, show tunes. She just saw music as being one long continuum, which is what I inherited from her. I don't like the ghettoization of music."

Resisting the boundaries imposed on him by heritage, history, and geography, Sting ventured out. He has been called a "citizen of the world" for his humanitarian work with groups like Amnesty International and his own Rainforest Foundation Fund. Sting always believed the world was vast, yet he sensed that for his parents and his ancestors who came before them, their circumscribed world afforded them safety. It turned out their world was much bigger than he'd ever imagined, and safety was often in short supply.

■ Sting knew little about his ancestors, and admitted that he hadn't always been particularly interested in them. He recognized that they were hardworking English people, his father the embodiment of that heritage. Ernest Matthew Sumner was born in Sunderland, England, on September 24, 1926. For much of Sting's life, Ernie Sumner was a milkman. "That's what he did seven days a week, 364 days a year—delivered milk. I think he was a smarter man than that would have indicated, and I think he resented the fact that he hadn't had opportunities to use his mind." Although emotionally distant, Ernie fulfilled his responsibilities. "He'd go out there in all weathers. He'd never have a day off, and he would work and work and work and work. He'd work for us. There were four siblings. We needed feeding. We needed clothes, needed to go to school, and he was the one who was the breadwinner. I admire that to this day," Sting said. "He gave me a work ethic, that work is honoring, that it honors the individual." Ernie did his duty as a father, but Sting believes it took its toll on him and on their relationship. He has written that he felt there was always "a veiled accusation that my father had been trapped in this life by us all." "I always had this sense," Sting said, "and he didn't disabuse me of that belief throughout his life."

Like many men of his generation, Ernie Sumner saw the world through military service. He served as a private in the British Army of the Rhine after Germany's surrender in 1945. Sting said that his father looked back on his time in the army with great nostalgia. "He occupied Germany, as he called it. He would show us pictures, these black-and-white shots of him in his uniform, usually in a bar with some *Fräuleins* and some beer and a cigarette. He looked like a happy young man." In the army he learned a trade, engineering. Prior to his work as a milkman, according to Sting, Ernie Sumner had worked in the shipbuilding industry.

Shipbuilding was the family trade. Sting's grandfather, Thomas Matthew Kirk Sumner, was born on March 5, 1899, in Sunderland, England, like his son, and worked as a shipwright, or shipbuilder. Sting's father spoke little of his own father. "There was a kind of separation between the generations," he said, "and his relationship with his father was reflected in our relationship, too." As a shipwright, Tom Sumner helped design, build, and repair ships. Northern England was one of the shipbuilding capitals of the world, and his hometown of Sunderland was dominated by a firm called Swan Hunter & Wigham Richardson, one of the largest shipyards on the River Tyne at the time. Locally known as Swan Hunter, the firm built the RMS *Mauritania*, then the largest ship in the world, and the RMS *Carpathia*, which rescued survivors of the *Titanic* in 1912. Even the children of the town took pride in these accomplishments—their fathers' accomplishments.

But the shipyards were dangerous places to work, and generations of men, women, and even children toiled in Dickensian conditions to build and maintain the ships that allowed Britain to control so much of the earth. "The shipyard was a very unpleasant place, noisy and toxic," Sting said. "They dealt in all kinds of toxic substances like red lead, asbestos. The health and safety record was appalling, yet there was this immense pride in being able to point to something and say, 'Look, we built that with our hands; we made that.' In modern society, we have few things that we can do that with. Everything we do is kind of ephemeral. We sit at the computer."

Sting's great-grandfather Richard Kellett Halfnight Sumner also worked in the shipyards. He was a coal trimmer, a dirty and dangerous job that involved shoveling coal into the hold to maintain the ship's balance. According to the 1911 national census of England and Wales, at age forty-four, Richard was a married man employed by the River Wear Commissioners, a father of eight children, four of whom worked themselves while still in the household.

Sting's grandfather's name was not listed among his working siblings'. In 1911, Tom was twelve years old, still in school and enjoying some semblance of a childhood. In the absence of powerful child labor laws, it was not uncommon for young children to be put to work early in life. While Richard allowed his twelve-year-old son, Sting's grandfather, to enjoy at least a rudimentary education, he himself had worked from a young age. In 1880, when Richard was about thirteen years old, he was the subject of an article that appeared in the *Shields Daily Gazette and Shipping Telegraph* on August 24. "Accident at Sunderland Docks," the headline read. "Shortly before 6:00 in the morning, a teemer named Richard Sumner was bringing, down the spout, a wagon of coal when, in turning a curve, the wagon went off the line. Sumner, who had hold of the brake, was violently thrown over the drop side to the ground below, a distance of some 45 feet. When picked up, he was found to be seriously injured and had to be conveyed to the infirmary on a locomotive." As we know, Richard survived the accident and went on to work, still in the shipyards, for many years. He died on January 8, 1933, at the beginning of the Depression, at age sixty-six.

When Sting's great-grandfather sustained his injuries, he was a child working in a very dangerous business. A trip back one more generation on Sting's family tree explained why this adolescent boy might have been compelled to seek employment. In the census record for Sunderland in 1861, the year the Civil War broke out in America, we found a listing for Henry and Ann Sumner, Sting's great-great-grandparents and the parents of Richard, who had suffered such grave injuries on the docks. Sting's great-great-grandfather Henry Kirk Sumner was born around 1824. On December 29, 1870, records showed, "Henry Sumner, born in Nottingham," joined the crew of a trade ship called *The James* as a mate. In this capacity, the forty-six-year-old Henry would have been responsible for the ship's cargo and deck crew. According to maritime records, *The James* carried cargo from northern England to ports in the Netherlands. By the standards of the day, this was a good job. It was a comparatively short route, and Henry and his crew mates were lucky to be well paid and well fed. Less than a year after he joined the crew of *The James*, however, the crew's luck ran out. *A Register of Accounts of Wages for Seamen* from 1871 reported the tragic news: "Particulars of the deceased: Henry Sumner, mate, aged 46, drowned on

September the 30th, 1871, at sea." Everyone on board perished, and Henry left behind a wife and nine children. Sting's great-grandfather Richard was only about four years old when his father died.

The sea played a complex and defining role in the history of Sting's family. It had everything to do with their destinies. His third great-grandparents, the parents of Henry, who was lost at sea, were George Sumner, born on February 13, 1799, and Mary Kirk, born on May 2, 1803, both in Nottinghamshire, England. They died, however, in Lower Wakefield, South Australia. Sting had never heard of an Australian connection at all and couldn't speculate on why they may have traveled there. "I'm fearing the worst," he joked. It's a well-known fact that in 1788, the British founded Australia as a penal colony. In the 1830s, however, a second settlement was established for British citizens seeking a fresh start, individuals who moved there of their own free will. George and Mary Sumner were not convicts. "I wouldn't be ashamed if they were," Sting added. "You could be a convict for stealing a loaf of bread."

So what brought these early-nineteenth-century Sumners to the other side of the world? They were both born in Nottinghamshire, as were eight of their children, yet they left their home, never to return. Painstakingly searching through countless ship manifests, we could find no evidence of their arrival. But a newspaper article from the *South Australian Register*, published on September 6, 1848, brought us closer to our answer. "Shipping intelligence," Sting read. "Arrived: Saturday, September 2. The ship *Harpley*, carrying the following refugee emigrants from France: George Summer, his wife, and three children." Because the article spelled the surname wrong, we searched the baptismal records at St. John the Evangelist Roman Catholic Church in Nottingham, where George and Mary had been married, to confirm that these were indeed Sting's ancestors. They were. George and Mary had three daughters, Elizabeth, age eighteen; Hannah, age twelve; and Jane Ann, age ten.

It was curious that their point of origin was France, not England. Sting's third great-grandparents were forced to relocate not once but twice, it turned out, as a result of economic hardship. "The *Harpley* arrived at Holdfast Bay in safety," continued the newspaper account. "She brings 25 agricultural laborers. The rest are lace workers with their families." Nottingham, we learned, had a rich history of lace making. George and Mary Sumner most likely toiled in small workshops using hand-operated frames to make lace. But when towering factories and steam-driven machines began to replace them in the 1840s, they, along with thousands of others, were forced out of work. En masse they headed to Calais, France, just across the English Channel, where lace workshops flourished and there was still a demand for their skills—for a time. In 1848 the French Revolution proved a disaster for the English lace makers. The political and social upheaval of their adopted home left the immigrants, including Sting's ancestors, unemployed, their future uncertain. A book titled *The Date-book of Remarkable and Memorable Events Connected with Nottingham and Its Neighbourhood: 1750–1850* detailed the aftermath of the Revolution in the English expatriate community. "The Revolution in France produced great distress among the lace hands of Nottingham extraction at Calais. The mayor and the other gentlemen, sympathizing with them, commenced a public subscription, which amounted, in the total, to about 600 pounds. With the assistance of the government, a considerable number of men and their families were conveyed to Australia." More than seven hundred lace makers relocated to Australia in that year with the help of the assisted passage scheme. Initiated by the government for British migrants too poor to pay their own passage to the developing colony, the assisted passage scheme aided the migration of nearly one hundred thousand Brits by 1850, their passage repaid through the garnishing of wages.

For Sting's ancestors, their second migration in a decade was a success. A Title of Land dated 1867 revealed that Sting's third great-grandfather, once a destitute lace maker who had been forced to flee the homeland of his birth as well as his adopted homeland, had found success in Australia as a farmer and landowner, "now sized of an estate contain[ing] 50 acres or thereabouts." George's son Henry stayed behind in England and lost his life at sea, and Henry's other descendants, Sting's English family, would struggle for generations to come, but the branch of the family that moved to Australia thrived. The three daughters who accompanied George and Mary on the *Harpley* started their own families in Adelaide. After Mary died in 1861, Sting's third great-grandfather remarried and had more Sumner children. Had George, a commoner, stayed in England, he never would have become a landowner or achieved this level of prosperity.

Sting had always known that the sea played some role in his family history, but not that it was so fundamental in his bloodline. It shaped the destiny of his ancestors, in their work and in their migration. "I knew this dimly. There was always a sense that we'd been involved with it, but never with such specificity," he said. "This is a total revelation to me, a completely different landscape for me to occupy."

■ On Sting's direct paternal Sumner line, we had followed his ancestors to the farthest outpost of the British Empire, Australia. Our journey into his father's mother's line would lead us closer to home, to one of the empire's most contested corners, Ireland. In Sting's autobiography, he mentions that his grandfather Thomas married a woman named Agnes White, a servant who came from an Irish Catholic family. Unfortunately, we found no trace of the existence of a woman of this name anywhere at that time. A marriage document filed in Sunderland, dated 1926, the height of the Jazz Age, corrected a long-held mistake. "Thomas Matthew Kirk Sumner, 27 years of age, shipwright, and Agnes Wright, 20 years old, are married on the 14th of August 1926."

He'd gotten her surname wrong, but Sting knew his grandmother Agnes very well otherwise. "She was the only person I knew with a bookshelf with piles of books. She aspired to the life of the mind, and she would always tell me that if I had any talent, it was because of her." He and his grandmother remained close until her death in 1998. "She taught me to do crosswords, which I do to this day, the British cryptic crossword. She would do the *Times* crossword every day, with a pen." He laughed. "Once you get the answer, there's no other answer."

Finding the correct spelling of Agnes's last name was the first step in recovering her Irish ancestry. While Agnes Wright's father's line was English, her mother's line put us on a path that headed straight back to Ireland. Agnes's grandparents, Sting's great-great-grandparents John Murphy and Eliza Cody, were married in Sunderland, England, in 1872, but their marriage certificate, which was written in Latin, revealed that their fathers, Sting's third great-grandfathers Michael Murphy and John Cody, still remained in Ireland. Despite the notorious difficulties of tracing Irish genealogy—many of Ireland's public records were pulped during World War I for paper or burned during the Irish Civil War in 1922, and for centuries the British had systematically destroyed birth, death, and marriage certificates kept by local church parishes—we were able to follow a paper trail for Sting's Irish ancestors that clued us in as to what had precipitated Sting's great-great-grandparents' move from Ireland to England.

Tax and property records revealed that both of Sting's third great-grandparents were tenant farmers, a situation typical throughout Ireland during the seventeenth and eighteenth centuries, whereby land that had been confiscated from the native Irish was given to absentee English landlords, who then leased so-called tiny-acre plots back to Irish tenant farmers, most of whom struggled mightily just to sustain or even feed their families. The records for John Cody, Eliza's father, indicated that while he did rent his home and land in County Waterford, a major trading center first established by Viking raiders in the year 853, he was not destitute.

The Murphys, however, were desperately poor. A baptismal record for Sting's great-great-grandfather John Murphy from 1850 in the parish of Inniskeen in County Monaghan provided proof of Sting's ancestors' hardscrabble existence. "John Murphy, baptized on the 21st of June in the year 1850 to father Michael Murphy and mother Mary Goodman, NIL." The designation "NIL" meant that Sting's third great-grandparents Michael Murphy and Mary Goodman were too poor to make the customary donation to the church on the baptism of their son John. The register revealed countless other couples in the same position. In 1847 the commissioner of public works, Samuel Ussher Roberts, shared his observations of the hopeless conditions in which County Monaghan's residents were living. "Hundreds spend days without food," he wrote in a letter dated February 20. "Their forlorn and distressing look with pain and sickness so dreadfully depicted in every countenance is horribly painful to look at, and with all this human misery, there is no person putting his shoulder to the burthen. No proper efforts are being made to relieve the people. How will it end? God only knows."

The commissioner was, of course, describing the infamous Irish potato famine, and Sting's great-great-grandfather was born in its midst. Between 1845 and 1851, the failure of the potato crop in Ireland year after year deprived Irish farmers of their primary source of food. Though the peasants were starving, the British crown demanded that the Irish continue to export wheat, oats, and barley to England. The famine was both a man-made and a natural disaster. One out of every eight Irish people died of either starvation or disease. At least a million others—about a quarter of the population—fled the country. Many went to America, while others, like Sting's second great-grandparents, fled to England.

Not everyone in the Murphy family was able to escape. Sting's third great-grandmother, John Murphy's mother, died in the most dire of circumstances. Sting read from her death certificate: "May the 12th 1881.

Mary Murphy, widow, 68 years of age at last birthday. Occupation: Pauper. Her residence: Occupier Workhouse, Carrickmacross." One of 130 such facilities built across Ireland between 1840 and 1843, Carrickmacross was known as the "poor man's jail." Mary Murphy, the widow of the poor tenant farmer Michael Murphy, had been left to survive on her own, and this was surely her last resort. Irish tradition at the time dictated that a widowed mother live with one of her married daughters, but the only daughters we could identify had, like their brother, immigrated to England. Mary's name never appeared on census records as part of any of her children's households, and she spent her last days in what we would call the poorhouse. Sting was brokenhearted to learn of his ancestor's fate. "The designation of pauper, it's just such shame attached to that, and yet it certainly wasn't her fault." The British had put the structure in place that ensured both the failure of the Irish and their punishment. "Seeing my great-great-great-grandmother in a poorhouse actually makes me feel very compassionate for her. It's part of my DNA, my history, and somehow who I am is very related to who these people were." The long journey into Sting's father's roots ended on a very sad note.

■ The sea played a prominent role on Sting's mother's side of the family, as it had on his father's. Sting's mother, Audrey Cowell, was born on June 25, 1931, in North Tyneside, England. She left school at age fifteen to work as a hairdresser. Her son adored her. "I'm a romantic. I'm a dreamer. They're the qualities she gave me," Sting said. "She gave me music." She had a flair about her, a sense of glamour, that both he and other people responded to. One of his earliest memories of his mother was of "people whistling at her in the street. She was very attractive, and she looked after herself. Her hair was always well done. She always wore nice clothes, so people would think of her, or she thought of herself, as a cut above everybody." He laughed. "Perhaps she was justified." His mother's demeanor was the opposite of his stoic father's, and in his autobiography, *Broken Music*, Sting described her as "spontaneously emotional and as prone to tantrums and tears as she is to the laughter and the joys of life." She died of breast cancer at the age of fifty-six, but she had lived to enjoy her son's success. In fact, Sting said, "she loved it."

Audrey never lived far from home. Her birthplace, her husband's, and her son's were all in the same northeastern region of England, all intimately connected to the sea. Her father, Sting's maternal grandfather, Ernest Edgar Cowell, was born nearby as well, in Cullercoats, England, in 1909. Yet his work kept him on land. Initially self-employed as a credit draper—essentially a collector of weekly payments, with interest, from customers who had purchased drapes on installment plans—in 1956 he began a successful career in the insurance industry. In fact, Ernest Cowell was a top-selling agent in Newcastle for the Sun Life Canada Company. In his autobiography, Sting described his grandfather as "rather too elegant to escape the attention of the whispers in a small town." Something set him apart from the other men of the area. "He was a ladies' man, and he had a wonderful car," Sting recalled. "He had a Rover car with massive headlamps and a running board. There was a kind of mystery about him." It was evident to Sting that his grandfather, in his choice of occupation, was trying to leave behind the blue-collar work of his father, Sting's great-grandfather James Cowell, who was a saddler and an electric tramcar inspector; that he hoped to "aspire to the middle class."

In prior generations, Sting's maternal ancestors had answered the call of the sea. A census document from 1871 introduced us to his great-great-grandparents, both born in 1837 in Castletown on the Isle of Man: William Cowell, described as a mariner, and Jane Cowell, described as a mariner's wife. It turned out that the description of Jane Cowell as a "mariner's wife" didn't give the whole picture. While most of the sailing records from the Isle of Man have been lost or destroyed, maritime records for ferryboats called steam packets, which traveled the eighty-one miles from the capital Douglas to Liverpool, have survived, among them a crew list from October 23, 1893. "Name of crew member: Jane Cowell," Sting read. "Ship in which she last served and year of discharge therefrom: *Fenella*, 1893. In what capacity engaged: Stewardess."

We had become used to finding Sting's male ancestors at sea, but not their wives. At age fifty-six, Sting's great-great-grandmother was earning ten shillings a week tending to passengers as a stewardess, hard work that entailed long hours on the rough Irish Sea. Over the next eight years, Jane served as a stewardess on three boats—the aforementioned *Fenella*, the *Ellan Vannin*, and the *Queen Victoria*. In July 1913 she was honored for her long service at sea in the steam packet magazine *The Manxman*, recognized as "the oldest living chief stewardess." She was seventy-six years old at the time. Whether Jane Cowell's time at sea was fulfilling or merely done for practical reasons we don't know, but Sting suspected that she got something out of it. "She was moving," he laughed. "She wasn't stuck on a farm somewhere. Might explain my wanderlust."

■ Sting had just one macabre memory of his mother's mother, Margaret Espy Hill, who was born in Willington Quay, Northumberland, England, in 1909. She died in 1954, only forty-five years old. Sting was three at the time. "I remember her teeth in a glass by her bed," he said. "That's the only memory I have, this horrific image of teeth in a glass of water."

This was not quite the image of water we'd grown accustomed to in Sting's family, but, jumping back several generations, we found ourselves once again on familiar territory. Sting's third great-grandmother Mary Redhead was born in Wallsend, Sting's own birthplace, in 1815. In addition, her two-hundred-year-old baptismal record gave us the names of her parents, Sting's fourth great-grandparents Robert and Mary Redhead, as well as her father's profession. Sting's fourth great-grandfather was a river pilot, navigating ships through dangerous or congested waters, such as harbors and river mouths. Pilots were expert ship handlers who possessed detailed knowledge of local waterways, and they were usually very well compensated. Through extrapolation, we guessed that Robert's father was also a pilot. In the sixteenth century, Trinity House, a local charitable guild developed to support the town's growing maritime community, originated a custom of only recruiting the sons or relatives of former local pilots to carry on the trade, suggesting that there were river pilots on Sting's family tree even before his fourth great-grandfather. The paper trail for Sting's mother's mother's line ended here, further back in time but in the same place as his mother's father's line had, with ancestors who made their livelihood on the sea.

"This leitmotif is getting heavy," Sting said. "It doesn't surprise me emotionally, because I've always been fascinated by the sea, but to actually see evidence of it in these documents is astounding. I don't know these people, I've never heard of these people, and yet there they are, and they're part of me." And the sea was part of all of them.

■ Sting had deep, deep roots in the United Kingdom. We were able to trace his father's side all the way back to his fourteenth great-grandfather Henry de Appleby, who was born around 1555 in Morden, Durham, England. Shakespeare, from whom Sting borrowed the title of his second album, *Nothing Like the Sun*, wasn't even born until 1564. On his mother's side the oldest ancestor we identified was Sting's fifth great-grandfather John Redhead, the father of the river pilot who was most likely a river pilot himself. John Redhead was born in Northumberland, England, around 1756, nearly two decades before the start of the American Revolution. Before he began this journey, Sting had been somewhat detached from his ancestry. "I thought, I don't think anybody in my family knows anything about anything beyond two generations. So I'm heartened by it, and surprised by it, and actually very warmed by it. I feel a richer man because of it."

Both sides of his family, even the poorest of his Irish ancestors, had left impressive paper trails that allowed us glimpses into their lives. DNA, of course, would let us go even further back. We administered two DNA tests to Sting. The first was an admixture test, which would reveal his percentages of European, sub-Saharan, and East Asian / Native American ancestry back to the time of Columbus. Sting's results held few surprises. He was 100 percent European, and of that, 83.5 percent was British and Irish. As we had seen, all of the ancestors we could name were primarily from England, with some from Ireland as well. Other parts of Europe were represented as well, in significantly smaller amounts, from northern to southern Europe and points in between.

We also looked at Sting's Y-DNA, which is passed from father to son, from generation to generation. Y-DNA is an identical genetic signature, and all the Sumner men that we traced shared it. His paternal haplogroup, a genetic population group that shares a common ancestor, reaches its highest density in Scandinavia. Interestingly, 33 percent of the men in Denmark share Sting's identical Y-DNA signature, yet only 15 percent of men in England do. Geneticists believe that this paternal haplogroup was spread from Scandinavia to the British Isles by the Vikings. It's reasonable to surmise that Sting's direct Sumner line traces back to a Viking. In fact, in Sting's admixture, his second largest percentage of European DNA was coded as northern European, at 11 percent. Vikings were, of course, fearless sailors, and, Sting added, "Viking means pirate." He laughed. "It doesn't surprise me at all." There was one surprise regarding his Viking ancestry, though. Sting shared his paternal haplogroup, and therefore a common ancestor somewhere on his family tree, with one other participant in our series, the African American rapper Nasir Jones. The shared ancestor was obviously on the white side of Nas's family. Sting was happy to learn of his new, unexpected relative. "Can't wait for Thanksgiving when we all get together."

■ In exploring his boyhood in his musical *The Last Ship*, Sting had, by necessity, examined the sea and how it shaped his world. His journey today confirmed and illuminated what he had long intuited. "Some things about me are becoming clearer, and as the days turn over, more will transpire in my subconscious about where I come from and who these people are and what they mean to me." He said, quite simply, "They're my relatives." His family's connection to the sea was astounding—his word to describe it— but so was their connection to the land. For centuries, Sting's ancestors toiled for king (and queen) and country, building up the empire on ships and in shipyards. The sacrifices and successes of all of his ancestors had brought him to this place. "We're not just from one region. We are from the whole of the British Isles and then the whole of Europe, which means that everywhere is sacred."

If there was a vessel that he could board to take him back in time to meet one ancestor, Sting would steer it toward his great-great-grandfather Henry Sumner, whose death at sea haunted him. "Dying at sea, leaving a thirteen-year-old boy to work and support the family, I find that very moving, and I'd like to see what kind of man he was." As Sting had mentioned several times, his great-great-grandfather was a part of him, just as all his ancestors were. Genetically we knew this to be true, but did these ancestors make Sting who he is today? Was it DNA? Our experiences? Our immediate families? "All of those things make us who we are," Sting responded. "I think the act of remembering is an act of enlarging, and memory is an important thing, so being given these tools is enriching. It's who we are. It's who I am. I behave and I think the way I do because of many, many factors, and my ancestors are one of them."

Deepak Chopra (b. 1946)

Deepak Chopra is a man of science and spirituality. His unique blend of Western and traditional Indian medicine has struck a chord with millions of followers, and he is the author of more than eighty books, twenty-two of them *New York Times* best sellers. After fifteen years as a practicing physician in the United States, he became disenchanted with Western medicine and the lifestyle he was leading. At his peak he cared for seven thousand patients, but he began to question what that level of care actually was. "I remember one day going and looking at a medical chart, and it had my writing," he recalled. "I had resuscitated a patient with a heart attack, but I didn't remember. I had saved this person's life, intubated him, put him on the respirator. I didn't remember."

The man best known as a holistic health guru was running himself ragged, smoking and drinking. He was burned out, and he could no longer reconcile his life and work. In 1985, when he met the Maharishi Mahesh Yogi—best known as the guru of the Beatles—he decided to make a dramatic change. The Maharishi encouraged him to study an ancient Indian system of holistic medicine known as Ayurveda. "In many traditional systems in the world, including Ayurveda," Deepak explained, "the human body or biological organism was not seen as separate from nature or the universe. Rather than being an independent observer of the universe, I'm also an activity of the universe. This fascinated me."

It fascinated many, and within a decade, he accomplished what would have once seemed impossible: bringing alternative medicine into the mainstream. Now he prefers to call it "integrative medicine." "We still need mainstream medicine for acute illnesses. If you break your leg, you'd better see an orthopedic physician." But, he continued, "a holistic approach that looks at a human being not only as a physical body but as somebody who has emotions and feelings and thoughts and relationships and ideas and imagination and is in the context of a larger ecosystem is the only way to look at people and allow a process that allows for healing. Healing is therefore a return of the memory of wholeness." Deepak has always seen himself as part of something larger. "All my ancestors are right now in my genetic activity in every cell of my body," he said. "There's a feeling of reverence always when I think about it."

Deepak Chopra had an auspicious beginning, born on October 22, 1946, in New Delhi, India, during Diwali. The Hindu festival of lights is a celebration of the victory of light over darkness, good over evil, and knowledge over ignorance. "Deepak literally means 'light,'" Deepak explained. "In my tradition, there's only one light. It's the light of consciousness, awareness. Name and form—that's how we think in India. The name represents the form."

His birth coincided with a rebirth for India itself. Before his first birthday, eighty-nine years of British sovereignty over India had come to an end, but cultures mingled easily in his childhood home. "We had a very strong cultural influence that was our family with its history and stories and myths and religion and all of that, which was really stronger than what we learned in school." Hindi was Deepak's native language, yet "our native language was taught as a second language in school. We learned Shakespeare, and we learned British history. We learned Indian history as told by the British." His father, although proudly Indian, didn't balk at the "Western-style" education his son received. Educated himself in British medical schools, and having served in the British army, "he thought that the best education was in these schools," he said. "My parents were comfortable in both environments."

When Deepak was twenty-four years old, he and his wife, Rita, moved from New Delhi to America. He rose quickly in the medical field, within just a few years becoming chief of staff at Boston Regional Medical Center. "I did feel like I had something to prove," he said. "I was, after all, a foreigner. I was an outsider. There was pressure to prove and pressure to be a little bit better than the rest." Today he describes himself as "Indian by birth, American by choice."

When Deepak first joined with the Maharashi, he "began to realize that we have a personal identity, but there's a larger identity that is more dominant or even more eternal or more timeless." Deepak's own personal identity was part of something much larger itself, bearing traces of the many cultures present in the land of his birth and of the ancestors who lived on that land before him.

■ Deepak could not overstate his father's influence on him. In the foreword to his father's book, he wrote: "The person I call 'me' is actually a bundle of memories and desires, dreams and wishes cultivated so tenderly by this man."" He called Krishan Lal Chopra "a saint," a remarkable man whom he has always aspired to emulate. "He was a true healer, despite the fact that he was also trained in modern science," Deepak said. "He was a humanitarian, an amazing diagnostician. He was everything. When we left Jabalpur and moved to Shillong, there were two thousand people in the railway station on the platform to see us off."

Deepak became a doctor at his father's urging. "I wanted to be a writer. My father wanted me to go into medicine, and on my fourteenth birthday he gifted me a bunch of books, and they were all about physicians." When Deepak made the shift away from Western medicine, his father was disappointed. "I had to go back to India to explain to him that I wasn't moving away from science; I was only expanding my understanding of science." A professor of medicine and chief of cardiology at Armed Forces Medical College in Pune, India, and the head of the department of medicine and cardiology at the prestigious Khairati Ram Hospital in New Delhi for twenty-five years, Deepak's father never retired from medicine; he completed a final set of rounds on the day he died.

Krishan Lal Chopra was born in Rawalpindi, India. The records regarding his birth are contradictory, but we believe that he was born in December 1917. Indian culture had primacy in Deepak's childhood home, but a ship manifest that we found revealed the complicated nature of nationality in the aftermath of British India. Dated November 16, 1954, the manifest for the steamship *Batory*, bound for Bombay from the Port of Southampton in England, included Krishan Chopra among a list of British passengers. Nowhere on the manifest was he described as Indian. "Maybe that was his British army identity, I don't know," Deepak said. "They were all citizens of Great Britain before independence." Yet by the time of Krishan's voyage, India had been independent for nine years.

Deepak was about eight years old when his father went to London to live. Krishan was one of few doctors from the subcontinent ever accepted as a member of the Royal College of Physicians in Edinburgh, the most prestigious and rigorous medical institution in all of Great Britain. This raised the question: did Deepak's father feel that he was representing his people, his homeland, in achieving and accepting this terrific honor? Deepak said that his father felt this "for sure." His son had experienced this himself, on his arrival in America. "He was representing his country. He was representing a nation that had been subjugated for close to two hundred years."

How had this young doctor from India been able to ascend to such heights? Deepak had written in his autobiography that Lord Mountbatten, the last viceroy of India and its last British governor general, to whom Krishan served as an aide-de-camp in the earliest days of the Indian republic, personally smoothed the way for his father to attend the Royal College of Physicians. "I think when he was leaving he said to my father, 'My dear chap, you've done a great job. Do you have any desire, any wish?' And my father said, 'I would love to be a cardiologist one day.' Apparently shortly thereafter he got a telegram saying he had a scholarship to go to England." Krishan's own ambition and intelligence were not insignificant, nor was his connection to this supremely powerful Englishman. In fact, Deepak had written that "the Chopras attached their fortunes to the British." How so? "It was part of their history," he explained. "It was part of who they were. They grew up with a strong background of Indian culture and Indian history and Indian mythology, but were immersed in the atmosphere of what they considered royalty."

We looked more closely at Deepak's father's military service. In 1943, just three years before his son's birth, the twenty-six-year-old Krishan Lal

Chopra was a medic and a captain in the Medical Service of the Indian Air Force. "In the British army," Deepak explained, "Indians could only be soldiers, not officers. But because my father was a physician he was an officer in the British army. That in itself was a big deal for Indians, that he was an officer, one on an equal footing with the British."

The role of India in World War II is often overlooked in history books, but it was incredibly significant. In September 1939, the Indian army had only about two hundred thousand men on its rolls. But when Britain declared war on Nazi Germany, Indians loyal to the Raj volunteered in droves, and by 1945, India had mounted the largest all-volunteer army in the history of the world—some 2.5 million men strong. The enormous army fought valiantly on multiple fronts, nowhere more bravely than at the Battle of Kohima in northeastern India, the site of one of the most important battles of World War II, a battle in which Deepak's father would play a crucial role.

On his graduation in 1943 from King Edward Medical University in Lahore, which is now in Pakistan, Krishan joined the newly formed Emergency Army Medical Corps as a medic. World War II was at its height, and in the spring of 1944, Deepak's father's battalion was sent east, to cut off the encroaching Japanese army in one of the bloodiest war zones in Southeast Asia. The road between Imphal and Kohima was the sole supply route between Burma and India, and its loss would have been devastating to the Allies. The Battle of Kohima, referred to as the "Stalingrad of the East" for its crucial strategic importance and copious bloodshed, was fought in horrifically close quarters over the course of three months. Deepak's father and his fellow medics were ordered to the front line to set up a field hospital. Without adequate time to dig in, the medics were exposed to enemy fire. Krishan and his fellow medics worked fearlessly and saved countless lives, but even so, there were more than 4,000 British Indian army casualties, compared to the Japanese's 5,700. Thanks to the valiant fighting of the Indian soldiers, the Allies held the town and the road and preserved the supply line to Burma.

Today Kohima is considered one of the most impressive victories on any front in the entire war, and Deepak's father played a major role in it. "He talked about the brutality of humans to humans. He talked about starvation. He talked about facing death every day, and he talked about his anguish for those who were wounded. He was a doctor, and that's all he thought about," Deepak said. "He never considered himself a war hero, but I do."

According to an article from the *Times of India*, dated December 23, 1944, Deepak was not alone. "Gallant Deeds in Burma," the headline read. "On a football ground the Supreme Commander spoke to Indian troops in Urdu, saying their fame had spread around the world. Altogether, the Supreme Commander decorated nearly 100 British and Indian officers and men." The Supreme Commander was, of course, Admiral Mountbatten, and he was addressing the Seventh Indian Division at Kohima. It was here, either during or just after the Battle of Kohima, that Krishan Chopra and Lord Mountbatten may have crossed paths for the first time. Kohima figured prominently in Deepak's earliest days. His father had returned there to tend to the wounded after the war and didn't meet his eldest son until he was twenty days old.

Krishan Chopra's military service was remarkably impressive. He rose to the rank of lieutenant colonel in the Indian army, the seventh highest position a commissioned officer could hold, and after independence retired as a full colonel. Wartime necessity undoubtedly played a role in Deepak's father's decision to become a military doctor, but as we went back another generation on the Chopra line, we learned that it wasn't the lone factor.

Deepak's father experienced good fortune through his associations with the British Empire, but Deepak's paternal grandparents, like the majority of Indians at the time, had a very different experience. They were both born in Rawalpindi, in Punjab province, his grandfather Sagar Chand Chopra in 1885 and his grandmother Kesari Devi in 1899. They married in 1910, when Kesari was just eleven years old. Together they would have fourteen children, eight of whom survived into adulthood.

By the end of World War II, the years of growing unrest, sparked by Mahatma Gandhi's nonviolent independence movement, finally led the British to relinquish their control, and on August 15, 1947, British sovereignty over India came to an end. Violence raged in the months leading up to independence, and India's long-awaited freedom came at a high price, notably in Sagar and Kesari's hometown of Rawalpindi. On March 21, 1947, the *Manchester Guardian* detailed the atrocities. "The Punjab government announced today that up to yesterday, 2,049 people had been killed and 1,103 seriously injured in the recent communal disturbances. Figures from the Rawalpindi and Attock districts were not reliable, but it was feared they would be 'formidable.'"

That fear was well founded. Before the British left India, they divided the subcontinent into the Islamic republic of Pakistan and the Hindu and

Sikh union of India. This became known as the Partition, and it triggered one of the largest mass migrations in human history. Approximately 14 million people moved to join their religious majority, on one side or the other of an arbitrarily drawn boundary through the northern part of the subcontinent. Punjab province, Sagar and Kemari Chopra's home, was split in two, with Rawalpindi ending up on the north side of the line, placing it in Islamic Pakistan. An estimated 1 million people died in violent clashes during the process. For months leading up to Partition, Indians had suspected that their nation would be divided along religious lines. Rawalpindi had long been a religiously mixed city in which Muslims and Hindus coexisted peaceably. Now it was in the crosshairs. The fear and uncertainty of impending freedom and division sparked an explosion of intersectarian violence. Some Hindus and Sikhs were forced to convert to Islam to escape torture or death. The bloody episode reported in the *Manchester Guardian* is sometimes called "the Rape of Rawalpindi" for the terrible toll the violence took on the city's women. Hundreds of women chose to kill themselves and their daughters to avoid rape, abduction, and dishonor. In one instance more than ninety women drowned themselves. Death, they believed, was preferable to what lay in store for them.

Deepak's grandparents were fortunate. When Partition came, they fled Rawalpindi by fighting their way onto a dangerously overcrowded train, refugees making their way south through India, ultimately arriving in New Delhi. Sagar was about sixty-two years old when he and his wife made the harrowing journey. People died on that train. It seemed likely that no one came out of the experience unscarred. Although he passed away several years later, in 1954, many of Deepak's relatives believe that the Partition played a role in his death—that the experience was so stressful it weakened his heart. "It's very possible, yes," Deepak agreed. "He left everything he had. It was a big topic in the house, the trauma of the Partition. It was almost therapeutic for them to talk about it. I think it was a way of processing the trauma. But as far as I can remember, there was still more nostalgia than horror." Deepak also said that his grandparents bore little anger or resentment toward the mobs who terrorized their town. "When I was growing up, my grandparents would say human beings are capable of the most atrocious things, but when you see something like this, you learn how not to be." Deeply spiritual people, Deepak said, "they were very influenced by the literature of the Indian mythologies, which say in the midst of crisis, keep your values. We would call it enlightenment." They called it dharma, "the concept that no matter what happens, there is a calling that you have that you should never give up on, and that calling is higher consciousness, spirituality imbibed in a deep way in the biology."

Nor did Deepak detect resentment toward the British—"not overtly," he said. "I remember my grandmother would often say that the British are stealing our knowledge; that the knowledge of science, of astronomy, of philosophy, or mathematics existed in India long before the British came. They were very proud of independent India." The relationship between the British and the Indians was complex, and Deepak's grandparents were British subjects for much of their lives. In fact, Sagar Chand Chopra, like his son, had been a military man.

Sagar's service in the army seemed like a logical course of action for a young man from Rawalpindi. The town had been a permanent garrison since the British annexed India in 1849, and by the turn of the twentieth century, when Deepak's grandfather would have been about fifteen, Rawalpindi became the most important military base in all of the British Raj. At thirty-two years old, he was a *havildar*—the equivalent of a sergeant—in the Indian army during World War I. India would lose seventy-four thousand lives during the war, but because Sagar was a married man, he was not sent overseas, as some 1 million Indian soldiers were. Instead, he was stationed on the northern frontier of India and spent the war in relative peace, with his wife and family. On December 8, 1917, while he was in the army, Deepak's grandfather wrote a letter in which he alluded to "a pleasure trip" he had taken, to what he called "this sacred pool." This was Haridwar, a holy place that would bring us even further back into Deepak's ancestry.

■ For many of us, the key to our family histories lies in the oral tradition. Two of Deepak's cousins, independently, shared the same intriguing story about a Chopra ancestor who had been a tribal chieftain in the barren desert landscape of the Northwest Territory. He held out against British conquest with a cannon to protect his land, but was eventually killed. According to lore, the British were so impressed by his military prowess and determination that they offered his son a place among their ranks, and he accepted. His saddle and sword were reputedly taken by the British and placed with other spoils of war in a British museum. Deepak had heard the story and guessed that the chieftain was his paternal great-grandfather, but the timing didn't work out. When Deepak's great-grandfather, Sagar's father, would have been alive, from about 1850 onward, the East India

Company had already annexed India; in other words, he couldn't have been holding out against British conquest. Neither sword nor saddle turned up in the inventories of the British Museum, the Victoria and Albert, or any of England's many war museums and collections. Our search was exhaustive, but each time we came back empty-handed. Though verification proved impossible, our researchers attempted to piece this story together. Chopra, they explained, is not historically a tribal name. They surmised that Deepak's great-grandfather was more likely a type of landlord, known as a *chaudris*. Loosely translated, *chaudris* means "chieftain." Sagar's father quite possibly fought the British by refusing to pay taxes, waging a war on British coffers.

This was a wonderfully inspiring story that we believed to be true—some version of it, anyway. In India, however, one needn't rely solely on oral history to trace a person's ancestry. For centuries Hindus and Sikhs have gone to Haridwar, the holy city on the Ganges, the "sacred pool" to which Deepak's grandfather had referred in his letter, to perform rites for their dead. Haridwar means "Gateway to God," and Deepak himself took the ashes of his parents there, to immerse them in the Ganges. "When I went," Deepak recalled, "I wrote to my grandchildren not yet born: 'One day you'll come here and you'll remember that I was thinking of you, and the fragrance of your ancestors lingers here right now.'"

Deepak was only the most recent in a long line of Chopras to make the pilgrimage. In Haridwar, thousands of Brahman Pandit priests, popularly known as Pandas, maintain family records of everyone who has ever visited the River Ganges. The Pandas, unrelated to the family for whom they are keeping the ancestral records, write these scrolls in code, a combination of Sanskrit and ancient Hindi and Urdu, the responsibility for the record keeping passed from father to son, from one generation to the next. A translation of the code revealed the names of ancestors previously unknown to Deepak who had made the identical pilgrimage hundreds of years before. "Residents of Hafizabad, Moti Ram and Bhagwan Das and Ramji Mal and Hina Nanda are the sons of Karam Chand and grandsons of Dilbagh Rai's, great-grandsons of Chavve Ram. Son Sukh Ram and Moti Ram came to the Ganges River in Samvad 1864." Deepak's third great-grandfather Moti Ram made the 357-mile pilgrimage to Haridwar—today a nine-and-a-half-hour car ride—with his son, Deepak's great-great-grandfather, Sukh Ram Dass Chopra, in the year 1807. In the same record, incredibly, we could go back further still, to Deepak's sixth great-grandfather Chavve Ram Chopra, who was born in the year 1712, sixty-four years before the signing of the Declaration of Independence in America. "When you go that deep you realize this is just the doorway to that realization that I'm stardust going back to the beginning of time. There's a continuity of life, a chain that goes back 13.8 billion years, and there's not a break in that chain," he said. We had brought Deepak back three centuries in his family, in that unbroken line of Chopras. "I just look at my body and say this is history. But it goes back before that. It gives me a feeling of awe, of reverence, of humility, but also magnificence."

■ Whereas Deepak's father embraced both his Indian and British identity, Deepak's mother, Pushpa Anand, was accepting but less enamored of her land's connections to what Deepak called "the great civilization" of Great Britain. "I remember when my father went on a British steamer to England for training," Deepak recalled, "and my mother told him the first thing you have to do when you get to England is get a white man to shine your shoes, just as a payback for the one-hundred-plus years of the Raj."

His mother, Pushpa, was Deepak's earliest connection to ancient Indian traditions and mythology, to those cultural memories that he cherished. "She was a classic mythical storyteller," he said. "She could sing stories going back to the dawn on Indian civilization." Unfamiliar to Western audiences, these stories, Deepak explained, were "the equivalent of *The Odyssey* and *The Iliad*, bigger in volume and many more stories, much more voluminous and every possible theme of humanity, sacred and profane, divine and diabolical, sinner and saint. You name it, it's there. When you finish reading it," he said, "you will say nothing human can ever be foreign to me. She could sing those stories."

Pushpa Anand was born on February 20, 1929, in Agra, but she grew up in New Delhi. She had no official medical training, but she was intimately involved with her husband's work. Deepak's relatives painted a picture of a nurturing woman who sat on her porch knitting while her husband saw patients. She took note of their circumstances and made sure, if they were poor, that they had enough to eat for the journey home, or enough money for train fare. Once again, Deepak said, for his family, it was always about that higher calling. "Duty, dharma, calling," he said. "They were all compassionate people. It was never about me, ever. It wasn't part of our family culture."

Tradition was important to the family. Deepak's parents entered into an arranged marriage, as was the custom, and became husband and wife on December 12, 1945, not long after Deepak's father served in the army during World War II. "The tradition of arranged marriages, it's not just two people getting married; it's two families getting married," Deepak explained. He called Pushpa and Krishan "the matriarch and the patriarch of the extended clan. He was like Abraham, and she was like Sarah. They ended up basically, because of Partition, taking care of brothers, sisters, cousins, you name it, parents." To his mother, tending to her husband and his career and her children were more important than anything.

Yet in some ways this intensely traditional Indian woman bucked tradition. The sixth of twelve children, she graduated from high school and went to the Lady Irwin College in Delhi. Because she married at age sixteen, she never completed her degree, but that she went to college at all was extraordinary. Only between 2 and 6 percent of the Indian female population under the British Raj was even literate. Pushpa Anand, however, "could recite the classics by heart and was very well spoken in English, read poetry."

Nurturing, compassionate, and deeply intelligent, Pushpa was the daughter of Ram Nath and Jashodha Rani Anand. Deepak's grandfather Ram was born around 1885, his grandmother Jashodha ten years later, in 1895. Both of Pushpa's parents were born in Lahore, which is today a city in Pakistan. According to relatives, Jashodha had a great faith in homeopathic and herbal remedies and Ayurveda. On both sides of his family, we learned that his grandparents turned to *vaidyas*, or faith healers who used traditional Ayurvedic medicine.

In 1939 Deepak's grandparents built the house at Babar Road in which they would live for their whole lives, and in which their grandson would be born in 1946. In fact, Deepak's maternal uncle Virenda Nath Anand still lives there today. The house has always been a symbol of stability in Deepak's family. For his entire life, Ram Nath worked for the Singer Sewing Company, or Singer Asia as it was called, with factories in India, Pakistan, and Sri Lanka. "He was quite, in those days, wealthy," Deepak said, recalling his grandfather's reputation as a businessman. "He had lots of benefits and was, again, taken care of by the British and upper middle class, if not upper class." Working from the age of twenty-one in Lahore, he was promoted within a short time to supervising agent of all of northern India, and he relocated to New Delhi. His work as a traveling salesman required that he move frequently, but eventually Singer stationed him in Agra, which became the family's home. According to relatives, by the time he retired Singer had named him the first nonwhite general manager of the Singer Sewing Company in northern India.

Ram Nath earned a good living, collected a substantial pension, and owned a number of houses in Lahore. But his job with Singer provided his family with comfort and security that went beyond the financial. By settling in New Delhi in 1939, far from the border soon drawn between India and Pakistan, Deepak's grandfather kept himself and his family out of harm's way, away from the violence and upheaval of Partition. In fact, No. 17 Babar became a safe house for other Anand relatives seeking refuge during Partition.

The Anand family benefited greatly from Deepak's grandfather's position and largesse. Once again, we saw Deepak's ancestors shouldering the responsibility for each other. Their connections were clearly strong, and we wanted to go back in time. Haridwar held the key to her father's direct Anand line, just as it had for the Chopra line. (Women's lineages were not inscribed in the scrolls, which is why it was impossible to trace the ancestry of either of Deepak's grandmothers.) An entry from April 1923 took us back to a time before Partition. "The Anand Vasi of Lahore: Ramnath and Jagannath, Kedarnath, Harichand, sons of Lala Thakur Dass and grandsons of Megh Raj, came to the Ganges River to bathe. With him came Jashodha Rani, son Triloknath and daughter Manwati, and son Shivnath in Samvat 1980, during the month of Baisakhi." Here we see the narrative of Deepak's grandparents' pilgrimage, along with three of their children, to bathe in the holy water of the Ganges during Baisakhi, which means "spring" and is the second month on the Hindu calendar. It introduced us to Deepak's great-grandfather Thakur Dass Anand and his great-great-grandfather Megh Raj Anand.

Another scroll told of an earlier pilgrimage, taken at the beginning of the twentieth century. "I visited Haridwar on May 1901," Deepak read, "with the bones of my father, Thakur Dass, who died on the night of 18 April at 12:30. Malan joined her sons to immerse the remains of her husband in the Ganges on May 6. [Signed], Malan Anand." Deepak felt transported. "Here we are sitting in New York City, going back through the mists of time." This was an incredible document, not just for its specificity—providing the precise time and date of the death of Deepak's great-grandfather—but also because it was signed by Thakur Dass's wife, Deepak's great-grandmother

Malan Anand. The earlier scroll mentioned Deepak's grandmother by name as well. Wives were rarely mentioned in the scrolls at all, remembered only as "female."

Based on the information in the Anand family scrolls at Haridwar, we were able to reach back all the way back to Deepak's fourth great-grandfather Nidhi Anand, who was born around 1785, two years after the end of the American Revolution. According to family lore, after his death, Nidhi Anand's ashes were brought to the Ganges by Maharaja Ranjit Singh himself, the founder of the Sikh Empire, which came to power on the Indian subcontinent in the early half of the nineteenth century. After the Maharaja's death in 1839, the relative peace of the Sikh Empire began to crumble, and within a decade India was at war with the British. The descendants of Nidhi Anand would live under British rule for the next century. It was here, with Deepak's fourth great-grandfather, that the paper trail on his mother's side ended.

The Pandas have been keeping track of Indian lineages for centuries, the names of Deepak's male ancestors recorded in their own pilgrimages to the Ganges, or those of their children. Deepak had honored his own parents in the same way that the generations before him had done, scattering their ashes in the holy river. "I've told my son that when I die he can throw the ashes in the backyard," Deepak said, "but then in hindsight, I think we shouldn't break the tradition." Tradition, heritage, ancestry—each is revered in India. Why here particularly? "Because there was a sense of continuity of life," Deepak answered, "there was a sense of great mystery and reverence for life, because there was a sense that we were grateful to be here; that life should be a perpetual surprise and cannot be taken for granted." Gratitude was clearly something Deepak had inherited from those who came before him.

■ The scrolls at Haridwar, painstakingly kept for generations by priests preserving the ancestry of the Chopras and the Anands, brought us back to the eighteenth century on both sides of Deepak's family. We traced his paternal side back to Deepak's sixth great-grandfather Chavve Ram Chopra, who was born around 1712 in Hafizabad. On his maternal side, his oldest ancestor was his fourth great-grandfather Nidhi Anand, who was born around 1785 in Lahore. For Deepak, seeing his family tree, his ancestors' names, unfurled before him confirmed his beliefs about the continuity of consciousness.

To go even further back than the holy records had taken us, we turned to DNA to shed more light on Deepak's ancestry. We administered two tests to him. The first was an admixture test, which reveals an individual's percentages of European, sub-Saharan African, and East Asian / Native American ancestry from about the last five hundred years. Deepak was 93.8 percent South Asian, 4.1 percent Middle Eastern and North African, 0.5 percent European, and 0.4 percent East Asian. "I should have guessed this," Deepak said, considering the results. "I go back to the ancient Indian civilization. I should have thought of that—Ayurveda and all that." The designation South Asian referred to India and Pakistan. This follows the genealogy. We know from Deepak's *gotra*, the unbroken male clan line that we recovered from Haridwar, that the Chopra name originated in Hafizabad, which is now in Pakistan. Scientists believe that when modern humans first left Africa, they traveled along the coast of southern Asia, reaching South Asia very early. During the last few thousand years, South Asia has been a crossroads of sorts, influenced by both Europe and eastern Asia, hence the small contributions of European and East African in Deepak's admixture. His Middle Eastern ancestry appears to represent ancestry from Syria, Turkey, and Iran.

Finally, we looked at Deepak's Y-DNA, which is an identical genetic signature passed from father to son, generation to generation. Deepak's Y-DNA is the same as that of his sixth great-grandfather. Deepak's paternal haplogroup, a genetic population group of people who share a common ancestor, is found mostly in Russia, India, Pakistan, and Afghanistan, which, again, dovetails with all that we know of Deepak's genealogy.

■ We had taken Deepak on a journey of empire and exodus. Some ancestors gained in stature and security under the rule of the British, while others suffered terribly, losing their homes and all that they owned. But what all of Deepak's ancestors held on to, no matter their fortunes or misfortunes, was their deep connection to their ancient Indian civilization. Like his ancestors, Deepak was a blend of all those external forces, and our exploration of his ancestry only strengthened that feeling. "I'm proud to be an Indian," he said. "I'm proud of the civilization I come from, and I'm proud to bring that civilization to the world." But, he continued, "I speak English and I recite Shakespeare, so I'm obviously connected. It's part of my DNA as well. Contradiction and paradox is the essence of life."

More than any of our other participants, Deepak was already keenly aware of his ancestors' presence inside of him when we embarked on our journey. "I'm all of them squeezed into the volume of a body and the span of a lifetime," he said. "When I expand my identity to include all these and those that came before them, I realize I am the universe, and they live right in this moment here." At this point in our conversation, we usually proposed a hypothetical ride in a time machine that could transport our subjects back to any ancestor. Deepak didn't need a lift. He unhesitatingly said that he wanted to meet his legendary Chopra ancestor, "the one who stood up to the British and said, 'I'm not going to surrender to murderers and plunderers,' the one who drew the line." Even though Deepak acknowledged and embraced the British influence on his life and his family, his loyalties lay with India. "The Indian tradition has a richer history of culture, music, art, mathematics, science," he said. "But you have to give credit to a little island that so influenced the world."

For Deepak, science and philosophy had long blended to inform his approach to medicine and his approach to life. It also informed his analysis of what made us who were are, our DNA or our ancestors and the lives they led. "We are the collection of context," he responded, "meaning relationship and history. Therefore, our DNA is the embodiment of that collective karma. By karma I mean that collective experience of humankind that goes back to the dawn of history. Who we are is all of that."

Sally Field (b. 1946)

The eternally young Sally Field's acting career has spanned more than fifty years. The two-time Academy Award winner got her start on the small screen, starring in the lighthearted, now-iconic *Gidget* and *The Flying Nun*. The "turning point" came for Sally in 1976, when she was cast against type in the unforgettable TV miniseries *Sybil*, in which she portrayed the desperately ill title character, a woman struggling with dissociative personality disorder, or what was then known as "split personality." Sally played each of Sybil's thirteen competing personalities—ranging from a baby girl to a grandmother—with an authenticity that has marked all of the subsequent performances in her storied career, whether in drama or comedy. Of all the roles she has taken on, there are three she holds dearest (the first two of which earned her the Best Actress statue). "Something deep inside of me resonated with *Norma Rae* and *Places in the Heart*, even *Lincoln* to a degree," Sally said, "these southern women that somewhere rest inside me, some grit, some gnash-your-teeth, get-it-done."

Sally Margaret Field was born on November 6, 1946, in Pasadena, California, a self-described "all-American girl." It was this image that catapulted her to fame in the early years of her career. When asked to name her home, she identifies strongly with her birthplace. "First I'd say I'm from southern California," she said. "But 'your family'? I will inevitably say Deep South."

That was her mother's side of the family. As for her father's side: "There was a distance to them that I never got beyond, a kind of aloofness and arm's length." Sally's parents divorced when she was just four years old. "It wasn't consciously traumatic, because my brother and I were so very close," she recalled. "So he was always my comfort zone." She stopped short of laying the blame for the gulf between father and daughter on the end of her parents' marriage, yet it was a gulf they never managed to bridge during his lifetime. "My father was somehow never able to come through to us."

Her mother and father, grandmothers and aunts were, to a person, tight-lipped about the past. "I have had the feeling for a long time that if I could just see a picture of them in my mind, of what they came from, of how hard it was for them, that it would somehow give me what I'm looking for in owning all of myself." Having undertaken a search into her ancestry on her own, Sally was now eager to probe her past more deeply, to find the answers to questions she had asked for so long. In adulthood Sally had come to recognize the loss, the seeming permanence of severed connections—connections we intended to restore. "As a child I didn't know how to ever say, 'Can I know you?' I was too young to form the words," she said. "Now, as a grownup, I would say, 'God, if I could have anything, could you give me just three days with five different people, and let me finally be able to talk to them?'" Our journey into Sally Field's roots would give her far more than three days; it would give her centuries.

■ Distance permeated Sally's relationship with her father. "I never called my father Dad," she said. Instead, she called him by his nickname, Dick. Sally's father was born Richard Dryden Field on December 26, 1914, in Titusville, Pennsylvania. Her mother was the actress, but Sally was certain that some of her flair for show business came from her father. "They squashed it like a bunch of bugs and belittled it," she said of her straitlaced paternal side. "But I know it stayed in him." Sally always detected a note of regret in her father that permeated his whole family. "There was a kind of lament in him of not following something, but I also thought it might be handed-down missed dreams of his mother, who had wanted to be a concert pianist, and my aunt Betty, who had wanted to be a dancer, who then spent most of her time as an usher at a Broadway theater, who loved theater and would write me long letters about it as she led patrons to their seats with her flashlight."

It was as if these missed dreams, as Sally called them, bound the family together. Although Sally saw her father frequently despite her parents' divorce, she admitted, "I never knew him." She knew little of his growing-up years in western Pennsylvania beyond what she believed was a closeness among his siblings. "It seemed that they all lived in the same place, all together, all the time," she said. "They were a tight-knit group, but I don't think they were emotionally tight-knit."

A page from the 1900 federal census for Bradford City, Pennsylvania, brought us back another two generations from this group, into the home of Sally's great-grandparents. Sally's grandfather, Fleet Folsom Field, born on February 1, 1881, in Pithole, Pennsylvania, was nineteen at the time this census was taken. He was living with his parents, Sally's great-grandparents, John Quincy Field and Charlotte "Lottie" Berry. According to the census record, the head of household John Quincy's occupation was "oil producer," his son's "oil well laborer." We guessed that Sally's grandfather worked for his father. Today we don't think of Pennsylvania as oil country, but in 1900, throughout the western part of the state, oil was king. It was first discovered in Titusville, where Sally's father was born, in 1859, two years before the Civil War started. Oil was already a critical commodity at the turn of the century, even in the preautomobile era, because it fueled the nation's gas lamps. From all over the nation, people flocked to western Pennsylvania, looking to strike it rich. The influx of people rivaled the Gold Rush of 1849.

Sally's great-grandfather's unusual name gave her pause. She couldn't fathom where the unapologetically American name John Quincy came from. "I think they were from Canada originally," she guessed. "I believe the whole group migrated from England. I don't know why they would have been patriotic." Sally was right about her great-grandfather's homeland. John Quincy Field was born in 1851, in the small farming village of Grimsby, Ontario. Sally, it turned out, had four generations of Canadian ancestors: before John Quincy Field came her great-great-grandfather Adam Field, her third great-grandfather John Morden Field, and her fourth great-grandfather Gilbert Field. The Fields were farmers, hardworking people leading hardscrabble lives, presumably with their origins in farming villages in England. But Gilbert Field's wife, Eleanor Morden, Sally's fourth great-grandmother, was born in Pennsylvania, not in England, in a town called Mount Bethel, in the year 1771. Migration from Pennsylvania to Canada at this time was unusual, to be sure. Fortunately Eleanor had left a paper trail to help us get to the bottom of the mystery.

The 1772 tax list for Mount Bethel, located about ninety miles from Philadelphia and seventy miles from New York City, gave us the name of Eleanor's father: Ralph Morden. Other records from the time provided the name of her mother, a woman named Anne Durham. According to the tax list, Ralph was a laborer, in possession of no land of his own, living in what was then the undeveloped American frontier. Sally's fifth great-grandparents were poor people, and Ralph traveled great distances to find work chopping wood for farmers in order to support his wife and eight children.

Three years after this tax list was recorded, the "shot heard round the world" was fired at Lexington and Concord. The American Revolution had begun. Overnight, the Thirteen Colonies became a battleground, and both rich and poor found themselves confronting a choice that no British subject had ever faced before: Would they side with the Patriots, or become Tories and remain loyal to the British?

Our history books generally cast the Revolutionary War as a battle between the American Patriots and the British, but it was far more complicated than that. In many parts of the country, what ensued was a kind of civil war, with neighbors and even family members fighting against each other. The results were, predictably, devastating. Entire towns were sacked, homes destroyed, farms set on fire. It was very hard to stay neutral—and Sally's fifth great-grandfather, we would learn, didn't. In the aftermath of a bloody battle between Patriots and Tories in a town called Minisink in New York, sixty miles from Sally's fifth great-grandparents' home in Mount Bethel, the local Patriot militia ambushed a group of Loyalists in the Mordens' hometown. A Patriot lieutenant described the attack in a letter written to the president of the commonwealth of Pennsylvania in 1780. "Having received intelligence that a party of Tories has appointed to meet," the letter went, "Colonel Bond placed a few volunteers in ambush who fired upon them. Two were made prisoners, namely Ralph Morden." Sally's fifth great-grandfather was a Tory, and in 1780, he was captured by the local Patriot militia and held as a prisoner of war.

Sally's ancestor stood accused of treason and of bearing arms against the state of Pennsylvania. "Ralph Morden," the indictment went, "did maliciously and traitorously with a great number of traitors, being armed and arrayed in a hostile manner with force and arms, did traitorously assemble against this commonwealth and did give and send intelligence." Sally paused. "Oh, Ralphie," she scolded. He pled not guilty. After a ten-day trial, the verdict came down. "Ralph Morden is guilty of treason," it read. "Judgment that he be hanged by the neck until he be dead." For reasons that remain unclear, the commonwealth doled out an extremely harsh sentence to Sally's fifth great-grandfather; Tories who took up arms against the Patriots were typically given jail terms. Just two and a half weeks later, on November 26, Ralph Morden was executed. A British official detained in Pennsylvania made brief reference to the death of Sally's ancestor in his journal: "A man was hanged this morning for piloting some people through the back woods. He left a wife and nine children."

Although the information was brand-new to Sally, it surprised her less than one might expect. Ralph Morden was, after all, in her Field line, and she saw consistencies between this long-ago ancestor and his descendants. "There's some ringing bell that resonates all the way down the line," she said, "this sort of strict nature that they had of right and wrong. 'We're right, and you're wrong.' 'We're good, and you're bad.' We don't allow our children to go on stage. It's not the right thing; we're decent-brought-up folk." We couldn't know Ralph Morden's motives for remaining loyal to the Crown, but Sally truly believed that fear of change may have been behind them. "Even if you felt it was the right thing to do, to fight for this new land, this new freedom, this new place, to stand for something that you believed in, I always felt that they were a group of people that wanted a set of rules that they rigidly followed, and everybody would step up to that line." She admitted to relishing the dramatic story of her ancestor's crime and death. "I like the colorful nature of it. I feel bad, because I know that his children and his wife struggled, but sometimes struggle is not the very worst thing that can happen to you."

What became of Ralph Morden's wife, Anne, Sally's fifth great-grandmother, and those nine children, one of whom was Sally's fourth great-grandmother Eleanor? Patriot mobs often targeted the wives of suspected Tories, and as the family of a convicted traitor, the Mordens were in grave danger. Seven years after her husband's death, and four years after the end of the American Revolution, the forty-four-year-old Anne made a decision that would alter the future of Sally's Morden family for generations. In 1787, she gathered her children and headed north from the newly formed United States for the safety of Ontario, Canada, still a British colony. Because Ralph Morden had been executed as a Loyalist, his surviving family was entitled to two hundred acres of land, a gift from the British government to their subjects who remained true. Anne was one of the first homesteaders in her part of Ontario, and as a result, Sally's Pennsylvanian ancestors are revered in Canada as founding mothers and fathers. For eight years the Mordens lived as squatters on the land bequeathed to them on Ralph's death, but in 1795, Anne petitioned for ownership—and got it.

The American Revolution had become personal for Sally. The story of her ancestors presented a side of the war not usually seen in this country. "You are struck with the fact of where the women end up. The men are the ones that go fight, and bravo to them. Hopefully it's for what they believe in and all of that, but then the women are there, left with the children, and what now?" Sally's ancestor took matters into her own hands at a time when such matters were usually left to men. "I feel admiration that she was able to pick it up and move it on and get the land." Simply put, Sally said, "I like her."

■ Sally's fifth great-grandparents were as far back as we could go on this line of her father's father's family, who emigrated from the Colonies to Canada. Sally's father's mother's family tree, however, took us back to England. Sally knew that her father's mother, Jane Fox, had had dreams that went unfulfilled, one in a long line of paternal ancestors Sally believed to suffer that fate. "I remember hearing that my grandmother wanted to be a concert pianist but that her father wouldn't let her go on stage because it was unladylike," she recalled. She guessed that the root of their reticence lay in their origins. "I had heard that they came from Puritans," she said. "That strict behavior really clung to the family."

Sally's Puritan roots ran deeper than she ever imagined. On her grandmother's side, we traced Sally's paternal line all the way back to the sixteenth century, to Sally's tenth great-grandfather William Bradford, a Puritan who was one of 102 passengers to arrive at Plymouth Rock on the *Mayflower* on December 21, 1620. Sally was stunned. "Holy smoke! I've heard of that ship! As a child I colored pictures of that boat, the crayon thing."

It was quite possible that Sally colored pictures of her ancestor, too, with "the crayon thing," without knowing it, because he would go on to take part in one of the seminal events of American history. Before we sat down with him in America, though, we wanted to learn as much as we could about his journey to the New World. His baptismal record had survived for more than four hundred years in St. Helena's Church in a town called Austerfield, England. "William, son of William Bradford," Sally read, "baptized on the 19th day of March, year 1590." His early years were marked by tragedy. His father, Sally's eleventh great-grandfather William Bradford, died when William was just a year old; his mother, Alice, Sally's eleventh great-grandmother, followed a few years later. By the time young William was seven, he was an orphan. At about age sixteen, he was drawn into the emerging Puritan movement, which rejected the rituals of the monarchy's official religion, the Church of England, believing the practices had no basis in the Bible.

King James I vehemently resisted the radical reform of his church and vowed to suppress any dissenters. At the Hampton Court Conference in January 1604, he issued the following proclamation: "I shall make them conform themselves, or I shall harry them out of the land or else do worse." Authorities began a massive roundup of the rebels. Just before Christmas of 1607, officials descended upon Scrooby Manor, the little church in William's hometown where he had sought solace and found faith, and arrested all of the Puritans inside, seventeen-year-old William Bradford among them. They were all thrown in jail, with no sense of when they might be released. "At the age of seventeen, for religious persecution," Sally marveled. "You've just got to shake your head."

Although William and his fellow worshippers were all ultimately released, they knew they were neither safe nor free in England, and they resolved to leave their homeland behind. On September 6, 1620, William and another 101 passengers boarded the *Mayflower* in Plymouth, England, setting sail for the New World. Together they hoped to create a religious haven in the newly formed colony of Virginia. While Sally was impressed by her tenth great-grandfather's dedication to his cause, she described her feelings about his search for religious freedom as "twofold." "I appreciate his bravery and his commitment to moving into very dangerous territory because of something he believed in very strongly. But to me, the Puritans handed down to this country a lot of things we need to get over," she said. "Boy, how much has really been done in the name of religion."

The journey was tumultuous, the weather so daunting that some of the crew wanted to turn back. The *Mayflower* was blown so far off course that when it finally landed sixty-six days later, it was on the shores of present-day Massachusetts, not Virginia. A wilderness such as they had never seen before confronted them. "That's the kind of bravery that only few people can feel now, maybe those people who go off into space." The environment was brutal. That first winter, the Pilgrims were forced to huddle together in the hull of the *Mayflower* just to stay warm. Within four months of their arrival, half of them had died from starvation and disease.

Death and despair coexisted with determination. Although their numbers were significantly reduced, the Pilgrims made it through the calamitous winter only to find themselves, in springtime, without a leader. The man they had elected to govern the Plymouth Colony, John Carver, one day collapsed and died suddenly. Sally's tenth great-grandfather stepped in and was elected to fill his place. He would remain governor, continuously elected and reelected, for the next thirty-six years.

Finally, the Pilgrim community was able to get a foothold in the New World. They built homes on the shores of Plymouth Bay, and the local Native Americans, the Wampanoag, taught them to hunt, farm, and fish. William Bradford kept the colony running through it all. Not only was he a key figure in Sally's family, her first immigrant ancestor, but he also played an iconic role in one of the defining events of early colonial American history: he presided over the first Thanksgiving dinner. We unearthed a letter that described the now-familiar event: "Our harvest being gotten in," Sally read, "our Governor sent four men on fowling, so that we might after a special manner rejoice together after we had gathered the fruits of our labor, many of the Indians coming amongst us. And although it be not always be so plentiful as it was at this time with us, yet by the goodness of God, we are so far from want. Glory hallelujah." Sally laughed. "I've always loved Thanksgiving. It's always been a big deal." Descent from a *Mayflower* Pilgrim was a big deal, too—Sally was our first participant to date to boast such a distinction—but for Sally this ancestry was more than a source of pride; it was clarifying. "I feel like I should be really, really excited, but I just go, 'Well, yeah, that makes sense,'" she said. "I know that I'm quintessentially American, and this underlines it."

■ Sally's mother was, in the words of her daughter, "a magnificent soul." Margaret Joy Morlan was born on May 10, 1922, in Houston, Texas. Even before Sally was born, Margaret was a working actress, something that Sally always assumed had been a factor in her parents' divorce. "She was independent," Sally said. Featured in such films as *The Man from Planet X* and television classics including *Bonanza* and *Perry Mason*, "she just handed the ball off to me in some ways." Sally never had the sense of wanting to be just like her mother, but she didn't deny that show business "was in my blood." "What my mother handed me is this love for the craft of acting, of telling stories through your person," Sally explained. "I'm a storyteller. I am transfixed and illuminated and taken off the ground by stories, and that was really started by the language that I had with my mother."

Sally described her mother as one in "a long line of complicated women" bound by secrets and circumstance. Call it devotion or dependence, the women of Sally's family were inextricably linked. "They never were away from each other. Always, always, all of those women never were parted from each other. My mother cared for my grandmother till the day she died, I mean lived with her, as I did with mine." Sally paused. "It's what women do."

We began our journey into the lives of these women with Sally's grandmother, Joy Beatrice Bickley, who was born on March 31, 1894, in Alabama, and who grew up in South Carolina and Texas. In the 1910 federal census for Columbia, Richland County, South Carolina, Joy Bickley was listed as an "inmate, age 16," at Epworth Orphanage. Joy only shared stories of the orphanage with her granddaughter toward the end of her life. She lived there with her sister Gladys, and the two sisters were deeply, deeply connected. "It all sounded very Dickensian," Sally began. "Gladys's job was to get up in the morning and stand on a stool and pick the bugs out of the oatmeal, weevils and things like that. Gladys just didn't want to live, and Joy refused to let her die, and Joy would stuff rotten potatoes into her because that's all they had." All they truly had, it seemed, was each other. "They had a way with each other. They were never apart, and they lived together in this orphanage, from what I can ascertain, for quite a number of years."

Together they suffered under the brutally repressive conditions of the turn-of-the-century Epworth Orphanage. "It was a lot of hellfire and damnation," Sally's grandmother had told her, "a lot of Bible talk and a lot of preaching about hell and sin and sex and men and evil ways. I imagine it was because there were a lot of those 'evil ways' that had gotten these children placed here." As an adult, Sally's grandmother felt too ashamed of her time in the orphanage to speak of it. "My grandmother and my aunt Gladys, who were so deeply influential in my life, I know they were so deeply disgraced, as my wonderful Mimi, their mother, was." Suffering under the stigmas of the time, their shame bonded them. "The sisters and Mimi were woven together, like a chain-link fence. They were," she repeated, "never apart."

Conditions at Epworth Orphanage were deplorable. Sally's grandmother and great-aunt likely lived in a dilapidated bunkhouse, and overcrowding was extreme. Just one example: more than 225 children were regularly packed into a dining room designed to hold 90. While the girls were living in the orphanage, their mother, Redonia Ethel Bickley, lived in nearby Newberry, South Carolina. According to the 1910 census of that town, she was a thirty-six-year-old widow, struggling to make ends meet as a live-in housekeeper at a boardinghouse. "This broke my heart," Sally said of her beloved great-grandmother. "It was close enough to the orphanage that I think she tried to, in some way, stay close to her children."

It appeared that Sally's great-grandmother Redonia was simply too poor to care for her daughters. Redonia had been pregnant with another man's child when she married a man known to us only as L. Bickley. Although not Joy's father, Bickley gave Sally's grandmother his last name. He died quite young, leaving Redonia to care for their four daughters on her own. With no means of support and no way to make a living, it seems that the orphanage was the only choice Redonia had for Joy and Gladys; the younger two daughters went to live with relatives of their father.

Sally's family tree on her mother's side was complicated by the fact that the man who raised her grandmother, L. Bickley, was not her biological father. According to oral history and confirmed by DNA tests, that man was James Luther Bynum, whom Sally called "the dark-eyed devil." "He's my grandmother's big dark eyes, my mother's big dark eyes, and my eyes," she said. "It is my eyes, and I don't know him." Of all the stories on her family tree, it was James Luther Bynum's that she most wanted to learn. "These women I grew up with never told their stories," Sally said. "They were southern and strong and secretive." That secretiveness revolved around, was dictated by, this mystery man. The mystery was about to be solved, because the Bynum branch of Sally's family had left behind an incredible paper trail, which we followed to one of the most critical events in American history.

Tapley Bynum, James Luther's father and Sally's great-great-grandfather, was born in 1845 in Calhoun County, Alabama. A census from the year 1860 showed us that at age fifteen, he was living with his parents, Eli Bynum, born in Pendleton, South Carolina, in 1813, and Miranda Pace, born in 1810, also in South Carolina. Eli and Miranda were Sally's third great-grandparents. Just months after this census was recorded, on January 11, 1861, Alabama officially seceded from the Union, and the state soon became a Civil War battleground. In 1862, at age seventeen, Sally's great-great-grandfather Tapley signed up to fight for the Confederacy, a soldier in the Thirty-First Alabama Infantry.

Sally knew little about the Bynum family specifically, but her family had never kept their Confederate leanings a secret. "It was a thread in the fabric of my life that has remained and was handed down," Sally said. "There was a feeling always of being proud of being in the Confederacy. I believe that to the day they died they resented what happened."

Sally's Bynum ancestors, we learned, were slave owners. According to the Slave Schedule of 1860, which listed the name of every slave owner in the nation and catalogued anonymously all of their slaves by age, gender, and color, Sally's third great-grandfather Eli Bynum owned twelve slaves, ranging in age from one to seventy. "I didn't know he owned twelve slaves, because my grandmother did not acknowledge his existence in her life. But I knew it was all around. She would visit distant relatives who still owned a plantation in some form. They were all farmers, mostly pretty poor, but they had once owned slaves," she said. "She never got any politically correct language adhered in her brain, and she said she just played with all them little pickaninnies, loved them little pickaninnies. It was deeply ingrained in her. She embraced that. She was drinking the Kool-Aid."

It was a way of life that many southerners had a hard time letting go. After all, their husbands, brothers, and sons fought and died for it. Eli Bynum's son Tapley, Sally's second great-grandfather, was on the front lines of a famous battle called the Battle of Champion Hill, fought on May 16, 1863. It was a crucial part of the Union army's Vicksburg campaign, a strategy aimed at dividing the South in two. The total number of casualties on both sides was enormous—nearly 6,300—but the Union emerged victorious and took all Confederate survivors prisoner, Sally's second great-grandfather among them.

Just seventeen years old, Tapley Bynum was kept in jail for less than a month, paroled on the condition that he swore never to return to the Confederate army. He secured his release, but he never severed ties completely.

His whereabouts at the time of his death on August 19, 1911, proved it. According to the *Montgomery Advertiser*, "T. D. Bynum was killed by lightning while returning from the recent reunion of the Confederate Veterans last Thursday afternoon." Sally appreciated the irony. The California-born actress nominated for an Oscar for her portrayal of Mary Todd Lincoln had proud Confederates and slave owners up and down her mother's family tree.

■ Sally had incredibly rich stories on both sides of her family tree, stories that took us back to two of the defining wars of American history, the Revolutionary War and the Civil War, not to mention the founding of Plymouth Colony. The oldest ancestors we could trace on both sides of her family tree were born about 250 years apart but shared one thing in common: both were British subjects. On her father's side, we traced Sally's ancestors all the way back to Peter Bradford, who was born around 1460 in Bentley, Arksey, Yorkshire, England. On her mother's side, we went back as far as William Bynum, who was born around 1724 in Virginia.

Sally's DNA would take us further back still. We first administered an admixture test, which measured her percentages of European, sub-Saharan African, and East Asian / Native American ancestry from the past five centuries or so. Her results were compatible with her genealogy: 99.2 percent European. "Boy, am I dull," Sally laughed. "I'm so white, I'm translucent. It's just awful!" Her results showed very small Asian percentages as well: 0.7 percent South Asian, which was from India, and 0.1 percent Native American. Sally had distant ancestors from outside northern Europe, but, as we would have expected, when we broke down her European ancestry, the bulk of it—67.1 percent—was from the British Isles. Represented in much smaller portions were France, Germany, Scandinavia, Finland, and eastern and southern Europe. "I am a mutt; I know that," Sally said. "I'm just a messed-up mutt."

We also tested Sally's mitochondrial DNA, a genetic fingerprint identical to her mother's, which was identical to her mother's, and so on. Her maternal haplogroup, a genetic population group that shares a common ancestor, is found in central Europe, in Denmark, Ireland, and Cantabria, which is a province of northern Spain. As her admixture results showed, Sally's mother's line had its origins in one of the many parts of Europe found in Sally's genome—not the sort of diversity Sally might have hoped for, but diversity nonetheless.

■ Sally had jokingly described herself as a "mutt," but she was a mutt of primarily British extraction. She related to her British ancestry in a way that might have made her tenth great-grandfather William Bradford proud. "I do feel very much a connection, but in my DNA, somewhere in my history and my lineage, I feel the struggle to escape from that, to escape from their rules and to have some sense of freedom that this country offered," Sally said. "Then I feel the struggle to get away from what they brought."

Sally saw in herself a rebellious streak, a willingness to strike out on her own that may have begun with her Puritan ancestors, but was also squelched by them. Maybe, she thought, this was the sort of thing imprinted on a person's DNA. In her mind, it was certainly passed down through the generations. "Ways of being, of not necessarily teaching your children, but how children watch their parents survive and how difficult their own survival is within their family, that gets handed down. How you look at the world gets handed down to your sons and daughters." She didn't have to look far back on her family tree to see this. "I see a way of being from my father's side of the family, I swear to you handed down from those Puritans who came over on that boat. They lost the great strength and belief in that Puritanical system, but they held on to something that might not have been the best thing to hold on to."

On the subject of "that boat" and "those Puritans," Sally had one of the richest and most historic family trees we had ever had the pleasure of researching. If a time machine could take her back to the Plymouth Colony, would she have wanted a seat at the first Thanksgiving table? Or was there another ancestor she would like to break bread with? "Certainly I would be interested in meeting William, who had been on the *Mayflower*," she said, "but I'm so struck with Anne, whose husband was hanged and who scrambled with all of her children. I visualize her scrambling to figure out what to do, how to survive. I appreciate her for that."

Although she could visualize her fifth great-grandmother Anne Morden on her journey from the former colonies to Canada, Sally couldn't picture herself anywhere else but here, in America. Deep British roots notwithstanding, Sally saw herself as a true American. "Every detail of it is totally fascinating, but it validates this part of me that simply knows this is my home. You can go visit, and you can appreciate other places, but I am deeply rooted in this country. When I close my eyes and dream about it, it's everything I see in my vision." Her journey into her past enriched her understanding of herself and of her parents, where their silences and sadnesses came from. But more than anything, it confirmed for her what she had always known to be true. "It's like some part of me has always known how long this land has been mine, or I've had my feet on it. When people will say, 'Where is your lineage?,' in Europe and other places and God knows where, I have never been able to visualize myself in any of those other places, as coming from there. I can't visualize it. It was always here. I am from here. I come from here."

Though strangers to each other, Sting, Deepak Chopra, and Sally Field share a common history, their roots deeply planted in the soil of the British Empire. Their ancestors were devoted British subjects who worked and fought in the service of king and country, on land and sea, on "the blessed plot" itself and thousands of miles away from it. As complicated as it is, Sting, Deepak, and Sally each embrace the legacy of empire that they carry in their blood, but for all of them, that legacy is a source of both pain and pride.

CHAPTER NINE

Ancient Roots

Fewer than 1 percent of Americans have Greek roots. It's a shockingly small number for such a vibrant community. The comedian Tina Fey, the humor writer David Sedaris, and the journalist and political commentator George Stephanopoulos all grew up in similar environments, where their Greek heritage was celebrated, but their knowledge of their Greek ancestors was stunted. Greek ancestry is notoriously difficult to trace, and the reason why lies in Greek history itself. Beginning in 146 B.C. and continuing well into the twentieth century, Romans, Turks, Germans, and other foreign powers ravaged the country and subjugated the population, destroying the vital records necessary to trace family histories. Fortunately for Tina, David, and George, not everything was lost. For all three of them, we discovered that their Greek ancestors had made enormous sacrifices for the freedom of their ancient homeland. For Tina and David, who have roots that connect them to a different part of Europe, they both have ancestors who played a dramatic role in another struggle for independence as well.

Tina Fey (b. 1970)

At just twenty-nine, she became the first woman to be named head writer of the legendary *Saturday Night Live*, shattering the notion that the writers' room had to be a boys' club. She was the force behind the offbeat sitcom

30 Rock, which she created, wrote, and starred in, and she has been honored repeatedly with Emmys and countless other awards. In 2007 *Time* magazine named Tina Fey one of the 100 Most Influential People in the World. Simply put, Tina is smart and funny, and people admire her for it. She idolizes Carol Burnett and Mary Tyler Moore, but she also credits contemporary peers like Amy Poehler and Maya Rudolph for influencing her. Comedy, she said, is "a never-ending chain of robbery."

Born Elizabeth Stamatina Fey on May 18, 1970, in Upper Darby, Pennsylvania, Tina grew up with comedy in her home and, to an extent, in her blood. "We watched a lot of comedy, as you might suspect," she said of her childhood. "Some of it you learn from watching people on TV, but some of it is internal. I'm sure some of it comes from my mom. My mom has a very dry sense of humor. She's not out there working for a laugh; she's wry. And I think anything that I would have of that, I get from her."

Tina's mother, Jeanne Fey, born Zenobia Xenakis, is also her connection to Greece. Growing up in the middle-class Greek neighborhood of Upper Darby, just outside Philadelphia, Tina describes herself as "half Greek." "I was sort of a novelty kid. I was mixed-race in my neighborhood because I was half Greek, half German, and a little bit of Scottish," she explained. The Greek half dominated Tina's childhood home and community. "We were very proud of our culture," she recalled. Her parents both spoke Greek—for her mother it was her native tongue; her father was self-taught. "We did listen to Greek music, and there were books about Greek art. And all Greek Americans have the imitation statues and things." There wasn't, however, a deep exploration of ancient Greek culture. "We didn't really talk about philosophy. It should have been talked about more. It was just the everyday 'Our food is delicious! The music is good!' It was a lot more mundane."

Mundane or not, Tina treasured and respected her Greek heritage, honoring it by marrying her husband in the Greek Orthodox tradition in which she had been raised. Although she said her parents would have been content to have her married by a justice of the peace, "it did seem like a nice thing to do for them." When it came time to name her daughters, she again turned to Greece and to family, giving her firstborn daughter, Alice, the middle name Zenobia in honor of her mother. Her second daughter's name, Penelope, is old as Homer's *Odyssey* itself; her middle name, Athena, leads straight back to Mount Olympus and is one of Tina's mother's middle names. "That was so important to me," Tina said. "It does seem to make sense to look back for these names instead of pulling them out of the ether, because you have a kid, and then you realize, 'Oh, I am an extension of a family line.'"

Tina was about to learn how incredibly far back her family lines went.

■ Tina's mother came to America when she was just a baby. Born Zenobia Gustandina Athena Xenakes on December 6, 1930, in Piraeus, Greece, her name was changed to Jeanne when she was a young child. "When her mother, who didn't speak a word of English, went to sign her up for school in Philadelphia," Tina explained, "my grandmother was saying, 'Her name is Zenobia, Zenobia,' and the woman said, 'I'm just going to write Jeanne.'" Even with her Americanized name, Jeanne displayed the traits that Tina associates with Greek women. "Very social. My mom is very warm. She would hug you. She would be very uncomfortable if you didn't let her feed you."

Tina's mother created a home for Tina and her brother that was saturated in Greek culture. Now we wanted to take Tina back to her mother's childhood home. We started in America, with the 1940 federal census for the city of Philadelphia, where Jeanne lived with her parents, Gus and Bessie Xenakes, and her three younger brothers. Like their daughter, Gus and Bessie had adopted—or been given—Americanized versions of their Greek names.

Tina's grandfather Gus was born Constantine Xenakes on the island of Ikaria on June 30, 1890. Although we couldn't find a record of his arrival at Ellis Island, we knew he came sometime before 1917. When the United States entered World War I that year, Gus was a twenty-seven-year-old immigrant laborer living in Philadelphia. Drafted in 1918 under the name Gus Xenakes, he served in the 155th Depot Brigade as a cook. He would ultimately serve six years in the U.S. Army, using the money and skills he acquired during that time to open a restaurant in Philadelphia. "Very Greek," Tina commented. "What Greek person doesn't have a restaurant?" Tina's grandfather's military service made him a United States citizen, and it gave Tina's family a foothold in their adopted homeland.

Gus kept a foothold in his native land as well, which, much to Tina's surprise, was listed on his draft card as Turkey and not Greece. The tiny island of Ikaria sits just thirty miles off the coast of Turkey and is today considered part of Greece. When Greece gained its independence in 1832, after nearly four centuries of domination by the Ottoman Empire, Ikaria remained under Ottoman rule. The Turks considered the Greeks inferior, barely a step above cattle—they even called their Greek subjects *rayah*, which literally translates to "flock"—and they ruled them accordingly, stripping them of right after right under Ottoman law.

This was the environment in which Tina's grandfather came of age. In 1912, when he was twenty-one years old, the islanders rebelled against the empire, taking on the Ottomans and expelling their troops. Ikaria became part of Greece. Tina had long been aware of the tensions between the Greeks and the Turks, even in her own home. "Sometimes my mom will talk disparagingly about how Greeks are mostly fair-haired, blue-eyed people, and if it hadn't been for the Turks, if we hadn't all been raped by Turks in our ancestry . . . " She trailed off. "There's no fondness for Turkish people."

Yet Tina's grandfather felt an extreme fondness for his homeland. In many ways he never left it. Ikaria, continuously populated since 7000 B.C. and known for its healing hot springs, has been a destination for those seeking wellness since ancient times. Gus owned a hotel there, given to him in the 1950s by his father, Tina's great-grandfather Zacharias Xenakes. Locals called it the Embassy because of the American flags flying out front. Those American flags planted on Greek soil were emblematic of the dual life Gus Xenakes led. For most of the year Gus ran a restaurant in Philadelphia, but every summer he returned to Ikaria to run the Embassy. "Maybe if you've left your home country," Tina said, "you still long for time there." In 1967, on learning that he was terminally ill, the American citizen and U.S. Army veteran returned to Greece for good. He died there in 1969, in his wife's arms, on the island of his birth.

However strong Tina's grandfather's emotional connection was to Ikaria, tracing his ancestry there proved impossible. His father, Tina's great-grandfather Zacharias Xenakes, had given him the hotel. This gave us a name, and we even had an approximate birth date of 1870. But the obstacles to tracing Greek genealogy can be insurmountable. Government records and church records were destroyed routinely under the constant domination of foreign powers for more than a millennium, and as a result, many villages in Greece have no records of marriages, births, or deaths. Unfortunately, this was the case with Ikaria, and we could go no further on the Xenakes line than Tina's great-grandfather Zacharias.

■ Would we be equally stymied in our research into the ancestry of Tina's grandmother? Bessie Xenakes was born Vasiliki Kourelakos in Petrina, Greece, on February 10, 1902. She died when her granddaughter was just a year old. Tina knew Bessie only through old photographs. "I had a passport picture of my grandmother holding my infant mother. She seemed to be a stylish, elegant woman. She's got a fur coat and a beautiful ring, like 'I'm taking a transatlantic crossing.'"

In the Ellis Island archives, a passenger list dated February 28, 1921, gave us a glimpse into one such transatlantic crossing, and revealed a surprising fact. Just twenty years old, unable to speak English, Vasiliki Kourelakos paid her own passage and made the journey to America on her own. "I thought I was badass for moving to Chicago from Philadelphia at twenty-one," Tina quipped.

We found a marriage certificate in the Pennsylvania State Archives for Vasiliki and Gus. They married in March 1930 and sometime that year returned to Greece, where Vasiliki gave birth to Tina's mother in December. They didn't stay, and in 1931, Vasiliki returned with her young baby to the United States, where she and Gus would raise their family in Philadelphia. But what about the family she left behind in Petrina, an ancient village nestled in the foothills of the Taygetus Mountains in southern Greece? A town register had survived the destruction all too common among Greek archives, and it brought us back another generation on Tina's family tree. The names she read from the page were familiar: "Napoleon Kourelakos, peasant farmer, and Stamatina Stephenakos, wife; two daughters Vasiliki and Aphrodite." Napoleon and Stamatina were Tina's great-grandparents, the namesakes of her uncle and herself. Vasiliki's father, Napoleon, was born in 1851, and her mother, Stamatina, in 1872, both in Petrina, in the Lakonias province of Greece.

That we'd gotten back this far, to the middle of the nineteenth century, was nothing short of a miracle in Greek genealogy, but incredibly, a text had survived that allowed us to go back further still. The sole copy of a book called *Petrina from the Seventeenth Century* gave us the name of Tina's third great-grandfather Stephanos Hirtoularis, born around 1800 on the island of Chios, just four miles off the coast of Turkey.

In 1821, a Greek secret society known as the Friendly Society began to sow the seeds of revolution against the Ottoman Empire, setting its sights on Chios, at the time one of the wealthiest islands in the Aegean Sea and therefore extremely valuable to both sides in the escalating conflict between the ruling Turks and their Greek subjects. On January 1, 1822, the Greeks declared their independence. In response, the Ottoman ruler Sultan Mahmud the Second deployed a fleet of ships packed with forty thousand Turks to the island. What happened next would shock the world. The Dutch consul stationed in Chios bore witness to what became known as the Chios Massacre, and he detailed the horrors in his diary. "You don't see anything but fire and disaster and Ottoman ships full of spoils, slaves, children, oxen, goats, mules," he wrote. "The spectacle causes compassion and melancholy. The Turkish troops burn, enslave, massacre. Horror dominates in the city, heartbreak in the countryside. The roads are full of dead bodies. The Pasha's order is not to leave any Greek alive, to enslave the women and the children and sack the place." This was the first Tina had ever heard of the gruesome event. "I wonder how many people my age have any real sense of this," she said. It was this sort of history, she speculated, that contributed to making even contemporary Greeks "mistrustful of other cultures." She had heard the derogatory comments in her own home. "This is where we see the source of what to me is a sort of generalized prejudice."

The Chios Massacre raged for weeks. At the end, tens of thousands of Greeks had been slaughtered; others had been enslaved or died of starvation. Out of a population of roughly 120,000, just 20,000 survived the rampage by hiding out in caves or in the woods. Amid the catastrophe, most of the island's records were destroyed forever. But the book that had given us Tina's third great-grandfather's name in the first place contained information about his fate. "After the massacre," Tina read, "Stephanos Hirtoularis moved from Chios to Petrina." For generations Petrina would remain Tina's family's home.

Stephanos did not find a quiet life in Petrina. The Greek Revolution was under way. The horrors of the Chios Massacre had made headlines across the globe, awakening other nations to the plight of the Greek people. With the help of England, France, and Russia, the revolutionary army overthrew their oppressors, and in 1832, the war came to an end. Greece became an independent nation, and Tina's third great-grandfather had played a part. A document compiled in 1844 listed the men of Petrina who served with distinction in the Greek Revolution: "Stephanos Hirtoularis, bronze medal for military service." "I descend from a patriot. That's awesome," she said. "I feel a renewed interest and pride in this side of the family, because I've never known any of this."

Because Tina's third great-grandfather Stephanos was recognized as a war hero, contemporaneous historians were inspired to record his ancestry. As a result, we could identify by name Tina's seventh great-grandfather Dimitrios Tzanos, born in the province of Messenia all the way back in 1630. Greece was still in the grip of the Ottoman Empire, under Sultan

Murad IV. It would remain so for another two centuries, brought out of domination with the help of Dimitrios's third great-grandson, Tina's third great-grandfather Stephanos.

This was as far as we could go in the paper trail on Tina's mother's side. Tina felt more deeply connected to her Greek heritage than she ever had. "Knowing these people were just living their day-to-day lives is eye-opening," she said. "You feel this thread going all the way back. To be able to know that that goes all the way back, it's making me feel more Greek than I usually feel."

■ Tina was raised in the Greek Orthodox church, in a Greek enclave outside Philadelphia, but she also identified with her father's heritage. Donald Henry Fey was born on June 9, 1933, in Philadelphia, a fourth-generation Pennsylvanian. "I've always assumed that I have a little bit more of the German temperament," she said. "I'm the sort of person that if someone was cutting a line, I would feel the need to intervene and talk about the sanctity of the line at the airport." A fundraiser and grant writer at the University of Pennsylvania, and a talented painter on the side, he was always supportive of his daughter's desire to "do something creative" with her life.

We started our journey into her father's roots with his parents, Heinrich "Henry" Fey, born on September 15, 1906, in Pennsylvania, and Mildred Ada Ritchie, born on January 1, 1905, in Philadelphia like her son. Both died before their granddaughter was born. Ever conscious of "Greek looks"—"I can always spot a Greek person," Tina said, "because our eyebrows are really straight. There's something going on in here that's the same"—she laughed when she looked at a picture of her paternal grandmother. "If you were able to put me through a deflavorizing machine that took the Greek out of me, that's what I would look like."

The paper trail was long for this side of the family, and we moved back several generations, from Tina's grandmother Mildred Ritchie to Tina's fifth great-grandfather, whose handwritten baptismal record from a little church in London had survived since the middle of the eighteenth century. "Christenings in the Parish of West Ham, England, 1744," Tina read. "John Hewson, son of Peter and Catherine." Tina was shocked. "Scotland I knew. I had no idea we had any family in England." John Hewson, born more than thirty years before the Revolutionary War, was the first ancestor on this line of Tina's family to come to America, and he led a fascinating life.

As a young man, Tina's fifth great-grandfather learned the art of textile manufacturing, and he quickly distinguished himself at Talwin and Foster, London's leading producer of high-end quilts. Before long, he would take his business to the colony of Pennsylvania, with a letter of introduction, dated July 25, 1773, from one of its most prominent citizens. "This will be delivered to you by John Hewson and Nathaniel Norgrove, who are recommended to be sober, industrious young men," Tina read. "I therefore recommend them to your civilities and advice, as they will be quite strangers there." Addressed to one Richard Bache, the letter is signed, "Your affectionate father, B. Franklin." That "affectionate father," Benjamin Franklin, needs no introduction himself. Richard Bache was Franklin's son-in-law, a prominent citizen in his own right, who would succeed his father-in-law as postmaster general after independence. The two powerful men paved the way for Tina's fifth great-grandfather to build his own business in the Colonies.

But why was Benjamin Franklin so keen on Tina's fifth great-grandfather? Franklin, as we know, was a man of foresight. In the late eighteenth century, America had almost no textile factories, and it was largely dependent on imports from England. Franklin recognized the importance of developing homegrown industry and thus recruited Tina's very talented fifth great-grandfather to bring his skills to America. In 1774, John Hewson opened a quilting factory in Kensington, Pennsylvania, quickly establishing himself as the master quilter of the Thirteen Colonies. In early 1775, then-General George Washington and his wife, Martha, passed through Philadelphia. During the visit, Martha Washington commissioned Tina's ancestor to make a kerchief inscribed with the words "George Washington, Esq. Foundator and Protector of America's Liberty and Independency." Washington would accept command of the Continental army on June 15, 1775.

Today John Hewson's work hangs in the Met, and textile historians still study his work. He left behind an impressive artistic legacy, but it is her ancestor's connection to two of America's Founding Fathers that left the deepest impression on Tina. "I grew up in Philadelphia during the Bicentennial. I'm born in the 1970s. I was at the prime age to experience it," she said. "This is something I've learned about in school." And if she had known then that she had an ancestor with famous friends? "I would have been so braggy!"

Tina's fifth great-grandfather prospered in Pennsylvania. But less than two years after his arrival in the Colonies, on April 19, 1775, battles between colonists and British troops erupted in Lexington and Concord. The American Revolution was under way. John Hewson was an Englishman living in Pennsylvania. Which side was he on? The Revolutionary War records at the National Archives held our answer: "Full name of soldier: Captain John Hewson." Tina's fifth great-grandfather created and led a militia of his employees, men who served as Patriots in the fight against the British.

John Hewson's portrait hangs in the Historical Society of Pennsylvania—"a place I've probably been," Tina noted—and when we showed her a copy of it, she saw her father's face and her own in Hewson's. Yet this ancestor, well known in his time, acquainted with Benjamin Franklin and George Washington, had been completely lost to Tina before today, as had the whole of her English ancestry. "I would always see that era of portrait in a museum and feel that they were sort of comical, because they're so white and kind of British-y, so not what I think of myself having any connection to."

On the contrary, the connection was incredibly strong. John Hewson was her original immigrant ancestor on her father's side of the family, and the second patriot we had met in a short span of time. "Thinking of both of these men, Stephanos and John Hewson, living in times where the world was changing, it's fascinating to me that the bulk of their lives were during these times of tremendous change. The country they were in became another country." The Greek ancestor opened a window on a world she hadn't known about at all, while the English one reconfigured her concept of the history that had happened in her backyard.

In taking up arms against the Crown, thus drawing a line in the sand between the land of his birth and his adopted homeland, Tina's fifth great-grandfather set a new course for her family, one which for generations had had its roots planted firmly in British soil. Her ninth great-grandfather was also named John Hewson, and he was her oldest named English ancestor. He worked as a cobbler, born to a poor family in London in 1610, a decade before the Pilgrims landed on Plymouth Rock.

Tina's ninth great-grandfather lived through a tumultuous period of English history, marked by religious intolerance and sectarian strife. Between 1642 and 1651, the English Civil Wars raged, with King Charles I on one side and radical members of Parliament, led by Oliver Cromwell, on the other. Charles believed in the Divine Right of Kings to rule, unquestioned and uncontested, over the land. To Cromwell and his fellow Parliamentarians, known as the Roundheads, Charles was a tyrant, irresponsible in matters both financial and military, and they sought a republic in which the Parliament would hold ultimate power.

A workingman in his thirties during the wars, Tina's ninth great-grandfather had choices to make: did he fight at all, and if he did, which side was he on, that of the Parliamentarians' New Model Army or the king's Royal Army? A British military document, dated 1647, listed among the soldiers who served in the New Model Army "Lieutenant-Colonel Hewson (now Colonel)." By aligning himself with those set on overthrowing the Royalists, Colonel John Hewson had chosen the winning side, and in 1649 the victors jailed King Charles I on the Isle of Wight. What happened next was unprecedented: the Parliament charged the king with treason, murder, "and other high crimes," and a jury of 135 men sentenced him to death. London was aghast: a king sentenced to death by commoners. One of those commoners, known by British historians as the regicides, was Tina's ninth great-grandfather. The cobbler-turned-colonel signed his name to King Charles's death warrant — one of the most important, most astonishing documents in all of English history. Charles I was beheaded on January 30, 1649.

Tina's ninth great-grandfather rose quickly in the ranks. At what cost, though? Cromwell was a brutal leader, responsible for the conquest of Ireland and the subjugation of local Catholic populations that would persist for centuries, and John Hewson was his deputy, knighted in December 1657 in recognition of his "valor" in the Irish campaigns and appointed governor of Dublin. Within the next two years, fates began to change for Cromwell and his allies, including Tina's ancestor. The Parliamentarians who had risen to power as opponents of tyranny were soon reviled for the selfsame practices. In London, Tina's ninth great-grandfather was so reviled that he was hanged in effigy. In 1660, the backlash against the Cromwellians, John Hewson among them, became so strong that the monarchy was restored. The regicides — the men who had been instrumental in the execution of King Charles I — became public enemies. Tina's ninth great-grandfather had no choice but to flee his homeland. He died alone, in hiding in the Netherlands, in 1662. His family remained in England until his great-great-grandson of the same name, Tina's fifth great-grandfather, set sail for the American colonies, where he, too, would ultimately go to war against a tyrannical king.

■ Tina had known that on her mother's side of the family the paper trail would take her back to Greece. Most surprising from a genealogist's perspective was how uncharacteristically long the paper trail was for a person of Greek ancestry. Her oldest named ancestor on her Greek side was Dimitrios Tzanos, who was born in Messenia in 1630. On her father's side, among her English family, the oldest named ancestor we found was Peter Seddon, who was born around 1520 in Ringley, Lancashire, England. Tina was more shocked by the absence of Scotland on her family tree than anything else. "My family thinks we're Scottish, and we're not," she said. "There's no Scottish in here." If there were Scottish ancestors, they'd left no trace in the paper trail.

To go beyond the paper trail, we administered two DNA tests to Tina, one to look at her admixture, or her percentages of European, sub-Saharan African, and East Asian / Native American ancestry from the last five hundred years or so, and the other to look at her maternal haplogroup, a genetic population group of individuals who share a common direct maternal ancestor. When asked what she thought her admixture might be, she joked, "One hundred percent Chinese!" To her surprise, she was part Asian—a comparatively small but significant number. Tina's results were 94 percent European and 6 percent Asian. Of that 94 percent European, almost half of her DNA traced to Italy and Greece, and a full quarter came from Great Britain, with the remainder from different populations of northern Europe. Her European DNA was nearly equally split between northern Europe and southern Europe, and it dovetailed with the genealogy we had uncovered through her Greek mother and her English and German father. Her Asian percentage was also equally split between two different subcategories: 3 percent Caucasus and 3 percent Middle East. While Tina may have been surprised to see any Asian DNA at all in her admixture, according to our genetic genealogist, hers was a perfectly logical result. The Ottoman Empire was vast. At its peak, the Turks controlled a territory that reached from present-day Kuwait in the Middle East up to the Armenian highlands, which are part of the Caucasus Mountains, and over to Greece. It's likely that internal migrations within the Ottoman Empire allowed DNA from the Middle East and the Caucasus to enter Tina's family tree. Further, the result gave validity to Tina's mother's belief "about how we all got brown eyes."

The second test we performed on Tina focused on her mother's line, her mitochondrial DNA. Just like Tina's daughters inherited an exact replica of her mitochondrial DNA, Tina inherited the same from her mother, Jeanne inherited the same from Vasiliki, and so on. Tina's maternal haplogroup is found primarily in Italy, which is not surprising, because Italy and Greece share many genetic similarities.

Of all the participants we'd had in our series, we discovered, through an analysis of Tina's autosomal DNA, which an individual inherits from her parents and from all the men and women on her ancestral lines, that Tina was related to just one of them. Although they don't share Greek ancestry, he is a fellow Philadelphian known for his vast network of connections: Kevin Bacon. "That's six degrees of Kevin Bacon," Tina said. "Is this the answer for everyone, though?"

■ Tina had the blood of revolutionaries, artists, and working people running through her veins. Some of her ancestors risked their lives to improve their lot at home, while others set sail across a vast ocean to create something new. Were those the people who made her the person she is today? Was it her DNA? Her experiences, or theirs? "DNA is part of it, certainly," Tina said. "The thing I take away from this is that your choices contribute to who you are."

Of all those ancestors, there was one in particular that she would like to meet if given the chance, and she wouldn't even have to stray far from her childhood home: "the father of American quilts, John Hewson, my fifth great-grandfather, the one who knew Benjamin Franklin and participated in the American Revolution." The American Revolution had always been a part of her childhood, just as her Greek heritage was. Now she had a personal connection to that defining event in our nation's history that she had never imagined. "I physically walked those streets in Philadelphia. You go on every school trip, and you walk the cobblestone streets, and you go to Betsy Ross's house and all those places where he must have been."

Tina's journey into her roots was an amazing one. One lost story after another had been found and shared. On her Greek side the loss was understandable. Centuries of subjugation had led to such widespread destruction of records that connections were often impossible to restore. But on her English side, her fifth great-grandfather had rubbed shoulders with Benjamin Franklin; her ninth great-grandfather sent a king to his death. Their portraits hung in museums, and their names appeared in history books. How were their stories ever lost? "Is it specifically an American thing, that we refocus on being American?" she asked, unable to answer the question herself. "Are we so self-centered that we're not looking back enough at where we've come from?" The journey, she said, "has awakened me to pay attention to the past more. In every one of those stories," she continued, "are people who moved across the world or fought, literally, physical battles for what they thought was right." Tina promised that she would never *not* look back again.

For the humorist David Sedaris, dinnertime around the family table with his parents and five siblings was writing school. "Let's say someone is telling a story about their school day, and it's boring," David explained. "They pause, and you jump right in there. You learn to tell a story quickly; you learn to cut to the chase. You learn that you don't add a lot of detail that doesn't ultimately matter; you don't name characters who don't contribute to your story." Those lessons, and a generous helping of exceptional talent and timing, have made David Sedaris the preeminent humor writer in the country. He is a beloved fixture on the NPR airwaves and in the pages of the *New Yorker* and a regular at the top of the best-seller list, the author of such essay collections as *Barrel Fever* and *Me Talk Pretty One Day*.

For David, one of the benefits of being part of a family so large he called it "a tribe" was that "you were never the focus of attention. You could lose yourself. You could hide if you needed to." This was a skill that came in useful for David, growing up Greek American in the South. Born David Raymond Sedaris on December 26, 1956, in Johnson City, New York, he moved to Raleigh, North Carolina, with his family when he was in the third grade. For the first time in his life he was called a Yankee. "When you win the war you don't really think about it. You kind of move on with your life. It was shocking to have this new identity as a Yankee, because I never thought of myself that way. It never occurred to me that that was even a part of my identity." The most pronounced part of his identity came from his Greek heritage. He never felt discriminated against for his ethnicity, but it set him apart from much of the surrounding community. "You've got to hand it to the Greeks. They don't have a bad reputation," he said. "In Raleigh at the time, if you said to people, 'Greek,' they probably would have said, 'Hercules.' I don't know that they had a negative notion of Greece. I just think that they thought, 'Foreign.'" The experience his Greek American father had growing up in New York State was very different from his own. "In the North, Greek immigrants would all live in the same neighborhood, and that would be the Greek neighborhood. But in the South, if you were any kind of minority, you didn't want to draw attention to yourself. It was mainly just white and black in the South."

David's mother, who was, according to David, of indeterminate British origin, had converted to the Greek Orthodox religion. "I always felt like my mother was treated poorly in the Greek church because she wasn't Greek.

She learned to make Greek food and things like that, but they didn't count her as a complete person." Regardless, David and his siblings were raised in the church, in what he called "this little Greek bubble." In 1970, when he was thirteen years old, David and his older sister Lisa went to the Ionian Village in Greece, a summer camp for Greek American children. For the first time, David experienced being part of the majority. "To have people come up to you and speak to you in that language assuming that you know that language because you look like them" caught him off guard. "I had one eyebrow. That's what made me look Greek. As I got older it faded, but it just used to be a straight line from here to here, and that identified me as Greek." From childhood on, David said he did not develop strong attachments to places, but he acknowledged that there was something different for him when he stood on Greek soil. "It's always interesting when you go back to where your family is from and you look like people, and you had a name people could pronounce," he said. "I didn't have that feeling of 'Oh, I need to live here to be closer in touch with that,' but it was interesting to feel it. I hadn't expected it."

What speaks most to David about Greek culture is the value it places on family ties. "If you meet a Greek person, it's a matter of minutes before they say my mother, my father, my sister, my brother. They are all up in their family, whereas you can meet an American, and it can be months before they mention their siblings or their parents. That's a big part of what makes Greeks Greek to me. I always find those the most interesting relationships. I want to hear about their family." Now was David's chance to hear about his own.

■ "My father had a bumper sticker on his mirror in his bedroom that said 'Greeks are great,'" David recalled. "We would make such fun of that, because it's like, 'Who are you trying to convince?' I always wondered what the neighbors would think if they saw that." David's father, Louis Sedaris, was born on April 5, 1923, in Albany, New York, an only child and the son of Greek immigrants. Although intensely proud of his heritage, once the family relocated to the South, David's father took steps to obscure the sense of otherness or differentness that his Greek background gave him in his new surroundings. "It's always interesting to me how well my father fit in," David said. "In the South everyone has their country club. My dad is on the golf course, and he had all the country club clothes that other people wore. Granted," he paused, "there was a better country club that we were denied entry into because my father's last name was Greek and because we were Yankees."

David wondered about his father's motivations. "I don't know if it was because he was just that kind of a guy who can blend in or if it was a reaction to the way he had grown up, having the parents who don't speak English, having a mom who can't read, who I believe was illiterate in two languages." When he was a teenager, Louis's parents kept him as far from American youth culture as they could. "They didn't understand. My dad wanted to play football. They were horrified when they found out, and they prevented him from doing it. I don't think they understood what that could have meant for a kid in his community. Plus," he added, "they had this newsstand, and they wanted him to work. They had an employee."

David's paternal grandparents were hardworking immigrants focused on improving their child's lot while still keeping him close to home. Heracles "Harry" Siderakos was born in 1880, and Adamandia Thomakou was born around 1895, both in Apidia, a small city in southern Greece. Harry died in 1961, but Adamandia lived with David's family for several years before her death in 1976. His Yiayia was David's direct family connection to Greece. She spoke almost no English, and she always remained completely foreign to David and his siblings. "My grandmother communicated love in a grandmotherly way. She would pet your hand until the skin wore off, and she would kiss you and touch you and cry. But we couldn't converse with her," he said. "She didn't look like my friends' grandmothers," he added. "In America, when you're a grandmother, you have short hair and a perm. She had hair that went down her back. She would go into the neighbor's yard and pick dandelion greens and come home and boil them. She was out collecting nuts and weeds from people's yards and cooking them. We were so embarrassed. We wanted our food to come from the grocery store." She brought Greece into the Sedaris home, almost literally as David described it. "Her room was like Greece. You had to step up because she had so many carpets on the floor of her room. And it smelled like another country." Even in the "Greek bubble" of church, to David, she stood out. "We were in church. The service was all in Greek. Who knows what the priest was saying? My grandmother. So she goes down the aisle, she throws her cane down, and she crawls on her hands and knees up the aisle. She grabs the priest's feet and is kissing his feet." David and his sisters were mortified. "We were like, 'Did you have to crawl? Couldn't you have walked?'" David knew that this lack of understanding and appreciation was typical of children of immigrants, but he had regrets. "When I think about my grandmother now, she's exactly the kind of person who I would gravitate to. I love to hear about foreigners' miserable lives and what they expected as opposed to what they ultimately received. Instead I was in the other room making fun of her."

David's grandmother clung to her Greek ways for decades in America. Departing Patras, Greece, on July 15, 1921, aboard the SS *Megali Hellas*, Diamantou Thomakou, as her name was recorded on the ship's manifest, undertook the two-week journey entirely on her own, in first class, with no family accompanying her. At twenty-six years old, she left behind a nation in tatters.

In 1921, Greece was at war for the fourth time in the young century. On the heels of two Balkan Wars and World War I, in which Greece sided with the British, Greece was now fighting for its independence in the Greco-Turkish War. This was a period of mass immigration for Greeks, and the U.S. Congress took steps to curtail it, implementing a quota system the year David's grandmother came to America that cut the number of Greek immigrants allowed into the country by more than 70 percent. On July 30, 1921, the *Washington Post* ran an article about the ship which carried David's grandmother to America. "The *Megali Hellas* carried an excess immigration quota of Greeks," the report read. "Several days ago, it was announced Greece had sent into this country in July all the immigrants to which she was entitled under the new restrictive laws. So when the *Megali Hellas*—the first of several ships in this quandary—thrust her bow up to the theoretical three-mile mark, her skipper tossed over his anchor to wait for August."

David's grandmother was forced to wait on the hot, cramped ship, thankfully not in steerage, from July 29 until August 1. The *Megali Hellas* was one of several Greek ships in the same position, docked in the harbor for days and nights before their immigrant passengers could disembark. On the first of the month, David's grandmother was one of the lucky ones. On August 2, 1921, the *New York Tribune* recounted the fate of another ship that had been forced to wait. "Forty-seven of the Greek immigrants who arrived here yesterday on the *Calabria* of the Anchor Line are facing deportation because the August quota for their country is already exceeded. A total of 704 Greeks came in yesterday. The maximum number to be admitted is 657. The physical fact that the *Calabria* failed to reach quarantine until two minutes after the *Megali Hellas* makes her responsible for bringing in too many Greeks." The *Megali Hellas* had won the immigration race by a nose, and David's grandmother was able to step onto American soil for the first time. Adamandia, who was so hampered in her communications with her own grandchildren, made her intentions perfectly clear on her arrival in America. Under the column on her passenger record "Length of time alien intends to remain in the United States," she stated definitively, "Forever."

Adamandia married David's grandfather, Heracles Siderakos, on June 1, 1922, less than a year after her arrival. Heracles, who went by the name Harry in America, had been in this country for nearly seventeen years already when his future wife made her journey. He came to New York on the SS *La Gascogne*, on October 24, 1904, having made the weeks-long journey, as so many of his compatriots did, in steerage. His surname was not changed or shortened at Ellis Island, as the myth often went. The first time we would see the name Sedaris was in the 1940 census for Cortland County, New York. We suspected Harry had shortened his original Greek name in an effort to Americanize it. "It might be what somebody coming here might think would fit more into America," David said, "but then you wind up going to a town and living in a Greek community and surrounding yourself with Greeks, in which case you might as well have kept your last name." Furthermore, David noted, "Sedaris is only one syllable shorter than Siderakos. I love a long Greek name. Nothing is funnier to me than a seven-syllable Greek last name."

We couldn't authenticate the origin of the family's shortened surname, but the 1940 census told us an inordinate amount about the lives of David's grandparents and father at age seventeen. They owned their own business, a hat- and shoe-cleaning store that David remembered as "a long, narrow storefront on Main Street. They had this little newsstand. You're literally a kid in a candy store, and they had elevated seats that you would sit in while you were having your shoes shined." Harry Sedaris was the proprietor, Deamando, as his grandmother's name was spelled by the census taker, a hat cleaner, and Louis a shoe shiner. They worked incredibly hard. The census reported that David's grandfather worked "75 hours a week, 52 weeks per year." They lived in a tiny, rented apartment above the store, and they crowded eight lodgers into their home with them. David was unsure how to measure their success. "You'd think that if you were going to work that hard, it would have maybe gotten you a little more," he said. "I never saw my grandmother partaking of the fruits of America."

Both of David's grandparents, however, took the momentous step of becoming American citizens. Many Greek immigrants never became Americans; in fact, between 1908 and 1924, nearly half of all Greek immigrants returned to their native country with the money they earned here. On September 8, 1931, at age thirty-six, Deomando Sedaris became an American citizen. It would be twenty-four years before David's grandfather signed his name to his own certificate of naturalization, on November 25, 1955. By that time, he had been in the country for more than fifty years.

■ David's grandparents never had an easy life in America. Yet, unlike many of their countrymen, they never returned to live in their homeland. What made them leave in the first place, and what had they left behind? We explored David's grandfather's family tree for the answers.

Starting in the 1890s, when David's grandfather was about ten, Greece was hit by a severe economic crisis. His grandparents' hometown of Apidia was an agricultural community, and it suffered immensely. Between 1890 and 1914, nearly one-sixth of the Greek population immigrated, mostly to the United States; Egypt was the second most popular destination. Many members of the Siderakos family, however, stayed in Greece.

David's relatives owned a family cafe, or *kafeneio*, in Apidia's town square, and they had lived in Apidia for generations. In fact, their names were recorded in the town register, which fortunately still existed. In the entry for his grandfather's birth we learned the name of David's great-grandfather, Elias Siderakos, born around 1840 in Apidia. He and his wife, David's great-grandmother, Georgia Attilakou, had several children, among them sons Spyridon, the eldest; Panagiotis; and, of course, David's grandfather Heracles. Going up through the generations, we saw the names Elias and Spyridon repeating in an alternating pattern, an example of the traditional Greek naming custom of the firstborn son of each generation bearing the name of his grandfather. By using this naming pattern, we were able to take David's tree back two more generations, to his second great-grandfather Spyridon Sideris and his siblings, David's second great-grandaunt Anastasoula and his second great-granduncle Ionnais, and unbelievably to his third great-grandfather Elias Sideris, born about 1780, also in Apidia. David laughed. "They don't trip off the tongue, do they?"

What was the Greek world like at the turn of the nineteenth century, when his third great-grandfather was a young man? "I bet it had something to do with those darn Turks," David guessed. "We were always raised to hate Turks, because they did something to us in like the year 8." David, of course, bore no personal, contemporary animosity for "those darn Turks," but for many Greeks, the scars of history ran deep. "My hatred for Turks was instilled in me. Sometimes when I'm doing a book signing, someone will give me their last name, and I'll say, 'What kind of last name is that?,' and they'll say, 'Turkey,' and I'll say, 'I hate you.'"

David's third great-grandfather grew up and raised his own children under the crushing thumb of the Ottoman Empire. Over the centuries, deep tensions developed between the Muslim Turks and their Christian Greek subjects, fueled by cultural and religious differences. The heart of the empire was present-day Turkey, but at the time it stretched from what is today Tunisia to Baghdad, and from Yemen to Bosnia. This vast territory included David's ancestral home of Apidia.

In 1821, when Elias Sideris would have been forty-one, the situation had become untenable, and revolts erupted across Greece. Greek rebels took control of the southern part of the country, including Apidia. On January 1, 1822, in a town called Epidaurus, about one hundred miles away from Apidia, the rebels wrote a Declaration of Independence. "The Greek Nation," it read, "unable to bear the galling and oppressive yoke of tyranny under Turkish despotism, proclaims this day its political existence and Independence."

The landmark declaration was followed by utter chaos, and brutality reigned on both sides. The Ottomans moved to crush the revolution, and Greeks throughout the region attacked and killed the Muslims living among them. Based on a field report in the Greek Military Archives, one of the only remaining sources of documents for this turbulent period in Greek history, in 1824, Sultan Mahmud II sent a general named Ibrahim Pasha to crush the Greek insurgents and put an end to the rebellion. The following year, on September 13, 1825, the preeminent Greek general Theodoros Kolokotronis reported the horrors of Ibrahim's campaign. "The fire Ibrahim brought and brings each time he moved his troops are wretched for someone to tell and hear. Having burnt down all the villages, he settled in Apidia, where he spent the night." A report published in 1830, six years after Ibrahim Pasha stormed Apidia, corroborated Kolokotronis's overview. "When they found no more heads to cut off, their rage turned against the villages and houses. They chopped down all the trees, left nothing but ruins and ashes, and spread death and devastation all around."

Ibrahim Pasha showed no mercy. His army destroyed Apidia, and residents who were able to fled in fear. Elias Sideris's family, however, didn't get out in time. In light of the overwhelming absence of records that genealogists have frequently encountered in Greece, the document we found was utterly shocking. It was a list of captives taken by Ibrahim Pasha from the village of Apidia and the surrounding region. "Anastasoula, daughter of Elias Sideris. Age when captured: 20. At Mysiri." David's second great-grandaunt was taken to Egypt, then called Mysiri, as a slave. In a letter dated 1826, a British diplomat stationed there described the conditions under which the Greek slaves were kept. "The slaves belonging to Ibrahim Pasha and his officers were immediately sent off to await in the harems of Cairo," David read. "The most distinguished of the virgins were destined to people the harems of the Viceroy. The men are considered Prisoners of War, but may be more properly called Galley-Slaves. They are chained two and two by the leg and condemned to hard labor and all the other sufferings. A very small number have survived their torments." Some of these slaves were eventually returned to Greece, but not all, and it is not known whether Anastasoula ever reunited with her family. David's family not only sacrificed their home for the revolution; they literally gave a daughter.

The revolution raged on for almost another decade from the time of David's second great-grandaunt's capture, and in 1832 Greece finally achieved its hard-won independence. It was no wonder, David agreed, that the wounds of war were so long to heal for the Greek people. "To lose somebody by death, death that you know of, is one thing. But if they're brought off to become a slave or forced to be a prostitute among the people who you hate more than anything, that must be a kind of agony that just never dies."

Learning the tragic story of his ancestor Anastasoula gave David new insight into Greek history and into his family's past, their reasons for staying and his grandparents' courage in leaving. "I never understood the attachment to a place. The idea of being born there and staying there and raising your children and raising your grandchildren there is so foreign to me. It's so foreign to me that you wouldn't want more than that, that you wouldn't have heard that there's a sea thirty miles away and that you wouldn't have thought, 'Let's go try our luck there.' But if the land is soaked in your blood . . .," he said. If his grandparents felt those ties, they had severed them, and their bold action gave him a "different respect" for them. "It might not look like much, but they were someone there, even if they were someone in a village of fifteen houses. That's the immigrant experience, isn't it? To become nobody again." His ancestors' names restored, the tragic details of their lives retold, made people who had become invisible visible again. "I was in Greece a while ago," David recalled, "and somebody said, 'When a Greek American has some success in the United States, we always want to claim that person.' They said, 'How does that make you feel?' And I said, 'That makes me feel great.'" David was happy to be claimed by Greece, and happy to reclaim his lost Greek ancestors. "It's really kind of beautiful, even if we were mispronouncing their names, to read their names, because isn't that what you want? Just to be remembered in some way, even if it's going to be that your name was read on a television show in a language you don't speak three hundred years after you die. I'll take it. I'll take that."

■ David's mother, he said, told stories like no one else, and when she died in 1991, he said ruefully, "There wasn't a replacement for that. There wasn't anyone who interpreted the world in quite the same way that she did." She was the funny parent, the one who worked at a story until it was just right. "Something would happen—nothing major, just some little thing would happen, and my mother would talk about it on the phone. Then she would call somebody later on in the day, and the story would have changed a little. It would be a little bit better, a little shorter. Then all of a sudden there would be dialogue, and she would be saying the things she wished she'd said in the earlier version. It was like watching a writer go through five or six drafts." He paused. "It was about the story. It was always about the story."

What was his mother's story? Sharon Elizabeth Leonard was born on February 17, 1929, in Binghamton, New York. Greek traditions dominated his childhood home, but they were not his mother's traditions by birth. "She was from a tragic country where people couldn't handle their alcohol—England, Scotland," he joked. "There was never really a location. 'Old country' was never really discussed on my mother's half of the family."

David's mother had a difficult childhood. Her father, Ray W. Leonard, born on May 25, 1898, in Binghamton, New York, was, as David put it, "a pretty severe alcoholic but a nice guy." "As often was the case with an alcoholic parent," David said, "my mother adored him." Her mother, Elizabeth Beebe, born on August 19, 1894, in Ithaca, New York, was "kind of a scold." Though his maternal grandparents were born in this country, their lives weren't much easier than the lives of Harry and Adamandia Sedaris. "You wouldn't think that the American grandparents would be as vulnerable as the Greek grandparents, but they were," David said. "Their existence was a bit precarious. But they had more than my Greek grandparents, and they were American. They could talk to anyone, and no one ever said, 'Where are you from?,' or 'What kind of name is that?'"

He looked at his mother's family tree. "John Brown, Martin Beebe, Mary Hitchcock," he read. "That's so interesting. We couldn't pronounce the names from my father's side." David's ancestors on his mother's side, we learned, had been in this country for generations, and they left behind a long, unbroken paper trail. We followed one of David's grandmother's lines back to mid-eighteenth-century America, to Mansfield, Connecticut, where the birth record for David's fourth great-grandfather still existed in the town archives. Nathan Wood was born on April 16, 1761, the son of Samuel Wood, David's fifth great-grandfather, who was born in 1716, in a town called Windham, Connecticut. The record gave us the names of two ancestors born in America before the Revolution. David had no idea that he had such deep roots in America. "I guess when I think about my heritage, I'm inclined to think of the exotic part, so I think of the Greek side," he said. "I don't think of the American side, and I have absolutely no idea why."

When David's fourth great-grandfather Nathan was born, Mansfield was a lightly populated rural town, its residents primarily farmers and mill workers. All that changed in 1775. When Nathan was just fourteen, the colonies revolted. Connecticut remained largely neutral until April 1777, when a ruthless British general named William Tryon led his troops on a scorched-earth campaign through Nathan's home state. The British destroyed everything in sight and went on to win a battle against the Patriots in a town called Ridgefield, just seventy-five miles from Nathan's hometown.

With Connecticut in the crosshairs, David's ancestor, a sixteen-year-old boy at the time, joined the Patriot army, his name listed on the payroll for Captain Nathaniel Wales's company in Colonel Jonathan Latimer's regiment from the state of Connecticut. Nathan Wood, it turned out, fought in one of the pivotal battles of the Revolutionary War, the second Battle of Saratoga, an extremely bloody battle that saw thousands killed in fierce hand-to-hand combat. David's fourth great-grandfather was on the front lines and barely survived. A pension application filed years later detailed his military experience. He "was wounded severely by the point of a bayonet a little below his naval [sic] and he killed three Hessians with the point of his bayonet in less than two minutes from the time he was wounded." In the heat of battle, wounded himself, David's ancestor had taken three lives. Could David imagine ever killing another human being? "Not a stranger," he quipped. He became serious. "Doesn't that fundamentally change a person? There's a lot of hate on my family tree." On both sides of his family, David descended from patriots who joined the fight for freedom in their homelands, willing to make sacrifices and risking their lives for the cause. Sustained by bravery, belief, or both, the Patriots won the Battle of Saratoga, their victory on October 17, 1777, often cited as the turning point in the war, the moment when America gained the upper hand in its struggle for freedom.

■ Today David makes his home in England. He had unwittingly made the reverse migration of his maternal ancestors, who centuries ago left British soil to make a life in the Thirteen Colonies. On his maternal grandfather Ray Leonard's line, we found ancestors who made this journey in the seventeenth century. William Denison, born on February 3, 1571, in Stortford, England, would die shortly before his eighty-second birthday on January 25, 1653, in Roxbury, Massachusetts. Thomas Lord, one of the first medical doctors in the Connecticut colony, was born in Towcester, North Hamptonshire, England, and died around January 29, 1643, in Hartford, Connecticut. David admitted that when he moved to England, he experienced "a real connection when he saw it," different from anything he'd ever felt either in the country of his birth or in his ancestral home of Greece on his father's side. Yet in America, through all the years he lived here, he never experienced a strong sense of his English roots. "I remember somebody saying, 'My family came over on the *Mayflower*,' and I remember thinking, we moved with Mayflower; it was Mayflower Van Lines that moved us, but then realizing that they meant, 'We have the keys to the country.'"

David had the keys to the country, too; he just had never known it. He descended from some of the first settlers of the Thirteen Colonies, and his descent from a Patriot qualified him for membership in the Sons of the American Revolution. He was fascinated to learn of his English background and his extremely deep American roots, but he wasn't ready to abandon his Greek heritage. He liked the mix. "It's almost like you don't want to drink straight gin," he said. "You want to mix it with something else, because if you harnessed the straight form it would make you an unbearable snob. It's good to mix it with something."

■ David had a fascinating family tree on both sides, surprising in its depth and documentation. On his mother's line his oldest named ancestor was John Denison, the father of his immigrant ancestor, born around 1540 in Stortford, England, during the Tudor period, when Henry VIII was king. On his father's side, his oldest ancestor was Elias Sideris, born around 1780 in Apidia, Greece. Analysis of David's DNA would take us even further back in time.

We administered an admixture test to David, which measures an individual's percentages of European, sub-Saharan African, and East Asian / Native American ancestry from the last five hundred years or so. As would be expected from his genealogy, David was overwhelmingly European — 96 percent. The remaining 4 percent, however, was Asian. Of the European percentage, 42 percent of it came from Italy and Greece, with the rest being a blend of mostly northern European populations. For someone who is culturally half Greek and half British, these findings were predictable. We broke down the Asian percentage as we had the European. The findings underscored what we knew about the history of the region. David's Asian DNA came from the Caucasus region, which, of course, was home to "those darn Turks." David feigned horror. "The blood of my enemies flows in my veins?" Some of that Turkish ancestry likely made its way into his genome as a result of violence, but it may also have been inherited from his ancestors who lived in Apidia when it was ruled by the Ottoman Empire, the end result of voluntary intermarriage between cultures. "That 4 percent is my self-hatred ratio."

Analysis of David's autosomal DNA, which an individual inherits from both of his or her parents and from all of the individuals on all of their ancestral lines, told us which of the other participants in our series David was connected to genetically. One was, perhaps unsurprisingly, George Stephanopoulos, who shares David's Greek heritage. David also had a genetic cousin among our participants from the other side of his family. He shares a common ancestor somewhere far back on his family tree with the actor Kevin Bacon, a descendant of English ancestors. "Well, that's because everyone is connected to Kevin Bacon," David joked — everyone, including our other guest of Greek and British descent, Tina Fey. Tina and David share no matches themselves, but Kevin Bacon is their shared genetic cousin. "I love that this big book that you presented me with, every time I turn the page I would think, what on earth could be waiting for me? I love that the very last page is Kevin Bacon." Six degrees indeed.

■ We had come to the end of our journey through David's ancestry, and his overriding response to what he had learned surprised him. The son of two revolutions found himself more drawn to one. "I'm not necessarily proud to admit it, but I have to say that the American Revolution part satisfies something deep inside of me. It satisfies a little snob kernel deep inside of me." His mother would have been delighted to know that she was a Daughter of the American Revolution, that she had passed that heritage on to her children. "I remember people talking about how their ancestors had been in America for a long time and using that as a way of saying they were better than you were, that that's why they went to that country club and you weren't allowed to go to that country club," David said. "I have to say that left a kind of hunger in her. Out of everything, that would have made her happy. I think that really would have meant a lot to her to know that."

On both sides David had ancestors deeply connected to their heritage through blood as well as bloodshed, patriots who had sacrificed tremendously for their cause. But no one sacrificed more than his second great-grandaunt Anastasoula, who was kidnapped into slavery by the Turkish army, a human trophy of their victory over her village. It was she whom David would meet if he could go back in time to talk to any one of his ancestors. "If I think about everything that we've seen here, that seems like a movie to me. This woman's story seems so compelling to me, a fully realized tragedy," he said. "Is there ever a day when your sorrow subsides? At twenty she must have had children. Does a day come when you don't think about them and then you hate yourself for not thinking about them? Let's say one of your jobs is to raise this Egyptian child, and then you find yourself loving that child. Do you hate yourself for loving the child?" Her story, David said, "touches me in a very real way. I would have a lot of questions for her."

David had a lot of questions for everyone. He said he thought of his mother every time he did book signings. She had "the eye," as he put it, the gift of determining what made a person special. About his fans, he said, "I don't want them to leave the table until I see that they're unlike anyone else who's in that room." Before David left the table, we wanted to know what it was that made him special, made him who he was. Was it the DNA he had inherited from all those ancestors, his experiences or theirs? He didn't hesitate to answer. "It was my family, my immediate family, not even going any farther," David said. "I would include my parents in that. They created an environment, the perfect environment, the perfect little petri dish for me by having exactly the brothers and sisters that I had. If you had removed one of them, I wouldn't be the person I am now." He broadened his scope to include the centuries-old ancestors he had met for the first time today. "I will forever be grateful to them and basically to all the people in this book for creating that petri dish that I was allowed to grow in."

George Stephanopoulos (b. 1961)

George Stephanopoulos is one of the most sought-after political commentators in the country, the trusted chief anchor of ABC News and the cohost of the morning staple *Good Morning America*. His fourteen-letter name became a household one when he served as communications director for Bill Clinton's 1992 presidential campaign and later in the same position in Clinton's White House. George got his start in politics as part of Massachusetts governor Michael Dukakis's 1988 presidential campaign. Joining Dukakis's team, George said, was a given. "For Greeks this was a big deal. A Greek American about my size, the same hair, same eyebrows, Democrat from Massachusetts," he said. "How could I not work for him?" The first Greek American who had a shot at being president, George explained, "got a lot of support from a lot of Greeks who don't share his political views just out of pure pride."

George has enjoyed that same embrace throughout his career on the public stage. "One of the ways I feel it the most is that Greeks will often come up to me and say, 'I'm so glad you didn't change your name.' I always loved the fact that my name was longer than anybody else's. It was a badge of honor." For Greek Americans of an earlier generation, George said, "Just to see a name that so recognizably, obviously, can't be anything but a Greek name working in the White House or working at ABC News has meant something to the community, and I try to do what I can to make them proud."

Born George Robert Stephanopoulos on February 10, 1961, in Fall River, Massachusetts, he said, "I don't remember not being proud of being Greek." George was immersed in his ancient culture on both sides of his family. His mother was the communications director for the Greek Archdiocese's news service, and his father, grandfather, uncle, cousins, and godfather were all priests in the Greek Orthodox Church. In fact, until high school George expected to become a priest himself. "It was who I was." George has chosen to raise his daughters in the Greek Orthodox Church—"I love the structure, and I love the roots," he said—but their mother is not Greek, and their world is different from that of earlier generations. "It was just something in the air we breathed," he said. "When my parents were growing up, their entire social life, their entire family life and cultural life was Greek. They lived with Greeks, they worked with Greeks, they went to church with Greeks, they ate with Greeks. For my kids, it's a much more mixed experience."

The family culture of his early years was undeniably Greek, but George's experience was, in a sense, also mixed: his was a Greek American home, and the contributions that ancient Greece had made to our American way of life did not go unnoticed. The concept of democracy, after all, had its roots in his ancestral homeland. "That was something that I was brought up to be very proud of, to know that that was an important part of our tradition and an important part of our contribution to the United States," he said. "We would recite the Greek National Anthem and the American National Anthem before all dinners."

For George, his Greek heritage and the Greek community that shared it served "as both safety net and conscience." When he arrived at Columbia University as a college freshman, he had no family in New York City. His parents sought out the owners of two Greek diners nearby (one of which was made famous as Monk's on *Seinfeld*) and introduced their son to the owners. "If he ever runs out of money," Mr. and Mrs. Stephanopoulos said to the strangers, "can you just make sure he gets some eggs?" The owners, of course, said yes.

Although George knew the four Greek-born grandparents who were the first in his family to immigrate to America, he knew little about the ancestors who came before them. "I lose track after my grandparents," he said. His connection to those ancestors was nonetheless powerful, and he experienced a strong sense of belonging on his first trip to Greece, when he was just nine years old. "Getting off the train, and seeing thirty people greet us at the train station, and they all looked like us," he recalled, "that's the first time you get that feeling of, wow, I'm part of something a lot bigger."

That George felt connected to his Greek ancestry came as no surprise. What would surprise him, though, was how deep his roots went, and how intimately involved his ancestors were with the tumultuous events that defined modern Greek history.

■ George came from a family of priests. His father, Robert George Stephanopoulos, born Haralambos Stephanopoulos in Neohori, Greece, on November 19, 1934, was ordained in 1959. His devotion to his faith extended far beyond the boundaries of the Greek Orthodox Church. In 1967 Father Stephanopoulos appeared on a national television program called *The Holy Seasons* as one of a panel of religious leaders dedicated to finding common ground among their followers and their faiths. The series aired during the Vietnam War and a few months before the Detroit riots. America was coming apart at the seams, and George's father hoped to mend it. "He was especially active in trying to find the bridges that tied different faiths together. It's rooted in the very heart of our religion," George said. "We're all made in the image of God, and that makes every individual sacred and special and irreducible and worthy of tremendous respect. I think he was driven by that."

On August 18, 1939, George's grandmother Tassia Stefanopoulou, then twenty-seven years old, arrived in America, at Ellis Island, on the SS *New Hellas* with her three children, four-year-old Haralambos and his younger brother and sister. The journey from Greece was long, and Tassia still had more than half a country to cross before she would meet her husband. George's grandfather and namesake, George Stephanopoulos, had come to America on his own the year before, in 1938, his destination Great Falls, Montana. We tend to associate immigrants, especially those who came through Ellis Island in the twentieth century, with crowded urban ethnic enclaves established by the countrymen and -women who had arrived before them. Many Greek immigrants, however, went west in search of jobs on the railroads and in factories. By 1910, in fact, a third of Greek immigrants were employed west of the Mississippi. George's grandfather, born on November 13, 1908, in Kyllini Ilias, Greece, came to America as a priest, providing Greek immigrants with a link to their culture and community as they worked hard to establish themselves in a foreign land. "The Greek Orthodox Church, especially for that first generation coming in, was the center of all life. It was church; it was community center; it was welfare center; it was family," George said. "It was where you went when you weren't working."

George knew little about his grandparents' experience in Great Falls. "The only thing that stuck with me from Great Falls was my father getting the name Lamby and Bobby." George's father was a little boy when his name was Americanized to the English translation of his given name,

Haralambos. "His first teacher in Montana, I guess it was," George recalled. "It was the easiest way for him to be identified, and it kind of stuck."

Many Greek immigrants chose not to make America their permanent home, only saving enough money here to make a return to their homeland possible. But the Stephanopoulos family were here to stay, and on August 4, 1944, at the height of World War II, George's grandfather became an American citizen. In the photo attached to his certificate of naturalization, Father George Stephanopoulos can be seen wearing his clerical collar, a visual reminder of his dual identity. "I identify him much more as Greek. It seemed like he was holding on to that," George said. "To see this makes me want to know what exactly drove him to that and to do it then."

The paper trail for George's father's family ended here, with his namesake. George was shocked. We hadn't even gotten out of the twentieth century. There was oral history: relatives said that George's great-grandfather's name was Haralambos Stephanopoulos and that he was born in 1867 in Greece. It seemed plausible; Greek naming patterns were such that the firstborn son was given the name of his grandfather, which in this case fit: George's father and great-grandfather shared the name Haralambos. But there were no records to corroborate the family lore. George's genealogy for his paternal ancestors was cut short abruptly, a result of the pitfalls common to tracing Greek ancestry.

■ Tracing George's mother's ancestry would prove to be an entirely different experience. George's mother, Nickolitsa Gloria Chafos, was born on June 7, 1933, to Greek immigrants in Rochester, Minnesota. George had expected to follow in his father's footsteps as a priest, but instead he followed in those of his mother, the former communications director for the Greek Orthodox Archdiocese of America. George had written of the first time he came across his mother's picture in her high school yearbook: "a pretty girl with dark hair and a wide smile whose American friends called her Gloria, instead of her Greek name." She was the daughter of Greek immigrants, but her home was in the Midwest. "She seemed much more American to me than my dad did," George said. "She seemed fully involved in life outside of the church and the Greek community. I think she wanted to be both fully, and she was." At the University of Minnesota, she started to go by the name Nikki, short for Nickolitsa. "It's holding on to a little bit more of the Greekness, although it's a mix. It's not Nickolitsa; it's Nikki. So you can still get a little bit of both there."

Nikki's father was an established businessman in Rochester. Born Andreas Tsafoulias on January 31, 1894, in Kallithea, Patras, Greece, he owned the Boston Shoe Repair on Rochester's main street for decades. It still stands today, run by George's uncle Peter. As George's paternal grandfather Robert had done, Andreas, who Americanized his name to Andrew Chafos, got his start in America in the West. Eighteen years old when he arrived in the United States, in 1912, Andreas went first to Salt Lake City, then to Iowa, and finally to Rochester, Minnesota. He would go on to establish his own business and send his children to college. It was the American dream.

The painful parts of his journey, however, were, as George put it, "glided over." In the early 1900s, Greeks in America faced virulent racism. They were targeted by the Ku Klux Klan, particularly in the South and the Midwest. Individuals were attacked and businesses were vandalized, sometimes to the point where Greek-owned establishments were forced to close. Around 1924, the KKK staged a rally in George's grandfather's adopted hometown of Rochester. No one in George's family had ever hinted at the racism that had flared up so close to home, yet his grandfather took steps to combat it. In 1929, George's grandfather cofounded the Rochester, Minnesota, chapter of the American Hellenic Educational Progressive Association. AHEPA, as it is still known today, formed with the mission of promoting the image of Greeks in America, assisting them in assimilating into American culture, and supporting Greek businesses and charities. George himself had benefited from the generosity of the organization. AHEPA awarded him a small college scholarship, and he remains actively involved with the group today. Never once had George heard of his grandfather's involvement in the civic organization.

Andrew's Greek roots were clearly a source of pride to him, something to be protected and preserved. In 1931, already well established in Minnesota, Andrew returned to Greece to start his family. At the outset of the Depression, on July 27, 1931, Andreas Chafos (as his name appeared on the passenger list) arrived in New York on the SS *Vulcania*, accompanied by his new wife, Margarite Nicolopoulos. Born in Saravali, Patras, Greece, on January 15, 1912, Margarite and Andreas married in their home province of Patras before coming to the United States together. She was nineteen years old at the time, eighteen years her husband's junior. In fact, Margarite was born in the year her husband first immigrated to America.

As we had seen with George's father's family, the vital records necessary to trace Greek ancestry had been largely destroyed. This was all too often the case for Greek genealogy. Thankfully, his mother's family proved an exception, and we found municipal rolls in the Greek State Archives of Patras that covered the town of Saravali, George's grandmother Margarite's birthplace. Her entire immediate family was listed within its pages: her father, George's great-grandfather Konstantinos Nicolopoulos, born on June 2, 1880; her mother, George's great-grandmother Nickolitsa Giannakopoulos; and Margarite's siblings, George's great-aunts and great-uncles Eleni, Ioannis, Theodoros, Marina, Michail, and Vasiliki.

According to relatives who still lived in Greece, George's great-grandmother died in childbirth, and her husband, Konstantinos, a peasant farmer, was responsible for raising his brood alone. It had to be a difficult life, one made more so by the outbreak of World War II. "I know it was tough," George said. "I think for a lot of the Greeks who came here, that was something they wanted to put behind them." It was a devastating time. Although Greece had tried to remain neutral, it was occupied by the Axis powers from 1941 until 1944. The Germans seized control of the country's food supply, and in just a few years, more than a quarter million Greeks died of starvation. Another fifty thousand were executed. One of the worst atrocities of the entire occupation happened less than thirty miles from Saravali, George's great-grandparents' village, in the town of Kalavryta. On December 13, 1943, the Germans shot and killed the town's entire male population, more than five hundred civilians.

One month after the decimation of Kalavryta's men, the Nazis converged on Saravali itself. "In January 1944," George read from a history of the town, "the Germans blockaded Saravali and arrested all the men of the village and threatened to kill them all together. Finally, after the interposition of many forces, the great danger was avoided. The Germans kept sixteen people from their captives. Among these sixteen captives were Kostis Nicolopoulos, Ionnais Nicolopoulos, Mihailis Nicolopoulos, Marina Nicolopoulos."

These were George's relatives: his great-grandfather, here referred to as Kostis, three great-uncles, and a great-aunt. (His great-uncle Theodoros was also taken captive but was not listed here.) "It's hard for me to even believe that this is part of my family's experience," George commented, hearing the painful story for the first time. "It makes me want to know more. It makes me feel, oddly, more American." This was no random operation. The Nazis had targeted Saravali and taken George's Nicolopoulos ancestors captive for a reason. The region was a hotbed of resistance to the German occupation, a place where Greeks conducted a persistent guerrilla war against the Nazis, ambushing patrols and bases and bombing communication lines. George's ancestors were deeply involved with the resistance, among the most heroic of the freedom fighters. His great-uncle Theodoros was one of the first men from Saravali to join the Greek People's Liberation Army, and his great-aunt Marina, whom George had actually met, was part of the National Solidarity Organization, the NSO. She had never breathed a word of any of this.

George's great-grandfather and his children were ultimately released from prison, but they paid a high price for their heroism. Residents of Saravali who had collaborated with the Nazis enacted vengeance upon supporters of the resistance, and the Nicolopoulos home was burned to the ground by their neighbors. Thankfully the family lived to tell their story—yet, strangely, they never told it. George was incredibly proud of his ancestors, "proud and humbled," he said, "humbled because I would hope I would do the same thing in their circumstance. Can you imagine the courage, knowing that they would pay such a high price and doing it anyway? I'm so happy they did."

Konstantinos Nicolopoulos lived out the rest of his eighty years in Saravali. A record of his death, dated April 17, 1960, enabled us to go back another generation on George's mother's mother's line. The names of Konstantinos's parents were listed alongside the date of their son's death. George's second great-grandparents Anastasios and Panagiota Nicolopoulos were both born in Greece, Anastasios around 1850 and Panagiota around 1860, one year before the American Civil War began. Thanks to the preservation of records in the town of George's grandmother's birth, three generations of George's maternal ancestors were restored to us by name. It was here, in the middle of the nineteenth century, that the paper trail for George's mother's mother's line ended.

■ Sometime after arriving in this country, George's grandfather Andreas Tsafoulias changed his name to the shorter, more American-sounding Andrew Chafos. Before him, however, were a long line of Tsafouliases: George's great-grandfather Konstantinos Tsafoulias, born in Patras in 1864; his second great-grandfather Andreas Tsafoulias, also born in Patras in 1834; his third great-grandfather Demitrios Tsafoulias, born around 1815 in Kallithea, Patras; and Georgios Tsafoulias, George's fourth great-grandfather, born in 1785 in the village of Vytina, in Arcadia, Greece. George looked at the names before him, stretching back to the end of the eighteenth century. "On one level it makes you feel small. You're just one part of a large chain," he said. "But knowing you're part of the chain is encouraging. It gives you a tiny sense of what immortality might be like."

The village of Vytina, which lies in the mountains of southern Greece, was still under the thumb of the Ottoman Empire, as was most of the rest of the country. George knew of the brutal treatment the Turks had inflicted upon his ancestors. "Beyond second class," he said. "That was something that we were always aware of, that that time had been unconscionable, inhuman. I'm very proud of the Greeks who then stepped up and broke free." His fourth great-grandfather Georgios, born just two years after the end of the American Revolution, was one of those Greeks. The mountainous terrain of the little town in the central Peloponnese was an ideal hideout for a legendary band of Greeks known as the Klephts. These armed brigands roamed the countryside, fighting Turks and living off of stolen food and goods. To the Greeks, they were revered as popular heroes. "They were the Robin Hoods," George said. But to the Ottoman Turks who ruled over Greece, the Klephts were bandits who wreaked havoc.

In 1804, when Georgios was just nineteen, the Turks had had enough of the Klephts. Fed up with the roving bands, they assassinated one of the ringleaders, Zacharias Pentalakos, among the most famous Klephts in all of Greek history. It was a dangerous time for the rebels. An autobiography by the famous Klepht Theodoros Kolokotronis detailed the quandary in which the brigands found themselves. "The sultan issued a firman to slay all the Klephts," he wrote. "At the same time, the patriarch was compelled to issue an excommunication against them, in order to stir up the whole people. In the following January, in the year 1806, came the orders to hunt us all down." The deeply religious Klephts were now excommunicated from the Greek Orthodox Church and being targeted by the Turks by royal mandate. Zacharias's assassination had a direct impact on George's fourth great-grandfather. In a passage uncovered about the local history of Patras, we discovered that Georgios was one of Zacharias's comrades—in other words, a Klepht. "Georgios Tsafoulias," George read, "fellow of Captain Zacharias, left Kynouria in 1806, during the persecution of the Klephts, and fled to Triata, Achaia."

Georgios, along with countless other Klephts, went into hiding. By 1821, fifteen years after he had fled his hometown, the Klephts had regrouped, infiltrating the countryside and fanning the flames of the Greek War for Independence. The war was brutal. Over the course of eleven years, 105,000 Greek and Turkish civilians died, but in 1832, the Greeks emerged victorious. Finally, the Greek nation was recognized by the international community, free from Ottoman rule at last. And evidence contained in the Patras history books suggests that George's fourth great-grandfather played a very important role. "After the revolution," the text read, "Georgios's sons settled in Kallithea. He was to receive a National Endowment. The family still lives in the Area of Patras." The National Endowment was a piece of land awarded to Georgios for his service to the Greek nation. "It's kind of thrilling," George said. "It makes me proud to know that my family did the right thing when it counted. Then that last line, too, which is still true today. The family still lives there." In fact, in the main square in the town of Kallithea stands a church founded by George's third great-grandfather, the son of the patriot Georgios. "This temple was built 1879," the inscription above the entrance to the church reads, "during the Guardianship of Dimitrios Tsafoulias." Said to be a well-known and respected man in the village, Dimitrios lived to be 105 years old. After his father fought for his country's freedom, the son helped to rebuild it. George's Tsafoulias ancestors were not just a part of Greece's history in revolutionary times; they shaped it. And there were still relatives to this day able to retell the stories. "That there's a continuity to it is great," he said. "They actually walked the walk that we all talked about."

■ Greek ancestry is among the most difficult to trace. Oppressive regimes took away the rights of the Greek people as well as the records that made their history discoverable. George was fortunate in that large portions of his family history had somehow survived the destruction. The paper trail on his father's side had run out much earlier than George had hoped, but through oral history we determined that his oldest named ancestor was probably Haralambos Stephanopoulos, born in 1867 in Greece. On his mother's side, though, the paper trail took us back generations, to George's fourth great-grandfather Georgios Tsafoulias, hero of the Greek War for Independence, born around 1785 in Vytina, Arcadia, Greece.

What we couldn't learn from the paper trail we could learn through DNA. The first test we administered was the admixture test, which reveals an individual's percentages of European, sub-Saharan African, and East Asian / Native American ancestry from around the time of Columbus. George's admixture revealed few surprises: 98.9 percent European and just 0.9 Middle Eastern and 0.1 percent East Asian. "I'm as Greek as it gets!"

George laughed. In breaking down the European number, it's important to remember that there is no category specifically for Greece. The 64 percent Balkan, 20 percent Italian, and 13 percent southern European, however, were consistent with the findings for a Greek person.

We administered two other tests to George, one of his Y-DNA, which is passed down from father to son, unchanged, from generation to generation to generation, and one of his mitochondrial DNA, a genetic signature that mothers pass to their children, regardless of the sex of the child. Both his paternal and maternal haplogroups, genetic population groups sharing a common ancestor, took us directly back to Greece.

By comparing George's autosomal DNA to that of all of our other participants, we found a genetic cousin. George and David Sedaris, of Greek descent on his father's side, share a common Greek ancestor, who most likely lived between two hundred and three hundred years ago. "I've never met him," George said. "I've got to go meet my cousin."

■ George had always described himself as Greek. This was the heritage he knew and the culture he loved, and today's journey only confirmed what he had long felt. Amazingly, he said, he now felt more Greek. "To a surprising degree I didn't think that was possible," he joked. "It firms up the foundation. Being Greek has always defined me in so many ways. I just didn't know how Greek I was." His admixture results, however, gave him pause. "I'm fifty-three years old, but I married more outside the gene pool than five hundred years before," he said. "That's a pretty big shift. I guess a lot can be gained from that, but it makes me a little more aware of what's lost."

Far more had been gained than lost during George's journey. He had two ancestors who fought bravely and at great cost to themselves and their families in the wars that dominated Greece's past. If he could go back in time, he'd go as far back as he could, to his oldest ancestor on his mother's side, the Klepht, the Robin Hood of Patras, Georgios Tsafoulias. "He's the least familiar and the most radical," he said of his fourth great-grandfather. "It has to be the Klepht."

George's ancestor the Klepht was brash and brave, on the side of right (depending on which side you were on) and ruthless in his pursuit of freedom. Would George have behaved the same way? He hoped so, but he couldn't say for sure. George's fourth great-grandfather's DNA was part of his DNA, so what was it that made George Stephanopoulos George Stephanopoulos? Was it the DNA he had inherited from his ancestors? Was it their experiences or his own? "It's obviously a mix of them all," George answered. "But what it makes me aware of is almost a collective family subconscious that survives. Even if you don't know the stories per se, you know the feelings that are transmitted in thousands of different ways every single day from generation to generation." As he had said throughout, "You're part of a chain. You're very small, but you're part of something very big."

The impact of ancient Greece on our American culture is far-reaching. The pantheon of Greek gods looms large in every young child's imagination, and the names Socrates, Plato, and Aristotle have become watchwords for wisdom and intellect. Most of all, ancient Greece gave rise to many of the political ideals that shaped the course of Western culture—political ideals that the ancestors of Tina Fey, David Sedaris, and George Stephanopoulos fought bravely for, both in Greece and, in the case of Tina and David, here in America.

CHAPTER TEN

Decoding Our Past

Negotiating the politics of identity is not as simple as black or white. For every participant in our series, DNA analysis reveals the patchwork of ancestral regions they carry within their genomes, and we employ cutting-edge genetics to help us find the answer to the question "What makes us who we are?" We looked for the answer in the genetic branches of my own family tree, as well as those of the actor Jessica Alba and the former governor of Massachusetts Deval Patrick. For Jessica and Deval, their DNA results were as complex and revealing as any we'd ever seen. Their genomes paint vivid pictures of the intricacies and intimacies of America and remind us that on all our family trees, ancestors that may be lost to time are never truly lost.

Jessica Alba (b. 1981)

By the time Jessica Alba was twelve years old, she had attended eleven different schools. Her father's position as a personnel specialist for the U.S. Air Force was behind the family's frequent moves. "Having that nomadic background," Jessica said, "was why I felt good on a film set. Moving around and creating a life for myself, no matter where I was, was something I was used to." The star of blockbusters like *The Fantastic Four* and the *Sin City* series, Jessica has long been at ease reinventing herself, but her family ties were unwavering. "The more success you have, the more isolated you can feel, the more you need your family—or I did at least. As long as I had my parents and my grandparents and my brother, I was OK. They were my foundation, and they were my rock."

Born on April 28, 1981, in Pomona, California, Jessica Marie Alba grew up in the embrace of a big extended family on her father's side, Mexican Americans whose gatherings were saturated with music and dancing and warmth. She never knew her mother's side, which she believed to be Danish. Perhaps for this reason, she said, "I identify more with Mexican American, with my Latino side." On the census, however, when it comes time to check those telltale boxes, she said, "I check both, weirdly." What she calls her "very typical American upbringing" included, as it has for so many, a loss of native culture, including the Spanish language. "It was just about assimilation. I think we blended, the typical American food with the Mexican food."

Despite strong family ties, questions about her ancestry have always lingered, and she was eager to get some answers. "My mom always used to call me a mutt," she joked. "I feel like I'm a little bit of everything, a melting pot of all kinds of cultures and different kinds of people. I feel like it shouldn't be so ambiguous. It would be nice to be able to pinpoint who we are." She had long known that her heritage comprised many different cultures. But as we journeyed through her family tree, she would learn that her ancestry was far more diverse than even she had imagined.

■ Amid the chaos of multiple moves, Jessica's father's side of the family was always a dominant, organizing force in Jessica's life. "The thing that was most consistent was my relationship with my grandparents and my aunts and uncles, my dad's brothers and sisters, his cousins," she said. Pomona, California, gave Jessica a sense of permanence as well. It was the birthplace of three generations of her family: herself, her father, and her grandmother. Her father, Mark David Alba, was born on September 8, 1960, in Pomona, to Isabel Martínez, born on April 20, 1932, and José Alba Sánchez, born on March 19, 1930, in San Bernardino, California. Her grandparents, both children of Mexican immigrants, were incredibly ambitious people, popular entertainers in the artists' colony and theater of Padua Hills, where they performed traditional Mexican folk songs and plays. Her grandfather was a classical guitarist, her grandmother a dancer and singer. She was also a strikingly beautiful model to whom her granddaughter bears an uncanny resemblance, and Isabel became one of the biggest stars at Padua Hills, courted by Hollywood talent scouts to audition for high-profile projects like *West Side Story* and Elvis Presley's *Blue Hawaii*. She turned them all down, because, Jessica explained, "she didn't want to be away from her family."

Isabel's own mother, Jessica had heard, was fiercely protective of her children. Isabel's parents, Jessica's great-grandparents Daniel Martínez and Guadalupe Miranda, were her first ancestors on this line to immigrate to the United States from Mexico. Her great-grandfather Daniel was born on February 22, 1902, in Mexico, and her great-grandmother Guadalupe was born on August 5, 1910, also in Mexico, in El Cargadero, in Zacatecas. We were not the first to take an interest in documenting Jessica's ancestry. Jessica's second cousin, Michelle Martínez, the granddaughter of Daniel Martínez, had compiled an oral history of the Martínez family. An interview she conducted with her own father, Daniel's son Daniel Jr., gave us tremendous insight into Jessica's great-grandfather's immigrant experience. "Daniel walked across the border somewhere near San Diego," the history read. "At the time, there was little border patrol and few immigration restrictions. The U.S. was welcoming Mexican workers, so Daniel came to the United States to make money and find adventure." After working on a ranch for a few years, where he "acquired some cowboy customs, including a taste for beef," Daniel, now in his twenties, moved to Los Angeles, where he purchased his own grocery and meat market, El Danubio. The store would play a major role in the marriage of her great-grandparents, and would bring us back another generation on Jessica's family tree.

Like their daughter, Jessica's great-great-grandparents Juan Miranda and Silveria Miramontes were born in El Cargadero, Juan on March 8, 1884, and Silveria on June 29, 1887. According to Jessica's great-uncle's oral history, the twenty-eight-year-old Juan Miranda contracted typhoid fever and died suddenly in 1912, leaving behind his wife and three children, including Jessica's great-grandmother Guadalupe, who was only two years old at the time. Silveria found herself in a very precarious position. At the time of her husband's death, Mexico was at war with itself, with rebels fighting to the death to overthrow the Mexican government. The Mexican Revolution, which began in 1910, was well under way. Before the revolution ended in 1920, almost a million Mexicans would be killed. Silveria struggled to stay in her home, but gave up the fight after three years. "Bands of soldiers gradually began to terrorize the countryside," Jessica's great-uncle Daniel explained in the oral history. "Both the revolutionaries and the federal soldiers would come to raid, take food and animals. By 1915, Silveria could no longer remain alone in Mexico with the continued threat of the raids. She decided to leave Mexico for the border city of Juarez and find work in El Paso across the border." According to Daniel Jr., Silveria met and married a man named Eleutrio García.

At this point in Daniel Jr.'s oral history, he made little further mention of Silveria or Guadalupe, Jessica's great-great-grandmother and great-grandmother, respectively. Unbelievably, there was yet another oral history in Jessica's family, this one an interview recorded with Guadalupe's sister, Jessica's great-grandaunt Carmen Miranda Armendárez. Her first-hand view of her mother's marriage was devastating. "She fell in love with someone who said he'd be responsible for the kids," Carmen said. "The man wanted us kids because he worked with the circus and wanted us to be trapeze artists." There is no evidence as to whether Jessica's great-grandmother Guadalupe ever actually worked in the circus, but a border crossing manifest from 1923 charted her next step. When Guadalupe Miranda was thirteen years old, she immigrated to the United States to reunite with her mother and stepfather, who were by that time already living in Los Angeles.

Just one year later, Guadalupe married Jessica's great-grandfather Daniel Martínez. According to their marriage license, "Daniel Martínez, age 21, and Guadalupe Miranda, age 18, were joined in marriage on the 17th of April, 1924, in Santa Ana." Guadalupe's age had been fabricated. She was fourteen years old at the time of her marriage, not eighteen. Jessica had heard the story of her great-grandparents' marriage. "I heard that she got traded for a store in downtown L.A. when she was twelve." Daniel had a store in downtown Los Angeles, so what really happened? Jessica's cousin Matt García explained. Guadalupe's mother and stepfather, Matt said, were customers at Jessica's great-grandfather Daniel Martínez's butcher shop. Like most customers at the time, the couple bought meat on credit and settled the bill at the end of the month. But when the end of the month came, Guadalupe's stepfather couldn't pay off his debt. He had fallen on hard times and agreed to let Daniel marry his stepdaughter if he would forgive the debt.

Apparently Daniel forgave the debt. Jessica couldn't venture a guess at what her great-grandmother thought at the time of her marriage, and as distasteful as Jessica found the story, she accepted it. "It's part of your family history," she said. "It all makes you who you are at the end of the day. I wouldn't be who I am if it weren't for the circumstances that came before me."

Guadalupe's stepfather wasn't alone in his financial difficulties. Jessica's great-grandfather Daniel lost his meat market, and the family was forced to work as migrant farmers, harvesting citrus, grapes, tomatoes, and cotton and living in migrant cabins, often earning less than a dollar a day. As jobs became more and more scarce, anti-immigrant sentiment directed at Mexican Americans intensified. Mexican Americans would be vilified, systematically denied rights that other citizens enjoyed. Jessica's grandparents had not kept this part of the Mexican American story a secret. "My grandfather said that there were water fountains and bathrooms. Basically anything that was open to the public, it was segregated for Mexicans versus the white people," she recalled. "There were Mexican schools and schools for white kids, and my grandmother, half of her siblings were fair-skinned and had light eyes and light hair, blonde hair and red hair, so they got to go to the white schools, and then the darker-skinned siblings had to go to the Mexican schools."

Jessica had heard painful stories all her life about the prejudice her family faced. What they'd neglected to tell her, though, was their response to it. She had no idea how determined her great-grandfather Daniel had been to fight back. He didn't want his darker-skinned children to start life at a disadvantage. After suffering through hard years as a migrant worker, he found work as a gardener at Claremont College, and around 1927, he banded together with other Mexican American families and cofounded the East Barrio School, located in the Mexican American community of Arbol Verde on the outskirts of Claremont. Here Mexican American children could practice reading and writing in Spanish, and they even studied Mexican history. The East Barrio School offered a supplement to the education offered in public school. "They felt racism every day, but they still wanted to instill pride in the children about who they are and where they came from, so they didn't lose touch with their roots," Jessica said. "But weirdly, it didn't carry on." Even the next generation wouldn't follow through. Daniel's own daughter Isabel didn't speak Spanish in Jessica's father's childhood home, and as a result, Jessica had been cut off from this part of her heritage. But she understood. "Just the desire to assimilate was so strong, it overpowered the connection to their ancestry or their history."

■ Like African Americans throughout so much of the twentieth century, Mexican Americans in Depression-era California were relegated to the back of the bus; soda fountains wouldn't serve them because they were the wrong ethnicity. José Alba Sánchez, Jessica's grandfather and Daniel's son-in-law, remembered these offenses vividly. He had risen above the discrimination to become a well-loved classical guitarist at Padua Hills and then embarked on a successful career as a businessman. He had prospered, but Jessica said that both he and her grandmother still bore the scars of growing up during the Depression. "My grandfather was essentially the CFO of a big paper company, had five houses and belonged to a country club, and they were still reusing the butter containers instead of buying Tupperware." We were curious to learn more about his journey.

José Alba Sánchez was born on March 19, 1930, in San Bernardino, California. In 1940, when José was ten years old, according to the federal census for San Bernardino, he was living with his father, Catalino Alba; his mother, Francisca (listed as "Francis") Alba; and his seven siblings. Catalino and Francisca were Jessica's great-grandparents, her first immigrant ancestors on her father's father's line. Catalino Alba Morones was born on April 30, 1901, in Durango, Mexico, and his wife, Francisca Sánchez, was born on December 2, 1907, in Guanajuato, Mexico. According to a border crossing manifest dated 1920, Catalino Alba entered the United States as a nineteen-year-old laborer, his final destination Gallup, New Mexico, his purpose, he told border officials, "to seek work."

Jessica's great-grandfather made his way from Gallup to San Bernardino, where he would raise his family and work servicing boilers for the railroads. Catalino, however, pursued his American dream beyond the railroad, and in 1931, he became one of the founding members of the Mexican Players, the original name of the Padua Hills Troupe of which his son and future daughter-in-law were an integral part. Jessica's great-grandfather and grandfather played at Padua Hills side by side, and Catalino was regarded as a master of traditional Mexican folk guitar and violin. His popularity transcended the walls of the Claremont theater, and in 1950 he was cast in a film noir starring James Mason called *One Way Street*.

Jessica was not the first Alba to have made it to the silver screen. She had never known her great-grandfather; he was long gone by the time Jessica was born, passing away shortly after his film debut, in 1952. Yet she had always been cognizant of the tremendous debt she owed to all her family for her path in life. "I feel in my heart of hearts that I wouldn't have even wanted to pursue acting if it wasn't for everyone in my family being so creative," she said. "My aunts and uncles, their kids, everyone always sings, whether it's a barbecue or a birthday party or Christmas or anytime we can get the family together. My grandfather brings out the guitar, and everybody starts singing. My grandmother would dance around, always in a really good mood. It was just part of who they are." And of course, all those relatives are part of Jessica.

■ Jessica's bond to her father's family was unmistakable. They were always nearby, always present in her daily life. On her mother's side, that bond was more tenuous. "I literally didn't grow up with my mom's family at all," she said, "so I didn't have any connection to her history." Jessica's mother, Catherine Louisa Jensen, was born on October 8, 1961, in Alexandria, Virginia. In 1988, when Jessica was seven years old, her mother was a stunt double and stand-in for Diane Lane on the TV miniseries *Lonesome Dove*. "There was something dazzling about being in a movie and being able to play dress-up," Jessica said. "There was the energy around a film set. It's infectious, and I remember feeling that energy when I visited my mom."

To introduce Jessica to her mother's family, we began with the 1940 census, from a place called Lakewood, Ohio, where a woman named Catherine Tebault, who was listed as head of household, was living with her seventeen-year-old daughter Lou Tebault. Lou was Jessica's grandmother, Louisa Harrison Tebault, born on August 30, 1922, in Washington, D.C. Jessica's great-grandmother Catherine Tebault was born Catherine Louise Nichols on July 11, 1897, in Luray, Virginia. Catherine died the year Jessica was born, in 1981. According to Jessica's mother, Catherine's husband, Paul Tebault, had walked out on his family when Jessica's grandmother was a very young girl. Entirely absent from the lives of his wife and daughter, he had always been shrouded in mystery. Through Paul Tebault, however, Jessica would learn that she had incredibly deep roots in the American South and in American history.

Paul's grandparents, Jessica's third great-grandparents, were married in 1861, during the first year of the Civil War. Eliza Anne Bonney was born on April 9, 1836, in Seaboard, Virginia, and died on June 5, 1890, in Norfolk, in her home state. Dr. Alfred George Tebault was born farther south, in Charleston, South Carolina, on February 23, 1811, and died in Brambleton, Virginia, on August 27, 1895.

The Tebaults were very well established. A book called *The History of*

Norfolk, Virginia, 1736–1977 reported on the election of Alfred Tebault as president of the Virginia Medical Society, on November 11, 1873. An extremely prominent physician, Jessica's third great-grandfather was one of the leading researchers on scarlet fever who before the end of the Civil War had specialized in studying the deadly disease among Virginia slaves. We uncovered medical journals, handwritten by her ancestor himself, from 1843. "A slave infant was next infected," he wrote. "Her 23-year-old mother followed with malignant scarlatina, dead on the sixth day." In another journal entry, Tebault wrote, "A black boy, aged 14 years, was attacked by severe scarlatina anginosa. On the 12th day, I was attacked for three days. On the 15th day, my daughter, aged 2, was attacked with violent scarlatina anginosa." Miraculously, Jessica's ancestor and his daughter survived, but many individuals were not so lucky. Scarlet fever was a scourge, a severe streptococcal infection that inflicted misery on its sufferers and often culminated in death. Because of their wretched living conditions, slaves were at high risk for infection. In 1877 Louis Pasteur invented the antibiotic to cure scarlet fever, but at the time that Alfred Tebault was conducting his research and keeping his journal, more than thirty years earlier, the disease was still frequently fatal.

Dr. Tebault's motives, humanitarian or otherwise, in conducting this dangerous research were unknown to us. An entry we found in the 1860 Slave Schedule of the federal census, however, may at least partially explain his interest in the subject. Compiled twice, once in 1850 and again in 1860, the Slave Schedule enumerated every slave in the United States not by name but by age, gender, and color; the only names that appeared on these Slave Schedules were those of the owners. Dr. Alfred George Tebault owned ten slaves, ranging in age from two to seventy-two years, and he was a very wealthy man because of them. In 1860, the year before the Civil War broke out, his slaves were valued at seven thousand dollars, the equivalent of two hundred thousand dollars today.

It had never occurred to Jessica that she had ancestors in the Civil War at all, least of all on the Confederate side. "I had no idea I had relatives with that type of history in the United States," Jessica said. Her own husband has an African American parent; he and her daughters are of mixed ancestry. "It's pretty rich," she said, "how connected, interconnected, and complicated it all is."

■ The little that Jessica knew about her mother's ancestry revolved around an elusive French ancestor. "My mom had said, 'Oh, we have French descent,' I think because of the name Tebault," Jessica recalled. "Maybe because her grandfather had walked out on her mom, her mom may have tried to make it sound like some fantasy, like he was some nomad from Europe and just took off." Her mother was correct, although the French ancestry was more distant than her mother believed. Dr. Tebault's great-great-grandparents on his mother's side were born in France. These were Jessica's seventh great-grandparents: François Philippe de Marigny de Mandeville was born on October 10, 1682, and Marie Madeline Lemaire was born in 1702, both in Paris. François was Jessica's original immigrant ancestor on her mother's side.

Unbelievably, François was born 101 years before the United States gained its independence from Great Britain. Sometime around the turn of the eighteenth century, Jessica's seventh great-grandfather left Paris for Montreal, Canada, where he established a fur-trading post. In 1711, he moved to Mobile, Alabama, which had been founded as the capital of the French colony in the New World only nine years earlier. In 1803, President Thomas Jefferson would complete the Louisiana Purchase, buying 828 million square miles of land from France and doubling the territory of the young nation. Mobile, along with New Orleans, was part of an area once called New France.

Jessica's ancestors put down roots in the region. According to a marriage record preserved in New Orleans, in 1772, François's grandson Pierre Philippe de Marigny de Mandeville married Jeanne Marie d'Estréhan, Jessica's fifth great-grandparents. Although we think of New Orleans as a French city, it has a complicated history, and at the time of Jessica's fifth great-grandparents' marriage, it was controlled by the Spanish. New Orleans would change hands again, reverting to French control, but the marriage record of Jessica's fifth great-grandparents was, in fact, written in Spanish.

Three years after their marriage, war broke out in America. On June 21, 1779, the Spanish entered the fray, declaring war on the British. Having funneled money and materiel to the Americans during the first years of the Revolution, Spain opted for military intervention as a means of regaining territory they had lost to the British after the Seven Years' War and of checking the spread of their rival's power in the New World. Jessica's fifth great-grandfather Pierre de Mandeville, a New Orleans native of French descent, took up arms to fight with Spain against the British Crown. A military record dated 1792, which detailed his service throughout the Revolutionary War, identified him as a "holder of the Royal Military Order of St. Louis" and as being the aide-de-camp to the Spanish colonial governor of Louisiana, the celebrated military hero Bernardo de Gálvez. Jessica's ancestor was present at the major battles in Gálvez's campaign against the British in what we know as the present-day states of Louisiana, Alabama, and Florida. As Gálvez secured control of the Mississippi River Valley in the wake of British surrenders at Baton Rouge, Natchez, and Mobile, Jessica's fifth great-grandfather, in the culminating battle in the Spanish campaign, the Battle of Pensacola, successfully led a diverse militia, made up of Mexicans, Native Americans, New Orleanians, Spaniards, free blacks, and white immigrants, to victory.

The surrender of Pensacola spelled the end of British control in West Florida. By opening the southern front, the Spanish had frustrated the English, depleting their resources and manpower and forcing them to defend territory beyond the original Thirteen Colonies. In the Treaty of Paris that formally ended the American Revolution in 1783, Spain actually reclaimed control of East and West Florida and would hold this territory until the United States acquired it through the Adams-Onís Treaty, ratified in 1821. Though Bernardo de Gálvez is remembered as the hero of the southern campaigns, and the namesake of Galveston, Texas, Pierre de Mandeville's part in the Spanish victory over the British was considered so essential that a New Orleans–based chapter of the Sons and Daughters of the American Revolution, which Jessica now had the right to join, is named for him. She had an incredibly deep purchase on a part of American history often overlooked in discussions of the American Revolution.

■ One more French ancestor of Jessica's caught our eye. His name was Guillaume D'Lisle, and he was Jessica's eighth great-grandfather, born in 1676 in Paris. Her French ancestry went back more than three hundred years. Jessica's seventh great-grandfather François Philippe de Mandeville lived in the part of America then called New France; Jessica's eighth great-grandfather was responsible for the region's definitive map. He was the chief geographer for Louis XIV of France, who reigned from 1643 to 1715, and D'Lisle's maps helped the French colonize the New World. Until D'Lisle, cartography had been based on approximations of distances. Jessica's ancestor was one of the first to determine exact longitude and latitude by using astronomy and lunar cartography. Unlike her Mandeville ancestors, Guillaume D'Lisle did not settle in America, nor did he fight for its freedom. From his drafting table, however, he had a profound effect on the New World.

■ Jessica had deep roots in both the Old World and the New. On her father's side, we had been able to go all the way back to a man named Josef Antonio Caldera, who was born around 1730 in Mexico. On her mother's side, we went back to Paris, to an ancestor named Claude Souart, who was born on February 16, 1653, when Louis XIV, the Sun King, ruled France. Jessica's mother's claims to French ancestry had panned out. "I thought she was just trying to be fancy," Jessica laughed.

Jessica had begun our conversation by stating unequivocally that she identifies primarily with her Mexican American side. Culturally this made sense, but what would her DNA tell us? Today, almost two-thirds of all Mexicans identify as mestizo, or mixed. It's a genetic legacy of the country's colonial history. When the Spanish invaded Mexico in the 1500s, they fathered children with Native Americans and with their African slaves. The story in Jessica's family had always been that the Alba name was brought by a Spaniard to Mexico. An analysis of her father Mark's Y-DNA could confirm the family lore scientifically. Her father's Y-chromosome was inherited from his father, José, who inherited it from his father, Catalino, and so on. It was virtually unchanged through the generations. According to his Y-DNA analysis, Mark Alba's paternal haplogroup, a genetic population group that shares a common ancestor, is unique to people descended from the Native people in the Americas. In plain English, this meant that the Albas did not come from Europe at all. They were not the conquistadors. Jessica's direct paternal ancestors have been in the New World for centuries. "That's fantastic!" Jessica said. "My grandfather looks Native." Almost all of our participants, no matter what their ethnic background, have heard rumors of a Native American ancestor somewhere in their past. These stories are almost always just that: rumors. Jessica, however, could stand behind that claim.

Jessica's first DNA test, her admixture test, would determine her percentages of European, sub-Saharan African, and Native American ancestry since around the time of Columbus. The Native portion was quite substantial—22.5 percent. The bulk of her admixture was European, at 72.7 percent, and there was a small portion of sub-Saharan African at

2 percent. In breaking down her European results, we discovered that Jessica had an incredibly diverse ancestral breakdown—appropriate for someone whose mother called her a "mutt": 33.5 percent British, 5.1 percent French-German, 3.9 percent Scandinavian, 17.3 percent Iberian, and 1.4 percent Italian.

We are always able to provide our participants with a detailed analysis of their European results, and there are companies that could pinpoint the countries of Africa represented by sub-Saharan African DNA, too, but for the first time it was possible to do the same for a subject with Native American ancestry. Using the largest Mexican genetic database ever assembled, we were able to determine that Jessica's Mexican ancestry may date back to the initial founding of Mexico. The largest portion of her Native DNA is from southern Mexico and includes Mayan ancestry. Her genome also contains DNA from groups of northern Mexico and from the Seri tribe of Sonora.

Jessica's DNA continued to open windows into hidden worlds. In her mestizo roots resided a secret heritage she had never heard about. Her father's test revealed a small amount of Jewish ancestry, 0.7 percent; an Italian DNA reading of 0.6 percent; and Middle Eastern / North African DNA registering at 0.8 percent. The numbers are small on their own, but taken together, a result like this may suggest a history of hidden Sephardic Jewish ancestry. An examination of Jessica's father's mitochondrial DNA, which is the genetic fingerprint he inherited from Isabel Martínez, who inherited it from Guadalupe Miranda, who inherited it from Silveria Miramontes, and so forth, led back to Jessica's fourth great-grandmother, a woman named Carmen Carillo who was born in Mexico in 1820. The people in the DNA database who matched Mark Alba's mitochondrial DNA signature had maternal ancestry from Spain, Italy, Germany, Poland, and Ukraine, and had Sephardic Jewish ancestry on their direct maternal lines. In other words, Carmen Carillo was of Sephardic Jewish ancestry herself, at least on her direct maternal line.

Jessica's fourth great-grandmother's family was part of a fascinating history. In late fifteenth-century Spain, Jewish people were given a terrible choice: convert to Roman Catholicism, face execution, or leave the country. Some of those who converted fled to colonial Mexico, where they found refuge on the frontier of the Spanish empire and practiced their true faith in secret. They became known as Crypto-Jews. Jessica's ancestors were among those who left. Her DNA tells us so. Her autosomal DNA, which she inherited from both of her parents and from all of her ancestral lines, also tells us how she is related to other Jewish people. Of all the Jewish participants we have had in our series, Jessica is the genetic cousin of the attorney Alan Dershowitz. This was just the last of many surprises in Jessica's journey through her roots.

■ Jessica's ancestors had taken fantastic journeys to establish themselves in America. Some of her father's ancestors had come on foot, crossing land bridges thousands of years ago and in recent history crossing borders; on her mother's side they had crossed an ocean to get here, to a country that was still parts French, Spanish, and English. Jessica had met an amazing array of people. Her father's relatives had always been close to her, her mother's unknown. Learning the stories of all the people who came before her linked her equally to all of them for the first time. "I really feel connected to who I am and my history. I get to walk now for the rest of my life knowing where I came from," she said, "and when I visit different countries, I have a sense of really feeling the history in a different way, to think that my ancestors probably walked those streets." And even though we had confirmed through science that Jessica was indeed "a little bit of everything," and according to her DNA nearly three-quarters European, she would continue to perceive herself as Mexican American. "It confirms how I've always felt, and I feel even more connected to my roots and where I came from."

The characters who populated Jessica's family tree were as varied as the DNA she carried inside her—musician, model, slave owner, Revolutionary War hero, and the list went on. Was it these ancestors who made Jessica who she was today? Their DNA? Her experiences? "It's a combination of all of it," she said. "There is a bit of nature in there, and there's a bit of nurture. All of that influences who you are." And if a time machine could whisk Jessica away to meet just one of the ancestors we'd introduced her to, who would it be? It seemed an unfair question to ask—the list was so long—but she responded without hesitation. "It would have to be Guillaume D'Lisle, just because it's the furthest back in history. It would have been really cool just to see what that life was like at that time." Perhaps it wasn't surprising that she had chosen the mapmaker. He had, after all, charted the course for so many on their way to the New World, the land that Jessica's ancestors had called home for so long.

Deval Patrick (b. 1956)

In 2006 Deval Patrick made history when he became the first African American elected governor in the state of Massachusetts, and only the second black governor elected in the nation's history. "I never really doubted that people were ready for a black governor, but the pundits doubted it, and the pollsters doubted it," he said. "We beat the odds; we beat the establishment." The historic election was the culmination of a life spent navigating two worlds, learning how to succeed as an ambitious and talented black man in a predominantly white world.

Deval Laurdine Patrick's African American identity was shaped by the community in which he was raised. He was born on July 31, 1956, on Chicago's South Side, in a black world that has to a large extent ceased to exist. "For me, being African American is as much a cultural marker as it is a racial or ethnic thing, and maybe even more so," he said. "It means growing up on the South Side around all these families who treated you as if every child was under the jurisdiction of every single adult on the block. It was the church ladies at Cosmopolitan Community Church who wore hats and came to church with the notion that worship was serious business, and who showed so much love and care, even though you knew there was calamity in their own lives."

When Deval was growing up, integration was the goal. "My mother was determined, as were my grandparents, to pass on to us basic, middle-class aspirations," he explained. "Just get a good education, get a good job, move on, do better, and pass it on." Deval and his wife, Diane, have raised their two daughters "in an intentionally integrated experience, because that was part of the aspiration I grew up in." For Deval's mother, material gain wasn't her primary motivation. "Everybody was struggling," he said. "There wasn't a lot of talk about what you didn't have. It was more about where you were going." As the tumultuous sixties rolled on, the Chicago streets became dangerous. Gang violence was on the rise, and crime became rampant. "My mother was worried about raising a black teenage boy on the South Side of Chicago in that time."

During middle school, a teacher recognized Deval's promise and recommended him for a program that would change his life, and at age fourteen, he won a scholarship to one of the country's most prestigious private schools, Milton Academy in Massachusetts. "It was like landing on a different planet," Deval recalled, describing an instance that underscored his misunderstanding of the alien world he'd entered. "They had a dress code in those days. The boys wore jackets and ties to classes. So when the clothing list arrived at home, my grandparents decided to splurge on a new jacket for me. But a jacket on the South Side of Chicago is a windbreaker. The first day of class, everybody's putting on their blue blazers and their tweed coats, and I had my windbreaker. The whole language of the place was foreign to me."

Deval soon figured out how to thrive in the elite circles at Milton. But he also had to learn what an education in an elite white prep school meant for his black identity. His father, he said, was "deeply disapproving." He bought him a blue blazer, but his support essentially ended there. "He said that it was going to turn me white. It was going to make me lose touch with my heritage and ultimately break my heart." On his first visit home at Thanksgiving, his sister was equally skeptical. "My family, my grandparents are coming out to get me at the airport. I got home, and everybody was excited, and we'd all talk at once in the hall. My sister interrupted, and she said, 'Ooh, he talks like a white boy.'" Deval was crushed. His grandmother, though, "saved the day. She said, 'He speaks like an educated boy.'" Deval's father and sister had struck a nerve, giving voice to Deval's own concerns. He had as much difficulty communicating with his Chicago friends when he returned home as he had had with his Milton schoolmates on his arrival at the academy. "You start telling them what you're experiencing, and their eyes glaze over, because they have no context."

It was a time of great soul searching for Deval. "You were straddling these two worlds," he said, "and sometimes the price of admission to one was denying the other." Over time, Deval learned to make the two parts whole. "I learned, before my heart was broken, to figure out who I was and to be that all the time, and not try to be one person on the South Side of Chicago and somebody else at Milton Academy. Just be that all the time," he said, "and the people who really loved you would stick with you."

Deval admitted that luck had played a part in setting his course. "I've had so many blessings. I knew of those blessings even when I was on the South Side of Chicago," he said. Those blessings, he recognized, came from without his family and within.

■ Deval Patrick was just four years old when his father walked out on his family. "I remember the fight the day he split," Deval said. "I remember my father stalking out, and my chasing him down the street, and asking where he was going. And I remember his anger. He kept telling me to go home, go home, go home, and I kept coming, and in his anger, he turned around and hit me, and I fell. I remember the burning of my palms on the concrete, and I remember looking up and watching him walk away from that position, and that I will never forget." It was a long time ago, but some scars never heal entirely. "I missed having a dad. Or I missed what I thought having a dad was like, the kind of person who teaches you how to throw a baseball or advises you on how to date girls."

Although the two reconnected after Deval enrolled in Milton Academy, in many ways his father remained a stranger. Laurdine Kenneth Patrick Jr., known as Pat, was born on November 23, 1929, in East Moline, Illinois. Some critics consider Pat Patrick, a founding member of Sun Ra, one of the most important saxophone players of the twentieth century, and he played with some of the most illustrious figures in all of jazz, from Thelonious Monk to John Coltrane. Deval's impressions of his father came largely through his art. "I wouldn't say I knew him very well," Deval began. "In some ways, he is my definition of an artist, completely absorbed in his art. He was a Black Nationalist early, very militant, very edgy about the exploitation of artists and musicians, and he saw his art both in musical terms and in cultural terms." Pat's love of music was his consuming passion, and he once called it "my life, my drug, my habit."

Digging deeper into Pat Patrick's background, it didn't take long to find music. Deval, going into law and then politics, had chosen an entirely different path from his father's, but Pat had followed in his own father's footsteps. "He received his first musical training on trumpet from his father," his obituary, printed in 1991, explained. Although bonded by music, Pat's relationship with his father was also marked by absence. His parents, Deval's grandparents, divorced when Deval's father was twelve. His father, Laurdine Kenneth Patrick Sr., who shared the nickname Pat with his son, was born on May 30, 1905, in Kansas, and his mother, LaVerne Love, was born on October 14, 1910, in Mississippi. Although his father had taught him to play, after the divorce his mother became the main force in his life. She bought him his first saxophone and moved to Chicago expressly so that her son could attend DuSable High School and get the best public school music education available to a black child at the time.

Laurdine Sr. was the only child of George Patrick and May Straughthers, Deval's great-grandparents. We learned from an obituary for Deval's great-grandfather that ran in 1939 in the Kewanee, Illinois, paper the *Star*

Courier that May Straughthers died when her son, Laurdine, was just an infant. We searched for birth, death, and census records for clues about May Straughthers, but she had left no trace; the sole mention of her was in her husband's obituary, and it was impossible to go back any further on her line.

Fortunately, that was not the case with Deval's great-grandfather. George Patrick was born in Macon County, Missouri, on July 22, 1884, to Thomas and Amanda Patrick, Deval's great-great-grandparents. Amazingly, Thomas and Amanda's marriage record, registered thirteen years after the end of slavery, still existed. On March 2, 1878, Thompson Patrick, as he was called in the record, and Amanda Tidings were married in Macon County, Missouri. It seems that Deval's great-great-grandfather used both names, Thomas and Thompson, throughout his life.

No records existed for Thomas (or Thompson) and Amanda Patrick in Missouri after 1880. The 1900 federal census found them in El Paso County, Colorado, where they were living with their eight children, ranging in age from sixteen years to nine months. Deval's great-grandfather George was the eldest. The Patricks were part of a tiny minority. In Colorado in 1900, out of a total 539,700 residents, a mere 8,570 were African Americans. In other words, black people comprised 1.6 percent of the state's population. We wondered what brought the Patricks out West. The census provided three intriguing clues. In the column "Own or rent," the Patricks' answer was "Own"; in the column "Free or mortgaged," it was "Free"; in the column "Farm or home," it was "Farm." At the turn of the twentieth century, Deval's ancestors owned their own farm in Colorado outright. This was very unusual for African Americans of this era. In the year of the census, 1900, only 2 percent of all African Americans in the entire nation were farm owners. How had Thomas Patrick become part of this rarefied group?

According to a homestead application filed on June 15, 1891, in Eastonville, El Paso County, Colorado, Thomas Patrick had staked a claim to 160 acres of federal land there. Deval's great-great-grandfather was a homesteader, taking advantage of an extraordinary piece of legislation that Abraham Lincoln signed into law in 1862. The Homestead Act gave anyone, including former slaves and women, the right to file a homestead claim. Under the terms of the act, if an individual could live on the land they had claimed for five years and make certain measurable improvements to it, they could obtain the title to that land free and clear. This was no easy task. While it cost only sixteen dollars to file such a claim, turning 160 acres of untouched land into a working farm took planning, patience,

and substantial investment. Only 40 percent of homesteaders ever succeeded in proving their claims, and Thomas and Amanda Patrick were
among that 40 percent. "In those times, from this place," Deval said, "as
an African American, it's pretty great."

In 1898, Deval's ancestor filed a testimony that proved his claim. Legally,
he had to show that he and his family lived on and worked their homestead
themselves. Deval read his great-great-grandfather's words from a document that bore his signature, written in his own hand. "My house was built
in July 1891, began to reside in it July 1891, three-room house, 36′ × 14′
shingle roof, five windows, and five door frames. Barn, cellar, henhouse,
closet, well, whole tract fenced, total value $600." In today's dollars the
house would be worth $16,000. Further, the application indicated that
Thomas had sixty-five acres under cultivation, and by 1898, he had raised
crops for seven seasons already, most likely potatoes and other root veg-
etables. In the course of seven years, Thomas Patrick had literally built a
farm from the ground up. On September 14, 1898, thirty-three years after
the end of slavery, the clerk approved Deval's ancestor's application. "He's
living his American dream," Deval said proudly.

In the late 1800s, the West offered African Americans some refuge, its
wide-open spaces holding the promise of freedom and equality not available to them anywhere else, in the South especially. Was there something in
particular that drew Deval's great-great-grandparents to this area in east-
central Colorado? An account of black life in El Paso County at the turn
of the twentieth century describing race relations there held the answer:
"All persons, irrespective of color, were granted the same right to housing,
schools, public places, and equal justice under the laws." Elsewhere in the
United States the African American community was in the stranglehold of
Jim Crow, yet El Paso County was thoroughly integrated, with a thriving
black community. "It's not what you expect," Deval said. "This is a part of
Colorado I didn't know. You have this community with all kinds of people
who had made a choice to live differently than the conventions in most of
the rest of the country at the time, which is a pretty remarkable thing, and
a brave thing to do under the circumstances in those days."

In the immediate vicinity in which Thomas and Amanda Patrick established their own farm were six others, one owned by a man named George
Patrick, who, based on census data, we assume was the older brother of
Deval's great-great-grandfather, and another owned by a man named Anderson Tidings. Tidings was Amanda's maiden name, and Anderson was

her father, Deval's third great-grandfather. His homestead file shows that he moved to the area in September 1891, just a few months after his daughter and her husband. All had made their way from Missouri to Colorado to build their future together in a new world.

Their strong foundation began to crumble in the span of a few years. A land deed filed on October 1, 1902, documented the sad story. After eleven years spent building his farm and improving his homestead claim, Deval's second great-grandfather Thomas sold his land to a white man named Harry F. Cummings for "the sum of one dollar and other valuable considerations"—cash, a loan, or debt forgiveness that was part of the contract without being written into it. In another land deed from 1902, we learned that Anderson Tidings had died, and a similar fate had befallen his farm. His heirs sold Deval's third great-grandfather's farm to Harry Cummings's brother.

The Patrick family appeared to be in decline. Three years after they sold their land, on July 22, 1905, Deval's great-great-grandparents were written up in the *Colorado Springs Gazette*. "Cost him ten dollars to beat wife," the headline read. "Thomas Patrick fined by Justice Ruby for exercising his fists on his better half. Amanda Patrick was the complaining witness yesterday in the case of *People v. Thomas Patrick*, charged with beating and assaulting his wife." Articles that appeared in the local paper suggested that the fight started over money. Even if economic pressures had wreaked havoc on the marriage, Deval offered no excuses for his great-great-grandfather. "It's a tired old story, isn't it?"

Later that same year, the newspaper reported that Deval's second great-grandparents had divorced after twenty-seven years of marriage, an extremely rare occurrence for the time, particularly among African Americans. "Amanda Patrick was given a decree on the grounds of cruelty and nonsupport, and was awarded the custody of the three minor children." Following the divorce, the family scattered. Thomas took a job in a foundry and moved to Pueblo, Colorado, where he died in 1913. By 1920, Amanda had moved to Des Moines, Iowa, with one of her daughters, and she died in East Moline, Illinois—the birthplace of Deval's father—in 1928.

■ It was a sad ending to an inspiring story. After coming so far together, the nuclear family of Thomas and Amanda Patrick had ruptured. Their name, however, persisted through generations, and Deval was curious about it. "I almost never run into people whose last name is Patrick," Deval commented, "and I never meet black people whose name is Patrick." Thomas Patrick was not the last to carry the Patrick name, nor, we learned, was he the first. According to his baptism record, which was registered in Macon County, Missouri, in 1866, Thomas was the son of Thomas and Violet Patrick, who were born in slavery, Deval's third great-grandfather in 1818 and his third great-grandmother in 1821. (Thomas Sr.'s name also fluctuated between Thomas and Thompson in the documents we found, like his son's.) To understand how they had come by the name meant identifying the white man who owned them.

There were no slave owners in Macon County with the surname Patrick. Our search took us just south, to Howard County, Missouri, where in the archives we found an estate document from the year 1851, a full decade before the start of the Civil War, drawn up on the death of a slave owner named Garrison Patrick. The document was invaluable to our search: it tallied all of Garrison Patrick's property, including his twenty-four slaves, every one of them listed by first name, age, and value. "This is amazing," Deval said. "I see Thompson, aged thirty-three, valued at $800. I see Violet, aged thirty, valued at $550." There was no trace of the names of Thompson or Violet's parents, Deval's fourth great-grandparents.

We had gone astonishingly far back on Deval's father's family tree. He paused to absorb it all. "As a black man in America, you're descended from people who were viewed as property. It's pretty chilling to see a dollar figure right next to their names." For him, slavery was no longer abstract. "You don't have to imagine anymore. It gives names and dates and these cold numbers, and family connections to people of whom I am their flesh and their blood." His ancestors' journey was incredible, with no shortage of struggle and strife, but it had given Deval his family name, and it had brought him to this point. "As my grandmother would say," he said, "look at us now."

■ Whereas Deval's father's roots had always remained shrouded in mystery, Deval's connection to his mother and her family was ever-present. Deval's mother, Emily Mae Wintersmith, was born on July 26, 1933, in Chicago. After her divorce from Deval's father, she moved in with her parents, sharing a room with her young son and daughter. "I had been born in that two-bedroom tenement, in my grandmother's bed," Deval said. "The story went that after I was born, the doctor didn't get there in time, and they put me in a roasting pan, at the nurse's instructions, that they were still using at Thanksgiving." They lived in cramped quarters but made the best of it. "My mother, sister, and I shared one of those bedrooms and a set of bunk beds. We'd go from the top bunk to the bottom bunk to the floor, every third night on the floor. It was very fair, actually."

Life was difficult for Deval's mother, and her experiences were limited. "She had a wonderful laugh," Deval recalled, "but spent so much of her life in sadness and disappointment that we didn't hear that laugh as much as we'd like." In spite of her struggles, Emily set an example of determination for her children that Deval internalized and emulated. Having dropped out of high school to marry Pat Patrick, Deval's mother took on menial part-time jobs to support herself and her children after her husband left. Setting her sights on a job with benefits, she applied for a position at the post office and was denied because she lacked the requisite high school diploma. "She went at night and got her GED," Deval recalled. "She brought my sister and me, and we played in another classroom with the chalk while she was studying." Afterward, she got that job at the post office and worked there until she retired. When it came time to send her son to Milton Academy, she agreed to it sight unseen, less concerned about losing her son to the "white world" than her former husband was. "My mother, who had absolutely no context for this, didn't understand it, who I think in retrospect was enormously brave just to say go, had very much the view, 'You know what you have here. Try that. You can always come home.'"

We started our journey into Deval's mother's roots in that very home. Her parents were both born in Louisville, Kentucky, Reynolds Brown Wintersmith on February 2, 1907, and Sally Mae Embers on December 28, 1902. Deval described both his grandparents as "Victorian." "They had a great emphasis on decorum and etiquette and how you carried yourself and how you behaved." Deval's grandmother, whom he called Gram, was a homemaker, "very particular," very strong, very outspoken. His grandfather, whom he called Poppy, worked as a janitor for a Chicago bank for sixty years. He was a quiet man, "dignified and kind." "I hope to become the man my grandfather was," Deval said.

Gram and Poppy were also both southern. They were part of the Great Migration, the mass movement of more than 6 million African Americans between 1910 and 1970 from the rural South to the urban areas of the North, Midwest, and West. Deval described the South Side as "a southern town in those days. Everybody talked about going down home in the summertime, and everybody was cooking food from the South. One of my favorite meals was Sunday morning breakfast with my grandparents, and my grandmother would just lay it out—biscuits and gravy and grits and the rest of it. But," he laughed, "you couldn't have it until you'd come home from church." They brought their customs and traditions with them to their new home, but what had they left behind? To go deeper into Deval's past on his mother's side, we explored her family's Kentucky origins.

The birth register from Louisville, Kentucky, for the year 1907 noted the birth of Deval's grandfather, and it gave us the names of his parents, Deval's great-grandparents, William Rufus Wintersmith, born February 18, 1870, in Elizabethtown, Kentucky, and Christina Davis, born around 1875 in Louisville. Both of them were born after slavery had ended. (There was a discrepancy in the records. Deval's great-grandfather's birth date was listed here and in the Social Security Death Index as February 18, 1873, but whoever furnished the information had made a mistake; 1870 was the year of his birth, corroborated by census data.) Deval's great-grandmother passed away long before he was born, but he visited the man he called Daddy Will nearly every month, with his mother and grandparents, laden down with food for the long drive. "It was before the interstates," Deval recalled fondly, "and they'd pack up food for the trip, fried chicken and potato salad. My grandmother would also make these incredible hamburgers and wrap them in foil, and they would just be calling to you from the time you got into the car." The nourishment he got from his grandparents, both literal and figurative, was undeniable.

We traced Deval's Wintersmith ancestors through the 1870 census for Elizabethtown in Hardin County, Kentucky, the birthplace of Abraham Lincoln. The 1870 census was the first in which former slaves were listed by name. He read the entry aloud: "Horace Wintersmith, age 22, M; Elizabeth Wintersmith, age 17, M; William, 2 months, M; Emily Wintersmith, age 38, B." Deval paused. "I'm not sure what the 'M' stands for." Two-month-old William was Deval's great-grandfather Daddy Will, and Horace and Elizabeth were his parents, Deval's great-great-grandparents. The census taker had chosen for these two generations the racial designation "M," meaning "mulatto." Based on her age, we could guess that Emily Wintersmith, who was described as black, was Horace's mother, but we couldn't be sure.

Deval's great-great-grandparents were both born in slavery, Horace Wintersmith around 1848 in Jefferson County, Kentucky, and Elizabeth Kincaid around 1853 in Hardin County. The census revealed not only their names, ages, and birthplaces, but also the value of the property that each member of the household owned. Horace Wintersmith's real estate was estimated to be worth $200, his personal estate $150; in today's dollars, that is the equivalent of more than $3,600 and $2,700, respectively. Just five years after emancipation, Deval's great-great-grandfather was a landowner. It was extremely rare for a former slave to establish himself so quickly.

A land deed filed in Hardin County in 1868 by a white physician named Harvey Slaughter answered some questions, but raised several more. "I have this day bargained and sold, and by these presents convey, by general warranty, to Horace Wintersmith, and his mother, Emily Wintersmith, persons of color, a certain piece or parcel of ground within the present town boundary of Elizabethtown." The remarkable document continued: "It is agreed and understood between Horace and his mother Emily, that she is to make the above-mentioned premises and appurtenances her home during her natural life, and also the home of her children, until they become of age, when the right title and ownership to the above-mentioned premises is to be the sole and rightful property of the said Horace." Now we had confirmation that Emily was indeed Horace's mother. We were back another generation on Deval's family tree, to his third great-grandmother—an ancestor who bore the same name as his mother. "Gram and Poppy must have known this in naming my mother Emily," he guessed. "But they would answer no questions about family beyond Daddy Will."

Daddy Will wasn't yet born when the transaction between Dr. Slaughter and Emily Wintersmith took place, but the deed took into account future generations of Emily's family. While most former slaves had little choice at this time but to work as sharecroppers, the land described in this deed would give Emily and Horace both security and autonomy. There clearly was a connection between Dr. Slaughter and Emily after slavery; had there been a connection before as well?

We turned to the Slave Schedule of 1850, an addendum to the federal census that appeared this year and in 1860. It listed by name all the slave owners in the nation as well as their slave property, who were catalogued anonymously by age, gender, and color, either black or mulatto. According to the 1850 Slave Schedule, Harvey Slaughter owned twelve slaves. Emily had been thirty-eight in the 1870 census, Horace twenty-two. It was a matter of simple math, and indeed, belonging to Harvey Slaughter was a twenty-year-old female and a three-year-old male. We believed that Deval's ancestors were these two unnamed individuals.

Nowhere else was there a record of Dr. Harvey Slaughter selling land to his former slaves. The paper trail for Emily Wintersmith and her descendants was no longer of help. It seemed only logical to conclude that there was a family connection between Harvey Slaughter and his former slaves, but there was no way to determine that with the documentation we had. We would have to turn to DNA for our answer. But before doing that, we turned to Deval's mother's mother's line, where another mystery awaited us.

■ Deval's mother's mother, Sally Mae Embers, had fair skin and red hair. In his memoir, Deval had written that she could pass for white, and sometimes she did when traveling through the South with her family. "They would often go to a diner or something like that, and she would go in first and order the food," he said, recounting a family story that had become legend. "Once it was placed, she beckoned the rest of the family in through the window. Once the food was on the table," he explained, "the proprietors weren't going to make a big stink about them eating in the kitchen." Or so she thought. "At this one place, when the whole family came in and sat down, the food was on the table, the owner came up and said, 'I'm sorry, you can't eat here; you have to eat in the kitchen.' And her response was, 'We don't eat in the kitchen in our own home,' and they got up and left the food on the table and walked out." Deval reveled in telling this story, a small triumph over the demoralizing reality of the Jim Crow South.

As we had seen, Sally was born in Louisville, Kentucky, in 1902. The circumstances of her birth were hazy. According to some relatives, she was adopted, but no one knew the names of either her biological or adoptive parents. The story Deval had heard was that she was half white, "the product of a white Irish landowner and black charwoman." Deval's mother had left many blanks on her mother's death certificate when Sally died in Milton, Massachusetts, in 1997. "Father, Henry Embers, state of birth unknown," she had written, "and mother, Nannie Taylor, state of birth unknown." An exhaustive search through the archives turned up no child that fit Sally's description living with adults with those names anywhere in the entire United States. The paper trail had run stone cold on Deval's grandmother's line.

■ Now we had two mysteries that we would rely on DNA to solve. On Deval's mother's father's line, the paper trail evidence was so compelling that his third great-grandfather was a white man named Harvey Slaughter that we constructed his family tree. His mother was named Margaret

Gray, and his father was James Slaughter, a judge. We traced their ancestors all the way back to England, to a man named Francis Gray, who arrived in Maryland in 1637 and died around 1690. If Harvey Slaughter was the father of Horace Wintersmith, we would expect to see some of the doctor's ancestors' DNA in Deval's results from an autosomal DNA test. Autosomal DNA is inherited from our parents and from all of our ancestral lines in generations past. At the time we examined Deval, the DNA databases contained about 1.1 million people who have themselves taken this type of test. The task of the genetic genealogist was to look for people who shared a significant amount of DNA with Deval—in other words, people who were his genetic cousins. Through this research it was discovered that one of Deval's strongest matches in the database was the descendant of one Captain George Gray, the brother of Harvey's mother.

This, combined with the paper trail, was convincing evidence that Emily's master was indeed the father of her son Horace. Dr. Harvey Slaughter was Deval's third great-grandfather. Deval exhaled. "It takes my breath away," he said. Sexual relationships between masters and their female slaves were an undisputed fact, and there was no doubt that many, if not most, were nonconsensual. But this one, Deval acknowledged, defied the prevailing stereotypes. "It's not entirely consistent with the cruelty part, that Dr. Slaughter would then convey land to my great-great-great-grandmother and his son for life." It may have been founded in love and not violence, but Dr. Slaughter still owned Deval's third great-grandmother, and she was bound to him by the law.

"I'm not surprised that I share DNA with white people," Deval said, contemplating his new relations. "I'm surprised that I share DNA with white people on Poppy's side. We knew this, or thought we knew it, on Gram's side, because of the way she looked and the stories she told."

DNA science would be deployed to get to the bottom of Deval's mother's mother's elusive origins as well. Deval had taken several DNA tests, one of which tested his mitochondrial DNA, the DNA which is passed down, unchanged and in an unbroken line, from mother to child, generation after generation. Deval inherited his mitochondrial DNA from his mother, Emily; Emily inherited hers from her mother, Sally; and Sally inherited hers from the mysterious Nannie Taylor, the black domestic worker who gave birth to the child of her Irish employer. In our analysis of Deval's mitochondrial DNA, we looked for a maternal line going back to Africa.

Instead, we saw nothing of the sort. "I see Ireland," Deval said. "I see the U.K. I see Norway. I see the German-Netherlands line. I see France." This was Deval's direct maternal line genetically, and it was not African at all. Sally's mother had European ancestry on her mother's side. If Nannie Taylor was indeed his grandmother's biological mother's name, she was a woman of European maternal descent. This was a very unusual reading. Only about 2 to 5 percent of all African Americans descend from a white woman in this way, most likely the result of a relationship between a white indentured servant and a black man. Furthermore, looking at his autosomal DNA, the two exact matches we found in the database, the two individuals who share Deval's exact mitochondrial DNA signature, are both white.

"My grandmother thought of herself as a black woman," Deval said. "She sang like a black woman in church. She talked about white people in her own line, but not in this way." He paused to process the unexpected information. "We know what we think we know based on what we were told." It was quite possible, of course, that Deval's grandmother had no idea herself.

■ What other secrets might Deval's DNA be keeping? Through analysis of his autosomal DNA, we had confirmed that his third great-grandfather was the white man who owned his third great-grandmother. Through a test of his mitochondrial DNA, we discovered that he descended from a white woman on his maternal line. We conducted an admixture test to determine his percentages of European, sub-Saharan African, and East Asian / Native American ancestry from the past five hundred years or so. Of course it was no surprise that Deval had European ancestry; we were actually able to name several of his white ancestors, and almost no black person descended from slaves comes back with a 100 percent sub-Saharan African result. The question for Deval was, how prevalent was that European DNA, and how did it compare to his other percentages? It turned out that over a third of his DNA was from Europe, 38.9 percent. He had a small percentage of Native American DNA, 1.2 percent, which was substantially higher than the average for African Americans. This meant that more than half of his DNA, 58.9 percent, came from Africa.

Understandably, most African Americans want to know from where in Africa their ancestors came. Often this is accomplished through analysis of mitochondrial DNA, but Deval's maternal line went back to northern Europe, not to the mother continent. To restore this history that has been stolen from all African Americans, we turned to his Y-DNA, which is passed, identically, from father to son. Deval got his from Pat Patrick, who got his from his father, also called Pat Patrick, and so on. The map results for Deval's Y-DNA looked strangely familiar, and nothing like Africa. Just like his mitochondrial DNA, his Y-DNA traced back to Europe, to Ireland and England, Belgium and the Netherlands. "Come on!" Deval laughed. As was the case for 35 percent of African American men, his original paternal ancestor was a white man. Deval reflected the diversity of America and its complexity in the most intimate way.

It was against the odds that a black person could ever find the name of his white ancestor. On his mother's side, the paper trail had led us to a man named Harvey Slaughter, and DNA science corroborated the story our research told. Unbelievably, it happened again. In our database, Deval had multiple matches to people with the surname Wetmore or Whitmore. In the 1850 census we found a forty-year-old millwright named George Clinton Wetmore living in Saline County, Missouri. Saline County was just fifty miles away from Howard County, where Deval's enslaved paternal ancestors had lived. Originally from New York, George Clinton Wetmore appeared to be the only person with this surname living in the vicinity of Deval's ancestors. Our findings in Deval's autosomal DNA showed long shared segments of identical DNA with George Wetmore's descendants. Although we cannot pinpoint definitively when the Wetmore DNA entered Deval's family tree, we suspected that Deval's great-great-grandfather Thomas the homesteader may have been the son of this white man, the result of a union between him and Deval's third great-grandmother Violet. This would make him the stepson of the man who gave him his name, Thomas, or Thompson, Patrick.

After myriad roadblocks, we eventually got Deval back to Africa, by matching his DNA with populations in specific African countries today. The largest amount, at 30 percent, was from Nigeria, followed by Congo-Angola at 11 percent, the Ivory Coast and Ghana at 10 percent, and smaller but still significant percentages from Senegal, Benin and Togo, as well as Mali and Cameroon. His African origins reflected the slave trade, during which more than 16 percent of slaves shipped to North America came from what is now eastern Nigeria, and nearly a quarter came from the Congo-Angola region. "Thank God you got to the African continent!" Deval exclaimed. "I thought we were going to be stuck in Europe." As diverse as his DNA was, Deval had never once doubted his deep connection to Africa. "The experience of being in Africa, culturally, is that you're constantly encountering scenes and people that are familiar, rhythms that are familiar, even the lilt in language that's familiar." Descent from three white ancestors notwithstanding, Deval said simply, "I'm still me."

■ There was some irony in the fact that the second black person ever elected governor in this country, the first in Massachusetts, has direct maternal and paternal lines leading straight back to Europe, not Africa. His deep roots in this country, on both sides of his family, took him back to ancestors black and white. Where we had first traced his ancestry back on his mother's side to his third great-grandmother Emily Wintersmith, who was born in slavery around 1832, with DNA we went back much further, to the ancestor of Harvey Slaughter, the white man who had fathered her son. Deval's oldest named ancestor on his mother's side was Francis Gray, who emigrated from England to America in 1637, just seventeen years after the *Mayflower* reached Massachusetts. On his father's side, where we had at first traced Deval's ancestry back as far as his third great-grandfather Thomas Patrick, born in 1818, the evidence, again through DNA, was extremely strong that Deval's oldest named ancestor was a white man, Thomas Wetmore, who was born in England around 1615 and died in Middletown, Connecticut. "Think of the amount of distance traveled, the miles traveled, the cultures traveled in these times, from these places," Deval said. "It makes you feel small and big at the same time, humble but also very connected."

Genealogical research and DNA science could do amazing things, introducing us to ancestors who lived generations before us. The time machine hadn't yet been invented that could actually transport us back to another era, and Deval admitted that the questions he had about his ancestors' relationships could never be answered. He understood history; he understood the complicated, often painful legacy of relations between white masters and their black female slaves. "It provokes a lot of questions," he said. "You hope that these lines connect in love and not in violence. Life is complicated, and these times were very complicated. But you hope it was not just taking, that it was giving."

Deval was the product of complex relationships, in his history and in his home. His personal journey had taken him from the South Side of Chicago to the State House of Massachusetts. He had one of the richest, most surprising tapestries of DNA that we'd seen. So what was it that made Deval

Laurdine Patrick who he was? "It's probably a blend of all that. I think, in my case, my experience and my sense of history, my connectedness to history, which this has helped me with today." The lessons that had come down to him from his family, both those that he knew and those that had come long before, were his greatest gift. "A lot of my raising up was about optimism and about looking forward. That probably makes me who I am more than anything."

Henry Louis Gates Jr. (b. 1950)

In my day job, I teach African and African American literature at Harvard. To anyone who glances at my face, I'm obviously a black man, and I have proudly identified as one my whole life. But several years ago, when I took a DNA admixture test for the first time, my genome told a much more complicated, and fascinating, story: slightly more than half of my ancestors over approximately the last five hundred years weren't black at all. They came from Europe. In fact, both my direct maternal and paternal genetic lines (my mitochondrial DNA and my Y-DNA) trace back not to Africa but to Europe. This means that I am descended on my father's father's side from a white man who impregnated a black woman, most probably a slave, and on my mother's side from a *white woman* who was impregnated by a black man, also most probably a slave. (As we told Deval, only about 2 to 5 percent of African Americans have a direct maternal line that goes back to Europe instead of Africa; on the paternal line, direct European ancestry is much more common, about 35 percent, because of what we know about the history of slavery.) That startling bit of information is one of the reasons I started making this program, traveling the country to interview people about what they knew of their roots, and sharing with them what they didn't.

If DNA reveals that our ancestry is so mixed, why do people feel so strongly about embracing just one identity? Why does American society insist on labeling its citizens as belonging to a single race? It turns out that what we call "race" today is a relatively new concept. It wasn't until the 1800s that scientists began using skin color and other traits to classify human beings into what they called the "three great races": Caucasian, Negroid, and Mongoloid. Employing the limited scientific methods of the day, they ranked people in a strict racial hierarchy and began to define "race" as an immutable and all-determining trait, something a person is born with that will never change.

Does the latest DNA science support this conception of race? In my case, learning about the diversity of my genetic makeup set me on a quest to find the source of my European genes. Even though over half of my ancestors since around the time of Columbus were white—in other words, I am genetically as much a white man as I am a black man—I have never been able to identify any one of those white ancestors by name, nor have I ever identified myself as white. The lingering mystery in my family has always been the identity of the Irishman who fathered the five children of my great-great-grandmother, a black slave named Jane Gates. Jane Gates gave my family our name, but she took the identity of my white great-great-grandfather to her grave.

A new field in ancestry tracing, genetic genealogy, uses our autosomal DNA to find our unknown genetic cousins. Mitochondrial DNA passes from mother to child as an identical genetic signature from generation to generation to generation. Likewise, fathers pass their Y-DNA to their sons, virtually unchanged, in the same fashion. Autosomal DNA, however, is different and much further-reaching. An individual inherits autosomal DNA from both parents and from all of his or her ancestral lines. I have had my DNA tested by all three of the companies that offer autosomal DNA testing for genealogical purposes, and in those databases there are more than 2 million other people who have been tested, people in search of their own connections, their own unknown cousins. In analyzing my autosomal DNA, our genetic genealogist looked for commonalities in the family trees of the people who share my DNA—for geographic regions that appear frequently, for surnames, and for ancestral couples.

One family kept popping up again and again in the family trees of my list of genetic cousins on my father's side. They were called the Mayles. Two of my top matches were a woman named Beverly White and a man named Keith Johnson. They share more DNA with me than almost anyone else on my list. We traced the lines of both Beverly and Keith back to a white man named Wilmore Mayle. The DNA matches between the descendants of Wilmore Mayle and me went on and on. Since our DNA can only be inherited from our ancestors, this white man, Wilmore Mayle, had to be a direct ancestor on one of the lines of my family tree.

This was the first time I'd ever been able to identify any of my white ancestors by name. What more could we learn about Wilmore Mayle? We tracked down another descendant of Wilmore Mayle, a white woman named Alexandra Finley, who, through her own independent investigations into her ancestry, had become the Mayle family historian. Alexandra traced our mutual ancestor back to his birth year of 1755 using one of the tools that is most essential to our own team of genealogists when establishing a paper trail for an individual's genealogy: his baptismal record. It had survived for more than 250 years in a church in England. "St. James the Apostle Church, Dover, Kent, England," the record said. "Wilmore Mayle, son of William and Mary." Alexandra was never able to pinpoint the exact year that Wilmore came to the New World, but our genealogists estimated that it was around 1765. We know for certain that his arrival predated the American Revolution, as records show that he fought with the Twentieth Virginia Line in late 1776. This was my second named Patriot ancestor. My fifth great-grandfather, a free black man named John Redman, also fought in the Continental army.

Through the paper trail we were able to establish that the British-born Wilmore Mayle fought as a Patriot for the freedom of his adopted land. He was also, we learned, a slave owner. My new cousin Alexandra discovered that after his arrival in Virginia, Wilmore Mayle had found work as a farmer and then bought a slave named Nancy. We have seen this incongruity time and again in the course of the series, a contradiction illustrated most glaringly in our Founding Fathers. "All men are created equal," the Declaration of Independence proclaimed, "endowed by their Creator with certain unalienable Rights," including "Life, Liberty and the pursuit of Happiness"—yet the economy of the young nation was built largely on the backs of slaves, and, though a sunset was placed on their importation after the founding of the Republic, their status as slaves, for life, remained unaltered in the newly established United States. My ancestor Wilmore Mayle was not the first among our participants' ancestors to have risked his life in the fight for freedom, on the one hand, and, on the other, denied the blessings of that freedom to others based on the color of their skin.

But Wilmore Mayle, Alexandra discovered, had subsequently done a most remarkable thing. I had never seen a document like the one Alexandra showed me. "Record of emancipation, May 6, 1826," it read. "Be it known to all, to whom it may concern, that I, Wilmore Mayle, of the County of Hampshire in the Commonwealth of Massachusetts, do by these presents liberate, emancipate, and forever set free my Negro woman Nancy, on the condition that she remain with me during my natural life in the quality of my wife." It was illegal in Virginia for a white man to marry a black woman, but this emancipation document was a public pronouncement that Wilmore Mayle intended to do just that. What would be the impact of my ancestor's flagrant violation of the law on the life and livelihood of this mixed-race couple and their six children in slave-era Virginia, with its strict racial hierarchy?

Alexandra found a clue in the 1840 U.S. census: Wilmore Mayle was listed as "colored." His marriage to Nancy effectively changed his racial status. It became fluid. In document after document, Alexandra saw government officials moving our ancestor back and forth across the color line. Sometimes he appeared as a white man, sometimes black, and sometimes mulatto.

After reading the document in which Wilmore Mayle freed the woman he loved and declared his intention to marry her, maybe it shouldn't have come as a surprise to learn that he and his wife continued to chart their own course. They are believed to be among the founders of a mixed-race community outside Philippi, West Virginia, called Chestnut Ridge. Philippi was only about eighty miles away from where I grew up in Piedmont, West Virginia, yet I had never heard of Chestnut Ridge. Traces of my ancestors still lingered there: the Mayle family cemetery where they were buried, the school and church where they studied and prayed.

Chestnut Ridge isn't the type of place we read about in history books. In the rolling hills of West Virginia, the Mayles and other mixed-race families like them segregated themselves. It was a refuge built by my ancestors so they could avoid the degradation of the slave economy in a community of their own where everyone was black, white, and neither. Although most of the Mayle descendants are long gone from Chestnut Ridge, they still reunite each year in the little town to celebrate themselves and their forebears on a day they call Heritage Day. I was fortunate enough to participate in this day, with new family members who evince and embrace the great unity and diversity of the human community.

■ For Jessica Alba and Deval Patrick, and for many of our other participants, identity was a matter of choice, even though our ancestors weren't. Mathematically, Jessica was nearly equal parts northern European and Mexican (when tallying her Native and southern European DNA in one column), yet she would continue to identify most with her Mexican ancestry. The fact that Deval descended from white European ancestors on both his direct maternal and paternal lines would never change the fact that he has always identified strongly as an African American and would continue to do so. The same was true for me. "It's amazing," Deval said. "We have spent so much of our history trying to harden what turns out to be quite blurred lines among and between people, and probably the sooner we acknowledge how blurred they are, and how common our humanity is, the better off we will be."

Indeed, the only reason I was able to connect with this branch of my family was because of the clues buried deep in my genome, clues that prove that America's color line has always been blurrier than any of us ever imagined. Though it remains impossible to determine how exactly Wilmore Mayle fits into my family tree, he extended its branches beyond my wildest imaginings. And with each discovery of all of our DNA cousins, my own and my guests', I continue to be amazed by just how connected all members of the human family truly are.

ACKNOWLEDGMENTS

If there's one thing I've learned from all of my genealogy series, it's that behind every name that our research turns up, there are rich stories and full lives. For our purposes here, unfortunately, the names will have to suffice!

Our production team never ceases to amaze me, led by senior producer John Maggio and series producers Sabin Streeter and Leslie Asako Gladsjo. The rest of the individuals responsible for these ten weeks' worth of incredible films are Phil Bertelsen, Josh Gleason, Hazel Gurland-Pooler, Muriel Soenens, and Jesse Sweet, directors/producers; Nicole Bozorgmir and Hannah Olson, coproducers; Brittany Clemons, Jessica Xanthe Cran, Samantha Gowda, and Stephen Robinson, associate producers; Megg Farrell and Joey Fishman, researchers; Ilya Chaiken, R. A. Fedde, Jim Isler, Emir Lewis, Bruce Shaw, and Merril Stern, editors; Stef Gordon, line producer; Stephen Altobello, post-production supervisor; and Elyse Hughes, production coordinator.

Neither the television series nor the companion books could have happened without the brilliant minds and tireless efforts of Johni Cerny, our chief genealogy researcher, and CeCe Moore, our DNA consultant and genetic genealogy researcher. Additional research was conducted by Natalie Baur, Kristina Bedford, Linda Blankenship, Brigitte Burkett, Laura H. Congleton, Farley Crawford, Barbara Crissman, Jonathan Deiss, Alan Drust, Alexandra Finley, Glynnis G. Gilbert, Elena Granda Álvarez, Ainsley Henriques, Matthew Hovious, Anita Johnson, Roseann Kebles, Eddie Killian, Tiffany Lukashefski, José Antonio Matos Arévalos, Kathleen McClure, Aaron McWilliams, Tania Moriera, Mark Newton, Doug Nicol, Jenny Orgill, Nick Sheedy, Simeon Stachera, Julia Winters, and Paul Woodbury.

The following scientists were invaluable to my understanding of the application of DNA analysis to ancestry tracing, and I am indebted to them for sharing with me and my team their astonishing range of knowledge: David Altshuler and Mark Daly at the Broad Institute; Catherine Ball, Stephen Baloglu, and Ken Chahine at AncestryDNA; Kasia Bryc and Joanna Mountain at 23andMe; Carlos Bustamante at the Stanford University School of Medicine; and Janine Cloud and Bennett Greenspan at Family Tree DNA.

I would like to express my deepest gratitude to the following corporations, foundations, and individuals for providing the generous funding for this series that allows us to bring the wonders of genealogy and DNA science to an ever wider audience: Ancestry.com, Ford Motor Company, Johnson & Johnson, McDonald's, the Ford Foundation, Dr. Georgette Bennett and Dr. Leonard Polonsky, Candace King Weir, the Daryl & Steven Roth Foundation, the Corporation for Public Broadcasting (CPB), and PBS. I would like to thank especially Rob Singer and Tim Sullivan at Ancestry.com; Jim Farley and Shawn Thompson at Ford Motor Company and Richole Hall, Monique Nelson, and Marc Perry at Ford's agency UniWorld Group; Sarah Colamarino, Andrea Higham, Yoandra Mordan, and Michael Sneed at Johnson & Johnson; Anja Carroll, Jennifer Feldman, and Rob Jackson at McDonald's; and Darren Walker at the Ford Foundation.

I have nothing but the most heartfelt admiration and appreciation for my co-executive producers and partners Peter W. Kunhardt and Dyllan McGee, and Stephen Segaller from WNET in New York. At Kunhardt McGee Productions, thanks go to Jill Cowan, Mary Farley, Matthew Goldman, George T. Kunhardt, Teddy Kunhardt, Deborah Porfido, and Will Ventura. Thanks also to Bill Gardner, Beth Hoppe, and Paula Kerger at PBS; Patricia de Stacy Harrison and Jennifer Lawson at CPB; and Julie Anderson and Neal Shapiro at WNET.

Lastly, I would like to thank the dear family, friends, and colleagues who enrich my life immeasurably: my partner, Marial Iglesias Utset; my daughters, Maggie and Liza Gates; my sons-in-law, Aaron Hatley and Greg Parsons; the Princesses of Piedmont, Brenda Kimmel Davy, Elaine Walker Johnson, Debora Kilroy, Cindy Francis Leatherman, Connie Butler Lechliter, Brenda Junkins Long, Deborah Wilson Pamepinto, Thelma Rankin Rhodes, and Teresa Lupis Savage; Bennett Ashley, Paul Lucas, Brandon Proia, and Peggy Siegal; and Lawrence Bobo, Kevin Matthew Burke, Amy Gosdanian, Glenn H. Hutchins, Marcyliena Morgan, Abby Wolf, and Julie Wolf.

INDEX